SEVENTH EDITION

College Law
for Business

JOHN D. ASHCROFT, J.D.
ASSISTANT PROFESSOR OF BUSINESS AND
COORDINATOR OF JUDICIAL AFFAIRS
SOUTHWEST MISSOURI STATE COLLEGE
MEMBER MISSOURI BAR AND AMERICAN BAR ASSOCIATION

A. ALDO CHARLES LL.B., D.Ed.
LATE PROFESSOR OF BUSINESS LAW
UNIVERSITY OF GEORGIA

CONSULTING EDITOR
RONALD A. ANDERSON
PROFESSOR OF LAW AND GOVERNMENT
DREXEL UNIVERSITY

Author of *Anderson's Uniform Commercial Code;*
Anderson's Uniform Commercial Code Legal Forms

L89 SOUTH-WESTERN PUBLISHING COMPANY
CINCINNATI • CHICAGO • DALLAS • NEW ROCHELLE, N. Y. • BURLINGAME, CALIF.
BRIGHTON, ENGLAND

Standard Book Number: 0-538-12890-9

Library of Congress Catalog Card Number: 68-20540

4 5 6 7 H 7 6 5 4 3

Printed in the United States of America

Preface

Amid the population and knowledge explosions is a vast legal expansion in which all are participants. Developments which alter the law of the business world are appearing with increasing frequency as government awakens to expanding consumer demands and the needs of the business community. Recent legislative enactments, which have expanded the law of business and made it more uniform, are matched by court decisions and opinions attesting to societal rights-consciousness and the legal orientation of modern communities.

Attempts to teach students "the law" would require a course of study far exceeding the curriculum of most law schools. The more modest, but no less important, objective of COLLEGE LAW FOR BUSINESS, Seventh Edition, is to acquaint the reader with vitally important concepts from which business law is developing. New terminology replaces outdated labels and descriptions. Individuals exposed to this text will recognize and adapt to the changing law because the concepts that are presented are designed to represent the law as it is developing in the 1970's.

The specific improvements in the Seventh Edition include a thoroughgoing revision of text material involving the addition of legal concepts and principles heretofore not included; new and revised illustrative cases; revision of end-of-chapter materials; revision of preview questions and cases for each part of the book; expansion of the glossary; and revision of the supplementary materials—study reports, tests, and instructor's manual.

A continuing feature of the Seventh Edition is an introduction to each part of the text through the vehicle of Preview Questions for Part 1 and Preview Cases for the other nine parts of the text. These questions and cases are designed to whet the appetite of the student, to challenge him, and to provide a general idea of the nature of the legal principles and problems with which he will be concerned in his study of each part.

Because the Uniform Commercial Code has been almost universally adopted, several sections of this textbook are now entirely constructed on the basis of it. This is particularly true of the sections dealing with commercial paper, sales, and risk-bearing devices.

Many of the questions at the end of each chapter have been revised. There has been an extensive revision of the case problems for each chapter. Similarly, there has been an extensive revision of the summary cases that are designed for review of basic legal concepts at the end of each part of the text. Emphasis has been given in the end-of-chapter materials to challenging the reader's ability to recognize legal situations which will require professional legal counsel. While attention is focused on challenging the student to make rather sophisticated, intelligent responses, the text and illustrative case materials clearly and plainly state the law. Illustrative cases are sprinkled throughout the text. Such integration of text and cases provides immediate learning reinforcement of the textual material. The concepts of the text are finally nailed down when the reader again applies the principles of the text and cases to the exercises at the end of each part.

The Glossary of Legal Terms has been expanded and revised. The terms that are included in the glossary have been selected because of their helpfulness to the beginning student.

The supplementary items for COLLEGE LAW FOR BUSINESS have been thoroughly revised and strengthened in order to provide student and instructor with even more helpful study and teaching devices.

The authors acknowledge a debt of gratitude to those instructors who continue to share their experiences and helpful teaching aids. Their suggestions and comments are always welcomed, for they help to build a vastly improved text. The authors also express deep appreciation to Janet E. Ashcroft, attorney-at-law and instructor of business law at Southwest Missouri State College, for her help in research, writing, and editing. A special expression of appreciation is owed Ronald A. Anderson, consultant for this edition, for his unique contributions to this revision.

J.D.A.

Contents

Part 1. Law and Its Enforcement

Part 2. Contracts

Part 3. Sales

Part 4. Bailments

Part 5. Commercial Paper

Part 6. Agency and Employment

Part 7. Partnerships

Part 8. Corporations

Part 9. Risk-Bearing Devices

Part 10. Property

Part I.

LAW AND
ITS ENFORCEMENT

What is law?

What is business law?

What is the common law?

What is equity law?

What is law by judicial decision?

What is constitutional law?

What is administrative law?

What is criminal law?

>What is the function of a court?

>What is the jurisdiction of a court?

>What are the federal courts?

>What are the state courts?

>What are the functions of court officers?

>What is the procedure for filing suit?

>What is the basic procedure for trial?

>How may an appeal be made from a decision?

These are some of the basic questions that are answered in the chapters constituting Part 1. For an introduction to Parts 2 to 10, you will be given a number of interesting preview cases. Preview questions and cases are designed to set the stage for your study of the many important areas of the law.

Chapter I

INTRODUCTION TO LAW

DEFINITION OF LAW

Nothing so complex as law could be completely described in one short definition. Many authors have tried to define it, but none have excelled Blackstone's famous definition: "*Law* is a rule of civil conduct, commanding what is right and prohibiting what is wrong." There are many rules of civil conduct and there are many admonitions commanding what is right and condemning what is wrong, but rules and admonitions are not necessarily laws. Only when a sovereign state issues rules prescribing what is right and what is wrong can a rule be called a law. Even then rules would not be laws unless sanctions are applied when the rules are broken.

Religious teachings, the mores of society, habit, group pressures to conform—all contribute to social control of conduct, but only the rules of law are all-pervasive, applying with equal force to every member of society. A breach of some of these rules is a crime, and the sanction is a fine, a jail sentence, or both. The sanctions for the breach of the other rules of law are for the most part damages. Every deviation from prescribed rules of conduct has an appropriate penalty. *Business law* is concerned primarily with those rules of conduct prescribed by government for the performance of business transactions.

Law is an evolutionary process. The vast number of laws governing business transactions in America did not come into existence overnight. They are the result of man's changing concepts of what is right and what is wrong. For example, for several centuries in England and America one who owned land owned the soil and minerals below the topsoil and the air above the land "all the way to heaven." The law prohibited trespassing on one's land or in one's

3

air. A telephone company that wanted to string a telephone wire through one's air had to buy a right of way. When airplanes were invented, this law became a millstone about society's neck. By judicial decree the courts modified the rule or else a transcontinental airline would have to buy a right of way through the air of every property owner from New York to San Francisco. Our present laws are the result of man's reactions to changed circumstances.

THE COMMON LAW

Every student of law must have some concept of the common law, its origin and development. In all nations having some form of representative democracy, the legislative department of the government is separate and distinct from the judicial department. It is fundamentally the function of the legislative department to enact the laws and the function of the judicial department to enforce the laws. *Common law* is in reality custom which has come to be recognized by the courts as binding on the community. If we go back to the eleventh century in England, there were simply no statutory laws prescribing the proper rule of conduct in hundreds of business situations. If there was no statutory law governing the situation when a dispute was brought before the judge, the court prescribed a rule of its own. Over a period of several centuries, judge-made laws constituted the larger percentage of the law. The American Colonists brought judge-made laws to America. After America became a sovereign nation, most of these common laws were either enacted as statutory laws or continued as judge-made laws. Thus the common law is the source of much of our business law today.

EQUITY LAW

Equity law evolved somewhat in the same manner as the common law. In England by 1200 A.D. many common-law rules had been formulated. These rules were gradually formed into categories to which judges could refer to guide them in their decisions in particular cases. Uniformity in the common law spread throughout England because judges tended to decide cases the same way other judges had decided them in the past when the facts were similar. Emphasis developed upon the form of action so that after a few centuries, the form became more important than the law itself. The common law in its beginning was very flexible, too flexible to be called law or a system of law; but by the year 1500 A.D. it had gone to the other extreme and had become extremely rigid and inflexible.

In all social institutions man must strive to harmonize two conflicting desires—the desire for stability and the desire for liberty. Law must encourage the fulfillment of both desires. If stability is overemphasized, laws become so rigid and inflexible that many wrongs can exist for which there are no remedies. If law is so flexible that each judge is free to formulate his own law in each case, unbound by any rule except his own conscience, liberty is precarious. It is essential to both stability and liberty that the laws governing our social conduct, whether based on statutes or prior cases, be honored by judges.

Some flexibility must be maintained so that when justice and equity demand it, the judge may decide a particular case, not by some rigid rule of law, but by what his conscience tells him ought to be done. This was the function of equity law in its beginning. The equity judges were the keepers of the king's conscience. In America today we still have the concept of equity law even though some structure and formality have crept into it. The decision in each case is recorded and becomes a precedent in future cases of a similar nature. Lawyers cite these decisions in order to persuade the court to render a similar decision in the case that is presently before the court.

Courts of equity jurisdiction provide for preventive action to protect individuals from harm which is strongly likely to occur. In this type of case a court with equity powers may initially issue a restraining order and, upon a complete hearing, an injunction forbidding activities which would be detrimental to others.

If one party continually abuses the property of another, a court may grant relief ordering the offending party to cease his abusive activity.

Only a few states maintain separate equity or, as they are frequently called, Chancery Courts. In most states today, legal and equitable principles are applied to each case as the facts justify, without making any formal distinction between law and equity.

LAW BY JUDICIAL DECISION

Along with the development of both the common law and equity law, many statutory laws were passed. In England as Parliament gained supremacy over the king, statutory law became a major source of law. In America, most of our laws have been statutory laws from the beginning. Judicial interpretation is an important element of the application of law, whether common law or statutory law.

In their interpretations of the statutes, judges particularize statutes to individual cases. Interpretations by the various supreme courts become precedents and under the *doctrine of stare decisis* (stand by the decision) are binding upon all lower courts. Any state supreme court or the Supreme Court of the United States can reverse a decision of a lower court. If the law is to attain stability so that we can know what our rights are before we undertake a business transaction, the courts must generally adhere to the judicial precedents set by earlier decisions. However, changing business practices may make it necessary for the previous case law to be overturned and a new rule or practice to be established.

CONSTITUTIONAL LAW

A *constitution* is the system or document which defines the relationships of the parts of the government to each other and the relation of the government to its citizens or subjects. The United States Constitution is the supreme law of the land. State constitutions, as well as statutory law, must agree with it. The Supreme Court of the United States is the final arbiter in disputes involving the constitutionality of any state or federal law. This court is also the final authority on whether or not any state constitution, or any part of a constitution, is in conflict with the federal Constitution. A state supreme court is, of course, the final judge as to whether a state law violates the constitution of the state.

ADMINISTRATIVE LAW

Many of our governmental functions today are carried on by means of administrative agencies set up by our legislative bodies. Because of the complex nature of our economic order, these boards and commissions must be given wide latitude in setting up rules of procedure. They issue orders and decrees that have the force of law unless set aside by the courts after being challenged.

STATUTES

Statutes constitute the most important source of law. Constitutions are difficult to amend and, for this reason, are not very responsive to the changing demands of the people. Statutory laws may be enacted, repealed, or amended at any regular or special session of the lawmaking body.

The three chief classes of lawmaking bodies in the United States are the federal Congress, the state legislatures, and the city councils. The laws of the city councils are called *ordinances,* but an ordinance is properly called a statutory law. In the United States, if any law, whether federal or state, is in conflict with the federal Constitution, it is unconstitutional. If there is a conflict between a state law and a law of the United States passed by the United States Congress in accordance with the federal Constitution, the latter prevails.

In the field of business law the most important statute is the Uniform Commercial Code.* The Code regulates the fields of sales of goods; commercial paper, such as checks; secured transactions in personal property; and particular aspects of banking, letters of credit, warehouse receipts, bills of lading, and investment securities.

CRIMINAL LAW

Criminal law is that branch of the law which has to do with crimes and the punishment of wrongdoers. A *crime* is an offense of a nature that tends to injure society as a whole. Business law has to do with crimes only incidentally. There are certain criminal offenses, such as arson, forgery, fraudulent conveyances, embezzlement, and the like, that are closely related to business activities.

Crimes are usually classified according to the nature of the punishment as felonies and misdemeanors. Generally speaking, *felonies* are the more serious crimes and are usually punishable by death or by imprisonment in a penitentiary. *Misdemeanors* are offenses of a less serious character, which are punishable by a fine, or by imprisonment in a county or local jail. Committing a forgery is a felony, but driving an automobile in excess of the prescribed speed limits is a misdemeanor. The criminal statutes define acts that are felonies and those that are misdemeanors.

TORT LAW

A tort is a breach of the duty of care one individual has toward others. Courts make awards to injured individuals to compensate them for damages suffered when one person fails to exercise reasonable

---

* The Code has been adopted in every state except Louisiana. The Code has also been adopted in the Virgin Islands and for the District of Columbia.

care and thereby causes injury to another. It is tort law which allows an innocent motorist who is the victim of a careless or negligent one to sue for damages.

QUESTIONS

1. What is meant by the *doctrine of stare decisis?*
2. What is a *judge-made law?*
3. Are judges as free today to decide cases according to their ideas of what is right as they were 100 years ago?
4. Why are we justified in classifying law by judicial decision as a source of law?
5. If a common law and a statutory law are in conflict, which one prevails?
6. What is the legal effect of an order issued by an administrative agency?
7. Classify the following crimes into felonies and misdemeanors: murder, theft of 10 cents, drunkenness, robbery, overtime parking, and forgery.
8. What is a tort?
9. Describe the relationship between the U.S. Constitution, state constitutions, and state statutes.
10. What kind of law is not made by the courts or directly by the legislature?

Chapter 2

COURTS AND COURT PROCEDURE

FUNCTIONS OF THE COURTS

The function of a court is to declare and apply the judicial precedents or case law and enforce laws passed by the legislative arm of the government. This is not the whole story, however. Constitutions by their very nature must be couched in generalities. The statutes passed by the lawmaking bodies are less general than the wording of constitutions but still must be made specific to apply to a particular court case. It is one of the chief functions of the courts to interpret and apply the law of whatever source in a given situation. For example, the federal Constitution gives the federal Congress power to regulate commerce among the several states. In conformity with this constitutional provision Congress passes a law requiring safety devices on trains. The court must then decide whether this is a regulation of interstate commerce.

Similarly, an Act of Congress regulates minimum wages. A case may arise as to whether this applies to the wages paid in a sawmill located in a rural section of the country. The court must decide whether or not the sawmill owner is engaged in interstate commerce. The court's decision may become a judicial precedent that will be followed in the future unless the court changes its decision in a subsequent case.

JURISDICTION OF COURTS

A corporation's officials consist of a president, a vice-president, many subordinate officials, and employees. Each individual has very definite authority in his limited field, with the authority broadening as

9

one goes from the foreman up the scale to the president. To a certain extent courts follow a pattern, starting with justice-of-the-peace or magistrate courts and extending up to the Supreme Court of the United States.

The power or authority which each court has to hear cases is called its *jurisdiction*. This jurisdiction may involve the subject matter of the case before the court. If the claim is for damages due to an automobile accident, a probate court will not have jurisdiction since this court deals with wills and the distribution of property of deceased persons to the heirs. A court may have jurisdiction over the subject matter but not over the person. If a resident of Buchanan County is charged with trespassing on his neighbor's property in the same county, the judge in adjoining Tazewell County does not have jurisdiction over the person of the accused. Nor does the judge in Buchanan County have jurisdiction over the person of the accused if the accused has not been properly served with notice of the trial. Before any court can try a case, it must first be established that it has jurisdiction over both the subject matter and the person in the case at issue.

CLASSIFICATION OF COURTS

Courts are classified for the purpose of determining their jurisdiction. This classification can be made in a variety of ways. One classification can be made according to the governmental unit setting up the court. In this sense they are classified as (1) federal courts, (2) state courts, and (3) municipal courts. The same courts may be classified according to the method of hearing cases. In this sense they are called trial courts and appellate courts. The *trial courts* conduct the original trial of the cases and render their decisions. The *appellate courts* review the cases appealed from the decisions of these trial courts.

The federal government and the states have a separate court structure, and this structure is best understood by classifying first the federal courts and second, the state courts.

FEDERAL COURTS

The federal courts are classified as:

1. Federal district courts
2. Federal courts of appeals

3. United States Supreme Court
4. Special federal courts

(1) **Federal District Courts.** By far the largest class of federal courts consists of the district courts. These courts are strictly trial courts in which are tried all criminal cases involving a violation of the federal law. The federal courts also have jurisdiction of civil suits which are brought (a) by the United States; (b) by citizens of the same state where the amount in controversy is $10,000 or more and arises under the Constitution, federal laws, and treaties; (c) between citizens of different states; and (d) between citizens of one state and a foreign nation or one of its citizens or subjects.

(2) **Federal Courts of Appeals.** The federal courts of appeals hear only appeals from a federal district court or from a state supreme court decision if the case involves a federal constitutional question. If one is convicted in a state court for "unlawfully distributing pamphlets," he may appeal to the state supreme court. If he loses in the state supreme court, he may next appeal to the federal court of appeals since the federal Constitution guarantees freedom of speech. If only the state constitution is involved, no right of appeal to a federal court exists.

(3) **United States Supreme Court.** For the most part, the United States Supreme Court hears only appealed cases from the federal courts of appeals. Under certain circumstances a decision of a federal district court may be appealed directly to the Supreme Court. The Supreme Court is the highest tribunal in the land, and its decision is final until the Court reverses its own decision or until the Congress changes the effect of a given decision by a constitutional amendment or by a legislative enactment. A decision of a federal court of appeals is binding upon all lower courts within the jurisdiction of that circuit court unless the Supreme Court reverses that decision.

(4) **Special Federal Courts.** The special federal courts are limited in their jurisdiction by the laws of Congress creating them. For example, the Customs Court hears only cases involving the rates of duty on various classes of imported goods, the collection of the revenues, and similar controversies. The decisions of the Customs Court may be appealed to the Court of Customs Appeals. There is

also a Claims Court to hear cases involving claims against the United States government. The government, being supreme, cannot be sued without its consent, but this consent is seldom withheld. The federal government has in fact enacted a statute known as the *Federal Tort Claims Act* which guarantees persons the right to sue the government for certain types of harm committed by the government and its employees.

CONTROL OF APPEAL COURTS OVER LOWER COURTS

All federal courts derive their authority from the people, either through the Constitution or the Congress, but the appellate courts exercise considerable authority over the courts under them. A judicial trial calls for a verdict; and the basis for this verdict in all cases is the trial court's authority as set out by the Congress and the appellate courts. Rules for the admissibility of evidence, trial procedure, the manner of selecting the jury, and many other important matters are determined by the appellate courts. The district court must adhere strictly to these rules as well as those laid down by the Congress. Furthermore, the district court, which is the trial court, is bound by the decisions of the federal courts of appeals and the Supreme Court in cases where the facts are substantially the same.

One can say that the Constitution gave the Supreme Court authority to exercise authority over any inferior courts which Congress might establish and that the Supreme Court gave the federal courts of appeals the power to exercise authority over the federal district courts, subject to review by the Supreme Court.

CLASSIFICATION OF STATE COURTS

State courts can best be classified into the following groups:

1. Inferior courts
2. Courts of original general jurisdiction
3. State supreme courts
4. Special courts

(1) **Inferior Courts.** The inferior courts of the states hear only minor disputes between citizens and minor criminal offenses. In the counties and smaller towns the most common inferior court is the justice-of-the-peace or magistrate court. A justice of the peace or magistrate hears all claims between citizens up to the maximum

fixed by the state, usually $500 or less. In addition, he may try all criminal cases involving misdemeanors. In the cities the function of the justice of the peace may be performed by the mayor, small claims courts, and police courts. The loser in any of these courts may appeal to the court of original general jurisdiction.

(2) Courts of Original General Jurisdiction. Courts of original general jurisdiction are for the average citizen the most important courts of the state. These courts have broad general jurisdiction involving disputes between two or more parties as well as criminal offenses against the state. They are called *courts of original jurisdiction* because it is in them that the case is first instituted. On occasion they hear appeals from inferior courts, but this does not make them true appellate bodies because the entire case is retried at this level. Thus, such an appeal is actually treated as a case of original jurisdiction. An official, permanent record is kept of the trial showing the testimony, evidence, statements of counsel and the judge, the judgment, and the findings of the court. For this reason these courts are often referred to as trial courts and courts of record. The official name of such a court in most states is *Circuit Court*.

Circuit court, then, is the official name given to a court of record, a trial court, or a court of original general jurisdiction.

If the defendant in a criminal case, or both parties in a civil suit, are satisfied that the decision of the trial court is in accordance with the law and the evidence, the controversy ends here.

(3) State Supreme Courts. In all states provision is made for an appeal to an appellate court by the party dissatisfied with the final judgment of the trial court, or any of its rulings and instructions. Only a court which hears appeals from a trial court is an appellate court. Usually the name of such a court is *State Supreme Court*.

(4) Special Courts. Many states have special courts, such as *probate courts* to probate wills; *juvenile courts* to try cases when children, usually under fourteen years of age, are charged with a crime; and *domestic relations courts* to hear cases involving disputes between husbands and wives. These are not courts of general jurisdiction, but of special jurisdiction. In many states these courts are of the same level as the trial courts. When this is the case, they, too, are properly called trial courts and courts of record. In other states they are on the same level as the inferior courts and are not courts of record.

COURT OFFICERS

The chief officer of an inferior court is the *justice of the peace,* trial justice, or similar officer; while the executive officer is the *constable.* In a state court of record the chief officer is the *judge,* the executive officer is the *sheriff,* and the recorder is the *clerk of the court.* This is also true of the federal courts except that the executive officer is called a *marshal.*

Persons who are educated in the profession of the law and who are legally qualified to practice law are known as *lawyers* or *attorneys.* They are officers of the court and are subject to punishment for a breach of duty. Lawyers ordinarily represent the parties in a civil or a criminal action, although many states permit the parties to a case to conduct their own trial. The practice of conducting one's own trial, however, is usually not advisable.

PROCEDURE IN FILING SUIT

Courts with but few exceptions are powerless to settle disputes between individuals unless one of the parties petitions the court. This petition or complaint is the beginning of a civil suit. The one who institutes the action is called the *plaintiff,* and the one against whom action is brought is called the *defendant.* The order of events in bringing an action is generally as follows:

(1) The complaint or petition is filed with the clerk of the court. This petition sets forth the nature of the claim and the remedy sought.

(2) As soon as the petition is filed, the clerk issues a *summons* or, as it is sometimes called, a *process.* This merely summons the defendant to appear in court and file his answer to the petition. The complaint and the answer constitute the first pleadings or attempts to establish and define the issues. Before the case can be placed before a jury, the issue or issues of the suit must be clearly specified through these preliminary pleadings, answers, and motions.

(3) The jury is impaneled and the trial opens.

TRIAL PROCEDURE

The trial proceeds in the following order:

(1) The attorney for the plaintiff makes an opening statement to the jury indicating the nature of the action and what he expects to prove. This is usually followed by the opening statement of the defendant's attorney.

(2) The plaintiff presents his evidence in the form of witnesses and documents. This is followed by the defendant's evidence.

(3) The attorney for each side summarizes the evidence and argues his points in an attempt to win the jury to his version of the case.

(4) The judge instructs the jury as to the points of law which govern the case. The judge has the sole power to determine the points of law, and the jury decides what weight is to be given to each point of evidence except that it cannot disregard undisputed evidence.

(5) The jury adjourns to the jury room and in secret arrives at its *verdict*. This verdict may be set aside by the court if it is contrary to the law and the evidence. Unless this is done, the judge renders judgment in accordance with the verdict.

(6) If neither party requests a jury, the case may be tried before the judge alone who in such circumstances would act as both judge and jury.

APPEALS

If either the plaintiff or the defendant is dissatisfied with the jury's verdict and the court's judgment, he may generally appeal to the state supreme court. When an appeal is taken, a complete transcript of the trial is printed and the state supreme court reviews the entire proceedings. The attorney for each side files a brief setting forth the reasons which warrant the supreme court in either affirming or reversing the judgment of the lower court. The decision of the state supreme court becomes judicial precedent and is binding upon all lower courts in the state. The supreme court may, however, reverse itself in a future case. This is seldom done unless the personnel of the court changes, and even then, reversals seldom occur.

QUESTIONS

1. What is the function of a court?
2. Which is the most specific—a constitution, a statutory law, or a court decision?

3. A corporation located in Alabama commits an act in Alabama that is illegal in Georgia. Can a Georgia court punish the Alabama corporation for such act?

4. (a) Name the largest class of federal courts.
   (b) Name two special federal courts.

5. If the Supreme Court of the United States declares a law unconstitutional, how may that decision be changed?

6. Is a decision of a state supreme court binding upon all the lower courts in that state?

7. Name the court in which the following disputes would be settled: (a) a dispute over the interpretation of a will; (b) a claim for an unpaid bill of $10; (c) the claim of a wife that her husband refuses to support her; (d) a damage suit for $2,500; (e) an appeal from the decision in the preceding suit; and (f) a claim against the federal government.

8. Who are the officers of a court?

9. (a) What is the first step in bringing a civil suit?
   (b) What is the first step in a civil suit after the jury is impaneled and the trial opens?

10. Smith sues Jones for $5,000, and the jury renders a verdict for $3,000. Who may appeal from this decision?

Part 2.

CONTRACTS

Preview Cases for Part 2: Contracts

- Dewey was expressly employed by Harmon to work as a carpenter on Harmon's house for $40 for one day's work. The next day Dewey reported for work again. He worked for four days after the first day and Harmon made no effort to stop him. Must Harmon pay Dewey for the additional four days of work?

- Hall and Karl were rowing in a boat. The boat overturned. Hall could not swim. He called to Karl, "I will give you my sports car if you will save me." Karl risked his life to save Hall. Later Hall refused to give Karl the car. Is he obligated to do so?

- Hoover offered by letter to sell Harrell a new Plymouth for $309. Harrell accepted by letter immediately. The true price was $3,009, but the typist erred in writing up the offer. Could Harrell hold Hoover to the offer?

- Harold purchased a used car from Jarvis. He gave a check for $300 in payment. The check was a bad check, and Jarvis threatened to prosecute Harold. Later he said to Harold, "If you will buy a new car for $2,800 cash, I will refrain from prosecuting you." Harold accepted the offer but later wished to avoid the contract. Does he have the right to do so?

- Sanders, a minor, owned and operated a service station. In this capacity he purchased gasoline, tires, and other merchandise amounting to $3,000. He was sued on this account, and his service station was to be sold to satisfy the debt. Was Sanders liable for his debts?

- Alewine and Goodnoe form a contract whereby Alewine agrees to sell Goodnoe 10,000 shares of stock one month from date at $42 a share. They do not intend actually to buy and sell the stock, but they do agree to settle for the difference between $42 a share and the closing price on the date fixed in the contract. Is the contract valid?

- Robertson orally promised to deed his lakeside cottage to his daughter if she would marry Jones. After the marriage, Robertson refused to execute and deliver the deed, and his daughter sued him. Is Robertson legally obligated to transfer the property?

These preview cases are designed to serve as a springboard for the study of this part. As you read through each chapter in this part, you will find the actual decisions for all these preview cases. Of course, there are many more such illustrative problems as well as case problems for decision at the end of each chapter. And there are also a number of even more challenging cases for review at the end of the part.

Chapter 3

CONTRACTS—NATURE
AND CLASSES

DEFINITION OF A CONTRACT

A *contract* can be defined as an agreement between two or more persons that is enforceable at law. At first glance this seems like a very simple definition. In reality Chapters 4-9 are devoted exclusively to explaining and elucidating this definition. Making contracts is such an everyday occurrence that we are often inclined to overlook its importance, except when the contracts are of substantial nature. When one buys a cup of coffee during a coffee break, he has made a contract. When the purchaser agrees to pay ten cents for the coffee, the seller agrees not only to supply one cup of coffee but also agrees by implication of law that it is safe to drink. If the coffee contains a harmful substance that makes the purchaser ill, there has been a breach of contract that may call for the payment of damages.

Business transactions are the result of agreements. Every time a person makes a purchase, buys a theater ticket, or boards a bus, an agreement is made. Each party to the agreement obtains certain rights and assumes certain duties and obligations. When such an agreement meets all the legal requirements of a contract, the law recognizes it as binding upon all parties. If one of the parties to the contract breaches it by failing or refusing to perform, the law allows the other party an appropriate action for obtaining damages or enforcing performance by the party breaching the contract.

Contracts form the very foundation upon which all modern business rests, for business consists almost entirely of the making and performing of contracts. Business is conducted for profit, and valid, enforceable contracts are the source of this profit. Good contracts are made by people who understand the law of contracts.

CONTRACTS CONTRASTED WITH AGREEMENTS

A contract must be an agreement, but an agreement is not necessarily a contract. Whenever two or more persons' minds meet upon any subject, no matter how trivial, there is an agreement. It is only when the parties intend to be legally obligated by the terms of the agreement that a contract comes into existence. Ordinarily, the subject matter of the contract must involve a business transaction as distinguished from a social transaction.

> Mary and John promise to meet at a certain place at six o'clock and have dinner together. This is an agreement, not a contract, since neither intends to be legally bound to carry out the terms of the agreement.
>
> If Alice says to David, "I will pay you $25 to be my escort for the Spring Ball," and David replies, "I will accept your offer," the agreement results in a contract. David is legally obligated to provide escort service, and Alice is legally bound to pay the $25.

CLASSIFICATION OF CONTRACTS

Contracts are often referred to by many names or terms. Unless these terms are understood, the law cannot be understood. For example, the law may state that executory contracts made on Sunday are void. This law cannot be understood unless one clearly understands the words "executory" and "void." For this reason one must study classification of contracts before he studies contracts. Every contract may be placed in one or more of the following classifications:

1. Express and implied contracts
2. Valid, void, and voidable contracts
3. Formal and simple contracts
4. Executory and executed contracts
5. Unilateral and bilateral contracts

(1) **Express and Implied Contracts.** When contracts are classified according to the manner of their formation, they fall into two groups—express and implied contracts. An *express contract* is one in which the parties express their intentions by words, whether in writing or orally, at the time they make the agreement. Both their intention to contract and the terms of the agreement are expressly stated.

- Kemp by letter offers to purchase a particular typewriter for $300, and Sampson by letter accepts Kemp's offer. This is an express contract. An analysis of the contract, however, shows that many essential parts have been omitted. Is this a cash sale or a credit sale? When is delivery to be made? Since nothing is said about credit, it is implied that Kemp will pay cash. The seller implied he would deliver the typewriter within a reasonable time. That which is customary need not be expressed in an express contract.

An *implied contract* is one in which the duties and the obligations which the parties assume are not expressed but are implied by their acts or conduct. The adage "A man's actions speak louder than his words" very appropriately describes this class of contract. The parties may indicate so clearly by their conduct what they intend to do that there is no need to express the agreement by words to make it binding.

- Dewey was expressly employed by Harmon to work as a carpenter on Harmon's house for $40 for one day's work. The next day Dewey reported for work again. He worked for four days after the first day and Harmon made no effort to stop him. Harmon must pay Dewey for five days of work at $40 a day. They had an express contract for the first day. Since essentially the same relationship continued for four more days, each party implied by his actions that the terms of the express contract would apply to the four days for which they had no express contract.

(2) Valid, Void, and Voidable Contracts. If one wishes to classify contracts according to their enforceability, then all contracts would be valid, void, or voidable.

A *valid contract* is one that will be enforced by the courts. In order to be enforceable, that is, valid, a contract must fulfill the following definite requirements:

(a) It must be based upon a mutual agreement by the parties to do or not to do a specific thing.

(b) It must be made by parties who are competent to enter into a contract that will be enforceable against both parties.

(c) The promise or obligation of each party must be supported by consideration (such as the payment of money, the delivery of goods, or the promise to do or refrain from doing some lawful future act) given by each party to the contract.

(d) It must be for a lawful purpose; that is, the purpose of the contract must not be illegal, such as the unauthorized buying and selling of narcotics.

(e) In some cases, the contract must meet certain formal requirements, such as being in writing or being in writing and under seal.

These five requirements are the criteria by which one may test the validity of any contract. If the agreement fails to meet one or more of these requirements, the contract may be void or voidable but never valid. A layman can, in most instances, analyze all business transactions in the light of these five requirements to ascertain their enforceability.

A contract that is of no legal effect is a *void contract*. Since there is no contract in the first place, the agreement is not enforceable in a court of law and thus does not come within the definition of a contract. The term "void contract," however, is widely used by the legal profession and must be understood. A void contract must be distinguished from an *unenforceable contract*. If the law requires a certain contract to be in a particular form, such as a deed, and it is not in that form, it is merely unenforceable, not void; but it can be made enforceable by changing the form to meet the requirements of the law. An agreement between two parties involving an illegal act is a void contract. Nothing the parties can do will make it enforceable.

A *voidable contract* is one that may be set aside by at least one of the parties. Basically, a voidable contract is an enforceable agreement; but, because of circumstances or the capacity of one party, it may be set aside by one of the parties. The test of a voidable contract is the existence of a choice by one party to abide by or to reject the contract. A contract made by an adult with a person not of lawful age (legally known as a minor or infant) is often voidable so far as the minor is concerned. It is enforceable against the adult but not against the minor. If both parties to an agreement are minors, either one may avoid the agreement. Until the party having the choice to avoid the contract exercises his right to set the contract aside, the contract remains in full force and effect.

(3) **Formal and Simple Contracts.** A contract under seal is a *formal contract*. In olden days when very few men could write, contracts were signed by means of an impression in wax attached to the paper. As time passed, a small wafer pasted on the contract replaced the use of wax. The wafer seal was in addition to the written signature. This practice is still used occasionally, but the more common practice is to sign formal contracts in one of these ways:

John Doe (Seal); John Doe [L. S.]; John Doe

Today, it is immaterial whether these substitutes for a seal are printed on the document or typewritten before signing or whether the persons signing write them after their respective names. In jurisdictions where the use of the seal has not been abolished, the seal implies consideration, as will be discussed in Chapter 7, "Consideration."

In some states the presence of a seal on a contract allows a party a longer time in which to bring suit if the contract is broken. Other states make no distinction between contracts under seal and other written contracts.

All contracts other than formal contracts are informal and are called *simple contracts*. A few of these, such as an agreement to sell land or to be responsible for the debt of another, must be in writing in order to be enforceable; otherwise they need not be prepared in any particular form. Generally speaking, informal or simple contracts may be in writing, may be oral, or may be implied from the conduct of the parties.

A *written contract* is one in which the terms are set forth in writing rather than expressed orally. The law requires some contracts not only to be in writing but also to be in a particular form. Some writers classify these as *formal contracts* because of their required form. The more common practice is to restrict the definition of formal contracts to those contracts that are in writing and under seal.

An *oral contract* is one in which the terms are stated in spoken, not written, words. Such a contract is usually enforceable, but it is not so satisfactory as a written contract. When a contract is oral, disputes may arise between the parties as to the terms of the agreement. No such disputes need arise about the terms of a written contract if the wording is clear, explicit, and complete. For this reason most businessmen avoid making oral contracts involving matters of very great importance.

(4) Executory and Executed Contracts. Contracts are classified to indicate the stage of performance as executory contracts and executed contracts. An *executory contract* is one the terms of which have not been fully carried out by all parties. If a man agrees to work for another for one year in return for a salary of $650 a month, the contract is executory from its inception until the twelve months expire. Even if the employer should prepay the salary, it would still be an executory contract because the other party has not yet worked the entire year, that is, executed his part of the contract.

An *executed contract* is one that has been fully performed by all parties to the contract. The Collegiate Shop sells and delivers a suit to Benson for $85, and Benson pays the purchase price at the time of the sale. This is an executed contract because nothing remains to be done on either side, that is, each party has completed performance of his part of the contract.

(5) **Unilateral and Bilateral Contracts.** When an act is done in consideration for a promise, the contract is a *unilateral contract*. If Smith loans Johnson $1,000 and Johnson promises to repay the loan in 90 days, this would be a unilateral contract. It is unilateral in the promise made. Johnson promises to pay Smith for his act of loaning him $1,000. A *bilateral contract* consists solely of a mutual exchange of promises to perform some future acts—one promise is the consideration for the other promise. If Brown promises to sell a truck to Adams for $500 and Adams agrees to pay $500, then the parties have exchanged a promise for a promise—a bilateral contract.

QUESTIONS

1. Name the five requirements of a valid contract.
2. Would it be possible to conduct a business if it were not for the law of contracts?
3. May a contract be partly implied?
4. Relative to the enforceability of contracts, name the three groups into which they are classified. Define and give an example of each group.
5. Define:
   (a) a *unilateral contract*
   (b) a *bilateral contract*
6. (a) Illustrate three ways by which one may indicate that a contract is under seal.
   (b) Does a seal add anything of importance to a contract?
7. Is an oral contract usually just as valid as a written contract?
8. If one has ten witnesses to an oral contract, can he enforce it if the contract is required by law to be in writing to be enforceable?
9. (a) Define an executory contract.
   (b) Define an executed contract.
10. If one party to a contract has executed his part but the other party has not, is the contract executory or executed?

CASE PROBLEMS

When the concluding question in a case problem can be answered simply, such as "Yes" or "No," state the legal principle or rule of law which supports your answer.

1. John and Henry agree to go on a hunting trip, starting the next day at 6 a.m. John purchased a gun, some shells, and a hunting outfit. The following day Henry called John and told him he had changed his mind and would not go hunting. Was the agreement of the day before a binding contract?

2. Gentry owned a home in Augusta. Hall promised to build Gentry a fallout shelter under his house for $700. Gentry agreed to pay $100 before the work started and to pay the balance upon completion of the shelter. Hall agreed to have the job completed within two weeks.

  (a) Is this an express contract or an implied contract?
  (b) Is it void, voidable, or valid?
  (c) Is it executed or executory?
  (d) Is it formal or informal?
  (e) Is it unilateral or bilateral?

3. In a certain state all executory contracts made on Sunday are void. Bell purchased a pair of shoes from Reese on Sunday, had them wrapped, and paid for them but asked Reese to hold them until Tuesday for him. On Tuesday he refused to take the shoes and demanded a return of his money. To determine the rights of the parties it was necessary to classify this contract. Was it an executed contract or an executory contract?

4. Harper was a real estate broker. He entered into a contract with Cohen to sell Cohen's house for $22,500. Cohen was to pay Harper a commission of 5 percent "when the sale is consummated." The law required all contracts for the sale of land to be formal. Must this contract be formal to be enforceable?

5. Morehead, a minor, purchased a suit from Jensen for $75. Jensen, as a part of the sales price, agreed to alter the suit to fit. When the suit was ready, Morehead refused to take it and pay for it. (a) Since a minor is liable only on his executed contracts for necessaries, was he within his legal right in refusing to purchase it? (b) If your answer to the question above was yes, state how Jensen might have made this a valid contract at the time the agreement was made.

6. Kathleen was invited to a formal dance. Her mother engaged Mrs. Schwartz to make an evening dress for Kathleen for $150. After the dress was finished but before it was delivered, Kathleen's boyfriend canceled the invitation. Her mother then refused to accept and pay for the dress, claiming the transaction was a social obligation, not a business transaction. Do you agree with this interpretation?

Chapter 4

OFFER AND ACCEPTANCE

Usually there can be no valid contract unless the minds of the contracting parties are in complete agreement. This agreement is reached when one party makes an offer and the other party accepts the offer.

The parties may· expressly state, either orally or in writing, what they agree to do, or they may indicate their intentions by their actions. The innermost thoughts of a person's mind can be known only to himself. If his conduct reasonably leads another person to believe·that the party intends to enter into a binding contract, then that party is bound as effectively as if he had expressed his intentions. In business, seldom does one indicate his full intentions solely by his acts. In most cases he expressly states a part of the contract and implies the other part.

Furthermore, one may have an obligation imposed on him by law. This will be done only when a failure to do so would result in an unjust enrichment of one person at the expense of another. For example, suppose a tenant is obligated to pay rent of $100 a month but by mistake hands the landlord $200. The law requires the landlord to return the overpayment of $100 on the basis of a *quasi-contract* obligation; that is, the law creates an agreement for repayment even though no agreement exists. For the landlord to keep the money would mean that he would be unjustly enriched at the expense of the tenant.

Two essential elements of a contract are: (1) an offer, either expressed or implied; and (2) an acceptance, either expressed or implied.

THE OFFER

The beginning of a contract is the offer made by the offeror to the offeree. The *offeror* is the person who makes the offer; the *offeree* is the person to whom the offer is made. An *offer* expresses the willingness of the offeror to enter into a contractual agreement. There are three elements of an offer:

1. The offer must be definite
2. It must be seriously intended
3. It must be communicated to the offeree

(1) The Offer Must Be Definite. A contract will not be enforced unless the court can ascertain what the parties agreed to. The offeror's intentions are ascertained from the offer, and this cannot be done unless the offer is definite.

■ Harold wrote to Davis as follows: "I will lease your building at 564 Main Street, alterations and floor layout to be mutually agreed upon." Davis accepted the offer, but Harold changed his mind and refused to lease the building. There was no contract because the expression "to be mutually agreed upon" is too indefinite. Harold would not be bound even though Davis agreed to make any alterations Harold wanted. The offer must be specific from the beginning.

The Uniform Commercial Code modifies this strict rule somewhat as to contracts for the sale of goods. It is not always practical for a businessman to make an offer for the sale of merchandise that is definite as to price. The offeror may leave the price open, it being determined by the market price at a future date or being fixed by a third party. This would be considered a definite offer. Furthermore, an offer to sell is an acceptable offer under the Uniform Commercial Code even if the offeror states no price. If the contract does not specify the price, the buyer must ordinarily pay the reasonable value of the goods.

(2) The Offer Must Be Seriously Intended. One may make an offer in jest, banter, fear, or extreme anger; and if this fact is known or should be known by the offeree because of the surrounding circumstances, no contract is formed. A business transaction is ordinarily not entered into in jest or because of extreme fear or anger, and the offeree has no right to think that the offer is seriously intended when it is made under these circumstances. There are times, however, when the offer is not seriously intended, but the offeree has no way of knowing this. In that event, if the offer is accepted, a binding contract results. In the two examples that follow these points are illustrated.

- Hall and Karl were rowing in a boat. The boat overturned. Hall could not swim. He called to Karl, "I will give you my sports car if you will save me." Karl risked his own life to save Hall. Hall refused to give Karl the sports car. He was within his rights. An offer made under extreme emotional circumstances is not an acceptable offer.

As previously noted, the secret thoughts of a party have no effect. If the offeree with reason thinks that the offer is made in earnest and accepts it, a binding contract will result even though the offer is made in jest.

- Hendler in a serious manner offered Knapp a painting worth $250 for $10. Knapp, being a poor judge of the value of paintings, accepted the offer. Hendler contended that he had made the offer just as a prank to see if Knapp appreciated the value of the painting. Since there was no circumstance or act on Hendler's part to indicate that the offer was made in jest, Knapp was reasonable in believing that the offer was seriously made.

(3) **The Offer Must Be Communicated to the Offeree.** Until the offeror makes known his offer to the offeree, it is not certain that he intends that the offeree may accept and thereby impose a binding contract upon him. Accordingly, it is held that an offer cannot be accepted by the offeree until the offeror has communicated the offer to him. If one writes out an offer and the offer falls into the hands of the offeree without the knowledge or consent of the offeror, it cannot be accepted. Furthermore, an offer directed to a specific individual or firm cannot be accepted by anyone else. This is true because one has a right to choose the people with whom he deals.

- Henderson dictated a letter to be sent to Miller offering to sell him stock in an oil company. Before Henderson mailed the letter, he heard on the radio that the company had struck oil. Miller also heard the news. Miller called Henderson on the phone and orally accepted the offer, since he had previously learned of the unmailed letter from Henderson's secretary. There was no contract since the offer was never communicated to the offeree. The mere dictation of a letter was only a step leading to communication; but no communication was actually made.

INVITATIONS TO MAKE OFFERS

In business many apparent offers are not true offers. They are instead treated as invitations to the public to make offers at certain terms and prices. If the invitation is accepted by a member of the public and an offer is submitted embodying all the terms set out in the invitation, the inviter may refuse to accept the offer; ordinarily, however, as a practical matter and in the interest of maintaining goodwill, he will accept such offer. The most common types of general invitations are advertisements, window displays, catalogs, price lists, and circular sales letters. If a merchant displays in his store window a coat for $65, he is not bound to sell at this price. Most businessmen would consider refusal to sell a very poor business policy, but it is nevertheless a protection which the law gives a businessman who might otherwise find that he oversold his stock of goods, thereby subjecting him to many suits for breach of contract.

> ■ The Denny Shoe Store placed a pair of shoes with a price tag of
> $8.95 in the store window. Stephen saw the shoes and offered to
> purchase them at that price. The price, in fact, was in error; it
> should have been $18.95. Denny stated he would not sell at $8.95
> and that he was raising the price to $18.95. There was no contract
> since the window display was a mere invitation to Stephen to
> make an offer.

The general rule is that a circular sales letter is not an offer but an invitation to the recipient to make an offer. It is often difficult, however, to distinguish between a general sales letter and a personal sales letter. The fact that the letter is addressed to a particular individual does not necessarily make it a personal sales letter containing an offer. If the wording is such as to indicate that the writer is merely trying to evoke an offer on certain terms, this is not an offer but an invitation to the other party to make an offer.

> ■ Landis wrote Hall: "If I were offered $20,000 for my house, I
> would be delighted to sell." Hall wrote immediately accepting the
> offer. There was no contract because there was no offer that could
> be accepted. Landis was merely inviting Hall to make an offer.

An advertisement, however, may be an offer when it clearly shows an intent that it is one. This is primarily true with advertisements that offer rewards.

> ■ Foster placed the following ad in the newspaper: "I will pay
> $1,000 to anyone giving information leading to the arrest and con-
> viction of the person who set fire to my property." Brewer saw the
> ad and set out to find the guilty party. As a result of Brewer's informa-
> tion, Dunnaway was arrested and tried. There was strong circumstan-
> tial evidence of his guilt, but the jury acquitted him. Brewer
> demanded his $1,000. Foster did not have to pay because his ad laid

down two conditions, namely, that the guilty party be "arrested" and "convicted." Since Dunnaway was not convicted, Foster did not have to pay.

DURATION OF THE OFFER

When an offer is once sent out, a large number of laws come into play. Ignorance of any one of them may seriously affect one's rights. Here is a summary of the more important ones:

(1) The offeror may revoke an offer any time prior to its acceptance.

(2) The offer may state that it would be held open for a particular time. Ordinarily the offer may be revoked in spite of such a provision. Two exceptions exist to this statement. First, if the offeror receives something in return for his statement or agreement to hold the offer open, it is said to be an *option* contract and the offer cannot be revoked. Secondly, if the offer relates to the sale or purchase of goods by a merchant, a signed written offer to purchase or buy which states that it will be held open cannot be revoked, to the extent discussed in Chapter 13.

In states in which the seal has its common-law effect, an offer cannot be revoked when it is contained in a sealed writing which states that it will not be revoked.

(3) A revocation of an offer must be communicated to the offeree prior to the acceptance. Mere intention to revoke is not sufficient. This is true even though the intent is clearly shown as when the offeror dictates a letter of revocation but the letter is not in fact sent or is not received by the offeree.

▪ Davis wrote the Towns Tire Company offering to lease them a building for five years for $400 a month. He gave thirty days to accept or reject the offer. Ten days later Davis leased the building to the Bell Tire Company and the Towns Tire Company learned of this lease. This revoked the offer to the Towns Tire Company as it is irrelevant how the revocation is communicated to the offeree.

(4) An offer is revoked by the lapse of the time specified in the offer. If no time is specified in the offer, it is revoked by a lapse of a reasonable time after being communicated to the offeree. What is a reasonable length of time varies with each case depending on the circumstances. It may be ten minutes in one case and sixty days in another. Important circumstances are the fact that the price of the goods or services involved are fluctuating or not fluctuating rapidly,

or perishable goods are involved, or there is or is not keen competition
with respect to the subject matter of the contract.

> ■ A New Orleans cotton broker wrote the Gulf Textile Company
> as follows: "Because of the unstable world conditions, I am anxious
> to dispose of my stock of cotton. I will take $165 a bale f.o.b. New
> Orleans." The Gulf Textile Company waited 25 days and then ac-
> cepted. The offer had lapsed since its wording clearly indicated that
> the offeror wanted an immediate reply.

(5) Death or insanity of the offeror automatically revokes the
offer by operation of law. This is true even though the offeree is not
aware of the death or the insanity of the offeror at the time he accepts.
Both parties must be alive and competent to contract at the moment
the acceptance is properly communicated to the offeror or his agent.

> ■ Dean wrote Denny offering to sell Denny 1,000 shares of stock
> for $18,000. A few days later Dean was fatally injured in an auto-
> mobile accident. Denny, unaware of Dean's death, accepted the offer.
> There was no contract because Dean's death revoked the offer.

(6) Rejection of the offer by the offeree terminates the offer.
Ordinarily, if the offeree makes a counteroffer without saying anything about the original offer, the original offer is likewise terminated.
To some extent this last statement does not apply when the subject
matter of the offer is the sale or purchase of goods.

THE ACCEPTANCE

When an offer has been properly communicated to the party for
whom it is intended, and that party, or someone authorized to act for
him, accepts, a binding contract is formed. The acceptance must be
communicated to the offeror, but no particular procedure is required
for this purpose. The acceptance may be made by words, oral or
written, or by some act which clearly shows an intention to accept.
Silence does not, except in rare cases, constitute an acceptance; nor
is a mental intention to accept sufficient. If the offer stipulates a particular mode or time of acceptance, the offeree must meet those
standards in order for a contract to be formed.

COUNTEROFFERS

An offer must be accepted without any deviation in the terms of
the offer. If the intended acceptance varies or qualifies the offer, this

is a *counteroffer* and is a rejection of the original offer. This rule is changed to some extent where the offer relates to the sale or purchase of goods. In any case, a counteroffer may be accepted or rejected by the original offeror.

> ▪ Dale wrote Williams as follows: "I will sell you my insurance agency for $15,000." Williams replied by letter: "I accept your offer with the understanding you will agree not to enter the insurance business again in this town for two years." This was a counteroffer and thus a rejection of the original offer.

INQUIRIES NOT CONSTITUTING REJECTION

The offeree may make an inquiry without rejecting the offer. For example, if the offer is for 1,000 shares of stock for $10,000 cash, the offeree may inquire as follows: "Would you be willing to wait thirty days for $5,000 and hold the stock as collateral security?" This is a mere inquiry and is not a rejection of the offer. If the inquiry is answered in the negative, the original offer may still be accepted, provided it has not been revoked in the meantime.

OFFERS AND ACCEPTANCES BY CORRESPONDENCE

When a person makes an offer by mail, he may, if he wishes, state that the acceptance will not be valid until it is actually received. In that case the agreement is not completed until the acceptance is actually delivered to the offeror. If, however, a person sends an offer by mail but does not specify that the acceptance is not to be valid until it is received, he is considered to have authorized the acceptance to be sent in any manner the offeree chooses, which is reasonable under the circumstances. A properly mailed acceptance takes effect at the time it is mailed. The rule applies even though the acceptance is never received by the offeror. In any court case involving such a situation, it becomes a question of fact as to whether or not there was an acceptance.

Similarly, when an offer is received in a telegram, the delivery of an acceptance to the telegraph company completes the agreement, unless the offeror specifies otherwise or unless custom or prior dealings indicate that acceptance by telegraph is improper. In former years it was held that an offer could be accepted only by the same means by which the offer was communicated. But this view is gradually being abandoned in favor of this provision of the Uniform Commercial Code

(Sec. 2-206(1)) relating to sales of personal property: "Unless otherwise unambiguously indicated by the language or circumstances, an offer to make a [sales] contract shall be construed as inviting acceptance in any manner and by any medium reasonable in the circumstances."

Careful and prudent persons can avoid many difficulties by stipulating in the offer how it must be accepted and when the acceptance is to become effective. For example, the offer may state, "The acceptance must be sent by wire and be received by me in Chicago by 12 noon on June 15 before the contract is complete." If the acceptance is mailed, there is no acceptance until the accepting letter is received by the offeror. That is to say, the acceptance is not effective unless it is by wire and is actually received by the offeror and by the time specified in Chicago.

> ▪ Taul owned a negotiable option to purchase 500 shares of stock
>   in a uranium company at $12 a share. He wrote ten letters to ten
> different people offering to sell the option for $1,000. Three of these
> parties immediately accepted. Taul could be sued by two of them
> for breach of contract because he can sell to only one. He should
> have included a protective clause in the offer such as, "contract not
> to become effective until acceptance acknowledged by me."

QUESTIONS

1. What is a *quasi contract*?
2. If one receives an offer by letter and he wishes to accept the offer before the offeror revokes it, which would be better—to accept by letter or by telegram?
3. How would it be possible for one to be bound on a contract and not be aware of it for quite some time?
4. If John has only one stereo set but writes five letters to five different people offering to sell it for $300, could he find himself in considerable difficulty if he were ignorant of the law regarding offer and acceptance?
5. Under what conditions may one accept an offer that is made in the form of a newspaper advertisement?
6. (a) When may an offer be revoked?
   (b) What is the effect of death or insanity of the offeror on an offer?
7. What is the effect of a counteroffer?
8. How may an offer by mail be accepted?
9. How does one determine what is a "reasonable time" after which an offer would "lapse"?
10. If an offer is made by telegram and the acceptance is sent by letter, when is the contract formed?

CASE PROBLEMS

1. The Hargrove Milling Company wrote an offer to the A & B Bakery as follows: "We will sell you flour at $20 a hundred, terms 2/10, n/30." The Bakery replied, "I accept your offer for 1,000 barrels if we can get terms 2/10, n/60." The A & B Bakery waited 20 days and did not hear from the offeror. A new acceptance was then mailed: "I accept your offer for 1,000 barrels at $20 a hundred, terms 2/10, n/30." Was a contract formed?

2. The S & C Bank ran this advertisement in the local paper: "We will pay $500 for information leading to identification of the person who robbed this bank." Davis read the ad. He had written down the getaway car's license. He supplied this information, and the robber was apprehended. Is Davis entitled to collect the $500?

3. Dawson, the sales manager for the Builders Supply Company, offered to sell Dobbs Brothers 500 gallons of paint at $4 per gallon. On October 1 Dobbs Brothers accepted by letter with a stipulation that the paint was to be delivered 50 gallons a week. No reply was ever made to this acceptance. Was there a contract?

4. Carrol was arrested by the police and put in jail for an attempted robbery. Samuel saw a picture of Carrol in the local paper and recognized him as a suspect wanted for robbery in a distant city. There was a reward of $5,000 for "arrest and conviction." Samuel called the police department in the distant city and informed them that Carrol was in a local jail. He demanded the reward of $5,000. Was he entitled to it?

5. Uncle John promised Fred a new car if Fred passed the bar exam. After he took the exam, he was exultant over how easy it was. He assured his uncle he had passed, so Uncle John gave him the car. A few days later the results of the bar exam were announced, but Fred's name was not among those who passed. Uncle John demanded a return of the car. Fred claims there was no contract binding him to return the car. Do you agree?

6. A local corporation formed for the purpose of drilling for oil went out of business. The stock was considered by all the townspeople to be absolutely worthless. Hipps, the owner of 1,000 shares of this stock, offered to sell them to Hurley for 10 cents a share. Hurley accepted. A few minutes later a radio report stated that oil had been discovered on a tract of land adjoining the property of the defunct corporation. Hipps refused to sell Hurley the stock, claiming the offer was made in jest. Was there a contract?

7. Joel wrote Broadnax a letter, offering to sell him a tract of real estate owned by Joel. Twenty-four hours later Joel sold the land to Ledbetter without waiting to hear from Broadnax. As soon as Broadnax received Joel's offer, he accepted. Joel contended that his selling the land to Ledbetter was a revocation of his offer to Broadnax. Do you agree?

8. At 9 a.m. Potts wired Lemly as follows: "I will sell you 1,000 bales of cotton 1-inch middling at 35 cents a pound." At 3 p.m. Lemly sent an acceptance in writing by a messenger boy. Before the boy reached Potts' office, Lemly received a telephone call from Potts stating the offer was revoked. While Potts was talking to Lemly on the phone, the messenger boy delivered the acceptance. Was a contract formed?

Chapter 5

DEFECTIVE AGREEMENTS

MISTAKES THAT MAKE AGREEMENTS DEFECTIVE

As a general rule, a mistake made by one party without the knowledge of the other has no effect on the validity of the contract. There are, however, certain mistakes that make agreements defective:

1. Mistakes as to the nature of the transaction
2. Mistakes as to the identity of the party
3. Mutual mistakes as to the identity of the subject matter
4. Mutual mistakes as to the existence of the subject matter

(1) **Mistakes as to the Nature of the Transaction.** A mistake as to the nature of the transaction renders the contract void if the mistake was caused by the fraud of the other contracting party. If, through trickery, a man is induced to sign a deed under the impression it is a note, he is not bound by his signature. But to avoid the contract on the ground of mistake, he must not have been negligent. A person signing a contract without reading it and without taking reasonable steps to learn what it means may be prevented from claiming that the contract is void. A person who is unable to read must have someone read and explain the paper to him.

> ▪ Miller, an educated person, purchased real estate from Robinson. Miller signed the contract which he "half read." As a result, he did not notice the provision of the contract calling for payment of interest on the unpaid portion of the purchase price. Miller refused to pay the interest specified in the contract. Robinson sued and was allowed to recover on the basis that a person is ordinarily bound by a contract that he signs without reading it.

(2) **Mistakes as to the Identity of the Party.** Freedom of contract includes among other things the freedom to choose the parties

with whom one contracts. With but rare exceptions, the law does not compel one to contract with a person with whom he does not wish to deal. If one is mistaken as to the identity of the party with whom he is contracting, then the contract is void. When the mistake as to the identity of a party is induced by trick or deception of that party, however, the contract is voidable and may be set aside by the deceived party.

If a person contracts with another in a face-to-face relationship, he is presumed to have intended to contract with this particular individual even though he thought it was someone else. Even if the other party said, "I am Charles Greene," when in fact he was Francis Barlow, the contract would be valid if the party was mistaken only as to the man's name, not his real identity. If he deals with him at a distance, however, and the other party falsely represents himself to be someone who he is not, the contract is void. Under these circumstances he cannot ascertain through reasonable diligence that he was mistaken.

If the mistake as to the identity of the party involves an executory contract, then the remedy consists merely of refusing to perform the contract. If it is executed, then any innocent party may rescind the contract by returning anything of value which he received and demanding that the other party do likewise. As far as possible, the law requires that both parties be restored to their prior positions.

> ▪ Holden had once been defrauded by a salesman for the Handy
>   Book Company. A salesman for the Handy Book Company called
>   on Holden to sell him a set of encyclopedias. The salesman knew of
>   Holden's extreme distaste for the Handy Book Company. For this
>   reason, he told Holden the encyclopedias were published by the
>   United Book Company. Holden agreed to buy the books. When they
>   arrived he learned the identity of the true publisher. He rescinded
>   the contract, demanding return of his money. He was within his rights.

(3) **Mutual Mistakes as to the Identity of the Subject Matter.** Unlike the mistakes described in the two preceding sections, mistakes as to the identity of the subject matter of a contract must be mutual. If both parties do not have in mind the same subject matter, their minds can never meet; and thus there can be no contract. For example, if A offers to sell and B agrees to buy "all the pulpwood on my Barnett Shoals Road farm" and A has two farms on that road, the parties may not have the same farm in mind. This cannot become a binding contract until the farm described in the offer is clearly identified.

Often the parties correctly identify the subject matter of the contract but are mistaken about some other aspect of the transaction.

For example, John has two stacks of lumber. One is high grade and the other is low grade. John, pointing to the high-grade lumber, says, "I will sell you this lumber for $5,000." Henry, the offeree, accepts. They both thought the particular stack of lumber identified was the low-quality lumber. The contract is valid, however, since the offeror pointed to, that is, identified, one particular stack of lumber. They were not mistaken as to which stack was meant.

> ▪ Biddle was the purchasing agent for a steel mill. He called on the Loef Brothers Scrap Iron Company to purchase scrap iron. There were two piles of several hundred tons each, one valued at 4 cents a pound and the other at 6 cents. The seller pointed directly at the 6 cents scrap and said, "This is the 4 cents pile of scrap iron." Biddle purchased it. Later the seller learned of his error in identifying the cheaper pile of scrap. It was too late. Since there was no mistake as to the pile to which he pointed, the contract was binding.

(4) **Mutual Mistakes as to the Existence of the Subject Matter.** If two parties enter into a contract relative to a specific subject matter, but at the moment of the contract this specific subject matter does not exist, the contract is void. Again the mistake must be a mutual mistake, not a unilateral one. Such a mistake most often arises when the subject matter of the contract has been destroyed by flood, fire, tornado, or other means, but its destruction is unknown to either party when the contract is formed.

> ▪ Smith sold the Missouri Pacific Railroad 5,000 railroad ties for $1.50 each. Prior to the contract but unknown to either party, the ties had been destroyed by a forest fire. The contract was void since it was based on the assumed existence of a specific lot of 5,000 railroad ties as contrasted with a contract to supply any 5,000 ties of a particular grade.

It is evident from these four classes of mistakes that it is not the function of the law to save us from the consequences of all mistakes. These four classes of mistakes cover a very small percentage of those made in business transactions. Knowledge and diligence, not law, are the chief bulwarks against losses due to mistakes.

MISTAKES THAT DO NOT MAKE AGREEMENTS DEFECTIVE

Most of the mistakes in business transactions do not affect the validity of the contract. Two of these classes of mistakes need special emphasis.

1. Mistakes as to value, quality, or price
2. Mistakes as to the terms of the contract

(1) Mistakes as to Value, Quality, or Price. A contract is not affected by the fact that one of the parties was mistaken as to the value, quality, or price of the subject matter of the contract. If the buyer does not trust his judgment, he has the right to demand of the seller a warranty as to the quality, quantity, or the value of the article he is buying. His ability to contract wisely is his chief protection against a bad bargain. If Snead sells Robinson a television set for $350, Robinson cannot rescind the contract merely because the set proved to be worth only $150. This is a mistake as to value and quality. He should obtain as a part of the contract an express warranty as to the set's quality. Conversely, if the seller parts with a jewel for $50, thinking it is a cheap stone, he cannot later complain if the jewel proves to be worth $2,500.

Mistakes as to value, quality, and sometimes quantity are mistakes, as a rule, of judgment. Mistakes as to price, however, may be the result of errors in typing or in misunderstanding of an oral quotation of the price. But again the wheels of commerce could not run smoothly if either party could avoid the contract merely because he was mistaken as to price. If the E & S Tire Company offers by letter to sell 1,000 tires at $24 each, it cannot avoid the contract on the basis that the secretary incorrectly typed the price $24 instead of $26, the price dictated. The seller is bound on the contract for $24.

> ▪ McGregor dictated an offer to the Instant Typing Service and quoted a price for a certain grade of typing paper at 90 cents a ream. Mary, his secretary, by error typed the offer at 80 cents a ream. McGregor did not catch the error in signing his letters because he sold many grades. The Instant Typing Service immediately accepted the offer and ordered 1,000 reams. It was then that the error was discovered. The contract was valid.

Mistakes of quantity may also be mistakes as to price or value. If both parties are mistaken as to the quantity, there is no meeting of the minds and there is no contract.

> ▪ The Elite Jewelry Store sold Dennis a box of knives and forks for $160. The box was marked to indicate it contained eight knives and eight forks. There were actually six of each. The buyer and the salesclerk relied on the notations on the box, unaware that there were only six knives and forks. This was a mistake of fact as to quantity and value; therefore, there was no contract.

As an exception to the principles stated above, one party cannot hold the other to a contract if he knows that the other one has made a mistake.

> ▪ Hoover offered by letter to sell Harrell a new Plymouth automobile for $309. Harrell accepted by letter immediately. The true price was $3,009, but the typist erred in writing up the offer. The error was so gross and apparent to Harrell that he could not hold Hoover to the offer.

The mistake must be one of fact, not mere opinion. If *A* buys a painting from *B* for $10 that is actually worth $5,000, and *A* knows *B* is mistaken as to its value, there is a valid contract. *B*'s opinion as to its value is erroneous. He is not mistaken as to a fact as illustrated in the case below.

> ▪ The Vaugh Lumber Company sold the Hope Construction Company 10,925 feet of lumber at $187.75 per thousand board feet. The bookkeeper, because of his lack of knowledge of business arithmetic, prepared an invoice showing the total price to be $205.11. The correct amount was $2,051.17. After the purchaser had paid the $205.11, he received a bill for an additional $1,846.06. He must pay it because here there was no error in the unit price of $187.75. The error in calculation on the invoice should have been evident to the purchaser. There was, in fact, no error in the contract price.

(2) Mistakes as to the Terms of the Contract. One of the most common mistakes relates to the terms of the contract. Such a mistake is usually the result of a failure to read the contract if it is written or a failure to understand its meaning or significance. If the contract is oral, either of the parties may be mistaken as to the terms of the contract without the other party's being aware of it. Such mistakes in both written and oral contracts do not affect their validity; otherwise anyone could avoid his contract merely by claiming that he was mistaken as to its terms.

Frequently contracts are entered into orally and then reduced to writing. If through an error in typing the written form does not conform to the oral form, then the parties may not be bound by the written form.

> ▪ The Welch Auto Supply Company orally agreed to purchase some tires of a certain grade and size for $12.50 per tire. When the sales agreement was drawn up, the price was erroneously typed $14.50. Under these conditions the seller could not enforce the $14.50 price.

FRAUD

One who induces another to enter into a contract as a result of an intentionally or recklessly false statement of a material fact, is guilty of *fraud*. A contract so induced is voidable, not void, since the party defrauded intended to make the contract but was induced to do so through fraud.

Fraud may be perpetrated by:

1. Express misrepresentation
2. Concealment of material facts
3. Silence when it is one's duty to speak

(1) **Express Misrepresentation.** Fraud, as a result of express misrepresentation, consists of four elements, each one of which must be present to constitute fraud:

(a) A false statement of a material fact must be made.

(b) The false statement must be made by one who knew it to be false, or by one who made it in reckless disregard of its truth or falsity.

(c) There must be an intent to induce the innocent party to act by reason of the false statement.

(d) The innocent party was induced to make the contract by the false statement.

If these four elements are present, the injured party may, at his option, rescind the contract. If he has been damaged by reason of the fraud, he may, in addition to rescinding the contract, sue for damages.

> ▪ Simpson falsified his financial statements to induce a bank to make him a loan of $5,000 for ninety days. After the loan was made and the discounted value of the note was deposited to his account, the bank learned of the fraud. The bank was entitled to rescind the contract and demand immediate repayment. Had the bank acted to its detriment, it could have also sued for damages.

Statements of opinion, as contrasted with statements of fact, do not, as a rule, constitute fraud. The theory here is that the person hearing the statement realizes or ought to realize that the other party is merely stating his own view and not a statement of fact. But if the speaker is an expert or has special knowledge not available to the other party and should realize that the other party relies on his expert opinion, then a misstatement of opinion or value, intentionally made, would amount to fraud.

Such expressions as "This is the best buy in town," "The price of this stock will double in the next twelve months," "This business will net you $15,000 a year" are all statements of opinion, not statements of fact. If one says, "This business has netted the owner $15,000," this is not an opinion or a prophesy, but an historical fact.

(2) Concealment of Material Facts. If one actively conceals material facts for the purpose of preventing the other contracting party from discovering them, such concealment is fraud even though there are no false statements.

Merely refraining from disclosing pertinent facts unknown to the other party is not fraud as a rule. There must be an active concealment to constitute fraud.

■ A coal company had been prospecting for coal on A's land and found none. Later A filled up the excavations to keep B, a prospective purchaser, from discovering the failure to find coal. This active concealment was fraud if B, to the knowledge of A, thought there was coal on the land.

(3) Silence When It Is One's Duty to Speak. If one's relationship with another is that of trust and confidence, then silence may constitute fraud. Such a relationship exists between partners in a business firm, an agent and his principal, a lawyer and his client, a guardian and his ward, a physician and his patient, and in many other trust relationships. In the case of an attorney-client relationship, for example, the attorney has a duty to reveal anything that is material to the client's interests, and his silence has the same effect as though he had knowingly made a false statement that there was no material fact to be told to the client. The client could, in such a case, avoid the contract.

Silence, when one has no duty to speak, is not fraud. If Lawrence offers to sell Marconi, a diamond merchant, a gem for $500 that is actually worth $15,000, Marconi's superior knowledge of value alone does not impose upon him the duty to speak.

DURESS

For a contract to be valid, all parties must enter into it of their free will. *Duress* is a means of destroying another's free will by obtaining his consent to a contract by means of a threat to do him, or members of his family (near relatives, such as husband, wife, parent, child, brother, sister, grandchild), some harm. The threat may relate to one's property (such as threat to burn down his house) or to his earning power. When the effect of the threat is to prevent the exercise of free will, duress exists.

> ▪ Harold purchased a used car from Jarvis. He gave a check for $300 in payment. The check was a bad check, and Jarvis threatened to prosecute Harold. Later he said to Harold, "If you will buy a new car for $2,800 cash, I will refrain from prosecuting you." Harold accepted the offer but later wished to avoid the contract. He could do so because the contract was voidable on his part because of duress. His guilt was irrelevant. The threat destroyed his free will to contract.

UNDUE INFLUENCE

One person may exercise such influence over the mind of another that the latter does not exercise his own free will. Although there is no force or threat of harm (which would be duress), the contract is nevertheless regarded as voidable. If a party in a confidential or fiduciary relationship to another induces him against his free will to enter into a contract, the agreement is voidable because of *undue influence*. If, under any relationship, one is in a position to take undue advantage of another, undue influence may render the contract voidable. Undue influence may result also from sickness, infirmity, or serious distress. Examples of such relationships are family relationships, a guardian and his ward, an attorney and his client, a physician and his patient, and any other relationship where confidence reposed on one side results in domination by the other.

In undue influence there is never any use of threats to harm the person, property, or relations of the other party as in duress. Usually the party exerting undue influence upon another is suave and friendly rather than gruff and threatening as in duress. The relationship of the two parties must be such that one yields because his will cannot hold out against the superior position, intelligence, or personality of the other party. Whether undue influence exists is a question for the court (usually the jury) to determine. Not every influence is regarded as undue; for example, a nagging wife is ordinarily not regarded as exercising undue influence. In addition, persuasion and argument are not per se undue influence. The key element is that the dominated party is helpless in the hands of the other.

▪ John's father was ill and totally dependent upon John for his support and comfort. John made several insistent offers to buy his father's home at less than its true value. John made no threats, but his father was afraid to antagonize John for fear he would not care for him. This fear destroyed his free will to contract. The sale was voidable.

REMEDIES FOR BREACH OF CONTRACT BECAUSE OF FRAUD, DURESS, OR UNDUE INFLUENCE

Since fraud, duress, and undue influence render contracts voidable, not void, one must know what to do when he is a victim of one of these acts. If he does nothing, the right to avoid the contract may be lost. Furthermore, he may ratify the contract by some act or word indicating an intention to be bound. After the contract is affirmed or ratified, one is as fully bound on it as if there had been no fraud, duress, or undue influence. But still the innocent party may sue for whatever damages he has sustained.

If instead of affirming the contract, one elects to rescind it, he must first return or offer to return whatever he received under the contract. After this is done, he is in a position to take one of three actions depending upon the circumstances:

(1) He may sue to recover any money, goods, or other things of value he has parted with, plus damages.

(2) If the contract is executory on the part of the innocent party, he can refuse to perform. If the other party sues, he can then interpose fraud, duress, or undue influence as a complete defense.

(3) He may bring a suit in equity to have the suit judicially declared void and ask for damages.

▪ Darter, a shoe merchant, was induced through fraud to purchase some shoes for $6,500. The shoes were purchased on 90 days' credit. Darter's best remedy in this case probably is to affirm the contract but to refrain from paying for the shoes. When the seller sues him, he can set up the fraud as a counterclaim. If he could prove that he was damaged to the extent of $3,000 by reason of the fraud, then he would pay the balance of the account, or $3,500.

In no case can the wrongdoer set the contract aside and thus profit from his wrong. If the agreement is void, neither party may enforce it; no special act is required for setting the agreement aside.

QUESTIONS

1. How is a contract affected by a mistake as to the nature of the transaction?
2. What is the effect of negligence on the part of a person who attempts to avoid a contract on the ground of mistake as to the nature of the transaction?
3. (a) If one is mistaken as to the identity of the party with whom he contracts, may he avoid a contract in which the dealings were face to face?
   (b) Can the parties be in mutual agreement when they are honestly mistaken as to the identity of the subject matter of the contract?
4. If the subject matter of the contract did not exist at the time the contract was formed and both parties were unaware of this fact, is the contract valid or void?
5. What is a *material fact?*
6. May one party who knows the true value of an article take advantage of the other party's ignorance of the value of it?
7. If *A* buys a ring set with a zircon thinking it is a diamond, is he bound if the seller did nothing to mislead him?
8. Is a contract induced by fraud void or voidable?
9. Define *duress.*
10. If one does not rely on a misrepresentation, may he plead fraud as a defense when sued on the contract?

CASE PROBLEMS

1. Mary Jones was a secretary in the Hope Furniture Company's office. Gowen wished to purchase $10,000 worth of furniture. He inquired of Miss Jones, since her employer was out, what were the terms of sale. She replied, "2 percent discount for cash." Thereupon Gowen bought the merchandise and paid cash for it. The invoice read "$10,000, less 2% discount, or $8,000." Later the Hope Furniture Company learned of the error and attempted to collect the difference between the $2,000 discount given by Miss Jones and the correct discount of $200. Could it collect?

2. The Lapp Jewelry Company had a diamond necklace for sale. The price was $7,500. McLean, a prospective purchaser, inquired of the salesman as to the price. The salesman looked up the price and said "$750," thinking that was the price shown on the price list. Neither the salesman nor the buyer knew the true value of the necklace. McLean agreed to purchase it. Was the Lapp Jewelry Company bound on this contract?

3. Harris Bibb was office manager for the Griffin Wholesale Company. In this capacity he signed a contract with the Atlanta Collecting Agency to collect $50,000 of delinquent accounts receivable. The written contract with

the agency contained this clause: "The Griffin Wholesale Company agrees to pay the Atlanta Collecting Agency 25% of the aggregate listing as its collection fee." Bibb thought this meant that for each $1,000 collected, the agency would take $250 and remit $750 to the Griffin Wholesale Company. The true meaning was that the agency kept the first $12,500 collected and remitted all over that. Was the Griffin Wholesale Company bound on this contract?

4. Pearson owned a deep sea fishing boat. He agreed to sell it to Huntley for $10,000, delivery to be made as soon as the boat returned to port. At the time the contract was made, the boat had sunk during a storm. This fact was unknown by both buyer and seller. Was there a valid contract?

5. The Sailors Antique Shop displayed several old-style beds. Hargrove purchased one for $2,700, thinking it was a very valuable Louis XIV make. The seller knew Hargrove was mistaken about the antiquity of the bed but said nothing to enlighten him about his ignorance. The bed was of fairly recent make and actually worth only $150. When Hargrove learned of this fact, he attempted to rescind the contract. May he do so?

6. Barry, in an effort to sell Mr. and Mrs. Andrews a house, stated, "In my opinion this house could not be built today for $25,000." Barry, a building expert, knew the house could be built for less than $20,000. In a suit for fraud, Barry attempted to prove he had expressed only an opinion, not a fact. Was this a false representation?

7. Henrietta was secretary to the president of the Coulter Corporation. She had an invalid mother to support, and their only source of income was Henrietta's salary. Her employer by means of persuasive salesmanship sold her 500 shares of stock in the corporation and had her assign 50 percent of her weekly salary in payment. She now wishes to disaffirm this contract. May she do it?

Chapter 6

COMPETENCY OF PARTIES

CAPACITY TO CONTRACT

In order that an agreement may be enforceable at law, all parties must have the legal and mental capacity to contract. The general rule is that all parties are presumed to have this capacity. Some parties, however, in the eyes of the law, lack such capacity because of age, physical condition, or public policy. Among those whom the law considers to be incompetent to some degree are minors, insane persons, intoxicated persons, convicts, married women, and aliens.

MINORS

The common-law rule that persons under twenty-one years of age are *minors* has been retained by most of the states. In nine states laws have been passed making girls competent to contract at eighteen years of age. In a few other states all minors who are married are fully competent to contract. In still other states minors who are in business for themselves are bound on all their business contracts.

Contracts of Minors. A minor may make contracts freely, and many of these contracts are fully as valid and enforceable as those of an adult. Some of his contracts are voidable at the minor's option. If a minor desires, he may perform his voidable contracts. If a minor wishes to treat a contract made with an adult as valid, the adult is bound by it; the adult cannot disaffirm it on the ground that the minor might avoid the contract. Should the minor die, the personal representative of his estate may disaffirm the contract which the minor could have avoided.

Business firms that carry on business transactions in all the states must know the law dealing with minors in each of the fifty states. Mail order houses and correspondence schools are particularly susceptible to losses when dealing with minors. The significance of the law is that, with but few exceptions, one deals with a minor at his own risk. The purpose of the law is to protect minors from unscrupulous adults, but in general the law affords the other party no more rights in scrupulous contracts than in unscrupulous ones. The minor is the sole judge as to whether or not he wishes to be bound on a voidable contract.

Contracts of Minors for Necessaries. A minor is fully liable for the reasonable value of necessaries actually supplied to him. The dividing line between necessaries and luxuries is often a fine one. *Necessaries* are ordinarily food, clothes, and shelter, not already provided for the minor by his parents or guardian. But with the raising of standards of living, courts now hold that necessaries include medical services, including surgery, dental work, and medicine; education through high school or trade school, and in a few states through college; working tools for his trade; and other goods which are luxuries to some people but necessaries to others because of peculiar circumstances.

The minor's liability is quasi-contractual in nature in that he is required to pay the reasonable value of what he actually receives in order to prevent his being unjustly enriched. He is not, however, required to pay the contract price.

▪ Harold, a minor, purchased a suit for $80 from Hope Tailors. All necessary alterations were to be made without extra charge. After the alterations were made, Harold refused to take the suit and pay for it. Even though the suit be a necessary, Harold would not be held liable because delivery of the suit had not taken place.

Disaffirmance. The term *disaffirmance* means the repudiation of a contract, that is, the election to avoid it. A minor has the legal right to disaffirm a voidable contract at any time during his minority or within a reasonable time after becoming of age. An adult does not, however, have the right to avoid a contract because the other party is a minor.

If the contract is wholly executory, a disaffirmance completely nullifies the contract.

The minor, upon electing to disaffirm the contract, must return whatever he may have received under the contract, provided he is still in possession of it. The fact that the minor is not in possession of the property, however, regardless of the reason, does not prevent him from exercising his right to disaffirm the contract.

> ▪ Bowen, a minor, purchased a watch for $75 from the Brush Jewelry Company. About one month later the watch was stolen. Bowen disaffirmed the contract and demanded the return of his $75. He may do so. The fact that he cannot return the watch does not bar his right to disaffirmance.

As an exception to the right to disaffirm a contract during minority, a minor cannot fully disaffirm a transfer of real estate made by him until he reaches his majority. Before that time, he may partially avoid the transfer to the extent that he may retake possession of the property and use it or rent it to others, but he cannot set aside transfer of title until he becomes twenty-one.

> ▪ McGowan, a minor eighteen years old, conveyed a tract of land to Vinson. While still a minor, McGowan sought to avoid the conveyance and to recover the land. It was held that he was not entitled to avoid the conveyance fully. Prior to the time of reaching majority, he could partially avoid conveyance by retaking possession of the land and using it or renting it to others. But he cannot set aside technical transfer of title until he becomes twenty-one.

If an adult purchases an asset from a minor, the adult has only a voidable title to the property. If he sells the property to an innocent third party before the minor disaffirms the contract, the innocent third party obtains good title to the property.

> ▪ Wilson, a minor, owned a 1969 automobile which he traded to Steele for a 1971 car. Wilson drove the car for two weeks and found the car not as good as the 1969 car. He asked Steele to return his car but was told that it had been sold to Forrest. Wilson then sued Forrest for return of the 1969 car. Wilson was not entitled to recover. Although Wilson could avoid the sale to Steele, he could not do so against Forrest who acquired title to the car in good faith and for value.

Ratification. A minor may ratify a voidable contract only after he has attained his majority. By *ratification* is meant a restatement of one's willingness to be bound by his promises made during minority. It is in substance a new promise and may be oral, written, or merely implied by his conduct. He cannot ratify a part and disaffirm a part; he must ratify all or none of it. Ratification must be made within a reasonable time after majority. What is a reasonable time is a question of fact to be determined in the light of all surrounding circumstances.

It should be noted that there is a difference between a minor's executed contracts and his executory contracts. After he reaches majority, his silence ratifies an executed contract, while it disaffirms an executory contract.

> ▪ Clarke purchased 100 shares of stock in the Gulf Oil Company and paid cash for them. One week after reaching 21, he received a dividend check. He cashed the check and spent the money. Soon thereafter he attempted to disaffirm the contract. He could not do so. When a minor ratifies a contract by some act, as in this case, he cannot later disaffirm it.

Minor's Business Contracts. Many states, either by special statutory provision or by court decisions, have made a minor's contract relative to the business in which he is engaged or employed fully binding on him. If a minor engages in a business or employment in the same manner as a person having legal capacity, he will not be allowed to set aside contracts that arise from such business or employment.

> ▪ Sanders, a minor, owned and operated a service station. In this capacity he purchased gasoline, tires, and other merchandise amounting to $3,000. He was sued on this account, and his service station was to be sold to satisfy the debt. Sanders claimed he was not liable on his debts because of his minority. He was held responsible as though he were a person having legal capacity.

How One May Contract Safely with Minors. Since in general one deals with minors at his own risk, every businessman must know how to protect himself when contracting with minors. The safest way is to have an adult (usually parent or guardian) join in the contract as a cosigner with the minor. This does not bind the minor, but it does give the other party the right to sue the adult who became party to the contract. In addition, the adult who deals with a young person should, if in doubt, ask the other party if he is twenty-one, or eighteen, as the case may be. If he answers "Yes," in a majority of the states this is a tort if false and will either bind him on the contract or subject him to a suit for damages. Thirdly, a merchant must run some risks when dealing with minors. If he sells to a minor, the contract may be avoided by the minor years later and a refund of the purchase price demanded. Since few minors exercise the right, it is more profitable for a businessman to run this risk than to seek absolute protection against loss. The loss in profits in lost sales would exceed the refunds.

Minors' Torts. A *tort* is a legal wrong, such as negligently or willfully damaging another person or his property. Thus, a minor who negligently runs his car into another is liable for the damages which he causes. As a general rule, a minor is liable for his torts as fully as an adult. If a minor misrepresents his age and the adult with whom he contracts relies upon this misrepresentation to his detriment, this is a tort. The law is not uniform throughout the United States as to whether or not a minor is bound on a contract induced by misrepresenting his age. In some states, when sued, he cannot avoid his contract if he fraudulently misrepresented his age. In some cases he may be held liable for any damage to or deterioration of the property he received under the contract. If the minor sues on the contract to recover what he paid, he may be denied recovery because of the misrepresentation of age.

INSANE PERSONS

In determining an insane person's capacity, the status of his insanity must be fixed. If he has been examined according to law and been formally adjudicated insane, then in most states, his contracts are void without regard to whether they are reasonable or for necessaries. He is considered incapable of making a valid acceptance of an offer no matter how fair the offer is. If he is insane but has not been so declared by the court, then his contracts are voidable, not void. Like a minor, he is liable for the reasonable value of necessaries that have been supplied to him. Upon disaffirmance, he must return anything of value received under the contract which he still has.

If an insane person has not been so declared, he may, while in a sane or lucid interval, make a contract which is fully as binding as those of a normal person.

If he has been judicially declared insane, his contracts are void without regard to whether he was lucid at the time of contracting. When the insane person has not been judicially declared insane, his capacity to contract is the same as that of any other normal person if he regains his sanity. If he is declared insane, his contractual capacity is not restored until the court officially declares him to be competent.

- ■ Robert Stacey was judicially declared insane. A guardian was appointed for him. Later Stacey sold his car for $500, a fair price. His guardian sued for a return of the car. The court held that the buyer had to return the car because Stacey's contract was void. Stacey had to return any money which had not been lost or spent.

INTOXICATED PERSONS

Contracts made by a person who has become so intoxicated that he cannot understand the meaning of his acts are voidable. Upon becoming sober, he may affirm or disaffirm his contracts made while he was drunk. If one delays unreasonably in disaffirming a contract made while intoxicated, he may lose the right to have the contract set aside.

A person who has been legally declared to be an habitual drunkard cannot make a valid contract but is liable for the reasonable value of necessaries furnished him. If a person is purposely caused to become drunk in order to be induced to contract, the agreement will be held invalid.

CONVICTS

Laws of the various states differ with regard to the capacity of a convict (one convicted of a major criminal offense, namely, a felony or treason) to contract. In some states, for example, he may not make a valid transfer of his property. Some states place a partial disability on capacity to contract; others, a total disability. In any event, however, the disability lasts only so long as the person is imprisoned.

MARRIED WOMEN

Common law held that a married woman could not make a binding contract and considered her contracts to be void. Even though living apart from her husband, she was still held to be under the common-law disability. In most states, however, the common-law disability has been removed by statute with but a few restrictions on the right of a married woman to contract. For example, in some states a married woman may not contract with her husband; in some states she may not contract to act as surety for her husband.

ALIENS

An *alien* is a citizen or subject of a foreign country residing in this country. Originally subject to disabilities to contract, an alien is in most instances able to make binding contracts. As a rule, an *enemy alien*—subject or citizen of a country with which we are at war—may not make binding contracts or sue on an existing contract. But an enemy alien may defend himself when sued on an existing contract.

QUESTIONS

1. What classes of persons are considered by the law to lack full capacity to make contracts?
2. Why is it important for business firms to know the law dealing with minors in their own and other states?
3. If a minor wishes to treat a contract with an adult as binding, may the adult avoid it because the other party is a minor?
4. Name some necessaries for which a minor may be held liable for payment.
5. When may a minor disaffirm his contracts?
6. When a minor disaffirms a contract, must he return any benefit which he received from the contract?
7. When may a minor ratify a voidable contract?
8. If a minor purchases two articles by the same contract, may he disaffirm the contract for one of the items and ratify it for the other one?
9. How may a businessman protect himself when dealing with minors?
10. Are the contracts of an insane person void or voidable if he has been judicially declared insane?
11. If John purchases a car from Henry, a minor, and then sells it to Watson, may Henry demand that Watson return the car to him?
12. If a minor lies about his age, is he guilty of a tort?
13. Are the contracts of enemy aliens valid?
14. Are the contracts of married women generally governed by the common law?

CASE PROBLEMS

1. Holcomb, 18 years of age, was a cripple and was working his way through college with a paper route necessitating a car. He purchased one from A & H Motors for $900. Holcomb would not agree to buy the car unless A & H Motors would agree to repair a dented fender. They finally agreed that Holcomb was to have the car for $875 and that he would then pay the A & H Motors $25 for repairing the fender. Before the car was delivered, Holcomb attempted to disaffirm. May he do so?

2. Graff, a married minor 18 years of age, purchased a house from Ivan for $18,000. He lived in the house until he was almost 21 and then sold it for $13,000. The large depreciation in value was due entirely to a new highway having been built near the house since Graff bought it. As soon as he reached 21, he disaffirmed the contract and demanded that Ivan pay him the $5,000 he lost on the sale of the house. May he do so?

3. Burson, a minor, owned and operated the Red and Black Cleaners. He incurred about $5,000 in debts for rent, equipment, and cleaning materials. He failed to pay any of them, and his creditors brought suit to fore-

close on the business and his home in order to collect payment. Burson claimed that since he was a minor, he was not liable for these debts. Is this contention sound?

4. Towns purchased 500 shares of stock from Fain, a minor, for $3,000, a fair price. Towns held the stock for 15 months and then sold it to Dillard for $4,200. Fain had just passed his twenty-first birthday by one week. He disaffirmed the contract and brought suit against both Towns and Dillard to get a return of his stock. Discuss the rights of all the parties.

5. Frank Clark, aged 20 years and 10 months, became engaged and bought his fiancee an engagement ring costing $200. He paid $25 down and agreed to pay $2 a week on the balance. About three months after he reached his majority, his fiancee broke the engagement and returned his ring. Having no other prospects, he offered to return the ring to the jeweler and demanded the return of the $69 which he had paid and a cancellation of the balance of the debt.

(a) Did he have a legal right to do so? Discuss fully.

(b) Would your conclusion be different if he had paid cash in full at the time of the purchase and had demanded a return of his money within ten days after attaining his majority?

6. Howard was declared insane by the proper court, and the court appointed Sailors as his guardian. A few days later Howard purchased a suit on credit, but the guardian refused to pay for the suit. Was this a valid contract?

7. Paris, a boy 17 years old, left his home and rented a room in town for $50 a month. After one month, he refused to pay, claiming a room was not a necessary for him since he could have stayed at home. Is his contention correct?

Chapter 7

CONSIDERATION

Courts will compel compliance with an agreement only when it is supported by consideration. Consideration distinguishes mere agreements from legally enforceable obligations. *Consideration* is whatever the promisor demands and receives as the price for his promise. Generally, a promise is binding upon a person only when he receives consideration.

In most contracts, each party requires and is content with a promise by the other as the price for his own promise. For example, a homeowner may promise to pay a painter $1,000 in return for the promise of the painter to paint his house. Correspondingly, the painter makes his promise to paint, in return for the promise of the homeowner to make such payment. From its very nature, this exchange of a promise for a promise occurs at the one time.

For a promise to constitute consideration, the promise must impose an obligation upon the person making the promise. If a merchant promises to sell to a businessman all of the carbon paper he happens to order at a specific price in return for the businessman's promise to pay that price for any he orders, there is no contract. There is no certainty that the businessman will need any carbon paper. Likewise there is no certainty on the part of the merchant, for he may discontinue the line, go out of business, or buy from another supplier.

Consideration, when requested as the price for the promise sued upon, may be the making of a promise, the doing of an act, or the making of a promise to refrain from doing an act which can be lawfully done. Thus, a promise to give up smoking or drinking can be consideration for a promise to make a certain payment in return therefor. In contrast, a promise to stop driving an automobile in excess of the speed limit is not consideration because a person does not have a right to drive illegally; and his promise to drive lawfully does not add anything to that which he is already required to do.

ADEQUACY OF CONSIDERATION

As a general rule, the adequacy of the consideration is irrelevant. The law does not prohibit bargains. Except in cases where the contract calls for a performance or the sale of goods which have a standard or recognized market value, it is impossible to fix the money value of each promise. If the consideration given by one party is grossly inadequate, this is a relevant fact in proving fraud, undue influence, or mistake. Then, too, the inadequacy of the consideration may be a factor in a court of equity where the equity judge is not bound by strict rules of law but is free to decide the case according to what is right.

PART PAYMENT

A partial payment of a past-due debt is not consideration to support the creditor's promise to cancel the balance of the debt. This is because the creditor is already entitled to the part payment. Promising to give him something to which he is already entitled is not consideration.

There are several exceptions to this rule:

(1) If the amount of the debt is in dispute, the acceptance in full settlement of a lesser sum than that claimed will cancel the debt.

> ▪ Agee, an electrician, agreed to do some electrical work for Cooper. When Cooper received Agee's bill, he claimed the charge was higher than that agreed upon. Despite the difference of opinion, Agee accepted Cooper's check, cashed it, then sought to recover the balance he claimed he was entitled to. Agee was denied his claim on the basis that the check he accepted and cashed constituted a discharge of the disputed debt.

(2) If there are several creditors, and each one agrees to accept in full settlement of his claim a percentage of the amount due, this agreement will cancel the unpaid balance due these creditors. This is known as a *composition of creditors*.

■ Lind's creditors sign an agreement that they will accept 45 cents on the dollar in satisfaction of their claims. Later, Schneider, one of the creditors, sues Lind for the balance of Lind's debt to him. Schneider was not allowed to collect. When the creditors agreed to accept a fractional share of their claims against Lind, their agreements were supported by consideration, and Lind's debts were discharged.

(3) If the debt is evidenced by a note or other written evidence, cancellation and return of the written evidence cancels the debt.

(4) If the payment of the lesser sum is accompanied by a receipt in full and some indication that a gift is made of the balance, the debt may be canceled.

(5) If a secured note in a lesser amount is given and accepted in discharge of an unsecured note, the difference between the two notes is discharged, the additional security feature of a secured note being consideration for the discharge of the difference. The security is the consideration to support the contract to settle for a lesser sum.

INSUFFICIENT OR INVALID CONSIDERATION

Many apparent considerations lack the full force and effect necessary to make enforceable agreements. Consideration of the following classes is either insufficient or invalid:

1. Performing or promising to perform what one is already obligated to do
2. Refraining from doing or promising to refrain from doing what one has no right to do
3. Past performance

(1) **Performing or Promising to Perform What One Is Already Obligated to Do.** If the claim to consideration consists merely of a promise to do what one is already legally obligated to do anyway, consideration ·is said to be invalid. If the consideration is invalid, the contract is invalid. In such case, the promise gives to the other contracting party nothing to which he is not already entitled; and the promise is therefore held not to be valid consideration with the result there is no binding contract.

Parties to a contract may at any time mutually agree to cancel an old contract and replace it with a new one. For this new contract to be enforceable, there must be some added features that benefit both parties though not necessarily to an equal extent. If a contractor agrees to build a house of certain specifications for $20,000, a contract of the homeowner to pay an additional $1,000 is not binding unless the contractor concurrently agrees as a consideration for the $1,000 to do something the original contract did not bind him to do. The value of the additional act by the contractor need not be $1,000. It merely must have a monetary value.

If unforeseen difficulties arise that make it impossible for the contractor to complete the house for $20,000, these unforeseen difficulties may in rare cases be a consideration. Strikes, bad weather, a change in prices are foreseeable difficulties. Underground rock formations or a change in the law relative to the building codes and zoning laws are examples of unforeseen difficulties. The homeowner does not have to agree to pay more because of these unforeseen difficulties; but if he does do so, they will constitute a consideration even though the contractor does not agree to do anything additional. Also, the homeowner is not bound to agree to pay more merely because of unforeseen difficulties. The law merely says that if he does do so, he cannot later raise the issue of whether or not there was consideration.

(2) Refraining from Doing or Promising to Refrain from Doing What One Has No Right to Do. When one promises to refrain from doing something, his conduct is called *forbearance*. If the promisor had a right to do the act, forbearance is a valid consideration. Consideration is invalid when it consists of a promise to forbear doing something which one has no right to do, such as to commit an unlawful act.

Often the forbearance consists of promising to refrain from suing the other party. Promising to refrain from suing another for slander is a good consideration if one has a reasonable right to demand damages for slander and intends to file such a suit. If there is a basis for a suit for slander, but the promisor had no intention of filing such a suit, then a promise to refrain from suing is an invalid consideration.

▪ Morgan, a newspaper columnist, wrote and published articles highly critical of Senator Borgman. The article attacked the character of Senator Borgman and accused him of accepting bribes to vote for certain bills. Senator Borgman told several people he could sue Morgan for libel but that he was not going to do so because he probably could not collect anyway. Later he threatened Morgan for libel unless Morgan promised to donate $5,000 to his campaign fund for reelection. Morgan promised to do this but subsequently refused to make payment. He was within his rights. Promising to refrain from doing what one has no intention of doing is not a consideration.

(3) Past Performance. An act performed prior to the promise does not constitute a detriment to the promisee. If a carpenter gratuitously helps a neighbor build his house with no promise of pay, he cannot enforce a promise to pay made after the house is completed. The promise to pay must induce the carpenter to do the work, and this cannot be done if the promise is made after the work is completed.

> ▪ Barnes, a groceryman, supplied David with groceries on credit while David was unemployed. Later Thomas, a friend of David, promised Barnes he would pay the bill if David did not. This promise was unenforceable since it was past consideration.

A debt that is discharged by bankruptcy may be revived under certain circumstances, usually by the debtor's agreeing to pay it. Such promises are enforceable even though the creditor, the promisee, gives no new consideration to support the promise. The debtor is said to have waived his defense of discharge in bankruptcy; and the original debt, therefore, is deemed to remain in force.

EXCEPTIONS TO REQUIREMENT OF CONSIDERATION

As a general rule, a promise is not binding unless it is supported by consideration. Certain exceptions to the rule involve (1) voluntary subscriptions, (2) debts of record, and (3) promissory estoppel.

(1) Voluntary Subscriptions. When charitable enterprises are financed by voluntary subscriptions of many persons, the promise of each person is generally held to be enforceable. When a number of people make pledges to or subscribe to a charitable association or to a church, for example, the pledges or subscriptions are binding. One theory for enforcing the promise is that each subscriber's promise is supported by the promises of other subscribers. Another theory is that a promisor relies on the promises of others. Still another theory is that a subscription is an offer of a unilateral contract which is accepted by creating liabilities or making expenditures. Despite the fact that such promises lack the technical requirements of ordinary contracts, the courts will enforce the promises as a matter of public policy.

> ▪ Kelly, along with many other communicants, subscribed to a building fund for the First Methodist Church. The finance committee of the church let a contract for the construction of the church, the cost to be met from the subscriptions. Kelly attempted to revoke his subscription after the church was half finished because he did not like the architecture. He is legally bound on his promise even though his promise is not supported by consideration.

(2) **Debts of Record.** Consideration is not necessary to support an obligation of record, such as a judgment, on the basis that such an obligation is enforceable as a matter of public policy.

(3) **Promissory Estoppel.** Although not supported by consideration, some promises are enforced by the courts on the basis of *promissory estoppel*. According to this doctrine, if one person makes a promise to another and that other person acts upon the promise, the promisor will not be permitted to claim lack of consideration in order to avoid his promise. Enforcement is held to be proper when the promisor should reasonably expect to cause and does cause action by the promisee and it would be in the interest of justice to enforce the promise. The theory has gained support as a means of realizing justice.

QUESTIONS

1. What is *consideration?*
2. Must every contract have consideration to make it valid?
3. If a promise does not impose a legal obligation upon the promisor, can such a promise constitute a consideration?
4. If a boy promises his father that he will not own and operate an automobile until he is eighteen in exchange for his father's promise to pay him $2,000, is this a valid contract?
5. What is a *composition of creditors?*
6. During Halloween night, two young men promised not to damage Day's car if Day would agree to pay them $50. Is this contract enforceable?
7. Give two illustrations of when the inadequacy of the consideration would be relevant.
8. Give an illustration of when the court will enforce a contract even though no consideration is present.
9. If Davis owes Dennis $10,000 and Dennis offers to settle for $7,000, what must Davis do to make the contract binding?
10. What is *promissory estoppel?*

CASE PROBLEMS

1. Brodie owed the Lanier National Bank $5,000. The note was past due, and the bank was on the verge of suing Brodie. Mrs. Brodie executed a $5,000 first mortgage on the home that was in her name to secure the Brodie note. She did this in return for the bank's promise not to sue her husband. Four years later the bank brought suit against Mrs. Brodie to

foreclose on the mortgage since Brodie's note was still unpaid. Mrs. Brodie denied liability on the grounds of no consideration. Is this defense good?

2. Henry and Doris lived in a house owned by Henry's father. They paid a monthly rental of about 50 percent of its true rental value. Over a period of five years Henry spent $3,200 on the house and greatly improved its value. Henry's father, before he died, promised in writing that Henry should be paid from the father's estate for this $3,200. The administrator refused to pay it. Can Henry compel him to do so?

3. Branch was the bookkeeper for the Brown Lumber Company. His duties were not only to keep the books but also to prepare and file all tax returns. One year his employer felt that the company had paid too much excess profits tax and asked Branch to seek a refund. He promised to give Branch 50 percent of any refunds received. Branch worked many hours overtime preparing the application for a refund and finally received $24,000. He demanded his share of $12,000, and the Brown Lumber Company refused to pay. Must it do so?

4. The Brooks Construction Company had a contract with Kirby to build a 40-unit motel according to a certain blueprint for $500,000, "the building to be completed within a reasonable time from date." For several reasons progress in completing the motel was slow, and Kirby said to Brooks, "If you will make a special effort to complete the motel in 30 days, I will pay an extra $5,000." He modified Kirby's offer to include a neon sign not included in the original blueprints. Kirby refused to pay the $5,000. Is the Brooks Construction Company entitled to collect since it finished the building in 30 days and included the neon sign?

5. Baldwin agreed to help Murphy, his brother-in-law, who was unemployed, build a house with the understanding that Baldwin was to receive no pay. After the house was completed, Murphy said to Baldwin, "When I go back to work, I am going to pay you $400 for the work you did for me." Later Baldwin attempted to enforce this agreement. Was Murphy liable for the $400?

6. Desmond was unemployed and had no place to live. His aunt, feeling sorry for him, allowed him to live with her until he could find work. Desmond lived with his aunt for four months and then obtained employment with an excellent salary. After obtaining his new job, Desmond told his aunt that he would pay her for the board and room she provided him. When he subsequently failed to pay, the aunt sued. Was she entitled to collect?

7. In an effort to rehabilitate Bacon who habitually wrote checks which were not backed by funds in the bank, Hamden promised Bacon $100 if he would write no insufficient funds checks for a period of one year. Is the promise enforceable?

8. At an alumni reunion of graduates of Elay College, Barr agreed to donate $5,000 to the proposed Thomas library. Later, after a student demonstration, Barr attempts to revoke his promise. Is he bound to give the $5,000?

Chapter 8

ILLEGAL AGREEMENTS

ILLEGALITY

A contract, to be valid and enforceable, must among other things be for a lawful purpose, and this purpose must be achieved in a lawful manner. If this were not true, the court might be placed in the absurd position of compelling one party to a contract to commit a crime. If the act itself is legal, but the manner of committing the act which is stipulated in the contract is illegal, the contract is void.

A contract that is void because of illegality does not necessarily mean the commission of the act is a crime—it may consist merely of a private wrong, for example, a conspiracy by two merchants to drive a third out of business.

If the contract is entire and cannot be performed except as an entity, then illegality in one part renders the whole contract invalid. If the contract is divisible so that the legal parts can be performed separately, the contract is enforceable for these parts. For example, when one purchases several articles, each priced separately, and the sale of one of these articles is illegal for the reason that the price was cut in violation of a price-fixing statute, the whole contract will not fall because of the one article. When it is not possible to separate the legal from the illegal part, the entire contract is held void even though part of it standing by itself calls for a lawful performance.

> ▪ The Varsity Sports Center employed Fain as an accountant at $100 a week. He was to do all the accounting and, in addition, to handle all wagers on each week's football games. The latter act is illegal. Since it was not stated how much of Fain's salary was for his duties as an accountant and how much was for taking the wagers, the whole contract was void because of illegality. The legal part cannot be separated from the illegal part. Fain could not collect any salary.

61

CONTRACTS PROHIBITED BY STATUTE

Many types of contracts are declared illegal by statute such as:

1. Gambling contracts
2. Sunday contracts
3. Usurious contracts
4. Contracts of an unlicensed operator
5. Contracts for the sale of articles that cannot be the subject matter of an ordinary sale
6. Contracts in unreasonable restraint of trade

(1) **Gambling Contracts.** A *gambling contract* is a transaction wherein the parties stand to win or to lose based on pure chance. What one gains, the other must lose. Under the early common law wagering contracts were enforceable, but they are now generally prohibited in all states by statute. In recent years certain classes of gambling contracts, such as pari-mutuel systems of betting on horse races and dog races, have been legalized in some states.

In general the courts will leave the parties to a gambling contract where it finds them and will not allow one party to sue the other for the breach of his gambling debt. If two parties to a gambling contract pay over money to a stakeholder with instructions to pay the money over to the winner, the law varies with each stage of the transaction. The law encourages repentance. Consequently, if one of the parties to a gambling contract repents before the outcome of the gambling event is known, he can demand a return of his money. If the stakeholder pays the money over to the winner, then the loser may sue either the winner or the stakeholder for reimbursement. Some states permit the one who repents the right to demand a return of his deposit even after the outcome of the event is known. This is the minority view. No state will permit the stakeholder to keep the money, for he is considered to be merely a trustee of funds. The court in this event requires the stakeholder to return each wagerer's deposit.

Closely akin to gambling debts are loans made to enable one to gamble. If A loans B $100 and then wins it back in a poker game, is this a gambling debt? Most courts hold that it is not, but some hold otherwise. If A and B bet $100 on a football game and B wins, and if A pays B by giving him a promissory note for the $100, such a note may be declared void by some statutes.

Trading on the stock exchange or the grain market represents legitimate business transactions. But the distinction between such trading and gambling contracts is sometimes very fine. These two sets of facts illustrate the distinction:

- Alewine and Goodnoe form a contract whereby Alewine agrees to sell Goodnoe 10,000 shares of stock one month from date at $42 a share. They do not intend actually to buy and sell the stock, but they do agree to settle for the difference between $42 a share and the closing price on the date fixed in the contract. This is a gambling contract.

- Arnold agrees to sell Bolde 10,000 bushels of wheat to be delivered six months later at $1.70 a bushel. Arnold does not own any wheat, but he expects to buy it for delivery. At the end of the six-month period, the seller may not actually deliver the wheat; but if the price of wheat has gone up, the seller may pay the buyer the difference between the current price and the contract, or if the price of wheat has gone down, the buyer may pay the seller the difference. Nevertheless the contract is legal because the intention was to deliver.

The primary difference between the two situations is in the intention to deliver. In the second case Arnold intended at the time of the contract to deliver the wheat and Bolde intended to accept it. In the first case no such intention to deliver existed.

(2) Sunday Contracts. The laws pertaining to Sunday contracts are the result of statutory legislation and judicial interpretation. These laws and interpretations vary considerably from state to state. Some states prohibit all Sunday contracts except those involving works of necessity and charity. In others both labor (servile or manual labor) and transactions of business on Sunday are prohibited. In some states, a contract though made on Sunday is valid if it is ratified on another day and the law permits such ratification. However, other courts hold that such contracts are invalid because one cannot ratify an illegal contract. And it has been held that an offer made on Sunday and accepted the next day constituted a valid agreement because a contract was formed when acceptance was given.

The performance of an act on Sunday which is prohibited by law is a misdemeanor, but seldom are the violators prosecuted. For this reason the types of transactions one observes being carried on on Sunday are not good guides to the restrictions in these laws.

(3) Usurious Contracts. Nearly every state has enacted a law to limit the rate of interest which may be charged for the use of money. Frequently there are two rates, the contract rate and the legal rate.

The *contract rate* is the maximum rate which may be charged; any rate above that is *usurious*. The *legal rate,* which is a rate somewhat lower than the contract rate, applies to all situations in which interest may be charged but in which the parties were silent as to the rate. If merchandise is sold on thirty days' credit, the seller may collect interest from the time the thirty days expire till the debt is paid. Since no rate is ordinarily agreed upon in a situation of this kind, the legal rate may be charged.

The courts will ignore attempts to disguise transactions which in fact are usurious and will treat them as usurious when there is in fact a lending of money at a usurious rate even though disguised by the lender's:

(a) Requiring the borrower to execute a note for an amount in excess of the actual loan

(b) Requiring the borrower to antedate the note so as to charge interest for a longer period than that agreed on

(c) Requiring the borrower to perform some service or labor for the lender without charge

(d) Charging a brokerage fee for lending one's own money when no broker was used

(e) Requiring the borrower to purchase some article from the lender at an exorbitant price

(f) Requiring the borrower to sell the lender some property he owns at a price considerably below its market value

The penalty for usury varies from state to state. In most states the only penalty is to prohibit the lender from collecting the excess interest. In other states the entire contract is void, and in still others the borrower need not pay any interest but must repay the principal. If the borrower has already paid the usurious interest, the court will require the lender to refund to the borrower any money collected in excess of the statute.

In all states there are special statutes governing loans by pawnbrokers, small loan companies, and finance companies. In some states these firms may charge as much as 42 percent a year. Any rate above that fixed by statute is usurious. When a loan is to be repaid in installments, the borrower actually pays more interest than the item expressly described as interest in the loan calculation, for the reason that the borrower pays interest on the full amount of the loan for the total loan period but only has the first installment of the principal borrowed for the first loan period, the second installment for two loan periods, and so on. Although the sum charged the borrower for the amount of money actually "used" by him is thus greater than the legal rate of interest, it is held that the usury laws are not violated by such transactions.

- Solomon borrowed $300 from the City Finance Company, agreeing to repay it in 12 equal monthly payments. The maximum rate of interest is 16 percent. The City Finance Company added the $48 interest to the $300 loan and had Solomon sign a noninterest-bearing note for 12 months at $29 a month. Since he paid interest on all this loan for 12 months but had the use of only one payment for 12 months, the rate of interest was greatly in excess of 16 percent, but it was not usurious. The same law can apply to any installment loan.

- Dupree loaned North $1,000 at 8 percent, the contract rate of interest. They agreed to antedate the loan 90 days. This is a subterfuge to evade the usury law, and the court will look at the actual facts and hold the transaction to be usurious.

(4) **Contracts of an Unlicensed Operator.** Laws make it illegal to operate certain types of businesses or professions without a license. Most of these laws are made to protect the public from incompetent operators. The most common types of professional persons who must be licensed to operate are doctors, lawyers, certified and licensed public accountants, dentists, insurance salesmen, and real estate salesmen. If anyone performs these services without license, he not only cannot sue to collect for his services but he may also be guilty of a crime. A licensing law may be designed solely as a revenue measure by requiring payment of a fee for a license. If a person operates in one of the fields or businesses covered by such a law, his contracts are held valid even though he does not have a valid license; but he may still be subject to fine or imprisonment for violating the law.

(5) **Contracts for Sale of Prohibited Articles.** If a druggist sells morphine or a similar drug to one who does not have a prescription, he cannot sue to collect the price. One who sells cigarettes or alcoholic beverages to a minor when such sale is prohibited cannot sue on the contract. The court will leave the parties where it finds them.

(6) **Contracts in Unreasonable Restraint of Trade.** It is the policy of our government to encourage competition. Any contract, therefore, intended to restrain trade unreasonably is null and void. The dividing line between reasonable and unreasonable restraint of trade is often dim, but certain acts have by judicial decision become well

established as being in unreasonable restraint of trade. The most common acts in this class are:

(a) Contracts not to compete
(b) Contracts to restrain trade
(c) Contracts to fix the resale price
(d) Unfair competitive practices

(a) Contracts Not to Compete. When one purchases a going business, he purchases not only the physical assets but also the goodwill, which is often the most valuable asset of the firm. If the seller should attempt to regain any of the physical assets without paying for them, he could be prosecuted for larceny, robbery, or burglary depending on the method used to regain them. In the absence of a contract prohibiting his attempt to retake the asset "goodwill," he may do so by engaging in the same business again and seeking to have his old customers continue to patronize him. It is customary and highly desirable when purchasing a business to include in the contract a provision prohibiting the seller from entering the same business again in the trade territory for a specified length of time. Such a contract not to compete is legal if the restriction is reasonable as to both time and space.

The restriction as to territory should not go beyond the trade area of the business. As the restriction is sustained to protect the buyer of the business from competition of the seller, it follows that the seller should not be subjected to the restriction longer than is reasonably necessary for the buyer to establish himself as the new business, nor to reach out into areas where the buyer is now engaging in business. When the restriction goes further than is necessary to protect the buyer of the business, it is unlawful not only because oppressive to the seller but also because the business community and society in general are deprived of the benefit of the activities of the seller.

> ▪ The M and N Cafeteria was owned by Mooney. He sold all equipment and the goodwill to Cohen and agreed not to enter the restaurant business again in the state for two years. The time was reasonable, but the restriction as to territory was too large, making the provision null and void.

Closely allied to this type of contract is one whereby an employee, as a part of his employment contract, agrees not to work for a competing firm for a certain period of time after terminating his employment. These contracts must be reasonable as to time and space.

(b) Contracts to Restrain Trade. Contracts to fix prices, divide up the trade territory, limit production so as to reduce the supply, or otherwise limit competition are void. Such contracts which affect interstate commerce and which are therefore subject to regulation by the federal government are specifically declared illegal by the Sherman Antitrust Act and the Clayton Act. Most of the states have similar laws applicable to intrastate commerce.

(c) Contracts to Fix the Resale Price. An agreement between a seller and his buyer that the latter shall not resell below a stated price is generally illegal as a price-fixing agreement. The original seller can, of course, control his price if he sells directly to the public through outlet stores. The situation of fixing the price to the consumer has also been met by federal and state statutes which permit the seller and the buyer to agree that certain minimum resale prices will be maintained. In approximately one half of the states, such a price-maintenance agreement is binding not only upon the parties to such an agreement but upon all other dealers in the industry. Such statutes are described as "fair trade acts" and are limited to products sold under a trademark or brand name.

(d) Unfair Competitive Practices. The Robinson-Patman Act attempted to eliminate certain unfair competitive practices in inter-state commerce. Under this act it is unlawful to discriminate in price between buyers if the goods are of like grade and quality. Most states have passed similar laws for intrastate commerce. Some state statutes go further and prohibit the resale of goods at a loss or below cost for the purpose of harming competition.

Contracts Contrary to Public Policy. Many contracts are unenforceable because they are contrary to public policy. Many acts have been declared by statute to fall within this category; but, as a rule, the courts must determine from the very nature of the act whether or not it is contrary to public policy.

One court, in attempting to classify contracts contrary to public policy, defined them thus: "Whatever tends to injustice, restraint of liberty, restraint of a legal right, whatever tends to the obstruction of justice, a violation of a statute, or the obstruction or perversion of the administration of the law as to executive, legislative, or other official action, whenever embodied in and made the subject of a contract, the contract is against public policy and therefore void and not susceptible to enforcement." (Brooks v. Cooper, 50 N. J. Eq. 761, 26 A. 978.)

The most common types of contracts that are invalid because they are contrary to public policy are:

1. Contracts limiting the freedom of marriage
2. Contracts obstructing the administration of justice
3. Contracts injuring the public service

(1) **Contracts Limiting the Freedom of Marriage.** It is contrary to public policy to enter into any contract the effect of which is to limit freedom of marriage, and such contracts are void. The following provisions in contracts have been held to render the contract a nullity: (a) an agreement whereby one party promises never to marry; (b) an agreement to refrain from marrying for a definite period of time (an agreement not to marry during minority, however, is valid); (c) an agreement not to marry certain named individuals.

With the same purpose of preserving and protecting marriages it is held that an agreement to seek a divorce for a consideration is void as against public policy.

(2) **Contracts Obstructing the Administration of Justice.** The impartial administration of justice is the cornerstone of democracy. Any contract that may obstruct our legal processes is null and void. It is not necessary that justice actually be obstructed. If the contract has the tendency to do so, the courts will not enforce it.

The following provisions have been held to render contracts void: (a) an agreement to pay a witness a larger fee than that allowed by law, provided the promisor wins the case; (b) an agreement by a candidate for sheriff that he will appoint a certain individual deputy sheriff in return for his aid in bringing about the promisor's election; (c) an agreement to pay a prospective witness a sum of money to leave the state until the trial is over; (d) an agreement not to prosecute a thief if he will return the stolen goods.

(3) **Contracts Injuring the Public Service.** Any contract that may, from its very nature, injure public service is void. A person may contract as an attorney to appear before any public authority to obtain or oppose the passage of any bill. But a contract to use improper influence to obtain the desired result is void.

Contracts to use one's influence in obtaining a public contract which by statute must be let to the lowest responsible bidder, to obtain pardons and paroles, and to pay a public official more or less than the statutory salary are also void.

QUESTIONS

1. May a contract for a lawful purpose be enforced if it calls for performance by illegal methods? Explain.
2. What is the effect of a contract a part of which is illegal?
3. What are some of the types of contracts that are illegal?
4. What test is used to determine if an agreement is a wager?
5. If a law prohibits the making of a contract on Sunday, what effect does it have on a contract when the offer is made on Sunday and the acceptance made on Monday?
6. What is the difference between the contract rate of interest and the legal rate of interest?
7. Give three illustrations of attempts to disguise transactions to avoid the usury laws.
8. If a real estate agent who is not licensed sells a house, is the owner bound to pay the commission?
9. If John loans Henry $100 so that they can have a poker game, is this a gambling debt?
10. If John purchases the Trenton Shoe Store from Mitchell, may he include an enforceable clause in the contract binding Mitchell not to enter the shoe business again in the United States?
11. Donald promises to pay Henry $1,000 if he will leave the state so that he cannot be called as a witness against Donald. Is this a valid contract?
12. Give an illustration of a contract restricting the freedom of marriage.

CASE PROBLEMS

1. Hall entered into a contract with the Dale Plumbing Company to install an extra bathroom in his home. All the terms of this contract were agreed upon, and the contract was signed on Sunday. The Dale Plumbing Company installed the fixtures in a very haphazard manner so that the fixtures were unusable without expensive repairs. This condition was not discovered until after Hall had paid the contract price. May Hall recover damages from the Dale Plumbing Company for breach of contract?

2. Andrews entered into a contract with the Chapman Construction Company to build a garage for $60,000. The construction price included all labor, materials, and architectural services, the architectural designs having been prepared by an employee of the Chapman Construction Company. Neither the employee nor anyone connected with the firm was a licensed architect. After the Chapman Construction Company had done about $5,000 worth of work, Andrews ordered him to stop and refused to pay for any

work already done. Is Andrews liable? If the contract had called for the labor and materials to be $58,000 and the architectural fees to be $2,000, would your answer be different?

3. Frances, 30, was engaged to marry Leonard. Dr. Hoag, the grandfather of Frances, disapproved strongly of Leonard. He promised to pay her $15,000 if she would break the engagement. She agreed to do so and thereafter broke the engagement and never married Leonard. Dr. Hoag never paid the money. After a substantial period of time she sued him for it. Is she entitled to recover?

4. Lund was store manager for the Downtown Sporting Goods, Inc. Boland wished to purchase an expensive pistol the store had for sale. A state law made it illegal to sell pistols to anyone who did not have a police permit to carry one. Lund did not know of this law and sold the pistol to Boland on credit. Boland never paid for it, and the seller sued. Must Boland pay for it?

5. The Akin Trucking Company was in desperate need of a loan of $10,000 but could not obtain one without collateral security. It had no acceptable collateral security. The bookkeeper owned $10,000 worth of industrial bonds. He offered to loan these to the firm to use as collateral if the firm would pay him 10 percent a year for their use. The offer was accepted. Was this contract usurious?

6. Harrell was desperately in need of money. Fortson was willing to loan him some money if some way could be devised to enable him to charge more than 8 percent interest, the contract rate. Harrell suggested that he give a note for the loan but antedate it 6 months. Fortson accepted this offer and loaned him $500 for 6 months, but the note was made to read 12 months. Was this contract usurious?

7. Hunt contracted with the Blank Manufacturing Company to use his influence with the proper government officials to obtain a $10,000,000 government contract for the Blank Company. Hunt was to receive 5 percent of any contract he obtained, nothing if he was unsuccessful. Through bribery he obtained a $6,000,000 contract and then demanded a fee of $300,000. Was he entitled to collect?

8. Pearl Klug purchased and paid for a dress on Sunday in a state where contracts made on Sunday were void. She asked the seller to hold the dress a few days, and said she would call for it later. Two days later she took the dress home. A week later Pearl returned the dress and demanded the return of her money. Was she entitled to its return?

9. Adams owned a hardware store in a town of about 10,000 population. Many of his customers were farmers who lived in the surrounding territory. The street on which the store was located was a state highway. Therefore, he did a small amount of business with tourists and travelers. Adams sold the business, including the goodwill, to Baker. As a part of the selling price, Adams agreed not to engage in the hardware business in that particular county for five years. Three years later Adams again entered the hardware business in that county, and Baker brought suit to prevent his doing this. Discuss the legal rights of the parties, and state your conclusion.

Chapter 9

FORM OF CONTRACTS

All contracts of importance ought to be in writing, but only a few must be written in order to be enforceable. An oral contract is just as effective and enforceable as a written contract unless it is one of the few types specifically required by statute to be in writing.

A written contract has several advantages over an oral contract, provided it includes all the terms and provisions of the agreement. In the first place, the existence of a contract cannot be denied if it is in writing. If there were no witnesses when an oral contract was formed, one of the parties might successfully deny that any contract was formed. In the second place, one of the parties may die or become insane. The administrator or executor of an estate in case of death, or the committee or guardian in case of insanity, is tremendously handicapped in enforcing an oral agreement made previously by the deceased or insane person. Even when there are witnesses present at the time an oral contract is formed, the testimony may vary considerably as to the actual terms of the contract. Written evidence, composed in clear and unambiguous language, is always better than oral evidence.

For these reasons most businessmen prefer to have contracts pertaining to matters of importance reduced to writing as a matter of caution even when this is not required by law.

STATUTE OF FRAUDS

In the year 1677 the English Parliament enacted a statute known as the *Statute of Frauds*. The statute listed certain classes of contracts which could not be enforced unless their terms were evidenced by a writing. The fourth and the seventeenth sections of the Statute of

Frauds contained a list of these contracts. Most of our states have adopted these two sections with but slight variations.

It is well to remember that in our country it is not the English Statute of Frauds but its American adaptations that determine which contracts must be in writing. The general provisions of the fourth section are given below, while those in the seventeenth section relating to the sale of goods as covered by the Uniform Commercial Code will be discussed in Chapter 14.

The Statute of Frauds applies only to executory contracts. If two parties enter into an oral contract, which comes within the Statute of Frauds, and both parties have fully performed according to its terms, neither party can seek to set aside the transaction on the ground that there was no writing. The purpose of the Statute of Frauds is to prevent the use of the courts for enforcing certain oral or alleged oral agreements. It is not applicable in the case of an oral agreement performed by both parties or when the parties voluntarily perform the agreement.

FOURTH SECTION OF THE STATUTE OF FRAUDS

The fourth section of the Statute of Frauds provides that the following types of agreements must be in writing:

1. An agreement to sell land or any interest in or concerning land

2. An agreement the terms of which do not call for performance within one year from the time it is made

3. An agreement to become responsible for the debts or default of another

4. An agreement of an executor or administrator to pay debts of the estate from his personal funds

5. An agreement in which the promise of one person is made in consideration of marriage

(1) An Agreement to Sell Land or Any Interest in or Concerning Land. An agreement to sell any interest in land comes within the Statute of Frauds. The writing which is thus required is distinct from the deed which will later be executed by which the seller makes the actual transfer of title to the interest to the buyer.

One may wish to sell not the land itself, but only an interest in the land. The evidence of this contract also must be in writing. These sales usually involve rights of way, joint use of driveways, mineral rights, timber, and any other interest in land. A lease for more than one year must be evidenced by a writing to be binding.

- Truman orally agreed to permit Smith to build a driveway across his lot. The price was to be $500. Truman later refused to go through with the agreement. He is within his rights because such agreements must be in writing to be valid.

Frequently, oral contracts relative to land are performed before any question of their validity is raised. For example, one leases a building by oral contract for two years. He occupies the building for that period and then refuses to pay the rent, alleging that the contract is invalid because it is oral. The law will compel him to pay the rent orally agreed to for the time that he has occupied the premises. If one has paid money or performed a service under an oral contract, he may recover the money or the value of the service even though he cannot enforce the executory part of the contract.

(2) **An Agreement the Terms of Which Do Not Call for Performance Within One Year from the Time It Is Made.** The terms of a contract that cannot be performed in one year are likely to be forgotten. To minimize the need to resort to the courts to determine one's right, the law requires all contracts that cannot be performed within one year to be in writing.

This provision of the Statute of Frauds means that if the terms of the contract are such that by their nature they cannot be performed within one year from the date of the contract, then the contract must be in writing. The contract can be so worded that it may not be completed for fifty years, yet if it is physically possible to complete it within one year, it need not be in writing. If John agrees in consideration of $5,000 to care for Smith for "as long as he (Smith) lives," this contract need not be in writing because there is no certainty Smith will live one year. But, by contract, an agreement to manage a motel for five years will by its terms require more than one year for performance and therefore comes within the Statute of Frauds.

(3) **An Agreement to Become Responsible for the Debts or Default of Another.** The term "debt" here refers to an obligation to pay money; "default" refers to a breach of contractual obligations other than money, such as a contract to build a house. Under such an agreement the promisor undertakes to make good the loss which the promisee would sustain if another person did not pay the promisee the debt owed him or failed to perform a duty imposed by contract or by law. If A promises C to pay B's debt to C if B fails to pay, A's promise must be in writing; A's promise is to be responsible for the debt of another.

The Statute of Frauds does not apply to the promise if in fact it is an original promise by the promisor rather than a promise by him to pay the debt of another. For example, if A buys on his own credit from B and tells B to deliver the goods to C, A is not promising to pay the debt of another; he is promising to pay his own debt.

The Statute of Frauds does not apply if the main purpose of the promise is to gain some advantage for the promisor. This provision of the Statute of Frauds was designed especially for those situations where one promises to answer for the debt of another person purely as an accommodation to that person. There are situations where one person promises to answer for the debt or default of another because it is to the promisor's personal financial interest to do so.

> ▪ Ward owned and operated a farm. Robinson worked the crops on a share-crop basis. Ward said to a merchant, "Let my tenant, Robinson, have credit up to $50 a month during the crop season; and if he does not pay you in the fall, I will." This wording makes this a contract that need not be in writing. The main purpose was to assure Ward that there would be a crop from which he could receive a share.

The Statute of Frauds does not apply where the promisor promises the debtor that the promisor will pay the debt owed to the third person, as where an uncle promises his nephew that the uncle will pay the nephew's bill to a department store. The statute applies only where the promise is made by the promisor directly to the creditor, as when the uncle makes a promise to the department store.

> ▪ Durwood sold Kenney an air conditioner for $400 and gave him 90 days to pay for it. Kenney became ill and his Uncle Glen said to him, "Don't worry; when it falls due, I will pay it." When the uncle did not pay Durwood, Kenney demanded that he pay. The uncle claimed he was not bound because the promise was not in writing. This defense is not valid because the Statute of Frauds does not require a writing when the promise is made directly to the debtor.

(4) An Agreement of an Executor or Administrator to Pay the Debts of the Estate. When a person dies, his executor (if he left a will), or his administrator (if he left no will), takes over all his assets and from these assets pays all the debts of the deceased before distributing the remainder under the decedent's will or, in the absence of a will, to the heirs. The executor or the administrator is not expected to pay the debts of the deceased out of his personal funds. For this reason, his promise to pay the debts of the estate from his personal funds is in reality a contract to become responsible for the debts of another and must be in writing to be enforceable.

The Statute does not apply when the administrator or the executor enters into an original contract relative to the estate. For example, an agreement to cover burial arrangements for the deceased does not come within the statute.

(5) An Agreement in Which the Promise of One Person Is Made in Consideration of Marriage. An agreement by which one person promises to pay a sum of money or to give property to another in consideration of marriage or a promise to marry must be in writing. This requirement of the Statute of Frauds does not apply to mutual promises to marry.

> ▪ Robertson orally promised his daughter to deed her his lakeside cottage if she would marry Jones. After the marriage, Robertson refused to execute the deed and the daughter sued him. Robertson was not bound to execute the transfer since his promise was oral.

NOTE OR MEMORANDUM

The Statute of Frauds requires that either the agreement be in writing and signed by both parties or that there be a note or memorandum in writing signed by the party against whom the claim for breach of promise is made. With the exception of the case of the sale of goods, as will be discussed in Chapter 14, the contract and the note or memorandum required by the Statute of Frauds must set forth all the material terms of the transaction. For example, in the case of the sale of an interest in real estate the memorandum must contain the names of the parties, the subject matter of the contract, the basic terms of the contract, including the price and the manner of delivery, and it must be signed by the one to be charged.

The law states that the memorandum must contain all the essential terms of the contract; yet it differs materially from a written contract. Probably the chief difference is that one may introduce oral testimony to explain or complete the memorandum. Under the parol evidence rule, this is not true of a contract. The court held the following receipt was an adequate memorandum: "Received of Sholowitz twenty-five dollars to bind the bargain for the sale of Noorigian's brick store and land at 46 Blackstone Street to Sholowitz. Balance due $1,975."

The memorandum need not be made at the time of the contract. It need be in existence only at the time suit is brought. The one who signs the memorandum need not sign with the intention of binding himself. If Jones writes Smith, "Since my agreement to buy your Buick for $1,200 was oral, I am not bound by it," this is a sufficient memorandum and removes the objection based on the Statute of Frauds.

OTHER WRITTEN CONTRACTS

The five classes of contracts that are listed by the Statute of Frauds are not the only contracts required by law to be in writing in order to be enforceable. Every state has a few additional requirements. The more common ones are contracts for the sale of securities and agreements to pay a commission to real estate brokers.

PAROL EVIDENCE RULE

Spoken words, that is, *parol evidence,* will not be permitted to vary or contradict the terms of a written contract which appears to be complete unless there is evidence of fraud, accident, or mistake so that the writing is in fact not a contract or is incomplete. This is known as the *parol evidence* rule.

If a written contract appears to be complete, the parol evidence rule will not permit modification by oral testimony or other writing made before or at the time of executing the agreement. However, an exception is made when the contract refers to other writings and indicates they are considered as incorporated into the contract.

The parol evidence rule is based on the assumption that a written contract represents the complete agreement. If, however, the contract is in fact not complete, the courts will admit parol evidence to clear up ambiguity or to show the existence of trade customs which are to be regarded as forming part of the contract.

A contract which appears to be complete may, in fact, have omitted a provision which ought to have been included. If the omission is due to fraud, duress, or other similar conduct, oral testimony may be produced to show such conduct.

QUESTIONS

1. As a general rule, an oral contract is just as enforceable as a written contract. Why, then, should all important contracts be in writing?
2. What is the *parol evidence* rule?
3. Give an example of oral testimony that may be introduced to explain the terms of a written contract.
4. What contracts of an executor need to be in writing?

5. If an agreement is made in consideration of marriage, must it be in writing?

6. If one takes upon himself an original obligation, even though the benefits go to another party, must the contract be in writing to be enforceable?

7. Must a memorandum be made at the same time the contract is made?

8. Is a memorandum binding on the one signing it even though he never intended it to be a memorandum?

9. If the main purpose of a promise to answer for another's debt is to gain some advantage for the promisor, must the contract be in writing?

10. Name some types of contracts that must be in writing.

CASE PROBLEMS

1. By means of an oral contract Holcomb was appointed an agent for the Burlington Life Insurance Company for five years and was to be paid a commission of 12½ percent of premium on the first five years' premiums. The insurance company refused to pay any commissions after the first year, claiming no liability on the oral contract. Are they bound?

2. Kemp was a combination cashier and bookkeeper for the Kerns Brick Company. Since he handled all the money for the firm, he was required to furnish a $10,000 bond. Kemp's father-in-law, DuPont, orally promised the Company that he would be personally liable for any shortages that might be found in the company's funds. Kemp could not get a bond from a commercial bonding company and would have lost his job if DuPont had not supplied the bond. Kemp owed DuPont $3,000; DuPont was afraid Kemp could not pay him if he lost his job. The auditor discovered a $2,000 shortage in the company's accounts, and the shortage was traced directly to Kemp. Can DuPont be held liable on his oral promise?

3. The Cofer Office Equipment Company entered into a written contract with the Hunt Insurance Company to keep all the insurance company's equipment repaired for the next three years for a monthly fee of $100. This written contract was signed, and each party retained a copy. Before the contract was signed, it was orally agreed that the contract was not to become effective unless Congress passed a new accelerated depreciation law. Nevertheless, the parties signed the contract and each retained a copy. This law was never passed. The Cofer Office Equipment sued for breach of contract. The Hunt Insurance Company attempted to prove by parol evidence the existence of this oral side agreement. May it do so?

4. Casey was employed by a written contract to serve as bookkeeper for the Standard Block Company at a salary of $500 a month. The contract was to run for one year. After Casey went to work, he learned that he was expected to work 48 hours a week. He had expected to work only 40 hours. Casey attempted to prove by oral testimony that it is customary for bookkeepers in that community to work only 40 hours a week. May he do so?

5. John rented a house by oral contract for two years at $125 a month. He soon became dissatisfied with the deal since he learned he could rent

a better house for $100 a month. He did not learn that this oral contract was not binding on him until after two years. He then demanded that the landlord reimburse him $25 a month for two years. May he do so?

6. The Reed Paper Company had for some time been negotiating with Downs on a business deal of the utmost importance to the company. The parties finally reached an agreement. Paul Chapman, secretary to the president of the Reed Paper Company, made a written memorandum of the contract, and Downs signed it. Chapman filed the memorandum. Later Downs refused to conform to his agreement. The memorandum could not be found since Chapman could not remember how or where he had filed it. The contract involved the sale of several thousand acres of pulpwood and the processing of the wood into paper over a period of three years. Could this contract be enforced if the memorandum was not found?

7. Mosely was employed by the Crawford Company at $550 a month. A competing firm in a nearby city offered Mosely $600 a month. The contract was made on May 10 with the work to start on July 1 and was to last for at least twelve months from July. All the arrangements were made orally. Mosely resigned his position with the Crawford Company, sold his home, and had his furniture packed and ready to move when he was notified that the position was not available. What recourse did Mosely have?

8. John Barner was sales manager for the Patterson Motor Company. Billy Seabolt, a minor, agreed to purchase a secondhand car for $1,400. As a part of the contract Barner stipulated that an adult must "stand good" for the payment. Steedman, an uncle of Seabolt, said, "Let him have the car; and if he does not keep up the payments, I will." Seabolt wrecked the car and then demanded a refund. Could Barner look to Steedman for the selling price?

9. Pat Snow owned and operated the Snow Barber Shop. He orally contracted with Buddy Broadnax to give Broadnax, a druggist, and his three boys all the haircuts and shaves they needed for the next two years for $300 cash. Broadnax was to pay the money the next day, but he changed his mind and refused to pay it. Snow wrote Broadnax a letter and demanded that "you pay me the $550 as you promised." Broadnax immediately replied by letter, "I never agreed to pay $550. It was $300. Anyway it is an oral contract, so try to collect it." Snow claimed this constituted a sufficient memorandum. Do you agree?

10. Beverly Hick and Myrna Mathis were secretaries. On October 8 they rented an efficiency apartment where they could prepare their meals. To tidy up the apartment, they repapered it, painted all woodwork, and made various other improvements. The total cost of the improvements amounted to $180. Their oral lease was to run to December 31, the following year. On December 1 the landlord notified them that beginning January 1 the rent would be increased $25 a month. Could he compel them to pay it?

11. Darlington purchased a piano from Davey, Incorporated, for $560. A sales ticket was made out and contained a statement that delivery was to be made December 5 and that payment was to be made on delivery. When the truck drivers brought the piano, Darlington refused to receive and pay for it. Davey sued him for breach of contract. Was he liable?

Chapter 10

ASSIGNMENT OF CONTRACTS

RIGHTS AND OBLIGATIONS

A contract creates both rights and obligations. Initially, one who is not a party to the contract has no right to the benefits to be derived from the contract, nor has he any of the duties or obligations. Third parties, however, may acquire these rights or assume these duties.

A party to a contract may wish to transfer his rights or to delegate his duties under the contract, or to do both. If one party assigns the contract in its entirety, this is referred to as an assignment while in reality it is "a transfer of rights and a delegation of duties." The term "delegation" is used only to describe a transfer to another of his duty alone without a transfer of rights. Whether rights may be assigned and duties delegated depends upon their nature and the terms of the contract.

- ▪ Johnson made a contract with DeFoe whereby DeFoe was to wire Johnson's house. For this service Johnson agreed to pay DeFoe $325. DeFoe delegated the job to Harris. This is a valid delegation of duties without assigning the right to receive $325 upon the completion of the work.

ASSIGNMENT OF RIGHTS

As a general rule, the rights under a contract may be assigned, but the duties and obligations under a contract may not be assigned. One's rights under a contract may be transferred almost as freely as his property. Such a transfer is referred to in law as an assignment. An *assignment* may, therefore, be defined as the means whereby one party conveys his rights in a contract to another who is not a party to the original undertaking. The party making the assignment is known as the *assignor;* the one to whom the right is transferred is the *assignee.*

RESTRICTIONS ON ONE'S RIGHT TO ASSIGN

Rights under contracts are generally assignable although statutes may impose some restrictions. Statutes in a number of states prohibit employees from assigning their wages. Statutes also prohibit the assignment of future pay by soldiers, sailors, and marines. Many states and cities also prohibit the assignment of the pay of public officials. Employees on public works are in many states prohibited by law from assigning a certain minimum percentage of their wages. This is to protect the wage earner and his family from hard-pressing creditors.

Often one's right under a contract is to receive the services of the other party, such as a bookkeeper, salesman, or other employee. The right to this party's personal services cannot be assigned because the employees cannot be required to work for a new employer without his consent.

Rights transferred by assignment and duties transferred by delegation cannot be modified by the assignment or transfer and remain the same as though only the original parties to the contract were involved.

The parties may include in the original contract a prohibition of the assignment of rights thereunder. Such a prohibition, however, is not effective in some states when only the right to money has been assigned.

DELEGATION OF DUTIES

A party to a contract cannot delegate his duties under the contract as readily as he can assign his rights because there is more frequently a "personal" element in the performance aspect of a contract, and it would change the obligation thereof if it were performed by another. If Allen retains Bentley, an attorney, to obtain a divorce for him for a fee of $250, Bentley can assign his right to receive the $250 to anyone and Allen must pay. He may not, however, delegate his duty to represent Allen in the divorce proceeding. In those contracts that involve trust and confidence, one may not delegate his duties. If one employs the Local Wonder Band to play for a dance, the contract cannot be assigned even to a nationally known band. Taste, confidence, and trust cannot be scientifically measured. Nor is it material that a reasonable man would be satisfied or content with the substitution. But if one hires Horne to paint his house for $300, whether or not the house has been painted right can readily be determined by recognized standards in the trade.

Only when the performance is standardized may one delegate its performance to another. In the construction industry, for example, there are many instances of delegation of duties because the correct performance can be easily ascertained. Contracts calling for unskilled work or labor may in most instances be delegated.

In all cases of delegation the delegating party remains fully liable under the contract. He may be sued for any breach of contract even though another party actually performed. In such an event he may in turn sue the party who performed inadequately. The parties to the original contract may expressly prohibit the delegation of duties thereunder.

EFFECT OF AN ASSIGNMENT

The nonassigning party retains all his rights and defenses as though there had never been an assignment. For example, if the nonassigning party was incompetent to contract, or entered into the contract under duress, undue influence, fraud, or misrepresentation, he may raise these defenses against the assignee as effectively as he could have done against the assignor.

Most assignments involve claims for money. The Fair Deal Grocery Company assigned $10,000 worth of its accounts receivable to the First National Bank. The assignor warranted that the accounts were genuine. If a customer, therefore, refused to pay the bank and proved that he did not owe the grocery any amount, the grocery company would be liable. If he failed to pay merely because he was insolvent, most courts would hold that the assignor was not liable.

WARRANTIES OF THE ASSIGNOR

When one assigns his rights under a contract to an assignee for value, he makes three implied warranties:

(1) That he is the true owner of the right

(2) That the right is valid and subsisting at the time the assignment is made

(3) That there are no defenses available to the debtor which have not been disclosed to the assignee.

If there is a breach of warranty by the assignor, the assignee may seek to recover his loss from the assignor. In the absence of an express guarantee, an assignor does not warrant that the other party will perform his duties under the contract, make payment, or is solvent.

> ▪ The Harbottle Distributing Company owed the Norfolk Brewery $10,000. In payment Harbottle assigned $10,000 of its accounts receivable to the Norfolk Brewery in full satisfaction of the debt. The assignee was able to collect only $7,000 of these accounts because the debtors were insolvent. The brewery has no recourse to Harbottle. Had the $3,000 been uncollectible because the debtors had valid defenses to the claims, then the Harbottle Distributing Company would have had to make good the loss.

In the case above the Norfolk Brewery Company erred by taking these accounts receivable by assignment. In this case Harbottle Distributing Company paid its debt, not with cash, but by a transfer of title of its accounts receivable. From the brewery company's standpoint the same result could have been obtained, not by taking title to these accounts, but by taking them merely as collateral security for their debt with a provision that the brewery was to collect the accounts and apply the proceeds on the $10,000. Under this arrangement, the brewery could have looked to the assignor for the balance of $3,000.

FORM OF THE ASSIGNMENT

An assignment may be made either by operation of law or by the act of the parties. In the event of death, the rights and duties (except for personal services) of the deceased are assigned by law to the executor or administrator of the estate. In the event of bankruptcy, the rights and duties of the bankrupt are assigned by operation of law to the trustee in bankruptcy. These two types of assignments are automatic. The assignment is effective without any act of the parties.

When the assignment is made by act of the parties, it may be either written or oral. If the original contract is one which must be in writing, the assignment must be in writing; otherwise, it may be made orally. It is always preferable to make the assignment in writing. This may be done in the case of written contracts by writing the terms of the assignment on the back of the written contract. Any contract may be assigned by executing an informal written assignment. The following written assignment is adequate in most cases.

In consideration of the Local Finance Company's canceling my debt of $500 to it, I hereby assign to the Local Finance Company $500 owed to me by the Dale Sand and Gravel Company.

Signed at noon, Friday, December 16, 1970, at Benson, Iowa.

(Signed) Harold Locke

NOTICE OF AN ASSIGNMENT

Notice need not be given to the other party in order to make the assignment effective as between the assignor and the assignee. Business prudence demands that the original promisor be notified. The promisor has a right to assume that the claim has not been assigned unless otherwise notified. For example, F. Dodd promised to pay Hodges $500 in thirty days. When the account came due, Dodd, since he had no notice of assignment, was safe in paying Hodges. But if Hodges had assigned the account to Wilson and Wilson had not given Dodd notice, then Wilson would not have been able to collect from Dodd.

In the event the assignor assigns a larger sum than the debtor owes, there is no obligation on the debtor to pay the entire assignment. When the creditor assigns only part of his claim, there is no obligation on the debtor to make payment thereof, although he may choose to do so and reduce his liability to the creditor to the extent of such payment.

- In a certain state where wages are assignable, Carson assigned wages to both his landlord and, a few days later, to a department store. The store demanded payment from Carson's employer and received payment. Two days later, the landlord demanded payment but was not permitted to collect. The employer was protected in making payment to the *only* known assignee, the department store.

NOVATION

The party entitled to receive performance under a contract may agree to release the party who is bound to perform and to permit another party to take his place. When this occurs it is not just a matter of assigning the liability under the contract; rather, it is one of abandoning the old contract and substituting a new one in its place. The change of contract and parties is called *novation*. For example, if Adams and Burnham have a contract, they, together with Caldwell, may agree that Caldwell shall take Adams' place. If this is done, there is a novation. Adams is discharged from the contract, and Burnham and Caldwell are bound. To be effective, it must be shown that a novation was intended. When there is a novation, the original obligor drops out of the picture; and the new party, who otherwise would be an assignee, takes his place and is alone liable for the performance.

> ▪ If Goff owes Ratcliff $500, Goff cannot shift this obligation to Lester without Ratcliff's consent. Ratcliff, however, can consent to the release of Goff and the substitution of Lester. In this event there is not an assignment, but a novation.

THIRD PARTY BENEFICIARY CONTRACTS

At common law only the parties to a contract could sue upon it or seek to enforce it. It was held that strangers to a contract had no rights under a contract. But courts began to make exceptions to the rule when it seemed evident that the contracting parties intended to benefit a third person, called a *third party beneficiary.*

The rule today is that a third person who is expressly benefited by the performance of the contract may enforce it against the promisor if benefit to the third party was intended by the contracting parties. The third person may be either a creditor beneficiary or a donee beneficiary. A *creditor beneficiary* is a creditor of the person whose obligation will be discharged to the extent that the promisor performs his promise. A *donee beneficiary* is one to whom no legal duty was owed by the promisee but to whom performance is a gift. A good example of a donee beneficiary is the beneficiary named in a life insurance contract.

Not everyone who benefits by the performance of a contract between others is properly considered a third party beneficiary with rights under the contract. If a person is merely incidentally benefited by the performance of a contract, he is not entitled to sue for breach or to sue for performance. For example, if a town contracts with a contractor for the paving of a certain street and the contractor fails to perform, the property owners whose property would have been improved by the paving are not entitled to sue for damages for nonperformance because they were to be only incidentally benefited. The contract for the paving of the street was designed essentially to further the public interest, not to benefit individual property owners.

JOINT, SEVERAL, AND JOINT AND SEVERAL CONTRACTS

When two or more persons enter into a contract with one or more other persons, the contract may be joint, several, or joint and several.

Joint Contracts. A *joint contract* is one in which two or more persons jointly promise to carry out an obligation or one in which two or more persons are jointly entitled to the performance of another party or parties. If Sands and Cole sign a contract stating "we jointly promise . . . ," the obligation is the joint obligation of Sands and Cole. Unless otherwise expressed, a promise by two or more persons is generally presumed to be joint and not several.

Several Contracts. A *several contract* arises when two or more persons individually agree to perform the same obligation even though the individual agreements are contained in the same document. If Sands and Cole sign a contract stating "we severally promise" or "each of us promises" to do a particular thing, the two signers are individually bound to perform.

Joint and Several Contracts. A *joint and several contract* is one in which two or more persons are bound both jointly and severally. If Sands and Cole sign a contract stating "we, and each of us, promise" or "I promise" to perform a particular act, they are jointly and severally obligated. The other party to the contract may treat the obligation as either a joint obligation or as a group of individual obligations, and he may bring suit against all or any one or more of them at one time. By statute in some states, a joint contract is interpreted to be a joint and several contract.

QUESTIONS

1. What is an *assignment?*
2. Name and identify the parties to an assignment.
3. In what ways may an assignment be made?
4. Why may rights to personal services not be assigned?
5. If one delegates his duties under a contract, what is his liability under the contract?
6. What is the effect of an assignment upon each party involved?
7. Whom should the assignee notify of the assignment?
8. Give an illustration of a serious loss that might occur if a bookkeeper failed to make a record of the day, hour, and minute when he received notice of an assignment.
9. If one becomes dissatisfied with a contract, may he get rid of it by assigning it to someone else?
10. What is the difference between a third party beneficiary and an incidental beneficiary?
11. Explain the meaning of *joint, several,* and *joint and several contracts.*

CASE PROBLEMS

1. Hamblen Lumber Company made all its employees sign a contract agreeing not to make any assignment of their wages. In spite of this, Stover, an employee, assigned $80 of his wages to the Ferguson Company. This company immediately notified Donahue, the bookkeeper of the Hamblen Lumber Company, of the assignment. Donahue refused to honor it and paid Stover the full amount due him. The Ferguson Company sued the Hamblen Lumber Company for the $80 since Stover never paid the account. Was the lumber company liable?

2. Eugene Black was credit manager for a furniture store. Stine purchased some furniture and in payment assigned to the furniture store $800 which was owed to him by the Clarke Engineering Corporation. Since the $800 was not due until ten days after the date of the assignment, Black held it until that date and presented it for payment. Payment was refused because Stine had offered the Clarke Engineering Corporation a 10 percent discount if they would pay him before the account was due. This they did. Must the corporation also pay the furniture store?

3. The Holcomb Filling Station sold a lot of gasoline on credit to local business firms. One of these firms, The Apex Bakery, was in debt to the station for $450. The owner of the bakery offered to turn over to the station $500 of its accounts receivable if the station would not sue the bakery. The offer was accepted. The filling station was able to collect only $100 on the accounts receivable because the debtors were insolvent. The station sued the bakery later for $400, the uncollectible balance of the accounts receivable. Was it entitled to collect?

4. Delaney, who owned and operated the M & N Cafeteria, sold it to Harper for $30,000, with $10,000 cash and the balance paid by note. Sometime later Harper sold the cafeteria to Mitchell; and Mitchell, as a part of the purchase price, agreed to assume Harper's obligation to pay Delaney the $20,000. Mitchell operated the cafeteria profitably for several months during which time his net profits were $18,000, but he made no payment on the notes. He became ill and the business declined rapidly. Delaney demanded that Harper pay the balance due on the original selling price. Was Harper obligated to pay this?

5. Harder contracted with the Dixie Red Coat Band to play at a party she was giving. The charge was $800. At the time the party was to start, Sherman's Blue Coat Band appeared and presented a written assignment to play from the Dixie Red Coat Band. Must Harder honor this assignment?

6. The Marbut Office Supply Company had a contract with the Second National Bank to keep all its office machines repaired for $100 a month. The Marbut Company sold its business in bulk to the McGregor Corporation and assigned this repair contract to this company. The bank refused to honor the assignment. Must it do so?

7. Elson and Ransom entered into a written agreement by which Elson promised to name his son after Ransom in exchange for Ransom's promise to pay Elson's son $5,000. Elson performs his part of the agreement. His son then brings action to enforce payment by Ransom. Is he entitled to do so?

Chapter 11

TERMINATION OF CONTRACTS

The preceding chapters have dealt with the law relative to the formation of contracts. It is equally important to know the law dealing with the termination of contracts. Some contracts, like marriage, are easy to enter into but often are difficult to terminate. There are five common methods by which contracts may be terminated. These are (a) performance of the contract, (b) discharge by operation of law, (c) by voluntary agreement of the parties, (d) by impossibility of performance, and (e) by acceptance of a breach of contract. The first two methods are covered in this chapter; the others are treated in Chapter 12.

PERFORMANCE

When all the terms of a contract have been fulfilled, the contract is discharged by performance. Not all the parties, however, need be discharged simultaneously. Each party is discharged as soon as he has done all that he agreed to do. The other party or parties are not discharged if any material thing remains to be done.

It may seem to be a simple matter to determine when a contract has been discharged by performance. There are several factors to be considered, however. They are:

1. Time of performance
2. Tender of performance
3. Satisfactory performance
4. Substantial performance

(1) **Time of Performance.** If the contract states when performance is to be rendered, the contract provisions must be followed unless the court should hold that under all the circumstances, performance on the exact date specified was not vital. When performance on the exact date is deemed vital, it is said that "time is of the essence." If no time for performance is stated, then performance must ordinarily be rendered within a reasonable time.

(2) **Tender of Performance.** An offer to perform an obligation in satisfaction of the terms of a contract is called a *tender of performance*. If a contract calls for the performance of an act, a tender of performance will discharge the obligation of the one making the tender so long as the tender conforms to the agreement.

> ▪ Cook hired the Thomas Transfer Company to move his household furniture to Atlanta on Monday, June 6, at 8 a.m. On that day the Thomas Transfer Company sent a truck to Cook's residence to load the furniture. Cook told the driver he was not ready and asked him to return at 2 p.m. As far as the Thomas Transfer Company is concerned, the contract is terminated since it tendered performance at the time specified. The transfer company's rights are determined by the circumstances. If their truck was idle because of Cook's breach of contract, it can sue for damages, the profit it would have made. It is under no obligation to return at 2 p.m.

An offer to pay money in satisfaction of a debt or claim is a *tender of payment*. The debtor must offer the exact amount due, including interest, if any. He must also make an actual offer of the money. If he says, "I am now ready to pay you," he has not made a sufficient tender. He must pay or tender the creditor the amount due.

A tender in the form of a check is not a proper tender. The payment must be tendered in *legal tender*. With but few minor exceptions, this is any form of United States money. If a check is accepted, the contract is performed as soon as the check is honored by the bank on which it is drawn.

If the tender is refused, the debt is not discharged. Although a proper tender does not pay the debt if the tender is refused, it does stop the running of interest. In addition, if the creditor should bring suit, the person who has tendered the correct amount is not liable for court costs. The debtor must, however, hold himself in readiness to pay at any time.

(3) **Satisfactory Performance.** It frequently happens that contracts specifically state that the contract must be "satisfactory to" or

"to the satisfaction of" a certain person. What constitutes satisfactory performance is frequently a disputed question. Certainly one should not be permitted to avoid a contract on an arbitrary standard of satisfaction impossible to attain. The courts generally have adopted the rule that if the contract is performed in a manner that would satisfy an ordinary, reasonable person, the terms of the contract have been met sufficiently to discharge it. There is one exception to this rule: If the performance involves the personal taste or fancy of one of the parties, he may reject it on the ground that it is not satisfactory to him.

> ▪ Mary employed Janet, an expert seamstress, to make her wedding gown. It was to be made "to your absolute satisfaction." The wedding was called off, and Mary refused to take the gown on the ground "it doesn't look exactly right on me." This was sufficient ground for refusing to pay. Clothing generally, and a wedding gown in particular, involves personal satisfaction of the customer. The seamstress had expressly agreed that it was to be made "to your absolute satisfaction." If the customer was in fact not satisfied, it was immaterial whether a reasonable person would have been satisfied.

(4) **Substantial Performance.** Under the early common law, each party to a contract had to perform to the last letter of the contract before he was entitled to demand his rights under the contract. Such a rule was often extremely inequitable. If a contractor builds a $50 million office building, it would be grossly unfair to say that he could collect none of the $50 million because of some breach.

The law today can be stated as follows: If a contract is substantially performed, the party performing may demand the full price under his contract, less the amount needed to correct the defect in his performance. In the case of the office building, if the cost of completing the building according to contract would be $3,000, the contractor could collect $50 million minus the $3,000. Suppose, however, that the contractor completed the excavation and then quit. He would be entitled to collect nothing. Just how far he must proceed toward full performance before he has substantially performed is often difficult to determine. The performance must be so nearly complete that it would be a great injustice to deny the contractor any compensation for the work.

> ▪ Hartwell contracted with The Herald Press to run ten quarterpage ads on ten consecutive days at a cost of $4,000. On one day the ad was run upside down. Hartwell refused to pay any part of the $4,000. The court held The Herald Press had substantially performed and Hartwell must pay for nine ads.

DISCHARGE BY OPERATION OF LAW

Under certain circumstances the law will effect a discharge of the contract, or at least the law will bar all right of action. The most common ways by which the law operates to discharge contracts are:

(1) Bankruptcy
(2) Statute of limitations
(3) Alteration of written contract

(1) Bankruptcy. It is not uncommon for individuals and business firms to be overwhelmed with financial obligations. The law permits these individuals and firms to petition the court for a decree of voluntary bankruptcy. Creditors may, under certain circumstances, force one into involuntary bankruptcy. (Bankruptcy is treated fully in Chapter 49.) In either event, all rights of action to enforce the contracts of the bankrupt are barred except for certain classes of debts, such as wages for the preceding three months, taxes, alimony, and court costs. However, a creditor's right of action is revived by the debtor's promise to pay made after the discharge of the bankruptcy proceeding.

(2) Statute of Limitations. When one party to a contract breaches it, the other party has the right to sue for breach of contract, but he must exercise this right within the time fixed by a statute which is called the *statute of limitations*. This time varies from state to state and for different types of debts. For open accounts, accounts receivable, and ordinary loans, the time varies from two to eight years, while for notes it varies from four to twenty years.

After a person has brought suit and obtained judgment, the judgment must be enforced by having the property of the debtor levied upon and sold. If this is not done, the statute of limitations operates even against judgments in some states. In those states where the statute applies to judgments, the time varies from five to twenty-one years from date of judgment.

The time is calculated from the date the obligation is due. In the case of running accounts, as purchases from department stores, the time starts from the date of the last purchase. If a part payment is made, the statute begins to run again from the date of such payment. If the promisor leaves the state, the statute ceases to run while he is beyond the jurisdiction of the court.

■ On July 1, 1960, Dover purchased a set of encyclopedias on the installment plan. The total price was $269.50. He was to pay $10 a month. The last payment he made was on September 1, 1961, leaving a balance of $129.50. The statute of limitations in his state was five years. In December, 1965, suit was brought to collect from Dover. He claimed the suit was barred by the statute of limitations. The court ruled the time ran from the date of the last payment. The five years had not expired.

A debt that has been outlawed by a statute of limitations may be revived. This is done in some states by a written acknowledgment of or a promise to pay the debt, in others by part payment after it has been outlawed, and in still others by the mere payment of the interest. After the debt is revived the period of the statute of limitations begins to run again from the time of the revival.

(3) **Alteration of Written Contract.** If one of the parties alters the written contract, it is discharged if the alteration was done intentionally and without the consent of the other party. In most states the alteration must also be material. If a contractor who has undertaken to build a house by January 15 and realizes that because of winter conditions he cannot finish by that date, erases and changes the date to March 15, he will be guilty of a material alteration which would discharge the contract.

QUESTIONS

1. State the ways in which a contract may be terminated.
2. If one party does not perform every detail of a contract, is the other party released from his obligations under the contract?
3. If one party contracts to perform a contract "to your absolute satisfaction," may the other party avoid the contract if he is not satisfied even though there is no apparent basis for his dissatisfaction?
4. If a debtor tenders payment of money but payment is refused, is the debt discharged?
5. If a check is accepted in payment, when is the contract performed?
6. If a contract contains no provision for time of performance, when must performance be rendered?
7. Does a proper tender that is refused stop the running of interest?
8. If a contract calls for an act, what is the effect of a refusal of a tender of performance?

CASE PROBLEMS

1. Daniel tendered a certified check in payment of his account. Cohen refused the check "because the amount is incorrect." Later Cohen sued Daniel on the account. Daniel proved that he had tendered a certified check for $500 as the full amount due, and he offered before the trial started to pay this amount. Cohen refused to accept it, claiming $700. The jury awarded Cohen a judgment for $500. Who must pay the court costs? Did Cohen use his knowledge of law wisely in this case?

2. Harmon employed Darwin to paint his house inside and out for $800. Darwin finished the job but, through an oversight, failed to paint the eaves boards on one end. Harmon offered Darwin $750, claiming he was withholding $50 for damages. Darwin offered to return and complete the job, which would require about two hours' work. Harmon refused to let him complete the job, and Darwin sued for $800. Who, in your opinion, was entitled to win the case?

3. Harbin contracted with Campbell to wire Campbell's house for $300. One week later, Harbin with his two helpers called at Campbell's residence and reported ready to begin the wiring. Campbell refused to let them enter the house. Being unable to get anyone else to wire it for less than $350, Campbell called Harbin and told him to go ahead and wire the house. Harbin refused and Campbell sued him for breach of contract. Was Harbin liable for damages?

4. Jason entered into a written contract with the White Brewery Company to work as their bookkeeper for 12 months at a salary of $700 a month. Jason signed two copies of the contract and mailed them to the White Brewery Company for its signature and a return of one copy to Jason. When Jason's copy was returned, the figure 12 was crossed out and 6 written over it. This alteration was made without Jason's consent. Is Jason bound on this contract?

5. The Martin Construction Company contracted to build a house for Mason for $21,000. The specifications called for the use of yellow pine lumber throughout except the flooring. After the house was completed, it was discovered that the rafters were hemlock. Mason refused to pay any part of the $21,000, claiming the breach of contract released him. What is your opinion?

6. Hunter with three other men planned an extensive fishing trip starting at 5 a.m., June 4. He purchased a boat from the Lanier Boat Company. The seller agreed to deliver it by 5 p.m. on June 3. At 5:45 p.m., June 3, the boat had not arrived, so Hunter purchased one from Daniel. At 5:54 p.m. the first boat was delivered, but Hunter refused to accept it. Was he within his rights?

Chapter 12

TERMINATION OF
CONTRACTS (Continued)

A contract is a mutual agreement. The parties are as free to change their minds by mutual agreement as they are to agree in the first place. Consequently, whenever the parties to a contract agree not to carry out its terms, the contract is discharged. The contract itself may recite the events or circumstances which will automatically terminate the agreement. The release of one party to the contract constitutes the consideration for the release of the other. If Walker agrees to build a house for Troelson, and Troelson agrees to pay Walker $20,000 upon completion of the house, they may at any time mutually agree to terminate the contract.

IMPOSSIBILITY OF PERFORMANCE

If the act called for in a contract is impossible of performance at the time the contract is made, no contract ever comes into existence. Frequently, impossibility of performance arises after a valid contract is formed. This type of impossibility discharges the contract under certain circumstances. The most common causes of discharge by impossibility of performance occurring after the contract is made are:

1. Destruction of the subject matter
2. New laws making the contract illegal
3. Death or physical incapacity of person to render personal services

(1) **Destruction of the Subject Matter.** If the contract involves specific subject matter, the destruction of this specific subject matter discharges the contract because of impossibility of performance.

If the contract specifies that the goods are to be manufactured in a particular plant, the destruction of that plant renders the contract impossible to perform. If the contract does not specifically designate the plant in which the articles are to be manufactured, the destruction of the plant from which the seller intended to procure the goods does not discharge the contract on the ground of impossibility; the seller is obligated to procure the goods elsewhere regardless of the additional cost involved.

> ■ The Campbell Builders' Supply Company had a contract to manufacture and deliver to the Dade Construction Company 100 aluminum windows of a certain size. Before the windows were made, the Campbell Builders' Supply Company's plant was destroyed by a tornado. This did not terminate the contract. Had the offer specified that the windows were to be made in the Dalton plant, then its destruction would have rendered the contract impossible to perform.

(2) **New Laws Making the Contract Illegal.** If an act is legal at the time of the contract but is subsequently made illegal, the contract is discharged. Under local option laws alcoholic beverages may be banned if a referendum approves such action. All executory contracts for the sale of alcoholic beverages in that locality are discharged when the ban becomes effective.

> ■ The Gates Construction Company contracted with Segrest to build a service station on Segrest's property. After the contract was entered into, but before work began, the city council passed a zoning ordinance restricting the site of the proposed service station to residential purposes. The contract was discharged by this ordinance.

(3) **Death or Physical Incapacity.** If the contract calls for personal services, death or physical incapacity of the person to perform such services discharges the contract. The personal services must be such that they cannot readily be performed by another or by the personal representative of the promisor.

Such acts as the painting of a portrait, representing a client in a legal proceeding, and other services of a highly personal nature are discharged by death or incapacity. In general, if the performance is too personal to be delegated, the death or disability of the party bound to perform will discharge the contract.

> ■ Gutherie entered into a contract with his father whereby Gutherie agreed to support his father as long as his father lived. Gutherie performed this contract for two years and then died while his father

was still alive but mentally incompetent. The guardian for the father sued the administrator of Gutherie's estate to force him to continue supporting the father. The court held Gutherie was fully released by his death. This decision stressed the fact that in such a contract it is the intent of the parties that death of the promisor terminates it.

ACCEPTANCE OF BREACH OF THE CONTRACT BY ONE OF THE PARTIES

When one of the parties fails or refuses to perform the obligations assumed under the contract, there is a breach of the contract.

If one party, prior to the time the other party is entitled to performance, announces his intention not to perform, there is an anticipatory breach of the contract. If the innocent party accepts the breach of the contract, the contract is thereby discharged.

REMEDIES FOR BREACH OF CONTRACT

If there is a breach of contract, the innocent party then has three courses of action which he may follow:

1. Sue for damages
2. Rescind the contract
3. Sue for specific performance

(1) Sue for Damages. The usual remedy for breach of contract is to sue for damages. In a suit for damages there are really two suits in one. The first is to prove breach of contract. The second is to prove damages. There are four kinds of damages: (a) nominal, (b) compensatory, (c) punitive, and (d) liquidated.

(a) Nominal Damages. If the plaintiff in a suit for damages because of a breach of contract is able to prove that the defendant broke the contract but is unable to prove he sustained any loss because of the breach, then the court will award him *nominal damages,* generally one dollar. The reason for this is to throw the court costs on the loser, the defendant.

▪ Thoben Textile Company contracted with the Dale Warehouse to purchase 1,000 bales of cotton for $20,000. The Dale Warehouse failed to perform, and the Thoben Textile Company purchased 1,000 bales of cotton of the same grade elsewhere for $19,975. In a suit for breach of contract these were the undisputed facts. The court awarded the plaintiff nominal damages of $1 since it did win its case by proving a breach of contract, but it failed to prove it had sustained any loss. The defendant had to pay the court costs.

(b) Compensatory Damages. The theory of the law of damages is that an injured party is to be compensated for any loss he may sustain but should not be permitted to profit from the other party's wrongdoing. The law, when there is a breach of contract, entitles the injured party to compensation for the exact amount of his loss, but no more. Such damages are called *compensatory damages.* Sometimes the actual loss is easily determined, but at other times it is very difficult to determine. As a general rule, the amount of damages is a question to be decided by the jury.

(c) Punitive or Exemplary Damages. In most instances the awarding of compensatory damages fully meets the ends of justice. There are rare cases, however, where compensatory damages are not adequate. In these instances the law may permit the plaintiff to receive punitive damages. *Punitive damages* are similar to a fine, but the amount paid goes to the plaintiff rather than to the government. The purpose of punitive damages is to punish the defendant, not to compensate the plaintiff. If a tenant maliciously damages property he is occupying, the landlord may frequently recover as damages the actual cost of repairs plus additional damages as punitive damages.

(d) Liquidated Damages. When two parties enter into a contract, they may, in order to avoid the problems involved in proving the actual damages sustained, include a provision fixing the amount of damages to be paid in the event one party breaches the contract. Such a provision is called *liquidated damages.* Such a clause in the contract specifies recoverable damages in the event that the plaintiff establishes a breach by the defendant. Liquidated damages must be reasonable and should be provided only in those cases where actual damages are difficult or impossible to prove. If the amount of damages fixed by the contract is unreasonable and in effect the damages are punitive, the court will not enforce this provision of the contract.

> ▪ O'Dell employed the Dade Construction Company to build a house for him for $20,000, to be completed by November 1. The contract stipulated that for every day the contractor was late in completing the house, $500 in damages should accrue. The house was not finished until November 11. O'Dell's only actual loss was that he had to pay one more month's rent. The liquidated damages provision was excessive and not binding since the owner of a $20,000 house would not sustain $500 damage for each day's delay.

(2) Rescind the Contract. The aggrieved party, when a contract is breached, may elect to rescind the contract. He then is released from all obligations not performed by him. If he has executed his part of the contract, his remedy is to sue for recovery of what he parted with. If the aggrieved party rescinds a contract for the sale of goods, he may also request damages for the breach.

(3) Sue for Specific Performance. Sometimes neither a suit for damages nor rescission will constitute an adequate remedy. The injured party's remedy under these circumstances is a suit in equity to compel *specific performance,* that is, the carrying out of the specific terms of the contract.

This remedy is available in most contracts for the sale of real estate or any interest in real estate and for the sale of rare articles of personal property, such as a painting or an heirloom, the value of which cannot readily be determined. There is no way to measure sentimental value attached to a relic. Under such circumstances mere money damages may be inadequate to compensate the injured party. The court may compel specific performance under such circumstances.

- The Small Art Museum contracted with McCloud to purchase a famous work of art for $40,000. Before McCloud delivered the painting to the buyer, another museum offered him $50,000 for it. McCloud failed to deliver the painting to the Small Art Museum. The Small Art Museum's remedy was to sue for specific performance.

As a general rule, contracts for the performance of personal services will not be specifically ordered, both because of the difficulty of supervision by the courts and because of the restriction of the Constitution prohibiting involuntary servitude except as a criminal punishment.

QUESTIONS

1. Is a contract to fly to the planet Neptune invalid because of impossibility of performance?
2. If one cannot perform a contract on time because of a strike in the trucking industry, is this a legal impossibility?
3. If a singer contracts to sing at a party, is he released if he develops laryngitis just before the party starts?
4. May an employer sue for specific performance in employment contracts?
5. Will the courts always enforce provisions in contracts for liquidated damages?
6. Give an illustration of when the courts may award punitive damages.
7. Under what conditions may one sue for specific performance of a contract rather than sue for damages?

8. A professional performer agreed to put on a program for a club for a $200 fee. Due to illness, he was unable to perform. Could he be sued for breach of contract?

9. What are *compensatory damages?*

10. What are *nominal damages?*

CASE PROBLEMS

1. Hanson entered into a contract with Holcomb to construct a service station at the corner of Case and Mell Streets. Before Hanson could start construction on the project, the city passed a zoning ordinance prohibiting commercial properties in the area of the proposed service station. Holcomb bought a lot in another section of the city and the whole project at the new location cost him $2,000 more than the cost at Case and Mell Streets. He sued Hanson for damages of $2,000. Can he collect?

2. The Brunswick Molasses Company contracted with the Candler Feed Company to deliver 100,000 gallons of molasses on or before April 1. Due to a strike at the Brunswick plant, the company was shut down for two months and could not fulfill its contract with the Candler Feed Company. When sued for damages, it set up the defense of impossibility of performance. Is this a good defense?

3. Holcomb leased a Gulf Oil Service Station for seven years. One year later the Gulf Oil Company, due to no fault of Holcomb, canceled Holcomb's franchise. Holcomb was unable to obtain a franchise from any other oil company, so he notified the lessor that he was no longer bound on the lease. Does the cancellation of the franchise terminate the lease?

4. Kerr, a noted singer and entertainer, was engaged by Flossie to sing at an annual dance at her dance studio. One day before Kerr was scheduled to sing, he was afflicted with a throat infection that left him temporarily speechless. Flossie had already paid him in advance one half of the price for his services. Flossie sued him for a return of this advance payment plus damages. Is Kerr liable for both damages and a return of the payment?

5. Hobbs entered into a written contract with Raub to sell Raub his house for $17,500, deed to be delivered within two weeks, at which time payment was to be made. When the time came to complete the sale, Hobbs refused to execute and deliver the deed since another buyer was willing to pay $18,500. What were Raub's rights?

6. The Carson Construction Company had a contract to erect a $2 million office building. It called for bids to supply the wire for the electrical wiring needs for the building. The invitation for bids stated that time was an extremely important factor. The Heller Copper Company submitted a bid. It wished to include a clause such as "Performance on the date specified is to be waived if performance cannot be made due to fire, flood, tornado, or other acts of God." But Heller Copper Company knew its nearest competitor would not include a similar clause in its bid. The Heller Company used this clause: "This wire to be fabricated in our plant located at Watkinsville." This plant was destroyed by a tornado before the wire was fabricated. Was the Heller Company released from its contract?

7. Four college boys rented a house from Duncan at $120 a month. The term was for ten months. There were several heated disputes between the boys and Duncan over whether or not the terms of the lease were being broken. The boys, to get even with Duncan, deliberately let the bathtub overflow, causing $700 water damage to the building. What are Duncan's rights?

8. The Vaughn Paper Company contracted with the Guest Printing Company to supply the printing paper for the Guest Printing Company for 10 months for $20,000. The paper was to be supplied in 10 equal shipments. A clause in the contract stipulated, "If any one shipment is late in arriving by 48 hours, the Vaughn Paper Company agrees to pay damages in the amount of $20,000." One shipment was four days late in arrival, but there was no evidence the Guest Printing Company was inconvenienced since it had ample stock on hand. It sued the Vaughn Paper Company for $20,000. How much damages is the Guest Printing Company entitled to receive?

9. The Hope Manufacturing Company entered into a contract with the Georgia Well and Supply Company to fabricate for the latter company certain sizes of well casings. A given quantity was to be delivered on the first of each month. Due to a heavy flood which seriously damaged the Hope Manufacturing Company plant, it was unable to fill its order for several months. The Georgia Well and Supply Company sued it for damages, alleging breach of contract. Was it entitled to damages?

10. The N & O Restaurant had a contract with the O'Kelley Dairy Farm to purchase ten gallons of raw milk a day for ten months. About one month after this contract was signed, the city council passed an ordinance prohibiting the serving of raw milk in the city's public eating places. The N & O Restaurant stopped its purchases of milk from O'Kelley, and O'Kelley sued for breach of contract. Was he entitled to collect?

SUMMARY CASES

PART 2

1. Kershaw & Son wrote a letter to Moulton in which was this key section: "We are authorized to offer Michigan fine salt, in full carload lots of 80-95 barrels." Immediately upon receipt of this letter Moulton replied, "You may ship me 2,000 barrels Michigan fine salt as offered in your letter." Due to changed circumstances, Kershaw & Sons did not wish to be bound on their offer. They contended the letter was a mere sales letter inviting offers, not an offer itself. Was this an offer? (Moulton v. Kershaw, 59 Wis. 316, 18 N. W. 172)

2. Failing, acting as agent for Blakeslee, wrote Nelson, asking him, "Will you and your wife accept $49,000 for your property?" Six days later Nelson replied, "I will not sell for less than $56,000." One day after receiving this letter from Nelson, Failing wired Nelson, "Will accept your offer $56,000 net." Did Nelson make an acceptable offer? (Blakeslee v. Nelson, 212 App. Div. 219, 207, N. Y. S. 676)

3. The defendant Rosenbusch owned a 1/160 interest in an oil lease on some land in Oklahoma. Rosenbusch was a resident of Washington, D. C., and was not familiar with conditions in Oklahoma. She had never received any income from the lease. Deardorf wrote to her offering to purchase her "nonproductive royalty interest" for $10. She accepted the offer but later learned that some very productive wells had been drilled near her lease and that it was now a very valuable lease, a fact known to Deardorf when he wrote her. She brought suit to set the contract aside. Should the court grant rescission? (Deardorf et al. v. Rosenbusch [Okla.], 206 P. 2d 996)

4. Shoenung, while a minor 19 years of age, purchased from the defendant an automobile for $300, trading in an old car with an allowance of $50 and giving a note for $250. Shoenung lived with his parents on a farm and worked in town, three miles distant. He returned the car two months later and demanded his old car back and the return of his $250 note. Was he entitled to disaffirm the contract? (Schoenung v. Gallet, 238 N. W. 852, 206 Wis. 52)

5. The Midtown Motors employed Wise as an expert automobile mechanic for three years at a salary of $5,000 the first year; $5,500, the second; and $6,000, the third. After eight months Wise was discharged without justifiable cause. He sued for damages and obtained a judgment. He went to work in the meantime for another auto firm. To collect his judgment Wise garnisheed the Midtown Motors' bank account. The owner of the Midtown Motors went to Wise's new place of employment and engaged in considerable verbal abuse of Wise. He threatened him with legal action for garnisheeing the bank account. Wise's present employer joined in the verbal abuse and told him he was "fired" unless he accepted the proffered $200 in full settlement and signed a release for the balance. While in a state of extreme mental confusion as to what to do, he signed the release. The next day he changed his mind and repudiated the release and demanded the full amount due him. May he repudiate the signed release? (Wise v. Midtown Motors, 231 Minn. 46, 42 N. W. 2d 404)

6. Jaffray owed Davis $7,714.37. The debt was past due. Davis offered to settle the $7,714.37 if Jaffray would give him three promissory notes totaling $3,462.24 secured by a security interest in the stock and fixtures and other property owned by Jaffray. Jaffray accepted the offer and in due course paid the three notes as they fell due. Davis then brought suit to collect the difference between the original debt of $7,714.37 and the sum of the three notes. Is he entitled to collect? (Jaffray et al. v. Davis et al., 124 N. Y. 164, 26 N. E. 351, 11 L. R. A. 710)

7. Parker sold his bakery business to Thomas. As a part of the sales agreement, this clause appeared: "together with goodwill and bakery machinery in said bakery." Another clause stipulated, "Parker agrees that he will not engage in the bakery business directly or indirectly for a period of seven years within a radius of seven miles of Boston." About one year later Parker began working as a baker for the Boston Syrian Baking Company. Thomas brought suit asking that Parker be enjoined from working for the Syrian Baking Company. Is he entitled to the injunction? (Thomas v. Parker, Mass. 98 N. E. 2d 640)

8. The Tile Company sold Drake some of its stock. An officer of the corporation in an effort to induce Drake to buy the stock stated that the corporation owned land that contained clay peculiarly adapted to the manufacture of clay tile. It later developed that this clay was not suitable for the making of clay tile. This fact was unknown to the officer of the corporation at the time he made the statement. Drake relied upon the statement and purchased the stock. Drake brought an action to rescind the contract, and the Tile Company raised the defense, not that the statement was true, but that the officer innocently made the misrepresentation. May Drake rescind? (Drake v. Fairmont Drain Tile and Brick Company, 129 Minn. 145, 151 N. W. 914)

9. Lee was a student at Yale University. He rented a room from Gregory for 40 weeks. He occupied the room for about three months and then gave it up without alleging any breach of contract on Gregory's part. Gregory brought suit to collect for the balance of the 40 weeks' rent. Is he entitled to collect? (Gregory v. Lee, 64 Conn. 407, 30 A. 53)

10. Rich owed a board bill contracted while he was attending college. As he was unable to pay the board bill, he persuaded Kilgore to pay the board bill for him and promised to reimburse Kilgore. Rich failed to reimburse Kilgore and was sued for the money. Rich pleaded minority as a defense, claiming that a loan of money was not a necessary. Was Rich's defense good in this case? (Kilgore v. Rich, 85 Me. 305, 22 A. 176)

11. Chevalier entered into an oral contract with Lane's, Inc. to work for the corporation for a period of 12 months, work to begin shortly after the contract was made. Chevalier began work and continued for a period of six months. According to his oral contract, Chevalier was to be paid a monthly salary plus a bonus of $1,500 at the end of six months. He was laid off without cause at the end of the first six months without receiving his $1,500 bonus, although his monthly salary had been paid. He brought suit for his $1,500 bonus plus his damages for having been discharged without cause. Is he entitled to either the $1,500 or damages? (Chevalier v. Lane's, Inc., 1948, 147 Tex. 106, 213 S. W. 2d 530)

12. Kelley entered into a contract with Hance whereby Kelley was to construct a sidewalk and curb in front of Hance's property. The price for the work was to be $3 a running foot, or $420 for the 140 feet. Kelley was to start work within one week and complete it before cold weather. Although the contract was entered into in September, Kelley did not begin work until December 4. He continued to work until he had removed dirt to a width of 12 feet. He then discontinued the work and never returned. In March the following year, Hance notified Kelley that the contract was canceled. Kelley then brought suit to recover for the value of the work he already had done at the time the contract was terminated by Hance. Is Kelley entitled to any compensation? (Kelley v. Hance, 108 Conn. 186, 142 A. 683)

13. Somerville held a charter to an ocean vessel, the Henry S. Little. Somerville assigned his charter to this vessel to Piaggio whereby Piaggio agreed to pay Somerville $1,500 upon the clearance of the vessel at Mobile. At that time Germany was carrying on unrestricted submarine warfare, and the owners of the vessel refused to clear it for fear it would be sunk by a German submarine. Since Piaggio was unable to get clearance for the vessel, he refused to pay the $1,500; and Somerville brought suit to collect. Is Piaggio's defense of impossibility of performance valid in this case? (Piaggio v. Somerville, 119 Miss. 6, 80 So. 342)

14. Potter purchased lumber from the Pacific Coast Lumber Company. A dispute arose as to the amount owed. Potter paid for the lumber, one lot by check and one by a draft. In both instances a voucher was attached in which appeared these words: "In full settlement of account stated below." The amount paid was less than the amount claimed. The Pacific Coast Lumber Company accepted the check and the draft as written. It then sued for the difference between the amount claimed and the amount paid. Was the lumber company entitled to collect? (Potter v. Pacific Coast Lumber Company, 37 Cal. 2d 592, 234 P. 2d 16)

15. Silverstein and Silverstein held a three-year written lease on space in Dohoney's property to be used for cigarette vending machines. The lease provided for the payment of rent by means of a commission on all cigarettes sold, but the amount of the commission was not stated. Prior to this lease the plaintiff had a machine in Dohoney's property and had paid him commissions on all sales of cigarettes. In a suit involving this contract, the key question was whether or not oral testimony could be introduced to prove the amount of commissions that were to be paid. Should the oral testimony be admitted? (Silverstein v. Dohoney, N.J. Sup. Ct. 108 A. 2d 451)

Part 3.

SALES

Preview Cases for Part 3: Sales

- Martin entered into a contract with Case whereby Case was to receive 25 percent of the selling price of Martin's automatic vending machine. Martin licensed the manufacture and distribution of the machine to a manufacturer in Canada. Case demanded that he receive 25 percent of the license fees. Was Case entitled to the money?

- Jameson, a married minor, purchased $100 worth of groceries on credit from the Jackson Super Market. On two occasions the purchases included two bottles of wine. A state law prohibited the sale of wine to anyone under 21 years of age. The wine on the sales tickets was separately priced, so the illegal part could easily be separated from the legal part. What, if anything, would Jameson be obligated to pay?

- Madson orally promised to sell Flood a certain article for $675 and subsequently refused to deliver the article. Flood sued for breach of contract. Madson's defense was that the agreement was unenforceable because a contract to sell or a contract for the sale of goods with the price of $500 or more needed to be in writing to be enforceable. Was Flood entitled to collect?

- Owen told Snyder that he wished to buy Snyder's auto. He drove the car for about ten minutes, returned to Snyder, stated that he wanted to take the auto to show it to his wife, and then left with the auto but never returned. Later Owen sold the auto in another state to Pearson and gave him a bill of sale. Pearson showed the bill of sale to Lincoln, falsely told him the certificate of title for the auto was held by a bank as security for the financing of the auto, and then sold the auto to Lincoln. Snyder sued Lincoln to recover the automobile. Was Snyder entitled to the automobile?

- Webster ordered a bowl of fish chowder in the Blue Ship Tea Room. She was injured by a fish bone in the chowder. She sued the Tea Room for breach of warranty. Should Webster be allowed to recover for damages?

These preview cases are designed to serve as a springboard for the study of this part. As you read through each chapter in this part, you will find the actual decisions for all these preview cases. Of course, there are many more such illustrative problems as well as case problems for decision at the end of each chapter. And there are also a number of even more challenging cases for review at the end of the part.

Chapter 13

SALES OF PERSONAL PROPERTY

IMPORTANCE OF SALES CONTRACTS

In terms of the number of contracts as well as in the dollar volume, contracts for the sale of goods—movable personal property—constitute the largest class of contracts in our economic system. Every time one purchases a package of cigarettes, he enters into a sales contract. If the cigarettes contained some harmful substance, the sale could be the basis of a suit for thousands of dollars in damages. Sales of movable personal property are governed by Article 2 of the Uniform Commercial Code, effective in all states except Louisiana.

PROPERTY SUBJECT TO SALE

As used in the Uniform Commercial Code and in these chapters, "sale" applies only to the sale of movable personal property. Thus, it does not apply to (1) real property, (2) intangible personal property, or (3) choses in action. *Real property* is land, interests in land, and things permanently attached to land. *Movable personal property* consists of all physical items which are not real estate, such as merchandise, clothing, and furniture. *Intangible personal property* consists of evidences of ownership of personal property, such as contracts, copyrights, and stocks. Accounts receivable, notes receivable, and similar assets are *choses in action* or intangible personal property.

Sales contracts must have all the essentials of any other contract, but they have some features that apply only to this type of contract. As the subject is developed in this and the following chapters, it will be seen that there are many rules pertaining to sales of personal property that would have no significance to any other type of contract, such as a contract of employment.

SALES AND CONTRACTS TO SELL

A distinction is made between a sale and a contract to sell at a future date.

A *sale* of goods is an agreement whereby the seller transfers the title to goods to the buyer for a consideration called the price. It is a contract in which the ownership changes hands at the moment the bargain is made regardless of who has possession of the goods.

A *contract to sell* goods is a contract whereby the seller agrees to transfer the title to goods to the buyer for a consideration called the price. This is a contract in which one promises to buy or to sell in the future.

The important distinction between a sale and a contract to sell is that in the former the title, or the ownership of the subject matter, is transferred at once; in the latter it will be transferred at a later time. A contract to sell is not in the true sense of the word a sale; it is merely an agreement to sell.

Since in a sale title passes to the buyer immediately, and in a contract to sell, title passes at some future date, it is extremely important to distinguish between the two. There can be no such thing as an intervening period during which time title rests with neither the seller nor the buyer. The risk of loss, with the exceptions set out later in this chapter, is borne by the owner. Also, any increase in the property belongs to the one who has the title. It is essential, therefore, to have certain definite rules to aid the courts in determining when title and risk of loss pass if the parties to the contract are silent as to these matters. If the parties specify when title or risk of loss passes, the courts will enforce this agreement.

PRICE

The consideration in a sales contract is generally expressed in terms of money or money's worth and is known as the *price*. The price may be payable in money, goods, or services.

▪ Martin entered into a contract with Case whereby Case was to receive 25 percent of the selling price of Martin's automatic vending machine. Martin licensed the manufacture and distribution of the machine to a manufacturer in Canada. Case demanded that he receive 25 percent of the license fees. The court held this was not a sale because it did not involve the transfer of title to movable personal property.

The sales contract is ordinarily an express contract, but some of its terms may be implied. If the price is not stated, it will be held to be the reasonable price; and if the goods are sold on a regulated market, such as a commodity exchange, the price on such market will be deemed the reasonable price. If the parties indicate that the price must be fixed by them or by a third person at a later date, there is no binding contract if the price is not thus fixed.

In Chapter 4 it was stated that an offer must be definite and specific. An offer to sell goods must also meet this test; but because of the peculiar nature of sales contracts, the courts do not apply this rule strictly.

> ▪ The Angus Textile Company entered into a contract with the Williams Cotton Merchant to purchase "all its needs of raw cotton for the next twelve months, the price to be that quoted on the New Orleans Cotton Market on the day of each delivery, or the last day the market was open prior to delivery if delivery is on Saturday or a holiday." This was a valid contract even though the offer does not state a definite price. The market price can be used when there is an established market.

EXISTING GOODS

In order to be the subject of a sale, it is necessary that the goods be existing. This means that the goods must both be in existence, as contrasted with goods not yet manufactured, and be then owned by the seller. If these conditions are not met, the only transaction that can be made between the seller and the buyer will be a contract to sell goods in the future.

Future goods are goods which the seller does not now own. He expects to acquire them in the future by purchase or by manufacture. Any contract purporting to sell future goods is a contract to sell and not a contract of sale. Title to the goods does not pass to the buyer when the goods come into existence. To the contrary, some further action must be taken by the seller.

> ▪ Taylor, a shoe manufacturer, contracted to sell the Mitchell Shoe Store 2,000 pairs of shoes. At the time this contract was made, the shoes had not been manufactured. After they were manufactured but before they were shipped, Taylor's creditors levied upon the shoes. Taylor claimed they were not his shoes since he had sold them to the Mitchell Shoe Store. Since the shoes at the time of the contract were not in existence, they were future goods. Consequently, this was merely a contract to sell, not of sale. The title to the shoes

did not pass to Mitchell Shoe Store upon being manufactured since some further act had to be done by Taylor to transfer title.

BILL OF SALE

A *bill of sale* is written evidence of one's title to tangible personal property. It is generally not necessary to have such evidence of title; but should one's title be questioned, such evidence is highly desirable. If one buys a stock of merchandise in bulk, a house trailer, livestock, and many other relatively expensive items, such as jewelry and furs, he should demand that the seller give him a bill of sale. This serves two purposes: (1) If the buyer wishes to resell the goods and the prospective buyer demands proof of title, he can produce his bill of sale; (2) if any question arises as to whether or not he came into possession of the goods legally, he has his bill of sale as proof.

- Howard purchased a trailer from Henderson. A few months later he contracted to sell it to Tucker. Tucker would not pay Howard for the trailer unless he could produce a bill of sale showing he had title to it. This often is a wise precaution.

ILLEGAL SALES

Many difficulties arise over illegal sales, that is, the sale of goods prohibited by law, such as alcoholic beverages in a "dry" locality. If the sale is fully executed, the court will not intervene to aid either party. If an innocent party through fraud is induced to enter into an illegal sale, the court will compel a restoration of the goods he has transferred.

If the illegal sale is wholly executory, the transaction is a contract to sell and will not be enforced. If it is only partially executory, the courts will still leave the parties where it found them unless the one who has performed is an innocent victim of a fraud.

If the sale is divisible and a part is legal and a part illegal, the court will enforce the legal part. As a rule the nature of the contract, not the nature of the goods, determines its divisibility. If the individual items are separately priced, the sale is divisible. If the sale involves several separate and independent items but is a lump-sum sale, then the sale is indivisible. If any part is illegal, the entire sale is illegal.

▪ Jameson, a married minor, purchased $100 worth of groceries on credit from the Jackson Super Market. On two occasions the purchases included two bottles of wine. A state law prohibited the sale of wine to anyone under 21 years of age. The wine on the sales tickets was separately priced, so the illegal part could easily be separated from the legal part. Jameson had to pay for all groceries but not for the wine.

QUESTIONS

1. Distinguish clearly between a sale and a contract to sell.
2. Why is it important to make a distinction between a sale and a contract to sell?
3. If the price in a sales contract is not stated, what may the court consider to be a reasonable price?
4. (a) What are *future goods?*
   (b) Can future goods ever constitute the subject matter of a contract of sale?
5. (a) What is a *bill of sale?*
   (b) Is a bill of sale necessary to pass title?
6. Give three illustrations of choses in action.
7. Is an offer to sell wheat at the Chicago market price on June 7 an acceptable offer?
8. How does the court view an illegal sale that has been executed, as compared to one which is wholly executory?

CASE PROBLEMS

1. The purchasing agent for the Stanley Wholesale Grocery Corporation agreed to purchase sugar from the Domino Refinery over a period of six months, the price not to exceed 5 cents a pound nor to fall below 4¾ cents a pound, the current market price at the time of delivery to determine the price of each shipment between these two extremes. The question arose as to whether or not these terms violated the rule that an offer must be definite and specific to be accepted. Was the contract valid?

2. Bilko rented a fishing boat from a wholesale fish merchant for the purpose of a fishing expedition. He purchased provisions and supplies for the expedition from Wholesale Foods, Inc., and gave as security a bill of sale on all the fish he was to catch on the trip at 10 cents a pound. When the boat docked laden with several tons of fish, the creditors of Bilko attached the fish for the debts owed them by Bilko. Wholesale Foods produced its bill of sale to prove it had title to the fish. Who has superior rights in this case, the creditors or the Wholesale Foods, Inc.?

3. The Blue Goose Cafe served Mrs. Jones a dinner consisting of turkey with dressing. After Mrs. Jones had eaten a part of it, it was discovered that the dressing contained portions of a mouse. Mrs. Jones sued for breach of an implied warranty that in the sale of goods the seller warrants they are fit for human consumption. For this law to be used in this case, serving of food in a restaurant must be a sale. Was this a sale?

4. Lasher, the purchasing agent of the Hertz Company, purchased a used bookkeeping machine from the Adams Bookkeeping Service. The selling price of the machine was $3,200. About two weeks later, a representative of the manufacturer of the machine demanded possession of the machine claiming it was only rented to the Adams Bookkeeping Service. He showed Lasher the rental agreement as proof of his statement. What should Lasher have done to avoid this loss?

5. Paul, aged seventeen, purchased about $50 worth of groceries from the Burkhart Food Mart on credit. The $50 included $5 for cigarettes. There was a state law making it illegal for a merchant to sell cigarettes to one under 18 years of age. Paul learned of this and refused to pay any part of the $50 since the sales contract is illegal. Was he correct in his contention?

6. Before the pecan season opened in Albany, Georgia, Thompson Brothers entered into a contract with Davis, a pecan grower, to purchase all his pecans "at the market price." After Davis had delivered 20,000 pounds of pecans, he asked Thompson Brothers for a settlement. He produced a New York paper showing the market price for pecans in New York to be 19 cents. In Albany they were 17 cents a pound. Could Davis collect 19 cents a pound?

Chapter 14

FORMALITIES OF A SALE

FORM OF CONTRACTS PERTAINING TO SALES

All contracts to sell or contracts of sale must be evidenced by a writing when the sales price is $500 or more. If the sales price is less, the contract may be oral, written, implied from conduct, or a combination of any of these.

If a contract does not meet the requirements of the Statute of Frauds, it is not void, merely unenforceable. If both parties elect to abide by its terms even though they are not legally bound to do so, neither one can later change his mind.

- Madson orally promised to sell Flood a certain article for $675 and subsequently refused to deliver the article. Flood sued for breach of contract. Madson's defense was that the agreement was unenforceable because a contract to sell or a contract for the sale of goods with the price of $500 or more needed to be in writing to be enforceable. It was held that Madson's defense was good.

SALES WITHIN THE STATUTE OF FRAUDS

Frequently one makes several purchases the same day from the same seller. The question may then be raised as to whether there is one sale or several sales. If one purchases five items from the same seller in one day, each one having a sale price of less than $500, but in the aggregate they are in excess of $500, must this contract meet the requirement of the Statute of Frauds? If the several items are part of the same sales transaction, it is one sale and must meet the requirement of the Statute. If all purchases are made during the same shopping tour and with the same salesperson who merely adds up the different items and charges the customer with a grand total, the several items are considered to be part of the same transaction. But if a separate sales slip is written for each purchase as one goes through a department store, buying in different departments, each transaction is a separate sale.

WHEN PROOF OF ORAL CONTRACT PERMITTED

In some instances the absence of a writing does not bar the proof of a sales contract.

(1) Receipt and Acceptance. An oral sales contract may be enforced if it can be shown that the goods were delivered by the seller and were received and accepted by the buyer. Both a receipt and an acceptance by the buyer must be shown. *Receipt* is taking possession of the goods. *Acceptance* is the assent of the buyer to become the owner of specific goods. The contract may be enforced only insofar as it relates to the goods received and accepted.

(2) Payment. An oral contract may be enforced if the buyer has made full payment on the contract. In the case of part payment, a contract may be enforced only with respect to goods for which payment has been made and accepted. There is some uncertainty under this rule as to the effectiveness as "payment" by check or a promissory note executed by the buyer. Under the law of commercial paper a check or note is conditional payment when delivered, and it does not become absolute until the instrument is paid. The earlier decisions held that the delivery of a negotiable instrument was not such a payment as would make the oral contract enforceable unless it was agreed at that time that the instrument was to be accepted as absolute and not conditional payment. A modern contrary view, which is influenced by the fact that businessmen ordinarily regard the delivery of a check or note as "payment," holds that the delivery of such an instrument is sufficient to make the oral contract enforceable.

When the buyer has negotiated or assigned to the seller a negotiable instrument that was executed by a third person and the seller has accepted the instrument, a payment has been made within the meaning of the Statute of Frauds.

A check or promissory note that is tendered as payment but which is refused by the seller does not constitute a payment under the Statute of Frauds.

(3) **Judicial Admission.** No writing is required when the person alleged to have made the contract voluntarily admits in the course of legal proceedings that he has done so.

(4) **Nonresellable Goods.** No writing is required when the goods are specifically made for the buyer and are of such an unusual nature that they are not suitable for sale in the ordinary course of the seller's business. For this exception to apply, however, the seller must have made a substantial beginning in manufacturing the goods, or if he is a middleman, in procuring them, before receiving notice of a repudiation by the buyer.

NATURE OF THE WRITING REQUIRED

(1) **Terms.** The writing need only give assurance that there was a transaction. Specifically, it need only indicate that a sale or contract to sell has been made and state the quantity of goods involved. Any other missing terms may be shown by parol evidence in the event of a dispute.

(2) **Signature.** The writing must be signed by the person who is being sued or his authorized agent. The signature must be placed on the writing with the intention of authenticating the writing. It may consist of initials; it may be printed, stamped, or typewritten. The important thing is that it was made with the necessary intent.

When the transaction is between merchants, the Uniform Commercial Code makes an exception to the requirement of signing. It provides that the failure of a merchant to repudiate a confirming letter sent him by another merchant binds him just as though he had signed the letter or other writing. This ends the evil of a one-sided writing under which the sender of the letter was bound but the receiver could safely ignore the transaction or could hold the sender as he chose, depending upon which alternative gave him the better financial advantage.

(3) **Time of Execution.** A writing to satisfy the Statute of Frauds may be made at any time at or after the making of the sale. It may even be made after the contract has been broken or a suit brought on it, since the essential element is the existence of written proof of the transaction when the trial is held.

(4) Particular Writings. The writing which satisfies the Statute of Frauds may be a single writing or it may be several writings considered as a group. Formal contracts, bills of sale, letters, and telegrams are common forms of writings that satisfy the Statute of Frauds. Purchase orders, cash register receipts, sales tickets, invoices, and similar papers generally do not satisfy the requirements as to a signature and sometimes they do not specify any quantity or commodity.

AUCTION SALES

A sale by auction for any amount is valid even though it is from necessity oral. In most states the auctioneer is the special agent for both the owner and the bidder. When he or the clerk of the auction makes a memorandum of the sale and signs it, this binds both parties. The bidder is the one who makes the offer. There is no contract until the auctioneer accepts the offer, which he may do in several ways. The most common way is the fall of the hammer, with the auctioneer saying, "Sold" or "Sold to (a certain person)." In most auctions, however, the final bid is preceded by several lower bids. If a man makes a bid to start the sale, the auctioneer may refuse to accept this as a starting bid. If he does accept it and then proceeds to ask for a higher bid, he can later refuse to accept this bid as the selling price.

If a bid is made "while the hammer is falling" in acceptance of a prior bid, then the auctioneer may at his discretion reopen the bidding or declare the goods sold. His decision is binding.

Goods may be offered for sale "with reserve" or "without reserve." If they are without reserve, then the goods cannot be withdrawn after the bidding starts unless no bid is received within a reasonable time after the auctioneer calls for bids. Goods are presumed to be offered with reserve unless the goods are explicitly put up without reserve.

QUESTIONS

1. What contracts involving sale of goods must be in writing to be enforceable?
2. Is a check part payment as defined by the Statute of Frauds?
3. If A sells B 1,000 bushels of wheat by oral contract, is a token delivery of 100 bushels sufficient to make the contract valid?
4. What is *"receipt"*? What is *"acceptance"*?

5. Is a sales ticket that is signed by the buyer a sufficient writing?

6. Wherein does a contract for nonresellable goods differ from a contract of sale?

7. In order to satisfy the Statute of Frauds, must a writing be made at the time of sale?

8. What kind of writing meets the requirements of a written agreement for an auction sale?

CASE PROBLEMS

1. Henry and Harriet went shopping at the Shadow Discount House for furniture. They selected a living room suite for $450. After visiting another store, they returned to the Shadow Discount House and selected a dining room suite for $475. The seller was to deliver the furniture the following day at which time payment was to be made. Is this one or two sales for the purpose of the Statute of Frauds?

2. Joel, sales manager for the Dobbs Building Materials Company, sold Wilson $6,000 worth of building materials. Joel wrote down the items on a purchase order as Wilson listed them. Joel agreed to take in part payment a 60-day draft drawn by Downs Motor Company in favor of Wilson. This draft was assigned in writing to the Dobbs Building Materials Company. Joel interpreted this to meet the requirements of a memo under the Statute of Frauds. Wilson signed nothing else and made no other payment at the time. He later canceled the order and demanded a return of the draft. Was Wilson bound on this contract?

3. Horace purchased a piano from Walden and paid for it by indorsing a check to Walden which was made to the order of Horace. On the back of the check he wrote: "Pay to the order of A. Walden but I will not be responsible if the check is not paid. Signed: John Horace." Walden agreed to accept the check with this indorsement. Does this meet the test of part payment?

4. Duncan made out a purchase order to the Fulton Steel Company for some sheet metal costing $2,700. This order was mailed on July 7. There was no acknowledgment of the order. On August 3 the metal arrived, but in the meantime Duncan had purchased the metal elsewhere. He claims he is not bound on this contract because it is not in writing. Do you agree?

5. Carson sold his recorder to Douglas for $500. He gave Douglas the key to the room where the recorder was stored and told Douglas to pick it up when convenient. Before Douglas went for the recorder, the building in which it was stored was destroyed by fire. Douglas now refuses to pay for the set, claiming it is Carson's loss since this was an oral contract. Do you agree?

6. Mrs. Jane Langley inspected some carpet material on display at the Sinkwich Furniture Mart. The salesman quoted her a definite price per

square foot, the carpet material to be cut individually to fit her living room, a wall-to-wall type of carpet. She orally agreed to purchase it. Her living room had a very odd and unusual shape. After the carpet was cut and laid, Mrs. Langley was keenly disappointed in its appearance. She had faintly remembered from her business law course that an oral sales contract under certain conditions is invalid. She refused to pay for the carpet and demanded that the seller take it up. What were the rights of the parties?

7. The Glo-Coat Paint Company offered to sell the Lull Paint Store a quantity of paint of various grades and colors. The value of the bulk lot was $5,575. The owner of the Lull Paint Store orally agreed to buy it, but the seller insisted on a written memorandum of the sale to make it comply with the Statute of Frauds. Lull was in a quandary. He really wanted the paint as it was a very good price, but there was a possibility he would sell his paint store in a few days, in which case he would not want it. He drew up a memo as follows: "It is hereby agreed that were I to buy the paint herein described, I will pay cash on the day of delivery, which is to be not later than one week from today." Both parties signed the memo. Lull sold his paint store the next day and notified the Glo-Coat Paint Company that he would not buy the paint. The Glo-Coat Paint Company sued him for breach of contract, alleging that they were inveigled into signing a trick memo. Was the Lull Paint Store liable on this contract?

Chapter 15

TRANSFER OF TITLE AND RISK IN SALES CONTRACTS

In the vast majority of sales transactions the buyer receives the proper goods, makes payment, and the transaction is thus completed. However, several types of problems may arise. For the most part, these problems can be avoided if the parties by their sales contract expressly state what they intend. When the parties have not by their contract specified what results they desire, however, the rules stated in this chapter are applied by the law.

NATURE OF THE PROBLEM

(1) **Creditors' Claims.** Creditors of the seller may seize the goods as belonging to the seller, or the buyer's creditors may seize them on the theory that they belong to the buyer. In such case the question arises whether the creditors are correct as to who owns the goods. The question of ownership is also important in connection with resale by the buyer, or liability for or computation of certain kinds of taxes, and liability under certain registration and criminal statutes.

(2) **Insurance.** Until the buyer has received the goods and the seller has been paid, both the seller and buyer have an economic interest in the sales transaction. The question arises as to whether either or both have enough interest to entitle them to insure the property involved, that is, whether they have an insurable interest.

(3) **Damage to Goods.** If the goods are damaged or totally destroyed without any fault of either the buyer or the seller, must

the seller bear the loss and supply new goods to the buyer? Or is it the buyer's loss, so that he must pay the seller the purchase price even though he now has no goods or has only damaged goods?

NATURE OF THE TRANSACTION

The nature of the transaction between the seller and the buyer determines the answer to be given to each question noted in the preceding section. Sales transactions may be classified according to (1) the nature of the goods and (2) the terms of the transaction.

(1) **Nature of Goods.** The goods may be *existing goods,* which means that they are physically in existence and are owned by the seller. It is immaterial whether the existing goods are in the condition required by the contract or whether the seller must do some act or complete the manufacture of the goods before they satisfy the terms of the contract.

In addition to existing goods, there are the classifications of identified goods and future goods. The seller and buyer may have agreed which goods are to be received by the buyer, or the seller may have picked out the goods. When such a selection has been made, the goods are described as *identified goods.* If the goods are neither existing nor identified at the time of the transaction, they are *future goods.*

(2) **Terms of the Transaction.** The terms of the contract may require that the goods be sent or shipped to the buyer, that is, that the seller make shipment. In the latter case, the seller's part is performed when he hands over the goods to a carrier for shipment to the buyer.

Instead of calling for actual delivery of goods, the transaction may involve a transfer of the document of title representing the goods. For example, the goods may be stored in a warehouse, the seller and the buyer having no intention of moving the goods, but intending that there should be a sale and a delivery of the warehouse receipt that stands for the goods. In this case the seller is required to produce the proper paper as distinguished from the goods themselves. The same is true when the goods are represented by a bill of lading issued by a carrier or by any other document of title.

TRANSFER OF TITLE, SPECIAL PROPERTY INTERESTS, AND RISK IN PARTICULAR TRANSACTIONS

The kinds of goods and transaction terms may be combined in a number of ways. Only the more common types of transactions will be considered. The following rules of law apply only in the absence of a contrary agreement by the parties concerning these matters.

(1) **Existing Goods Identified at Time of Contracting.** The title to such goods that are not to be transported passes to the buyer at the time and place of contracting.

- Morrison sold growing grapefruit to Randall. The written contract specified: "All terms of this agreement have been reduced to writing herein." The contract provided for the harvesting of the crop nine weeks later and stated: "Seller agrees that if harvesting is paid by buyer, it is to be charged to seller's account." The crop was damaged by the failure of Morrison to care for and water the orchards after making the sale. Randall refused to take the grapefruit. Judgment was for Morrison and stated that the contract did not impose any duty upon the seller to care for the goods after the sale had been made, and no duty would be implied. Therefore, the seller had completed his performance under the contract and was entitled to sue for the breach of the contract by the buyer.

Since the buyer becomes the owner of the goods, he has an insurable interest in them. Conversely, the seller no longer has an insurable interest unless he has by agreement reserved a security interest to protect his right to payment.

If the seller is a merchant, the risk of loss passes to the buyer when he receives the goods from the merchant. If the seller is a nonmerchant seller, the risk passes when the seller tenders or makes available the goods to the buyer. Thus, the risk of loss remains longer on the merchant seller on the ground that the merchant seller, being in the business, can more readily protect himself against such continued risk.

The fact that "title" has not been transferred to a motor vehicle because of a statute making the issuance of a title certificate essential for that purpose does not affect the transfer of the risk of loss as between the seller and buyer.

(2) **Negotiable Documents Representing Existing Goods Identified at Time of Contracting.** In this case the buyer has a property interest, but not title, and an insurable interest in the goods at the

time and place of contracting. But the buyer does not ordinarily acquire the title nor become subject to the risk of loss until he receives delivery of the documents. Conversely, the seller has an insurable interest and title up to that time.

(3) **Seller's Marking Future Goods for Buyer.** If the buyer sends an order for goods to be manufactured by the seller or to be filled by him from inventory or by purchases from third persons, one step in the process of filling the order is the seller's act of marking, tagging, labeling, or in some way doing an act for the benefit of his shipping department or for himself to indicate that certain goods are the ones to be sent or delivered to the buyer under contract. This act is enough to give the buyer a property interest in the goods and gives him the right to insure them. However, neither title nor risk of loss passes to the buyer at that time but remains with the seller who, as continuing owner, also has an insurable interest in the goods. Thus, neither title nor liability passes to the buyer until some event, such as a shipment or delivery, occurs.

(4) **Contract for Shipment of Future Goods.** In this situation the buyer has placed an order for goods that will be shipped to him later. The contract is performed by the seller when he delivers the goods to a carrier for shipment to the buyer. Under such a contract the title and risk of loss pass to the buyer when the goods are delivered to the carrier, that is, at the time and place of shipment. After that happens, the seller has no insurable interest unless he has reserved a security interest in the goods.

> ▪ Donohue was a local distributor for the Acme Brewing Co. Under the distribution contract, sales were made at prices set by the company "all f.o.b. Acme Brewing Company's plant, from which shipment is made. . . . Distributor agrees . . . to pay all freight and transportation charges from Acme Brewing Company's place of business or to the delivery point designated by the distributor and all delivery expenses." Donohue wrote the company to deliver a quantity of beer to a trucker by the name of Stetson as soon as the latter would accept the goods. The company delivered the goods to Stetson. Snow delayed the transportation and caused the beer to freeze. Donohue rejected the beer and was sued by the company for the purchase price. Judgment was for the company. As the contract called for shipment f.o.b. the seller's plant, the risk of loss passed to the buyer at that time and place. The fact that the goods were damaged thereafter did not affect the buyer's duty to pay for the goods.

DAMAGE OR DESTRUCTION OF GOODS

Unless the parties agree otherwise, damage to or the destruction of the goods affects the transaction as follows:

(1) Damage to Identified Goods Before Risk of Loss Passes. When goods that were identified at the time the contract was made suffer some damage or are destroyed without the fault of either party before the risk of loss has passed, the contract is avoided if the loss is total. If the loss is partial or if the goods have so deteriorated that they do not conform to the contract, the buyer has the option, after inspection of the goods, (a) to treat the contract as avoided, or (b) to accept the goods subject to an allowance or deduction from the contract price. In either case, the buyer cannot assert any claims against the seller for breach of contract.

(2) Damage to Identified Goods after Risk of Loss Passes. If partial damage or total destruction occurs after the risk of loss has passed, it is the buyer's loss. It may be, however, that the buyer will be able to recover the amount of the damages from the person in possession of the goods or from a third person causing the loss. For example, in many instances the risk of loss passes at the time of the transaction even though the seller is to deliver the goods later. During the period from the transfer of the risk of loss to the transfer of possession to the buyer, the seller has the status of a bailee of the goods and is liable to the buyer under the circumstances for which an ordinary bailee would be liable.

(3) Damage to Unidentified Goods. So long as the goods are unidentified, no risk of loss has passed to the buyer. If any goods are damaged or destroyed during this period, it is the loss of the seller. The buyer is still entitled to receive the goods for which he contracted. If the seller fails to deliver the goods, he is liable to the purchaser for the breach of his contract. The only exception arises when the parties have provided in the contract that destruction of the seller's supply shall release the seller from liability or when it is clear that the parties contracted for the purchase and sale of part of the seller's supply to the exclusion of any other possible source of such goods.

(4) Reservation of Title or Possession. When the seller reserves title or possession solely as security to make certain that he will be paid, the risk of loss is borne by the buyer if the circumstances are such that he would bear the loss in the absence of such reservation.

SALES ON APPROVAL AND WITH RIGHT TO RETURN

A sales transaction may give the buyer the privilege of returning the goods. In a *sale on approval,* the sale is not complete until the buyer approves. A *sale or return* is a completed sale with the right of the buyer to return the goods and thereby set aside the sale. The agreement of the parties determines whether the sale is on approval or with return. If they fail to indicate their intention, it is deemed a sale on approval if the goods are purchased for use, that is, by a consumer. It is deemed a sale or return if purchased for resale, that is, by a merchant.

(1) **Consequence of Sale on Approval.** Unless agreed otherwise, title and risk of loss remain with the seller under a sale on approval. Use of the goods by the buyer consistent with the purpose of trial does not constitute approval by him. There is an approval, however, if he acts in a manner that is not consistent with a reasonable trial, or if he fails to express his choice within the time specified or within a reasonable time if no time is specified. If the goods are returned, the seller bears the risk and the expense involved. Since the buyer is not the "owner" of the goods while they are on approval, the goods may not be claimed by the buyer's creditors.

(2) **Consequence of Sale or Return.** In a sale or return, title and risk of loss pass to the buyer as in the case of an ordinary sale. In the absence of a contrary agreement, the buyer under a sale or return may return all of the goods or any commercial unit thereof. A *commercial unit* is any article, group of articles, or quantity commercially regarded as a separate unit or item, such as a particular machine, a suite of furniture, or a carload lot. The goods must still be in substantially their original condition, and the option to return must be exercised within the time specified by the contract or within a reasonable time if none is specified. The return under such a contract is at the buyer's risk and expense. As long as the goods are in the buyer's possession under a sale or return contract, his creditors may treat the goods as belonging to him.

(3) **Other Transactions.** A consignment is not a sale on approval or a sale with right to return. In the absence of any contrary provision,

it is merely an agency and denotes that property is in the possession of the consignee for sale. In the absence of some restriction, the consignor may revoke the agency at will and retake possession of his property. Whether goods are sent to a person as buyer or on consignment to sell for the seller is a question of the intention of the parties.

SALES OF FUNGIBLE GOODS

Fungible goods are goods of a homogeneous or like nature that may be sold by weight or measure. They are goods of which any unit is from its nature or by commercial usage treated as the equivalent of any other unit. Wheat, oil, coal, and similar bulk commodities are fungible goods since any one bushel or other unit of the mass will be exactly the same as any other bushel or similar unit.

Title to an undivided share or quantity of an identified mass of fungible goods may pass to the buyer at the time of the transaction, making the buyer an owner in common with the seller. For example, when a person sells to another 600 bushels of wheat from his bin which contains 1,000 bushels, title to 600 bushels passes to the buyer at the time of the transaction, giving him a 6/10ths undivided interest in the mass as an owner in common with the seller. The courts in some states, however, have held that the title does not pass until a separation has been made.

SALE OF UNDIVIDED SHARES

The problem of the passage of title to a part of a larger mass of fungible goods is distinct from the problem of the passage of title when the sale is made of a fractional interest without any intention to make a later separation. In the former case the buyer is to become the exclusive owner of a separated portion. In the latter case he is to become a co-owner of the entire mass. Thus there may be a sale of a part interest in a radio, an automobile, or a flock of sheep. The right to make a sale of a fractional interest is recognized by statute.

AUCTION SALES

When goods are sold at an auction in separate lots, each lot is a separate transaction, and title to each passes independently of the other lots. Title to each lot passes when the auctioneer announces by the fall of the hammer or in any other customary manner that the auction is completed as to that lot.

C.O.D. SHIPMENT

In the absence of an extension of credit, a seller has the right to keep the goods until paid, but he loses his right if he delivers possession of the goods to anyone for the buyer. However, where the goods are delivered to a carrier, the seller may keep his right to possession by making the shipment C.O.D., or by the addition of any other terms indicating that the carrier should not surrender the goods to the buyer until the buyer has made payment. Such a provision has no effect other than to keep the buyer from obtaining possession until he has made payment. The C.O.D. provision does not affect the problem of determining whether title or risk of loss has passed.

EFFECT OF SALE ON TITLE

As a general rule, a person can sell only such interest or title in goods as he possesses. If the property is subject to a bailment (personal property temporarily in the custody of another person) a sale by the bailor is subject to the bailment. Similarly, the bailee can only transfer his right under the bailment, assuming that the bailment agreement permits his right to be assigned or transferred. The fact that the bailee is in possession does not give him the right to transfer the bailor's title.

A thief or finder generally cannot transfer the title to property since he can pass only that which he has, namely the possession but not the title. In fact, the purchaser from the thief not only fails to obtain title but also becomes liable to the owner as a converter of the property even though he purchased in good faith.

- Owen told Snyder that he wished to buy Snyder's auto. He drove the car for about ten minutes, returned to Snyder, stated that he wanted to take the auto to show it to his wife, and then left with the auto but never returned. Later Owen sold the auto in another state to Pearson and gave him a bill of sale. Pearson showed the bill of sale to Lincoln, falsely told him the certificate of title for the auto was held by a bank as security for the financing of the auto, and then sold the auto to Lincoln. Snyder sued Lincoln to recover the automobile. Judgment was for Snyder. Owen had been guilty of larceny in obtaining the automobile, and no title had passed to him. The automobile could therefore be recovered even though the ultimate purchaser gave value and acted in good faith.

There are certain instances, however, when either because of the conduct of the owner or the desire of society to protect the bona fide purchaser for value, the law permits a greater title to be transferred than the seller possesses.

(1) **Sale by Entrustee.** If the owner entrusts his goods to a merchant who deals in goods of that kind, the latter has the power to transfer the entruster's title to anyone who buys from him in the ordinary course of business.

> ■ Al's Auto Sales sold and delivered a used car to Cross Motor Co. on December 18, the title certificate to be delivered when payment was made. Cross gave Al a bank draft for the amount of the purchase price on the same day. On December 23, Cross resold the car to Moskowitz. Al attached the certificate of title of the car to Cross' draft and sent it through another bank for payment on January 4. The draft was dishonored and returned to Al together with the certificate of title. Al then learned that the car had been resold to Moskowitz and sued him to recover the car. Judgment was against Al. By sending the certificate, Al had made it appear that Cross Motor had the authority to sell, and title could pass. Having done so, Al was estopped to deny the right of Cross to transfer title.

It is immaterial why the goods were entrusted to the merchant. Hence the leaving of a watch for repairs with a jeweler who sells new and secondhand watches would give the jeweler the power to pass the title to a buyer in the ordinary course of business. The entrustee is, of course, liable to the owner for damages caused by his sale of the goods and may be guilty of some form of statutory offense such as embezzlement.

If the entrustee is not a merchant, but merely a prospective customer trying out an automobile, there is no transfer of title when the entrustee sells to a third person.

(2) **Consignment Sales.** A manufacturer or distributor may send goods to a dealer for sale to the public with the understanding that the manufacturer or distributor is to remain the owner and the dealer in effect is to act as his agent. When the dealer maintains a place of business at which he deals in goods of the kind in question under a name other than that of the consigning manufacturer or distributor, the creditors of the dealer may reach the goods as though they were owned by him.

(3) **Estoppel.** The owner of property may estop (bar) himself from asserting that he is the owner and denying the right of another person to sell the property. A person may purchase a product and

have the bill of sale made out in the name of a friend to whom he
then gives possession of the product and the bill of sale. He might
do so in order to deceive his own creditors or to keep other persons
from knowing that he made the purchase. If the friend should sell
the product to a bona fide purchaser who relies on the bill of sale
as showing that the friend was the owner, the true owner is estopped
or barred from denying the friend's apparent ownership or his authority to sell.

(4) **Documents of Title.** By statute, certain documents of title,
such as bills of lading and warehouse receipts, have been clothed with
a degree of negotiability when executed in proper form. By virtue of
such provisions, the holder of a negotiable document of title directing
delivery of the goods to him or his order, or to bearer, may transfer
to a purchaser for value acting in good faith such title as was possessed by the person leaving the property with the issuer of the
document. In such cases it is immaterial that the holder had not
acquired the documents in a lawful manner.

(5) **Recording and Filing Statutes.** In order to protect subsequent purchasers and creditors, statutes may require that certain
transactions be recorded or filed and may provide that if that is not
done, the transaction has no effect against a purchaser who thereafter
buys the goods in good faith from the person who appears to be the
owner or against the execution creditors of such an apparent owner.
Thus, if a seller retains a security interest in the goods sold to the
buyer but fails to file a financing statement in the manner required
by the Code, the purchaser appears to be the owner of the goods free
from any security interest; subsequent bona fide purchasers or creditors of the buyer can acquire title from the buyer free of the seller's
security interest.

(6) **Voidable Title.** If the buyer has a voidable title, as when he
obtained the goods by fraud, the seller can rescind the sale while the
buyer is still the owner. If, however, the buyer resells the property
to a bona fide purchaser before the seller has rescinded the transaction, the subsequent purchaser acquires valid title. It is immaterial
whether the buyer having the voidable title had obtained title by
fraud as to his identity, or by larceny by trick, or that he had paid

for the goods with a bad check, or that the transaction was a cash sale and the purchase price has not been paid.

QUESTIONS

1. What are *existing goods*? *Identified goods*? *Future goods*?
2. If the terms of a sales transaction require that the goods be shipped by the seller to the buyer, when is the seller considered to have completed his performance?
3. As a general rule, when does risk of loss pass to the buyer from a merchant seller? From a nonmerchant seller?
4. When do title and risk of loss pass to the buyer in a contract for shipment of future goods?
5. If Judson sells 500 cases of a cola drink to Goodman "f.o.b. Judson's plant," when does risk of loss pass?
6. If damage occurs to identified goods before risk of loss passes, what options does the buyer have?
7. (a) Distinguish between a "sale on approval" and a "sale or return." (b) Why is it important to make a distinction?
8. What are *fungible goods*? When does title to fungible goods pass?
9. If Jackson lends his lawn mower to his neighbor, Tilton, may Tilton pass good title in a sale of the mower to a third person?
10. If Holmes leaves his portable television set for repair with Ace TV (repair shop and dealer in new and used sets), and Ace sells the set to Lodder, would the buyer get good title?

CASE PROBLEMS

1. Warren enters into a contract to buy 25 sheep out of Thacker's flock. The next day Warren learns that the entire flock has been sold and delivered to Siever. Warren sues Thacker for conversion of the 25 sheep which he alleges belong to him. Is he entitled to judgment on this or any other basis?

2. Lowell agrees to purchase a certain quantity of cotton that Sturgis, the seller, agrees to bale. The cotton is destroyed before it is baled. Upon whom does the loss fall in each of the following situations? (a) Sturgis is an ordinary seller. (b) Sturgis is a merchant seller.

3. Owens directs Hunter to send him 1,000 bushels of corn by railroad freight. When does title to the goods pass?

4. When Ryan ships merchandise purchased by Martin, Ryan makes out the bill of lading to his (Ryan's) agent. Who bears the risk of loss during the shipment?

5. Johns orders goods from Barnett on trial for 15 days. The goods are destroyed during this period. The seller brings an action for the price contending that Johns has title to the goods during this period subject to his right to revest the title in Barnett by returning the goods. Do you agree?

6. A manufacturer sells five vending machines of a new type to a dealer. The terms of the agreement provide that the buyer can return the machines within 60 days if he does not succeed in selling them. Twenty days later the machines are destroyed by fire. Upon whom does the loss fall?

7. Lindsey, who has 30 tons of coal in a bin, sells 10 tons of it to Monroe. Before Monroe calls for his coal, who has title to the coal in the bin?

8. Dunham orders a specified number of sacks of cement mix from Neltner who, according to agreement, marks the goods C.O.D. and delivers them to the carrier. The goods are lost in transit. Who must suffer the loss?

9. Eastern Supply Co. purchased lawn mowers from the Turf Man Sales Corp. The purchase order stated on its face "Ship direct to 30th & Harcum Way, Pitts., Pa." Turf Man delivered the goods to Helm's Express, Inc. for shipment and delivery to Eastern at the address in question. Did title pass on delivery of the goods to Helm or upon their arrival at the specified address?

10. Barrett fraudulently induced Corning Bros. to sell him a horse. Three months later Barrett sold the horse to Price, a bona fide purchaser. Corning sued Price to obtain the horse on the theory that because of Barrett's fraud he never obtained title and Corning Bros. still owned the horse. Decide.

Chapter 16

WARRANTIES OF THE SELLER

NATURE OF WARRANTIES

In making a sale, a seller often "warrants" or "guarantees" that the article will measure up to a certain standard or will operate in a certain manner. The statement of the seller in which he "warrants" or "guarantees" the article is known as an *express warranty*. It is a warranty because it is a representation about the goods; it is express because the seller actually and definitely expresses it. By his warranty the seller agrees in effect to make good any loss or damages that the purchaser may suffer if the goods are not as they are represented. The Code specifically provides that any affirmation of fact or promise made by the seller to the buyer which relates to the goods and becomes part of the basis of the bargain creates an express warranty.

If a warranty is made at the time of the sale, it is considered to be a part of the contract and is therefore binding. If a warranty is made after a sale has been completed, it is binding even though not supported by any consideration; it is regarded as a modification of the sales contract.

Certain warranties, such as a warranty or guarantee that the seller has the right to sell the goods and can pass good title to the buyer, are imposed by the law on all sellers. Since they are not expressed by the seller, they are called *implied warranties*.

EXPRESS WARRANTIES

No particular words are required to constitute an express warranty. The words "warrant" or "guarantee" need not be used. If a statement or a promise is such that a reasonable interpretation of the language leads the buyer to believe there is a warranty, the courts will construe it as such. A seller is bound by the ordinary meaning of his words, not by his intentions.

The seller can use the word "warrant" or "guarantee" and still not be bound by it if an ordinary, prudent man would not interpret it to constitute a warranty. If the seller of a car says, "I'll guarantee that you will not be sorry if you buy the car at this price," no warranty exists as this is mere "sales talk," even though the word "guarantee" is used.

REPRESENTATIONS

Most so-called representations are mere "sales talk" or "puffing." The law holds that a seller may praise his wares, even extravagantly, without obligating himself on his statements or representations. If the representations can be classed as "opinions," "sales talk," "puffing," or similar expressions, they do not give cause for legal redress. Some "shady" merchants have made an art of making opinions sound like warranties. A person should not be misled by such borderline expressions as "best on the market for the money," "these goods are worth $10 if they are worth a dime," "experts have estimated that one ought to be able to sell a thousand a month of these," and many others which sound very convincing but which have been held to be mere expressions of opinion.

If the buyer sues for breach of warranty, the seller is not allowed to prove that he made the statement in good faith. This is irrelevant. If the buyer sues for a tort, alleging a fraudulent representation, he must prove the seller made the false statement with a knowledge of its falsity.

The rule that a statement of opinion or belief does not constitute a warranty must be qualified. Although an expression by the seller of what is clearly his opinion does not constitute either a warranty or a basis for fraud liability, the seller may be liable for fraud if he in fact does not believe the opinion which he states that he has. Secondly, one who is not an expert may rely on the opinion of one who is an expert. An expert refrigerator mechanic says, "In my opinion this refrigerator, which I have personally checked, is in A-1 condition." The purchaser who knows little or nothing about the mechanics of refrigerators may rely on this expert's opinion.

■ Hopkins, a long-established dealer and heating engineer, sold
  Ringgold an oil heater for his ten-room house. Hopkins tried
  to explain the meaning of BTU's to Ringgold, but it was not very

clear to Ringgold. Ringgold selected a heater, and Hopkins expressed the opinion it would be adequate to heat his house. It proved to be totally inadequate to heat the house. Ringgold had a right to rely on Hopkin's opinion since he seemed to be an expert.

DEFECTS

If there are defects that are actually known to the buyer, or defects that are so apparent that no special skill or ability is required to detect them, an express warranty cannot be invoked to cover them. If Ross says, "I guarantee this car to be in first-class condition in every respect," there is no breach of warranty if the car clearly has four bald tires. The courts assume that the clear implication of his words is, "except for the defects which you can clearly see." This would not be true if the seller used any scheme or artifice to conceal the defect. The seller must not do anything for the purpose of diverting the attention of the buyer from the defects.

IMPLIED WARRANTIES

An *implied warranty* is one that was not made by the seller but which is implied by the law. In certain instances the law implies or reads a warranty into a sale although the seller did not make it. That is, the implied warranty arises automatically from the fact that a sale has been made. Express warranties arise because they form part of the basis on which the sale has been made.

The fact that express warranties are made does not exclude implied warranties. When both express and implied warranties exist, they should be construed as consistent with each other. In case it is unreasonable to construe them as consistent, an express warranty prevails over an implied warranty as to the same subject matter, except in the case of an implied warranty of fitness for a particular purpose.

WARRANTIES OF ALL SELLERS

A distinction is made between a merchant seller and the casual seller. The Uniform Commercial Code provides for a greater range of warranties in the case of the merchant seller. The following warranties apply to all sellers:

(1) **Warranty of Title.** Every seller, by the mere act of selling, makes a warranty that his title is good and that the transfer is rightful.

A warranty of title may be specifically excluded, or the circumstances may be such as to prevent the warranty from arising. The latter situation is found when the buyer has reason to know that the seller does not claim to hold the title or that he is claiming to sell only such right or title as he or a third person may have. For example, no warranty of title arises when the seller makes the sale in a representative capacity, such as a sheriff, an auctioneer, or an administrator. Likewise no warranty arises when the seller makes the sale by virtue of a power of sale possessed by him as a pledgee or mortgagee.

(2) **Warranty Against Encumbrances.** Every seller by the mere act of selling makes a warranty that the goods shall be delivered free from any security interest or any other lien or encumbrance of which the buyer at the time of the sales transaction had no knowledge. Thus there is a breach of warranty when the automobile sold to the buyer is already subject to an outstanding claim that had been placed against it by the original owner and which was unknown to the buyer at the time of the sale.

This warranty refers to the goods only at the time they are delivered to the buyer and is not concerned with an encumbrance which existed before or at the time the sale was made. For example, a seller may not have paid in full for the goods which he is reselling and the original supplier may have a lien on the goods. The seller may resell the goods while that lien is still on them, and his only duty is to pay off the lien before he delivers the goods to the buyer.

The warranty against encumbrances may be excluded expressly or by the circumstances of the case in the same manner as a warranty of title. By definition, a warranty against encumbrances does not arise if the buyer knows of the existence of the encumbrance in question. Knowledge must be actual knowledge as contrasted with constructive notice, which the law presumes everyone knows by virtue of the fact that an encumbrance is filed or recorded on the public record.

(3) **Warranty of Conformity to Seller's Statement or Promise.** Whenever a statement or promise made by the seller constitutes an express warranty, it is binding on the seller regardless of the type of seller involved.

(4) **Warranty of Conformity to Description, Sample, or Model.** When the contract is based in part on the understanding that the seller will supply goods according to a particular description or that

the goods will be the same as the sample or a model, the seller is bound by an express warranty that the goods shall conform to the description, sample, or model. Ordinarily a *sample* is a portion of a whole mass that is the subject of the transaction. A *model* is a replica of the article in question. The mere fact that a sample is exhibited in the course of negotiations does not make the sale a sale by sample, as there must be an intent shown that the sample be part of the basis of contracting.

(5) **Warranty of Fitness For a Particular Purpose.** If the buyer intends to use the goods for a particular or unusual purpose, as contrasted with the ordinary use for which they are customarily sold, the seller makes an implied warranty that the goods will be fit for the purpose when the buyer relies on the seller's skill or judgment to select or furnish suitable goods, and when the seller at the time of contracting knows or has reason to know the buyer's particular purpose and his reliance on the seller's judgment. For example, where a government representative inquired of the seller whether the seller had a tape suitable for use on a particular government computer system, there arose an implied warranty, unless otherwise excluded, that the tape furnished by the seller was fit for that purpose.

The fact that the seller did not intend to make a warranty of fitness for a particular purpose is immaterial. Parol evidence is admissible to show that the seller had knowledge of the buyer's intended use.

ADDITIONAL WARRANTIES OF MERCHANT SELLER

In addition to the warranties made by every seller, a merchant seller makes the following additional implied warranties.

(1) **Warranty Against Infringement.** Unless otherwise agreed, every seller who is a merchant regularly dealing in goods of the kind which he has sold warrants that the goods shall be delivered free of the rightful claim of any third person by way of patent or trademark infringement.

(2) **Warranty of Merchantability or Fitness For Normal Use.** A merchant seller who makes a sale of goods in which he customarily deals makes an implied warranty of merchantability. The warranty is in fact a group of warranties, the most important of which is that the

goods are fit for the ordinary purposes for which they are sold. Consequently, when the seller of ice-making and beverage-vending machines is a merchant of such machines, an implied warranty of fitness for use arises. Also included are implied warranties as to the general or average quality of the goods, and their packaging and labeling.

The implied warranty of merchantability relates to the condition of the goods at the time the seller is to perform under the contract. Once the risk of loss has passed to the buyer, there is no warranty as to the continuing merchantability of the goods unless such subsequent deterioration or condition is proof that the goods were in fact not merchantable when the seller made delivery.

There is no warranty that customers of the buyer will want to buy the goods, that is, "merchantability" does not mean that the buyer will be able to resell the goods.

Warranty of fitness relates only to the fitness of the product that is made or sold. It does not impose upon the manufacturer or seller the duty to employ any particular design or to sell one product rather than another because another might be safer.

> ■ Adams purchased a Chevrolet station wagon made by General
>   Motors. While driving the station wagon, he was struck on the
> left side by another vehicle. The left side of the station wagon
> collapsed and inflicted fatal injuries. An action was brought on
> behalf of his estate against General Motors, claiming that the station
> wagon had been negligently constructed in that it was built on an
> X-frame (of two supporting rails crossing diagonally under the body
> of the car) and that the collapse of the left side would have been
> avoided if General Motors had added side rails to the X-frame.
> Judgment was for General Motors. The requirement that the auto-
> mobile be fit for its intended purpose did not mean that it must be
> made accident-proof, particularly in view of the fact that the purpose
> of the automobile is not engaging in collisions. The fact that some
> competitors put side rails on the frames, and that some expert stated
> that this would be safer, did not create liability for failing to do so.

WARRANTIES IN PARTICULAR SALES

Particular types of sales may involve special considerations.

(1) **Sale of Food or Drink.** The sale of food or drink, whether to be consumed on or off the seller's premises, is a sale. When made by a merchant, the sale carries the implied warranty that the food is fit for its ordinary purpose, that is, human consumption. Under the prior law some authorities held that there was no breach of warranty when

a harmful object found in the food was natural to the particular kind of food, such as an oyster shell in oysters, a chicken bone in chicken, and so on. Other cases regarded the warranty as breached when the harm-causing substance in the food was such that its presence could not be reasonably expected, without regard to whether the substance was natural, or foreign, as in the case of a nail or piece of glass.

The Code does not end the conflict between courts applying the "foreign-natural" test and those applying the "reasonable-expectation" test. The significance of the two is that in the first test a buyer is barred from recovery as a matter of law where he finds the "natural" substance in the food, as a cherry pit in a cherry pie; whereas under the reasonable expectation test, it is necessary to make a determination of fact, ordinarily by the jury, to determine whether the buyer could reasonably expect the object in the food.

It is, of course, necessary to distinguish the foregoing situations from those in which the preparation of the foods contemplates the continued presence of some element which is not removed, such as prune stones in cooked prunes.

> ▪ Webster ordered a bowl of fish chowder in the Blue Ship Tea Room. She was injured by a fish bone in the chowder. She sued the Tea Room for breach of warranty. It was shown that when chowder is made, the entire unboned fish is cooked. The court held that as the soup was typically made with whole fish, it was apparent that the presence of fish bones in the soup should be foreseen by a reasonable person. Consequently, the warranty of merchantability was not broken.

(2) **Sale of Article With Patent or Trade Name.** The sale of a patent- or trade-name article is treated with respect to warranties in the same way as any other sale. The fact that the sale is made on the basis of the patent or trade name does not bar the existence of a warranty of fitness for a particular purpose when the circumstances giving rise to such a warranty otherwise exist.

It is a question of fact, however, whether the buyer relied on the seller's skill and judgment when he made the purchase. That is, if the buyer asked for a patent- or trade-name article and insisted on it, it is apparent that he did not rely upon the seller's skill and judgment and therefore the factual basis for an implied warranty of fitness for the particular purpose is lacking. If the necessary reliance upon the seller's skill and judgment is shown, however, the warranty arises in that situation.

▪ Sperry Rand Corp. agreed to convert the record-keeping system
of Industrial Supply Corp. so that it could be maintained by a
computer and to sell a computer and nine other items necessary
for such a record-keeping system. The computer and the equipment
were ordered by identified trade name and number. When the
system did not work, Industrial Supply sued Sperry Rand for breach
of implied warranty of fitness. Sperry Rand raised the defense that
there was no such warranty because the equipment had been ordered
by trade name and number. The court held that the fact that the
equipment was ordered by trade name and number did not show
the buyer was purchasing at its risk. The circumstances showed
the sale was made in reliance on the seller's skill, and with appreciation of the buyer's problems, and the sale of the particular
equipment to the buyer was made as constituting the equipment
needed by it. Under such circumstances, a warranty of the fitness
of the equipment for such purpose was implied.

The seller of automobile parts is not liable for breach of the implied warranty of their fitness when the parts were ordered by catalog
number for use in a specified vehicle and the seller did not know that
the lubrication system of the automobile had been changed so as
to make the parts ordered unfit for use.

(3) **Sale on Buyer's Specifications.** When the buyer furnishes the
seller with exact specifications for the preparation or manufacture of
goods, the same warranties arise as in the case of any other sale of
such goods by the particular seller. No warranty of fitness for a particular purpose can arise, however, since it is clear that the buyer is
purchasing on the basis of his own decision and is not relying on the
seller's skill and judgment.

In sales made upon the buyer's specifications, no warranty against
infringement is impliedly made by the merchant seller. Conversely,
the buyer in substance makes a warranty to protect the seller from
liability should the seller be held liable for patent violation by following the specifications of the buyer.

(4) **Sale of Secondhand or Used Goods.** No warranty arises as
to fitness of used property for ordinary use when the sale is made
by a casual seller. If made by a merchant seller, such a warranty may
sometimes be implied. Prior to the Code a number of states followed
the rule that no warranty arose in connection with used or secondhand goods, particularly automobiles and machinery; whereas some
courts found a warranty of fitness for ordinary use in the sale of

secondhand goods, particularly airplanes. It is likely that this division of authority will continue under the Code.

EXCLUSION AND SURRENDER OF WARRANTIES

Warranties may be excluded or surrendered by the agreement of the parties, subject to the limitation that such a provision must not be unconscionable. It is proper for the jury to consider the purchase price in determining the scope of the warranty of fitness, as where coal was bought for one-half or less the price of standard coal.

If a warranty of fitness is excluded in writing, it must be conspicuous to assure that the buyer will be aware of its presence. If the implied warranty of merchantability is excluded, the exclusion clause must expressly mention the word "merchantability" and must be conspicuous.

(1) **Particular Provisions.** Such a statement as "there are no warranties which extend beyond the description on the face hereof" excludes all implied warranties of fitness. Implied warranties are excluded by the statement of "as is," "with all faults," or other language which in normal common speech calls attention to the warranty exclusion and makes it clear that there is no implied warranty. For example, an implied warranty that a steam heater would work properly in the buyer's dry cleaning plant was effectively excluded by provisions that "the warranties and guarantees herein set forth are made by us and accepted by you in lieu of all statutory or implied warranties or guarantees, other than title. . . . This contract contains all agreements between the parties and there is no agreement, verbal or otherwise, which is not set down herein," and the contract had only a "one-year warranty on labor and material supplied by seller."

In order for a disclaimer of warranties to be a binding part of an oral sales contract, the disclaimer must be called to the attention of the buyer. When the contract as made does not disclaim warranties, a disclaimer of warranties that accompanies the goods which are delivered later is not effective because it is a mere unilateral attempt to modify the contract.

(2) **Examination.** There is no implied warranty with respect to defects in goods that an examination should have revealed when the buyer before making the final contract has examined the goods, or a model or sample, or has refused to make such examination.

(3) **Dealings and Customs.** An implied warranty may be excluded or modified by course of dealings, course of performance, or usage of trade.

CAVEAT EMPTOR

In the absence of fraud on the part of the seller or circumstances in which the law finds a warranty, the relationship of the seller and buyer is aptly described by the maxim of *caveat emptor* (let the buyer beware). Courts at common law rigidly applied this rule, requiring the purchaser in the ordinary sale to act in reliance upon his own judgment except when the seller gave him an express warranty. The trend of the earlier statutes, the Uniform Commercial Code, and decisions of modern courts has been to soften the harshness of this rule, primarily by implying warranties for the protection of the buyer. The rule of caveat emptor is still applied, however, when the buyer has full opportunity to make such examination of the goods as would disclose the existence of any defect and the seller is not guilty of fraud.

PRODUCT LIABILITY

When harm to person or property results from the use or condition of an article of personal property, the person injured may be entitled to recover damages. This right may be based on the theory that there was a breach of warranty or that the person sued was negligent.

(1) **Breach of Warranty.** At common law the rule was that only the parties to a transaction had any rights relating to it. Accordingly, only the buyer could sue his immediate seller for breach of warranty. The rule was stated in the terms that there could be no suit for breach of warranty unless there was a privity of contract (a contract relationship) between the plaintiff and the defendant.

In most states an exception to the privity rule developed under which members of the buyer's family and various other remote persons not in privity of contract with the seller or manufacturer can sue for breach of warranty when injured by the harmful condition of food, beverages, or drugs. The right to sue the manufacturer of a bottled or packaged food might be denied where there is evidence that another person has or might have tampered with the item before it reached the buyer or consumer.

The Code expressly abolishes the requirement of privity to a limited extent by permitting a suit for breach of warranty to be brought against the seller by members of the buyer's family, his household, and his guests, with respect to personal injury sustained by them. Apart from the express provision made by the Code, there is a conflict of authority as to whether privity of contract is required in other cases, with the trend being toward the abolition of that requirement. In many states, the doctrine is flatly rejected when suit is brought by a buyer against the manufacturer or a prior seller. In many instances, recovery by the buyer against the remote manufacturer or seller is based on the fact that the defendant had advertised directly to the public and therefore made a warranty to the purchasing consumer of the truth of his advertising. But while advertising by the manufacturer to the consumer is a reason for not requiring privity when the consumer sues the manufacturer, the absence of advertising by the manufacturer does not bar such action by the buyer.

■ Dennis purchased Lestoil, a household detergent, from Farrell. She was severely burned by it and sued the seller and its manufacturers, the Lestoil Corporation and the Adell Chemical Company. The manufacturers had extensively promoted the product by television, radio, and newspapers, stating that it could be used safely for household and cleaning tasks and that it was "the all-purpose detergent—for all household cleaning and laundering." The manufacturers defended on the ground that Dennis had not purchased the bottle of Lestoil from them. The court held that the fact that the plaintiff had not purchased the product from the defendant was not a defense. The sale of the product had been promoted by mass media advertising appealing directly to the consumer; therefore, the manufacturer could not raise the defense of lack of privity when the consumer responded to its advertising.

Recovery may also be allowed when the consumer mails to the manufacturer a warranty registration card which the manufacturer had packed with the purchased article.

(2) **Negligence.** Aside from the provisions of the Code, a person injured through the use or condition of personal property may be entitled to sue the manufacturer for the damages which he sustains on the theory that the defendant was negligent in the preparation or manufacture of the article. Historically, such suits were limited by the concept of privity of contract so that only the buyer could sue the seller for the latter's negligence; the buyer could not sue the

manufacturer for the latter's negligence. This requirement of privity has generally been abolished. The modern rule is that whenever the manufacturer as a reasonable man should foresee that if he is negligent a particular class of persons will be injured by his product, the manufacturer is liable to an injured member of that class without regard to whether such plaintiff purchased from him or from anyone.

(3) **Effect of Reprocessing by Distributor.** Liability of the manufacturer or supplier to the ultimate consumer, whether for warranty or negligence, does not arise when the manufacturer or supplier believes or has reason to believe that the immediate distributor or processor is to complete processing or is to take further steps that will remove an otherwise foreseeable danger. Accordingly, although the supplier of unfinished pork to a retailer should realize that it might contain trichinae and be dangerous to the ultimate consumers, he is not liable to an ultimate consumer who contracts trichinosis when the retailer in purchasing the unfinished pork told the supplier that he would finish processing it. The processing would have destroyed any trichinae, and the supplier did not know or have reason to know that the retailer failed to do so.

IDENTITY OF PARTIES

The existence of product liability may be affected by the identity of the claimant or of the defendant.

(1) **Third Persons.** Historically, third persons, meaning persons who were not "buyers" from anyone, such as guests, employees, or total strangers, were denied recovery because of the absence of privity. The Code, however, permits recovery for breach of warranty by the guests of the buyer but makes no provision as to recovery by employees or strangers.

There is a conflict of authority as to whether an employee of the buyer may sue the seller or manufacturer for breach of warranty. In some jurisdictions the employee's right to recover is denied on the ground that he is outside of the distributive chain, not being a buyer. Others allow recovery in such a case. By the latter view, an employee of a construction contractor may recover for breach of the implied warranty of fitness made by the manufacturer of the structural steel which proved defective and, falling, injured the employee.

In some states, the courts have ignored privity of contract when the injured person was not even a subpurchaser but a member of the public or a stranger at large by adopting a doctrine of strict tort liability. This doctrine makes a manufacturer liable to anyone who is injured because of a defect in the manufacture of the product when such defect makes the use of the product dangerous to the user or to persons in the vicinity of the product and the person injured or killed is such a user or person in the vicinity. There is also a growing trend to allow recovery by the "stranger" on the theory of breach of warranty. It has been held that a repairman fixing an automobile who is injured because of a defect in the automobile may sue the manufacturer for breach of implied warranty of fitness.

(2) **Manufacturer of Component Part.** Many items of goods in today's marketplace were not made entirely by one manufacturer. Thus the harm caused may result in a given case from a defect in a component part of the finished product. As the manufacturer of the total article was the buyer from the component part manufacturer, it followed that the privity rule barred suit against the component part manufacturer for breach of warranty by anyone injured. In jurisdictions in which privity of contract is not recognized as a bar to recovery, it is not material that the defendant manufactured merely a component part. That is to say, the manufacturer of a component part cannot defend from suit by the ultimate purchaser on the ground of absence of privity. Thus the purchaser of a tractor trailer may recover from the manufacturer of the brake system of the trailer for damages sustained when the brake system failed to work. Likewise, a person injured while on a golf course when an automobile parked on the club parking lot became "unparked" and ran down hill can sue the manufacturer of the defective parking unit.

NATURE AND CAUSE OF HARM

The law is more concerned in cases where the plaintiff has been personally injured as contrasted with economically harmed. That is, the law places protection of the person of the individual above that of property rights. The harm sustained by the product-liability plaintiff must have been "caused" by the defendant, regardless of whether suit is brought for the negligence of the defendant or on the theory of breach of warranty.

There is no liability when harm is not foreseeable. For example, when the law requires that a particular product be used with a safety device, the manufacturer of the product is not negligent when the product is used without the safety device required by law. Thus the manufacturer of grinding wheels had the right to anticipate that the danger of injury from flying fragments of the wheel would be reduced or eliminated by the use of a protective shield as was required by law and was therefore not under any obligation to make the wheels "accident-proof" when used without a protective shield.

In many states, an injured plaintiff has the choice of suing for breach of warranty or for damages for negligence. The importance of the distinction between the two remedies lies in the fact that to prove his case for breach of warranty the plaintiff is required only to prove facts of which he has direct knowledge or about which he can readily learn. That is, he need only show that there was a sale and a warranty, that the goods did not conform to the warranty, and that he was injured thereby. In the case of the action for negligence against the manufacturer, the plaintiff figuratively must also go into the defendant's plant or factory and learn how the given article was made and prove in court that there was negligence. Unless the plaintiff is able to show that the design of the manufacturer's product or his general method of manufacture was faulty, it is likely that the plaintiff will be unable to prove that there was negligence. It has been the recognition of this difficulty which, to a large degree, has led the courts to expand the warranty liability under which proof of negligence is not required.

A manufacturer or seller may assume by the terms of his contract a liability broader than would arise from a mere warranty.

> ▪ Spiegel purchased a jar of skin cream from Saks 34th Street. It had been manufactured by the National Toilet Co. The carton and the jar stated that it was chemically pure and absolutely safe. When Spiegel used the cream, it caused a severe skin rash. She sued Saks and National. Judgment was for Spiegel. The statements on the carton and the jar constituted an express warranty binding both the seller and the manufacturer. The statement that it was safe was an absolute undertaking that it was safe for everyone; as distinguished from merely an implied warranty of reasonable fitness, which would be subject to an exception of a particular allergy of a plaintiff.

QUESTIONS

1. Must an express warranty involve a material fact before there can be a breach of warranty?
2. May one make a warranty even though he has no intention of doing so?

3. If an oral warranty is not included when the contract is written up, may the purchaser prove it by oral testimony?

4. Distinguish by examples the difference between an implied warranty of fitness for a particular purpose and an implied warranty of merchantability.

5. Is the statement, "This fish bait is so good you will have to hide behind a tree to put it on a hook," a warranty or sales talk?

6. Is an expression of an opinion ever a warranty?

7. What warranty does the seller make when he sells by sample?

8. Explain the difference in the "foreign-natural" test and the "reasonable expectation" test as applied to the sale of food or drink.

CASE PROBLEMS

1. While negotiating the sale of a parakeet to Heck, Sheridan states, "This bird is healthy, as far as I know." Heck purchases the parakeet in reliance on Sheridan's statement. In an action against Sheridan, Heck proves that Sheridan knew at the time of the sale that the bird was diseased. Is Heck entitled to judgment?

2. Morris, a dealer, purchased a poultry feed additive called Gro-good Poultry Supplement from Stratton Laboratories. The public did not buy the supplement. When Stratton sued Morris for the purchase price, he claimed that there was a breach of warranty of merchantability because the goods did not sell. Was he correct?

3. Margaret deposited a dime in a soft drink dispensing machine and purchased a bottled drink. When she had finished drinking about half of it, she discovered a dead insect in the bottle and became so ill she was not able to work the rest of the day. She sued the local bottling company for damages. Was she entitled to collect?

4. Sullivan was the purchasing agent for the Swanson Clothing Store. While on a New York buying trip, he inspected some suit samples. The seller assured him, "They are the very latest Ivy League style;" "They will sell like hot cakes;" "You will need to reorder before the season is half over." Sullivan purchased 1,000 suits, but the store could sell only 300 suits. The store sued the seller for breach of warranty. Were any or all of these statements warranties?

5. The Elkhorn Motor Sales Corporation sold Kirby a car for $1,200. He was given a written guarantee that the car was in "A-1 condition" and provided that if anything went wrong with the car within 12 months, the Elkhorn Motor Corporation would repair it, charging only the wholesale cost of parts plus labor. What is the weakness in this warranty?

6. Branch, a cattleman, purchased from the Hay Seed Company 2,000 pounds of reseeding crimson clover seed. The seller said, "This is the Dixie strain of reseeding clover, and I guarantee you won't have to worry about

its reseeding." There are several strains of crimson clover, some reseeding, some not. The Dixie strain is the most reliable. Branch later learned his seed was not the Dixie strain. It did reseed satisfactorily, but Branch could not market his seed as Dixie seed. He sued the Hay Seed Company for breach of warranty. Was he entitled to collect damages?

7. Larsen orders a certain quantity of a specified grade of leather. He plans to use the material in making luggage. When he discovers that the leather is not suitable for that purpose, he brings an action against the seller for damages arising out of a breach of warranty. Is he entitled to judgment?

8. Young was branch manager for the Free-Fit Shoe stores. He purchased 1,000 pairs of overshoes that were expressly guaranteed to be waterproof and seamless. The shoes delivered had two seams and were not 100 percent waterproof. The purchase price was $5,000, and Young estimated that the shoes were not worth more than $4,000. The shoes had been purchased on credit. Young kept the shoes and withheld $3,000 from the purchase price as damages. The seller sued for $3,000, less a credit of $1,000 for the damages, and obtained judgment for $2,000. What error did Young commit in selecting his remedy?

9. The defendant wrote to the plaintiff for information and prices on a road-finishing machine. In his letter he stated that the machine must be for 16″ x 18″ finishing work on a concrete pavement and "must pass the specifications of the Michigan State Highway Department." The machine that was delivered failed to do the work. The defendant refused to pay the notes that he had given in payment of the purchase price.

(a) Did the purchaser expressly or impliedly make known the purpose for which the machine was to be used?

(b) Did the buyer rely on the seller's skill or judgment?

10. The Heller Typewriter Exchange sold McBroom a secondhand typewriter. McBroom wanted the typewriter just for personal use. He used the "hunt-and-peck" system. The seller assured McBroom that a good typist could attain a speed of 150 words a minute on this machine although he knew it was impossible to make over 80 words a minute. He also guaranteed that it was in perfect condition, that it was "the best buy in town," and that McBroom could no doubt sell it for $15 more than he was paying for it. McBroom later learned that he could buy a similar machine for $5 less and that it was impossible to attain a speed of more than 80 words a minute; otherwise, the machine was just as represented. He offered to return the machine and demanded the return of his money. The seller refused so McBroom brought suit. Who was entitled to win the case?

11. A salesman in an effort to sell a college student an encyclopedia set for $70 showed him proofs of advertisements that were to be run soon fixing the price for the same books at $210. "This is the last chance to buy at this price" was repeated over and over. The salesman also said, "I guarantee that you can pass any business law exam if you learn all the answers in this encyclopedia." The college student bought the books but failed his examination. Also, the price did not go up. The purchaser wished to rescind the contract. Could he do so?

SUMMARY CASES

PART 3

1. John Low and Sons sold to Alfred Low and Company all the halibut that might be caught by the fishing schooner on which they were going on a fishing trip. Before the fish were delivered, John Low and Sons went into bankruptcy, and the question arose as to whether or not this sale of the halibut was valid. Was this a valid sale? (Low v. Pew, 108 Mass. 347)

2. The city of Boscobel, Wisconsin, sold two bailers, two engines, two steam pumps, and other equipment to the Muscoda Manufacturing Company. The total selling price was $1,800, $200 in cash and the balance "to be paid before taking out of the plant." This property was located in a frame building. Before the balance of the $1,600 was paid and the property was removed, the building and all its contents were destroyed by fire. The city of Boscobel brought suit to collect the balance due, and the Muscoda Manufacturing Company denied liability on the ground that risk of loss to the property had not passed to it at the time of the fire loss. Had title passed? (City of Boscobel v. Muscoda Manufacturing Company, 175 Wis. 62, 183 N. W. 963)

3. The Kramer Brothers offered by wire to sell Hunter Brothers Milling Company 1,600 sacks of bran at 73 cents a hundred pounds f.o.b. destination. The Hunter Brothers Milling Company accepted by wire, and the bran was shipped by railway freight in four cars. Only two of the cars arrived, the other two having been destroyed by flood. The buyer sued to recover damages for the failure of the seller to deliver the four carloads as agreed. Is the buyer entitled to damages? (Hunter Brothers Milling Company v. Kramer Bros., 71 Kans. 468, 80 p. 963)

4. Plummer sold a car for $800 cash to Davis. Davis paid for the car by check. Plummer delivered the car to Davis together with a certificate of title but with the understanding that there was to be no sale until the check was cleared through the bank. The check turned out to be a bad check. Davis in the meantime had sold the car to Kingsley who knew nothing about the arrangement between Plummer and Davis. Plummer brought suit against Kingsley to recover the car, claiming that since Davis did not have good title to the car, he could not transfer good title to Kingsley. Did Kingsley obtain good title? (Plummer v. Kingsley, 190 Oregon, 378, 226 P. 2d 297)

5. Saunders purchased a canvas tent from Cowl, a merchant, paying $250 down. Saunders inspected the tent, but at the time of the inspection it was folded and not easily inspected. Furthermore, the evidence showed that Saunders would not have been able to perceive the defects in the canvas even if he had inspected it thoroughly. The seller stated, "It is to be in good condition when delivered." The tent was so defective that it was in reality worthless. Saunders alleges a breach of warranty and sues to recover his $250. Was there a breach of warranty? (Saunders v. Cowl et al., 201 Minn. 574, 277 N. W. 12)

6. Hodge Chile Co. negotiated for the purchase of food cartons from Interstate Folding Box Co. Interstate sent samples of its boxes to Hodge without making any statement as to their qualifications. Hodge subjected the samples to various tests and then placed an order for the boxes with Interstate. Hodge did not pay for the boxes and, when sued for their purchase price, claimed that there was a breach of an implied warranty of fitness of the boxes for use for their intended purpose. It was shown that the defects of which Hodge complained had not been revealed in the tests because the cartons had been filled by hand instead of by machine and the chile put in the boxes was poured at a lower temperature than when poured by machine. Did Hodge have a valid defense? (Interstate Folding Box Co. v. Hodge Chile Co., [Mo.App.] 334 S.W.2d 408)

7. Mrs. Hirth, at the request of her mother, Mrs. Burkhart, purchased a can of corned beef from the Great Atlantic and Pacific Tea Company. The beef had been processed by Armour and Company. The can of beef contained imbedded in the meat a piece of tin which Mrs. Burkhart swallowed. She became ill and soon died from the effects of this act. Her next of kin brought suit against both the seller and the processor. The complaint alleged that both were negligent and that both the seller and the processor had committed a breach of warranty. (a) Was either or both guilty of negligence? (b) Was either or both guilty of a breach of warranty? (Burkhart v. Armour & Co., et al., 115 Conn. 249, 161 A. 385)

8. Lentz was a cripple and could walk only with great difficulty. Through an agent he purchased a horse from the Omar Baking Company. The agent made clear to the seller that because of Lentz's physical condition the horse must be gentle. He was assured that the horse was gentle. The first time the horse was hitched to a buggy with Lentz as the driver, it ran away; Lentz received severe injuries that rendered him a helpless invalid. He sued the bakery for doctor bills, pain and suffering, and the loss of earning power, alleging a breach of warranty. Was there a breach of warranty? (Lentz v. Omar Baking Company, 125 Neb. 861, 252 N. W. 410)

9. Braun of Philadelphia contracted to sell and deliver a barge load of coal to McNeal of Burlington, New Jersey. The contract clearly stipulated that the coal was to be delivered by the seller to the buyer at Burlington. The coal was loaded on the barge and shipped. The barge arrived safely and was tied securely to the wharf. Soon thereafter and before McNeal had an opportunity to unload it, the barge sank and the coal was lost. Braun brought suit to compel McNeal to pay for the coal. Who must bear the loss in this case? (McNeal v. Braun, 153 N. J. 617, 23 A. 687)

10. The Standard Stevedoring Company purchased a crane from Jaffe that Jaffe had widely advertised as having a lifting capacity of 15 to 20 tons. There was no evidence that this statement was made orally when an agent of the buyer came to inspect the crane. The seller was aware that the buyer became interested in the crane as a result of the advertising. The purchasing agent of the Standard Stevedoring Company made no attempt to verify the lifting capacity of the crane due to the impracticality of doing so. The purchaser learned after he bought the crane that it would not lift anywhere near 15 to 20 tons and brought suit to rescind the contract. Was there a breach of an express warranty? (Standard Stevedoring Company v. Jaffe, Tenn. App. 302 S. W. 2d 829)

Part 4.

BAILMENTS

Preview Cases for Part 4: Bailments

- Fleeman borrowed Brown's truck expressly for the purpose of hauling a load of cotton to the cotton gin. After the cotton was ginned, Fleeman drove about ten miles further to another town to get some farm machinery parts. The truck was wrecked on this part of the trip due to no fault on the part of Fleeman. Who must bear the loss for damage to the truck?

- Webster shipped some perishable freight by the Georgia Central Railroad. The freight was intended for Athens, Georgia, but by error in the address written on the package by Webster it was sent to Athens, Tennessee. Before it could be returned, the freight was a total loss. Who must bear the loss?

- Johnson was traveling by plane to Cedar City. The plane made a brief stop at Cedar City, but Johnson was asleep and did not hear the pilot's announcement. Johnson awoke after the plane had gone 100 miles beyond Cedar City. Is the airline liable to Johnson for the inconvenience he suffered?

- Jason entered the Ridge Manor Motel to register as a guest. He was told there were no vacancies but that he could wait awhile if he wished to see if anyone checked out. This he did. While he was waiting, his baggage was stolen. Is the motel liable for the loss?

These preview cases are designed to serve as a springboard for the study of this part. As you read through each chapter in this part, you will find the actual decisions for all these preview cases. Of course, there are many more such illustrative problems as well as case problems for decision at the end of each chapter. And there are also a number of even more challenging cases for review at the end of the part.

Chapter 17

BAILMENTS IN GENERAL

CHARACTERISTICS OF A BAILMENT

A *bailment* is the transfer of possession, but not the title, of personal property (never real property) by one party, usually the owner, to another party on condition that the identical property will be returned to him or his agent at a future date or that it will be delivered to a person designated in the agreement. The one who retains title but gives up possession is called the *bailor*. The one who acquires possession but not the title is called the *bailee*.

Bailments are generally classified as ordinary and extraordinary. *Extraordinary bailments* are those in which the bailee assumes unusual duties and liabilities imposed by law, as in the case of hotelkeepers or common carriers. *Ordinary bailments* include all other bailments.

In a bailment two conditions are always present:

(1) There must be both a delivery and an acceptance of property.

(2) The parties to the bailment agree that the bailor is to get back the same property, thought it may be greatly altered in form.

Also, the property may be delivered with the understanding that the bailee is to deliver it to a third party or sell the item for the bailor. In this case the bailee would not expect to get the property back, but would expect it to be disposed of in the way designated. If either one of the preceding conditions is absent, the transaction is not a bailment.

Some typical business transactions resulting in a bailment are:

(a) A motorist leaves his car with the garage for repairs.

(b) A family stores its furniture in a warehouse.

(c) A student borrows a dinner jacket to wear to a formal dance.

(d) A hunter leaves his jewelry with a friend for safekeeping while he goes on an extended hunting trip.

THE BAILMENT AGREEMENT

A bailment is based upon an agreement, express or implied, between the bailor and the bailee. If the agreement is the result of written or spoken words, the bailment is express. If the agreement is indicated by the conduct of the parties, the bailment is implied. When a man checks his hat and coat as he enters a restaurant, nothing may be said, but the bailment is implied by the acts of the two parties.

DELIVERY AND ACCEPTANCE

A bailment can be established only if there is delivery accompanied by acceptance of personal property. The delivery and acceptance may be actual or constructive. They are actual when the goods themselves are delivered and accepted. They are constructive when there is no physical delivery of the goods but when control over the goods is delivered and accepted.

There is a constructive bailment when someone finds lost property. The owner does not actually deliver the property to the finder, but the law holds this to be a bailment. A constructive bailment also occurs when property of one person is washed up on the land of another, the latter being constituted the bailee for the goods of the former.

- Dieball had a painting on exhibit at an art show. Hauchin, a furniture merchant, offered to rent it for 60 days to place on display in his store. Dieball wrote out a statement notifying the manager of the art exhibition to deliver his painting to Hauchin. The delivery of this writing to Hauchin constituted constructive delivery.

RETURN OF THE BAILED PROPERTY

In a bailment the bailee must return to the bailor the identical goods bailed. If a farmer delivers wheat to a miller, a bailment is established if he is to get back flour made from the same wheat. If he is to get back flour made from any wheat of like grade, there is an exchange of personal property (a sale, with the purchase price for the flour being the delivery of a certain quantity of grain), but not a bailment.

- The Apex Freezer Company delivered 10 home freezers to the Gerhart Appliance Company to be sold on a 20 percent commission. Any freezers unsold were to be returned. This was a bailment even though the contract contemplated that the freezers would never be returned. If they were not sold, they would have to be returned.

CLASSIFICATIONS OF BAILMENTS

For convenience, bailments are usually divided into the following three groups:

1. Bailments for the sole benefit of the bailor
2. Bailments for the sole benefit of the bailee
3. Bailments for the mutual benefit of both parties

(1) **Bailments for the Sole Benefit of the Bailor.** If one is in possession of another's personal property for the sole benefit of the owner, a bailment for the sole benefit of the bailor exists. The bailee receives no benefits in the way of compensation or else it would not be a bailment for the sole benefit of the bailor. For example, a man asks a friend to keep his piano in his home until he, the owner, is able to rent larger quarters. The friend may not play the piano or otherwise receive the benefits of ownership while it is in his possession. If a farmer agrees, gratuitously, to haul a load of hay to town for a neighbor, this is clearly a bailment for the sole benefit of the bailor. Another example of a bailment for the sole benefit of the bailor occurs when one person loses an article and another person finds it. In this case the loser is the bailor, and the finder is the bailee.

During the time that he has possession of the goods as a bailee, even though the bailment is for the sole benefit of the bailor, he nevertheless assumes certain responsibilities. He is liable for lack of reasonable care with respect to the property.

(2) **Bailments for the Sole Benefit of the Bailee.** If the bailee has possession of another's personal property, and the owner of the property receives no benefit or compensation for its use, a bailment for the sole benefit of the bailee exists. This type of bailment arises as a rule through borrowing someone else's property. The bailee must exercise reasonable care over the property and is liable for negligence if he fails to do so. The bailee is not an insurer of the bailed property since any loss or damage due to no fault whatsoever of the bailee falls upon the owner. If Petras borrows Walker's diamond ring to wear to a dance and is robbed on the way to the dance, the loss falls upon Walker, the owner. Petras was not negligent.

Even though the bailor receives no benefit from a bailment for the sole benefit of the bailee, he must inform the bailee of any known defects. If the bailee is injured by reason of a defect, the bailor is liable for damages, provided he knew of the defect and failed to inform the bailee.

> ■ Orr borrowed a power saw from Temple to make certain repairs in his store. Orr was injured because of a defective part (unknown to Temple) in the tool and claimed that Temple was liable. Temple was not liable because in a bailment for the sole benefit of the bailee, the bailor is obligated to inform the bailee of only those defects of which the bailor is aware.

(3) Bailments for the Mutual Benefit of Both Parties. The largest volume of bailments are those for the mutual benefit of both the bailor and the bailee. Some common bailments of this type are: machinery left with a mechanic to be repaired, laundry and dry cleaning contracts, the rental of personal property, such as an automobile or a typewriter, and material left with a fabricator to be converted into a finished product for a price. The bailee must take reasonable care of the bailed property.

> ■ Green rented a You-Drive-It automobile from Trestle Motors Company. While driving to Denver, he collided with a car driven by White, and both cars were wrecked. The roads were coated with ice, and at the time of the collision Green was driving down a fairly steep grade at about forty miles an hour. Visibility because of snow was about 200 feet. Green was liable to the Trestle Motors Company for damages to the car. Forty miles an hour, under the conditions described, was faster than an ordinary, prudent man would have driven his own car.
>
> Had the Trestle Motors Company furnished Green with a car which had a defect that caused the accident, not only would Green not have been liable, but the Trestle Motors Company would have been liable to Green for any damages sustained by him. In a mutual-benefit bailment of this type, the bailor must furnish safe property, not just inform the bailee of any known defects.

In mutual-benefit bailments the bailee makes a charge for services rendered. This is true in all repair jobs, laundry, dry cleaning, shoe mending, and storage bailments. The bailee has a lien against the bailed property for his charges. If these charges are not paid, the bailee is under no obligation to return the bailed goods. After a reasonable time, the bailee may advertise and sell the property for his charges. If any money remains from the proceeds of the sale after expenses and his charges are paid, he must turn it over to the bailor.

If the bailee parts with possession of the property before he has been paid, in most states he loses his lien. If he later regains possession of the same property, his lien is not reestablished for the old charges, except where, by special statute, this right is given to the bailee.

CARE OF BAILED PROPERTY

As a general rule, any loss due to the theft or damage of personal property falls upon the owner. This may not be true in the case of a bailment. Thus it is important to ascertain if there is in fact a bailment. If there is a bailment and the loss was caused by the negligence of the bailee, the owner can hold the bailee responsible for the loss.

In ordinary bailments, the standard of care required of the bailee is: *reasonable care under the circumstances,* that is, the degree of care which a reasonable man would exercise in order to protect the property from harm.

The chief factors in determining what is reasonable care in a bailment are (a) time and place of making the bailment, (b) facilities for taking care of the property, (c) nature of the property, (d) bailee's knowledge of its nature, and (e) extent of the bailee's skill and experience in taking care of goods of that kind. The bailee is also liable for the negligence of his employees or servants with respect to the property. Whether or not a bailee is negligent is ordinarily a question of fact to be decided by a jury.

USE OF THE BAILED GOODS

When a bailment is for the sole benefit of the bailor, the bailee has no right to use the property for his own purpose. This rule may be altered if use of the goods is for their benefit or is necessary to preserve them.

If the bailment is for the sole benefit of the bailee, the use is strictly limited to the use agreed upon by the parties at the time the bailment was effected. If the bailee uses the property in any other way, he is liable for any resulting damage regardless of his negligence.

■ Fleeman borrowed Brown's truck expressly for the purpose of hauling a load of cotton to the cotton gin. After the cotton was ginned, Fleeman drove about ten miles further to another town to get some farm machinery parts. The truck was wrecked on this part of the trip due to no fault of Fleeman. He must bear the loss, since he used the truck for a purpose for which it was not bailed.

In any bailment the wrongful use of the property makes the bailee liable for any damages caused by that use. The only question is whether the bailment permits the use. For example, does a bailment to repair a car give permission to the repairman to drive the car for the purpose of a road test?

DUTIES AND OBLIGATIONS OF THE BAILOR

The bailor must always inform the bailee of any defects known to the bailor; and if the bailor benefits from the bailment, he must also make reasonable efforts to discover the existence of any unknown defects. For example, when A borrows or rents B's truck, B must inform A if the brakes are deficient. If B fails to do so and A is injured, B is liable for damages. When the bailment is for the sole benefit of the bailee, the bailor is liable for any injury due to a failure to inform the bailee of any known defects. The bailor is not liable if the injury is due to an unknown defect.

BAILEE'S DUTY TO PROTECT PROPERTY

Often bailed property is damaged or destroyed not by any negligence by the bailee in the use of it, but by some act having nothing to do with its use. One of the most common causes of loss is the failure to insure the property. In the absence of a promise supported by a consideration to insure the property, the bailee is under no obligation to insure it. But the bailor may as a part of the contract of bailment obligate the bailee to insure the bailed property. Under such circumstances a failure of the bailee to do so subjects him to full liability for all losses due to a failure to insure.

■ Inglis rented some stage decorations for a play he was staging. After the play was over but before the decorations were returned, they were destroyed by fire due to no fault of Inglis. He had no fire insurance on them. In a mutual-benefit bailment the bailee must exercise that degree of care that an ordinary, prudent man would exercise. Since the contract did not require Inglis to insure the property and since Inglis was not negligent, he has no liability to the bailor.

Another cause of loss not due to the use of property is a failure to return it on time or returning it to the wrong party in good faith. In both cases the bailee is liable if the loss is due primarily to this failure to return the property on time to the owner. The bailee is liable for all loss due to the wrongful use of the property regardless of negligence.

SALE OF BAILED PROPERTY BY THE BAILEE

Possession of property is not proof of ownership. One who purchases property from a bailee ordinarily does not get good title to it. There are situations, however, where the bailor may not deny that the bailee had the right to sell the property. This is particularly true in goods put out on consignment with a commission merchant or factor. In these cases a mutual-benefit bailment exists even though the bailor does not expect to get the bailed property back. The purpose of the bailment is to have the property sold and the proceeds remitted to the bailor. The bailee has the power to sell all goods under these types of contracts regardless of any restriction upon his right to sell, unless the buyer knows of the restriction.

The bailor may by his act mislead an innocent third person into believing that the bailee owns the property. An instance of this type is shown in the following illustration:

> ▪ Donovan purchased a typewriter from the Dodd Office Equipment Company. He paid for the machine but asked the seller to leave it on display until he was ready to pick it up. Dodd sold it to Dooley. Dooley got good title to it even though the seller was merely the bailee of the typewriter. Donovan's act of making it possible for the Dodd Office Equipment Company to perpetrate a fraud upon an innocent party estops him from denying the company had a right to sell it.

PLEDGE OR PAWN

One type of bailment is the deposit of personal property as security for some debt or obligation. If the security is tangible property, such as livestock, a radio, or an automobile, it is a *pawn*. If the security is intangible property, such as notes, bonds, or stock certificates, it is a *pledge*. In each case the transaction is a mutual-benefit bailment.

QUESTIONS

1. In a bailment, is the owner the bailor or the bailee?
2. (a) If one sends a suit to be cleaned, is this a bailment?
   (b) If one enters a restaurant and hangs his coat on a hook provided for the convenience of the customers, is this a bailment?
3. Give an example of a contract of bailment without an actual delivery of the goods to the bailee.
4. If the owner of a car has it in B's garage and he gives the keys to C and instructs him to get the car, is this a bailment?

5. Should a bailee carry fire insurance on the property he has in his possession that belongs to another?

6. What is the extent of liability of a bailor with regard to defects in property loaned for no compensation to the bailee?

7. If Jones loans his car to Smith as a favor and Smith is injured because the car had very defective brakes, what remedy does Smith have against Jones?

8. In a bailment for the sole benefit of the bailor, how may the bailee use the goods?

9. In a bailment for the mutual benefit of both parties, the bailee used the property contrary to the agreement. Is the bailee liable for damages if the property is damaged due to no negligence on the part of the bailee?

10. (a) Define a *pawn*.
   (b) Define a *pledge*.

CASE PROBLEMS

1. Crutchfield ran the following advertisement in a daily newspaper: "Found one palomino horse. Owner can get it by paying for the cost of this ad and a reasonable price for feed and caring for it." Must the owner pay before obtaining the horse?

2. Ramsey placed an expensive fur with the Snow Fur Storage Company. Ramsey wrote a note to the bailee asking him to deliver the fur to John Harlee. Mrs. Harlee obtained the note, took it to the Snow Fur Storage Company, and asked to receive the fur. Grace, the secretary for the bailee, delivered the fur to Mrs. Harlee. It developed that Mr. and Mrs. Harlee were divorced and neither Mrs. Harlee nor the fur coat could be located. Was the Snow Fur Storage Company liable for this loss?

3. Lucille entered an exclusive coat and dress shop intending to purchase a coat. Preparatory to trying on a coat, she removed the one she was wearing and laid it with her pocketbook on the store counter. The pocketbook, containing $500 in money and a $150 watch, was stolen by an unknown customer. The owner of the dress shop contended he was not liable for the loss because there was no delivery of the articles to him or his agents. Do you agree?

4. The Dupree Garage, over a period of one month, did about $1,500 repairs on several trucks owned by the Brown Trucking Company. The $1,500 repair bill was past due. Two trucks were later brought in for minor repairs. Mr. Dupree refused to let Brown have the trucks until the old bill for $1,500 plus the current repair bill was paid. Brown paid the current repair bill and demanded possession of the trucks. Was he within his rights?

5. The Bronson Typewriter Exchange sold an electric typewriter to Holmes, who was to pick up the machine the following day. The next day Holmes telephoned the Bronson Typewriter Exchange and asked that the machine be delivered to 237 Hull Street. Marion, the secretary, attached a memo to the machine showing that it was to be delivered to 237 Hull Street. Because of her poor penmanship, the truck driver read it 237 Hall Street. He delivered it at that address. The machine was stolen before the error was detected. Who must bear the loss, Holmes or the Bronson Typewriter Exchange?

6. The Bailey Transfer and Storage Company received from Hill some household furniture to be stored in their brick warehouse. About one month later the storage company, without Hill's knowledge or consent, moved the furniture to a new location in a nearby fireproof building. Hill's fire insurance policy showed the location of his furniture as 1416 Main street, the location of the brick warehouse. The policy also contained a clause which limited the company's liability if the property was moved to a new location without the insurance company's consent. The property was destroyed by fire through no negligence on the part of the storage company. The fire insurance company refused to pay. Could Hill collect for the loss from the Bailey Transfer and Storage Company?

7. The Bargain Corner had a stock of merchandise valued at $20,000. Of this amount $15,000 belonged to the proprietor, and $5,000 was stocked on consignment. There was a fire insurance policy of $10,000 on the stock owned by the Bargain Corner proprietor but none on the consigned merchandise. A fire loss results in a damage of $8,000 on the stock, $2,000 of which was on the consigned goods. The proprietor of the Bargain Corner was in no way negligent in causing the loss. Must he use $2,000 of the insurance proceeds to apply on the loss of the consigned goods?

8. Hicks orally sold Smith all his spring lambs and gave Smith one week to take them away. Hicks agreed to care for the lambs without charge until Smith came for them, at which time Smith was to make payment. Two days later the lambs were frozen to death in a blizzard. Hicks made no effort to get them to shelter, and there was some evidence to indicate that he might have saved some of them had he put them in shelter. Smith refused to pay for the lambs. Must he pay for them?

9. Henry asked to borrow his employer's car to drive to Booneville on personal business. There were two roads to Booneville. By the usual route, the distance was ten miles; by the other route, it was twenty miles. Henry went the long way so that he could pick up his girl friend and take her with him. While driving at forty miles an hour around a bad curve, he ran into another car parked on the wrong side of the road. There was conflicting evidence as to whether or not he was driving with both hands. His employer demanded that Henry pay the $575 repair bill. Was he legally bound to pay it?

10. Nixon owned a warehouse used for storing wheat for his customers. Wheat of like grade was deposited in bins, and the owner was given a warehouse receipt showing the number of bushels and grade of wheat left with Nixon. It was the custom to return to the wheat owner the correct number of bushels of wheat of like grade that was left in the warehouse, but no promise was made to return exactly the same wheat. Rice deposited wheat with Nixon, and soon thereafter the warehouse and all the wheat was destroyed. Rice demanded payment from Nixon for the value of the wheat contending there was a sale, not a bailment. Do you agree?

Chapter 18

COMMON CARRIERS

DEFINITION

A *carrier* is engaged in the business of transporting either goods or persons, or both. A carrier of goods is a bailee. Since a fee is charged for such service, the bailment is one for the mutual benefit of both parties. The general law of bailments, however, does not apply to all carriers of goods. For this reason it is necessary to classify carriers so that the laws governing each class may be set out.

CLASSIFICATION OF CARRIERS

Carriers are usually classified into three groups:

1. Contract carriers
2. Private carriers
3. Common carriers

(1) **Contract Carriers.** A *contract carrier* is one who, for a fee, undertakes to transport goods or persons. He does not hold himself out to the public as being able and willing to serve all who apply. He transports only under special instances and special arrangements. Since he conducts his business for profit, he is anxious to serve all as far as it is profitable for him to do so. He is free to refuse service if it is unprofitable, a freedom denied to common carriers. The most usual types of contract carriers are trucks, moving vans, railroads, ships, and delivery services.

Contract carriers' contracts for transporting goods are mutual-benefit bailments, and the general law of bailments as well as of contracts governs them. A contract carrier may limit liability for loss to the goods whether caused by its negligence or by the fault of others. In the absence of such a limitation the law of mutual-benefit bailments applies. Any state or city may impose certain limitations upon these contract carriers, but such limitations are seldom extensive.

(2) **Private Carriers.** A *private carrier* is a carrier owned by the shipper, such as a truck fleet owned and operated by an industrial firm or a fleet of ships owned by an oil company for transporting its own products.

(3) **Common Carriers.** A *common carrier* is one who undertakes to transport goods or persons, without discrimination, for all who apply for that service, assuming that the carrier transports proper goods and that facilities are available for transport. One who ships goods by a common carrier is called the *consignor*; the one to whom the goods are shipped is called the *consignee*; and the contract between the parties is called a *bill of lading*.

A common carrier must serve all who apply without discrimination. If he fails to do so, he is liable for any damages resulting from such a refusal. He may refuse service because it is not one for which he is equipped. For example, an express company does not have to accept lumber for transportation. Also, a common carrier may refuse service if its equipment is inadequate to accommodate additional customers in excess of the normal demands.

Provided he has room, a common carrier of persons must carry without discrimination all fit persons who may apply for passage. He is not, however, required to transport (a) any person who requires unusual attention, such as an invalid, unless that person is accompanied by an attendant, (b) any person who intends to cause an injury to the carrier or the passengers, (c) any person who is likely to harm passengers, such as a person with a contagious disease, or (d) any person who is likely to be offensive to passengers, such as an intoxicated person.

The usual types of common carriers of persons are railroads, bus lines, airplanes, ships (both ocean and river), and street railways. Common carriers are public monopolies and are subject to regulations as to prices, services, equipment, and other operational policies. This public regulation is in lieu of competition as a determinant of their prices and services.

LIABILITY OF COMMON CARRIER OF GOODS FOR LOSS

With but five exceptions noted below, a common carrier of goods is liable for loss or damage without regard to negligence or intentional fault of the carrier, its employees, or third persons. He thus is an insurer of the safety of the goods except when the loss arises from the excepted causes.

The common carrier is not liable as an insurer for losses arising from:

1. Acts of God
2. Acts of a public authority
3. Inherent nature of goods
4. Acts of the shipper
5. Acts of public enemy

These exceptions do not excuse the carrier if the carrier is also negligent in failing to safeguard the goods from harm.

(1) **Acts of God.** If the loss to goods being transported is due to floods, snowstorms, tornadoes, lightning, or fire caused by lightning, the carrier is not liable since these are considered acts of God.

▪ A flash flood weakened the pillars of a railroad bridge. Soon after the waters began to recede, a freight train started across the bridge, causing it to collapse and plunge into the raging waters. The company did not have the bridge inspected before dispatching the train across. Many carloads of freight were badly damaged by water. The railroad denied liability on the ground this was an act of God. The railroad was not excused from liability since its negligence in failing to inspect and repair the bridge contributed to the harm. Therefore, it was not excused by the initial occurrence of an act of God in the form of a flash flood.

(2) **Acts of a Public Authority.** Any loss to goods being transported due to public authority is borne by the shipper, not the carrier. Illicit goods may be seized by public officials, or health officials may seize goods that are a menace to health. The carrier is not liable for such loss.

(3) **Inherent Nature of the Goods.** Some goods, such as vegetables, are highly perishable. If the carrier uses proper care, he is not liable for damage due to the inherent nature of the goods. The most

common types of loss due to the inherent nature of the goods are: decay of vegetables, fermentation or evaporation of liquids, and the death of livestock as a result of natural causes or the fault of other animals.

(4) **Acts of the Shipper.** If the loss is due to the act of the shipper, the carrier is not liable. The most common cause of this type of loss is improper packing. If the packing is clearly improper, the carrier should refuse to accept the goods. If the improper packing cannot be detected by inspection, and a loss results, the carrier is relieved from liability. Other instances are misdirection of the merchandise and failure to indicate fragile contents.

■ Webster shipped some perishable freight by the Georgia Central Railroad. The freight was intended for Athens, Georgia, but by error in the address written on the package by Webster it was sent to Athens, Tennessee. Before it could be returned, the freight was a total loss. This loss must be borne by the shipper.

(5) **Acts of Public Enemy.** If the loss or damage to goods is the result of organized warfare or border excursions of foreign bandits, the carrier is not liable. This cause of loss has all but vanished in America. Mobs, strikers, and rioters are not listed as public enemies in interpreting this exclusion.

LIMITATIONS UPON THE CARRIER'S LIABILITY

A carrier may attempt to limit or escape the extraordinary liability imposed upon him by law. This is most often done by a contract between the shipper and the carrier. Since the bill of lading is the written evidence of the contract, the limitations on the carrier's liability are set out in this document. Since the shipper does not have any direct voice in the preparation of the bill of lading, the law requires all carriers to have the printed bill-of-lading form approved before it is adopted. For interstate commerce this approval is given by the Interstate Commerce Commission. The states have similar bodies to regulate purely intrastate commerce. These bodies have approved a few provisions whereby the carriers limit their liability. But in addition to the uniform limitations set out in the printed form of bill of lading, space is left for any additional limitations which the shipper and the carrier may agree upon. The Federal Bills of

Lading Act governs this matter as to interstate shipments, while the Uniform Commercial Code controls with respect to intrastate shipments. In general the limitations upon the carrier's liability permitted by these acts fall into the following classes:

(1) A carrier is permitted to limit by agreement his loss to a specified sum or to a specified percent of the value of the goods. To obtain the benefit for itself, a carrier must give the shipper the choice of shipping at the lower rates subject to the limited liability or at the ordinary rate without any limitation of liability.

(2) Most states permit the carriers to exempt themselves from liability due to certain named hazards. The most common named hazards are: fire, leakage, breakage, spoilage, and losses due to riots, strikes, mobs, and robbers. Some states specifically prohibit an exemption for loss by fire. Before these exemptions are valid, they must be specifically enumerated in the bill of lading or shipper's receipt. In all cases the exemptions are not effective if the loss is due to the negligence of the carrier. No consideration in the form of a reduced rate need be given to justify these limitations.

(3) Livestock shipments create many problems for carriers, and delay in transportation for any cause may result in serious losses or extra expense for feed. Most states allow some form of limitation upon the carrier's liability if the loss is due to a delay over which the carrier has no control.

The Uniform Commercial Code specifically provides that the Code does not change or alter in any way those liabilities imposed upon the carrier for losses not the result of the carrier's negligence. In those cases where the carrier is held liable only for loss due to negligence, the Uniform Commercial Code provides for liability only for ordinary negligence.

DURATION OF CARRIER'S LIABILITY

The carrier is subject to the high degree of liability stated only during transportation. If the goods are delivered to the carrier for immediate shipment and are received from the carrier promptly upon arrival, the goods are regarded as being transported during the entire transaction. There may, however, be a delay in the beginning or at the end of the shipment, during which interval the carrier is regarded as merely a warehouseman of the goods with its liability measured by the bailment law.

(1) **Carrier as Bailee Before Transportation.** Frequently, goods are delivered to the carrier before they are ready for transportation. The carrier may be instructed to hold the goods until shipping instructions are received, or the carrier may delay shipment until the freight charges are paid. In either event, the carrier is liable only as a warehouseman, that is, a mutual-benefit bailee. The carrier's role as an insurer, therefore, does not arise until the goods are ready to be transported.

(2) **Carrier as Bailee After Transportation.** When the goods arrive at their destination, the consignee is given a reasonable time to accept delivery of the goods. Express companies must deliver the goods to the consignee's place of business, but railroads need only place the goods in the freight depot, or, in case of car lots, set the car on a siding where the consignee can unload the goods. If the consignee does not call for the goods within a reasonable time after being notified by the carrier that the goods have arrived, the carrier is liable only as a warehouseman.

INITIAL AND CONNECTING CARRIERS

The initial carrier and the final carrier are each liable for a common carrier loss occurring on the line of a connecting carrier. The terminal carrier may then compel the connecting carrier to reimburse it. This liability of the terminal carrier is in addition to the liability of the connecting carrier on whose line the loss occurs, when such carrier remains liable as at common law.

BILL OF LADING

A *bill of lading* is a document of title and sets forth the contract between the shipper and the carrier. Title to the goods described in the bill of lading may be passed by transferring the bill of lading to the purchaser. Since the bill of lading names the consignee, the carrier should deliver the goods to him only, or to one whom he has designated as the proper person to receive the goods.

The Uniform Commercial Code defines a bill of lading as "a document evidencing the receipt of goods for shipment issued by a person engaged in the business of transporting or forwarding goods, and includes an airbill." It is the contract between the shipper and the transportation company.

There are two types of bills of lading:

1. Straight, or nonnegotiable, bills of lading
2. Order, or negotiable, bills of lading

(1) **Straight Bills of Lading.** Under this type of bill of lading the consignee alone is designated as the one to whom the goods are to be delivered. The consignee may transfer his rights to another, but as a rule the third party obtains no better title than the shipper or the consignee had. He may under certain circumstances get larger rights than the consignee. If the bill of lading contains a recital as to the contents, quantity, or weight of the goods, the carrier is bound to a bona fide transferee as to the accuracy of these descriptions unless the bill of lading itself indicates that the contents of packages are unknown to the carrier.

As with all assignments, the assignee should notify the carrier of his assignment when the original consignee sells the goods before receipt. The carrier is justified in delivering goods to the consignee if it has received no notice of assignment.

- McDougal shipped by a straight bill of lading reciting shipment of 1,000 reams of typing paper to the Yuma Printing Company. The consignee sold this bill of lading to the Guest Printing Company. When the cartons were opened, there were only 800 reams of paper. The railroad must make good the shortage as it should have checked the accuracy of the count.

(2) **Order Bills of Lading.** The bill of lading may set forth that the goods are shipped to a designated consignee or his order, or merely "to the bearer" of the bill of lading. In such case the bill of lading is an order or negotiable bill of lading and must be presented to the carrier before the carrier can safely deliver the goods. If the goods are delivered to the named consignee and later a bona fide innocent purchaser of the bill of lading demands the goods, the carrier is liable to the holder of the bill of lading.

- The Clark Milling Company shipped a carload of flour to Rose and Rogers in South Carolina. The order bill of lading was attached to a draft and sent to a bank at the point of destination. The consignee, without paying the draft or obtaining the bill of lading, was permitted to receive the flour. The carrier was held liable for delivery of the flour without demanding that the consignee surrender the bill of lading. (N. & W. Ry. Co. v. Aylor, 153 Va. 575)

RIGHTS OF COMMON CARRIERS OF PERSONS

Common carriers of persons have the right to prescribe the place and time of the payment of fares, usually before boarding the train, bus, or other vehicle. They also have the right to prescribe certain rules of conduct while transporting passengers so long as these are reasonable. They may stop the vehicle and remove any passenger who refuses to pay his fare or whose conduct is offensive to the other passengers. They also have the right to reserve certain coaches, seats, or space for special classes of passengers, such as Pullman cars and sleeper coaches.

> ■ Scott boarded a boat for a coastal trip south. When the ship master
>   called for all tickets, Scott could not locate his. Upon his refusal
> to pay for his passage, he was removed at the first mooring. He sued
> the ship line owner for damages after he later located his ticket. He
> did not succeed in his claim for damages since he could not produce
> a ticket when required. The carrier was not required to take his
> word for it.

LIABILITY OF COMMON CARRIER OF PERSONS

The carriers of passengers are not insurers of the passengers' safety, but they are required to exercise the highest degree of care possible, consistent with practical operation. The liability of the carrier begins as soon as the passenger enters the station or waiting platform and does not end until he has left the station at the end of the journey. The degree of care required is only ordinary care while the passenger is in the station. After the passenger boards the bus, train, plane, or other vehicle, the utmost care is required.

DUTIES OF COMMON CARRIERS OF PERSONS

A carrier's duties to its passengers consist of two broad groups:

1. Duty to provide reasonable accommodations and services
2. Duty to provide reasonable protection to its passengers

(1) Duty to Provide Reasonable Accommodations and Services. When a traveler purchases a ticket from a common carrier, a contract is formed between the carrier and the passenger. Historically, the contract entitled the passenger to a seat. If there was no seat available, he could get off at the next station and demand a refund of his fare. He could also sue for damages for breach of contract. However, the better view today is that the carrier's duty is to make reasonable efforts to provide sufficient facilities so that the public can be accommodated, which may be merely standing room; and there is no guarantee that a passenger will have a seat in the absence of an express reservation, as in the case of air travel. The carrier must also notify the passenger of the arrival of the train, bus, or airplane at his destination and stop long enough to permit the passenger to disembark. A personal notice is not necessary, only a general announcement. If this is not done and a passenger is carried beyond his destination, he may sue for any damages suffered.

(2) **Duty to Provide Reasonable Protection to Its Passengers.** Common carriers of passengers are not insurers of the absolute safety of passengers but must exercise extraordinary care to protect them. Any injury to the passenger by an employee or fellow passengers subjects the carrier to liability for damages, provided the passenger is without blame. The vehicle must stop at a safe place for alighting, and passengers must be assisted when necessary for alighting. Transportation may be denied to invalids unless someone accompanies them; but if accepted, reasonable assistance must be rendered to them.

> ▪ Johnson was traveling by plane to Cedar City. The plane made a brief stop at Cedar City, but Johnson was asleep and did not hear the pilot's announcement. Johnson awoke after the plane had gone 100 miles beyond Cedar City. The carrier was not liable for Johnson's inconvenience and delay in reaching his destination since the pilot announced the arrival at Cedar City.

DEFINITION OF BAGGAGE

Baggage consists of those articles necessary for personal convenience while traveling. Articles carried by travelers on similar missions and destinations constitute the test rather than what passengers in general carry. For example, fishing paraphernalia is baggage for a man on a fishing trip, but not for the ordinary traveler. Also, a lady's watch is not baggage when carried in a traveling bag by a man. Any article carried for the accommodation of one who is not a passenger is not baggage. The carrier is, of course, liable for the loss of articles the same as for baggage, but the passenger is not entitled to have them transported without extra charge. They are freight, not baggage.

LIABILITY FOR BAGGAGE

The liability of a common carrier for baggage is the same as that of a common carrier of goods. The common carrier is an insurer of the baggage with the five exceptions noted in the section on common carriers of goods. It is necessary to distinguish between baggage retained in the possession of the traveler and that carried in the baggage car or other space. In the first type, the carrier is liable only for lack of reasonable care or for willful misconduct of its agents or employees.

A reasonable amount of baggage may be carried as a part of the cost of the passenger's fare. The carrier may charge extra for an amount in excess of a reasonable value, usually $100.

QUESTIONS

1. What law governs contract carriers?
2. Is a common carrier liable for the loss or damage to goods being transported regardless of negligence?
3. Must a common carrier serve all who apply?
4. Name some acts which the law tends to call acts of God.
5. What acts of the shipper will relieve a common carrier of liability for loss?
6. When does the common carrier's liability begin?
7. When goods must be transported by two or more carriers before reaching their destination, which carrier is liable?
8. (a) What is a *bill of lading*?
   (b) What is the difference between a *straight bill of lading* and an *order bill of lading*?
9. To what extent are common carriers responsible for the safety of passengers?
10. What is the liability of a common carrier for baggage carried by a passenger?

CASE PROBLEMS

1. The Case Equipment Company purchased 10 tractors from the Case Manufacturing Company. The tractors were shipped by railroad freight with a negotiable bill of lading. The consignee borrowed money on the tractors from Finley Finance Company and indorsed the bill of lading to the lender as security for the loan. When the tractors arrived, they were delivered to the consignee without demanding that he produce the bill of lading. The Finley Finance Company sued the railroad for its loss. Is the railroad liable?

2. Stanley shipped several cartons of books by air freight. In one package was a painting valued at $10,000. The cartons were all marked: "Contents—Books." The carton containing the painting was stolen. Is the carrier liable?

3. The Blue Ridge Airlines had a rule that no dogs were to be taken aboard one of its planes. Miss Wiley persuaded the pilot to make an exception for her tiny Fifi. The little poodle looked so innocent that the pilot permitted Miss Wiley to carry it aboard. It bit a lady passenger severely on the ankle. Did the carrier have to pay damages because of its failure to protect the safety of its passengers?

4. The Devon Seed Company ordered a carload of seed from the Newberry Seed Corporation. When the seed arrived, the car was placed on a siding where the consignee by agreement was to load it onto his truck and at his expense. The car was placed on the siding at 10 a.m., but the Devon Seed Company was not notified that day. During the night a riot occurred, and the seed was thrown out of the car by the rioters and destroyed by a heavy rain. Loss by riot had not been excluded in the bill of lading. Is the carrier liable for the loss?

5. The Baxter Machine Company shipped an expensive machine to the Buford Mining Company in Denver by a straight bill of lading. An agent of the Buford Mining Company called at the office of the Stern Engineering Corporation and offered to sell them the machinery, stating that their plans had been altered and they would have to return it. The Stern Corporation purchased the machinery and received the bill of lading by indorsement. Three days later they inquired of the railroad if the machinery had arrived and were told that it had already been delivered to the consignee, the Buford Mining Company. It developed that this latter company, after it got possession of the machinery, had sold and delivered it to the Rocky Mountain Mining Company. The Stern Engineering Corporation sued the railroad for the value of the machinery, alleging it had delivered the machinery to the wrong party. Was the railroad liable?

6. Hardin delivered 42 bales of cotton to the Georgia Railroad with instructions to hold them until the following day when an additional 58 bales would be delivered, making a total shipment of 100 bales. The 42 bales were stacked on the loading platform. That night a fire destroyed the 42 bales. There was no negligence on the part of the railroad in starting the fire or in preventing its spread. Hardin sued the railroad for the value of the cotton, alleging that it was liable as a common carrier. Was Hardin entitled to collect?

7. Thomas owned a large truck in which he hauled fresh vegetables for a produce exchange from Florida to Atlanta. On the return trip he often carried freight at rates considerably below that charged by the railroad. On one of these return trips, the Glenn Jewelry Company shipped two cases of jewelry valued at $2,500 to its branch store in Orlando. The jewelry was stolen through no fault of Thomas. The Glenn Jewelry Company sued Thomas as a common carrier for the value of the jewelry. Was he liable?

8. A jewelry salesman was traveling on a train to a college town to sell class rings, fraternity and sorority pins, and other types of jewelry to college students. His bag containing $1,000 worth of samples was stolen. The baggage was given to the porter and he stacked it with the baggage belonging to the other passengers. Was the carrier liable for its loss, assuming no extra charge was paid for the baggage?

9. Roberts purchased a ticket for a trip to Denver. He boarded the train and took a seat. When the conductor called for his ticket, he could not locate it. The conductor required him to pay his fare in cash, and Roberts refused. At the next station Roberts was ordered to leave the train, but he refused to do so. The train policeman was called, and Roberts was forceably removed. As a result he was twenty-four hours late in keeping an appointment, resulting in a loss of some business. He sued the railroad for the loss plus additional damages for his injured pride in being forceably removed from the train. Was the carrier liable?

10. The Associated Farmers Warehouse Corporation shipped a load of wheat by riverboat to St. Louis. The boat struck a tree trunk that had been washed into the river channel by a recent flood. The boat sank, and all the wheat was destroyed. Was the carrier liable for this loss?

11. Mrs. Julia Hasbrouck obtained passage on the New York Central and Hudson Railroad to make a trip to Natick, Massachusetts, to visit her daughter, a college student in that city. In her baggage were four rings valued at about $1,500. Mrs. Hasbrouck was socially prominent and was in the habit of wearing expensive jewelry at all social functions. The baggage was checked with the railroad and the usual excess value was declared and the charges paid. When she arrived at her destination, her baggage was returned to her, but the jewelry was missing. The railroad refused to pay her claim, contending that so much jewelry, four diamond rings, was not properly baggage, and therefore the railroad was not liable for its loss. Was the railroad liable for the loss?

Chapter 19

HOTELKEEPERS AS BAILEES

SPECIAL BAILMENTS

When a guest registers at a hotel, the hotelkeeper enters into a special relationship with him with respect to the guest's luggage and other personal property. Since early times, the innkeeper has been held to an extraordinary degree of liability for the safety of the personal property of his guest, the traveler, or the transient. Since the hotelkeeper's occupation is that of a public calling, the law exacted from him a higher degree of care than it did from a bailee in an ordinary mutual-benefit bailment. Like those of carriers described in the preceding chapter, the contracts of hotelkeepers were specially designated exceptional bailments. For this reason a hotelkeeper's liability for the safety of a guest's property could not be determined from the general law of bailments alone.

The common law is the basis of most of our laws dealing with hotelkeepers, but as conditions change, the law must change. The traveler today is not at the mercy of the hotelkeeper as was the case prior to our modern system of transportation and communication. Much of the change in the common law has been by statute. Today most states have laws permitting hotelkeepers and motel keepers to limit their liability. These statutes vary so widely that only a few general statements can be made about them. Limitation upon his liability usually is accomplished by some kind of public notice to the guest, usually a notice posted in the guest's room. Some statutes simply declare that the law of mutual-benefit bailments applies. Other statutes require that the hotelkeeper, in order to escape full liability, provide a vault or other safe place of deposit for valuables, such as furs and jewelry. Even with all these statutory modifications of the common law, the hotelkeeper still owes his guest a high degree of care for

171

both his property and his person. In the absence of a valid limitation, the hotelkeeper is generally an insurer of the safety of goods entrusted to his care. As exceptions to the general rule, the hotelkeeper is not liable for loss caused by an act of God, a public enemy, act of public authority, the inherent nature of the property, or the fault of the guest.

WHO IS A HOTELKEEPER?

Under the old common law an innkeeper was one who provided a traveler with lodging, food, drink, and a stable for the traveler's horses. If any one of these services was not supplied, one was not an innkeeper, and thus not held to strict accountability for the care and safety of the guest. This narrow common law rule has been so modified that today "innkeeper" is synonymous with "hotelkeeper." Today a *hotelkeeper* is one who is regularly engaged in the business of offering living accommodations to all transient persons. He may supply food or entertainment, but providing lodging to the transients is the cardinal test.

THOSE WHO ARE NOT HOTELKEEPERS

If one provides rooms only or room and board to permanent guests, but does not hold himself out as able and willing to accommodate transients, he is not a hotelkeeper and thus is not held to the strict accountability of the common law. A tourist home is not an inn if the owner does not hold himself out as willing to accommodate all transients who apply. Modern motels, auto courts, and tourist cabin establishments are usually classed as inns. Hotels that cater only to permanent residents are not inns, although a hotel may cater to both permanent guests and transients. A hotel owes the typical duties to its transient guests; but to its permanent guests it owes the duties of a landlord.

DUTIES AND LIABILITIES OF A HOTELKEEPER

The duties and liabilities of a hotelkeeper are:

1. Duty to serve all who apply
2. Duty to protect a guest's person
3. Duty to care for the guest's property

(1) **Duty to Serve All Who Apply.** The basic test of a hotel-keeper is that he holds himself out as willing to serve all who apply without discrimination. He is liable for damages to the person rejected. He may turn people away, such as a drunken person who would be highly offensive to his other guests. If his rooms are all filled, he may turn all other applicants away without liability for damages. Today hotels of all classes are so numerous and competition for business is so keen that this duty is seldom breached.

If a hotel refuses accommodations for an improper reason, it is liable for damages, including exemplary damages. In addition, it may be liable under a civil rights or similar statutory provision, and it may also be guilty of a crime. By virtue of the Federal Civil Rights Act of 1964, neither a hotel nor its concessionaire can discriminate against patrons nor segregate them on the basis of race, color, religion, or national origin. The federal act is limited to discrimination for the stated reasons and does not in any way interfere with the right of the hotel to exclude those who are unfit persons to admit because they are drunk or criminally violent, nor persons who are not dressed in the manner required by reasonable hotel regulations applied to all persons. When there has been improper discrimination or segregation or it is reasonably believed that such action may occur, the federal act authorizes the institution of proceedings in the federal courts for an order to stop such prohibited practices.

(2) **Duty to Protect a Guest's Person.** A hotelkeeper is not liable as an insurer of a guest's safety. He must use ordinary care for the safety of those who are on his premises as guests, but not for a mere visitor or a patron of the newsstand or lunchroom. The hotelkeeper's liability with respect to the condition of the premises is the same, regardless of the identity of the victim. The difference in duty arises only in connection with the "property" of the victim.

A hotelkeeper must provide fire escapes and also have conspicuous notices indicating the direction of the fire escapes. He is not liable for an injury due to a fire if he was in no way negligent in starting the fire. If he is negligent in preventing the spread of the fire or in directing the guests to fire escapes, he is liable. Fire prevention practices, such as steel doors leading to stairways between floors, are required of all hotels. If a fire starts due to no negligence of the hotel-keeper or his employees, he is not liable to the guests for their personal injuries unless they can show that the fire was not contained because of a failure to install the required fire safety features. In one case the court held the hotelkeeper was not liable for the loss of life on the floor where the fire started, but was liable for all personal injuries on the four floors to which the fire spread because of the negligence of the hotel.

(3) **Duty to Care for the Guest's Property.** The hotelkeeper is an insurer of the guest's property except for losses occurring from:

(a) Act of God
(b) Act of public enemy
(c) Act of public authority
(d) Act of guest
(e) Inherent nature of the property

Under the common law the innkeeper was an insurer of the guest's property unless the loss or damage was due to one of the five acts listed. By statute in every state this liability has been modified to some extent.

The hotelkeeper may provide a safe where a guest may deposit his valuable articles. If the guest fails to do this, the hotelkeeper is released from liability as an insurer. Notice to this effect must be posted either in the room or at the registration desk. Also, most statutes limit a hotel's liability to a designated sum. Other states permit the hotelkeeper to limit his liability by contract with the guest. This is usually done by posting a notice.

WHO ARE GUESTS?

Before a hotelkeeper can be held liable either for injury to the person or for loss of property, the injured party must be a guest. To be a *guest* one must be a transient, not a permanent resident. Also, he must have been received as a transient guest. If one enters the hotel to attend a ball or other social function or to visit a guest, he himself is not a guest. Likewise, a person going to a hotel restaurant for dinner is not a "guest" of the hotel, but merely a "patron." The essential element in the modern definition of *guest* is that he is a transient. Under this definition a guest need not be a traveler nor come from a distance. A person living within a short distance of the hotel who engages a room at the hotel and remains there overnight is a guest.

The relationship of guest and hotelkeeper does not begin until a person is received as a guest by the hotelkeeper. The relationship terminates when the guest leaves or when he ceases to be a transient, as when he arranges for a more or less permanent residence at the hotel.

> ▪ Jason entered the Ridge Manor Motel to register as a guest. He was told there were no vacancies but that he could wait awhile if he wished to see if anyone checked out. This he did. While he was waiting, his baggage was stolen. The motel was liable since he entered the premises with the intention of becoming a guest and was tentatively accepted as a guest.

LIEN OF THE HOTELKEEPER

A hotelkeeper has a lien on the baggage of his guests for the value of the services rendered. This lien extends also to all wearing apparel not actually being worn, such as an overcoat, a fur coat, or an extra suit. If the hotel knows that the property belongs to a third person, it is not subject to the lien in some states; while in other states the lien of the hotel may be asserted if the property has been entrusted to the guest by the owner with knowledge or reason to know that it might be taken to a hotel.

The lien of the hotelkeeper attaches only to baggage. It does not apply to an automobile, for example. If the hotel provides storage facilities for the guest's car, the car cannot be held if the guest fails to pay his hotel bill. If there is a separate charge for car storage, this charge (but not the room charge) must be paid before the car can be removed. In some states, statutes make the automobile subject to the hotelkeeper's lien.

If the charges are not paid within a reasonable time, the hotelkeeper may sell the baggage or other goods and pay the charges. Any residue must be returned to the guest. The lien terminates when the property is returned to the guest even though the room charges have not been paid. A minor is as fully bound by these laws as an adult.

> ▪ Garson registered at the Ridge Manor Motel in Florida and incurred a hotel bill amounting to $120. He paid the bill by check and departed, taking all his baggage and jewelry. The check was returned marked "Insufficient funds." The lien is not reestablished by a return of the check.

BOARDINGHOUSE KEEPERS

The laws of a hotelkeeper do not apply to boardinghouse keepers. The boardinghouse keeper has no lien under the common law, but most states have given this right to boardinghouses by statute. The chief difference in the common law relating to a hotelkeeper and a boardinghouse keeper is that the latter need take only ordinary care of the property of the boarder or lodger. He is in no way an insurer. Also, he does not have to accept all who apply.

CRIMES AGAINST HOTELS

Statutes commonly make it a criminal offense for a hotel guest, boardinghouse tenant, or similar lodger to attempt to defraud the hotel or boardinghouse by intentionally leaving without paying his bill, removing his property secretly, or engaging in similar fraudulent practices.

> ■ Dobson had been a guest at the Georgian Hotel for five days. He secretly left the hotel without paying his bill. The hotel owner had him indicted "for fraudulently leaving without paying his hotel bill." He was found guilty because the act of leaving secretly without paying showed that his intent was to defraud the hotel.

QUESTIONS

1. What is a hotelkeeper? A guest?
2. What are the duties of a hotelkeeper to his guests?
3. How may a hotelkeeper avoid liability for the loss of valuables carried by the guest?
4. Is the hotelkeeper liable for the injury to a guest by fire if the hotel was in no way negligent?
5. If a guest has $4,000 worth of jewelry and expensive clothes while staying at a hotel and the property is stolen from the guest's room due to no fault of the hotel, is the hotelkeeper liable for the loss?
6. If a guest's baggage is held by the hotel as a lien for the payment of the hotel charges, what disposition may be made of the property?
7. What is the chief difference in the liability of a hotelkeeper and a boardinghouse keeper?
8. May one be charged with a crime for fraudulently leaving without paying his board bill at a boardinghouse?

CASE PROBLEMS

1. Burke registered at the Devon Hotel. He was a minor. He ran up a hotel bill of $75. The hotel held his baggage and a hi-fi set until the

bill was paid. Burke attempted to disaffirm his contract, contending that there was no necessity for him to travel or to stay at a hotel. May he disaffirm?

2. Danner drove up to the King Cotton Motel. An attendant approached and he inquired about a room. He left two traveling bags with the attendant, stating he would return later to register. He changed his mind and returned for his bags. They could not be located. Is the motel liable for this loss?

3. Mr. and Mrs. North took two rooms at a motel fixed for light housekeeping. They were to pay rent by the month and planned to spend the winter in the city. While they were out, a thief entered the room and stole a necklace worth $1,500. They sued the motel owner for the loss. Is he liable?

4. Miss Seagraves, an actress, spent some time at an exclusive hotel in Florida. When she got ready to leave, she had an unpaid hotel bill of several hundred dollars. She was unable to pay the bill, and the hotel notified her that she could not remove her baggage from the room. Although the temperature outside was 96, she put on her expensive mink coat, adorned herself with all her expensive jewelry, and then attempted to leave without her baggage. The hotel contended it was entitled to a lien on her coat and her excess jewelry. Was its contention correct?

5. The Greenway Auto Court had signs along the highway soliciting all travelers to become guests. John L. Hewess, a labor leader, applied for accommodations. Because the owner of the auto court was violently opposed to unions, he refused Hewess accommodations although he had vacant rooms. Hewess sued for damages. Was the Greenway Auto Court liable?

6. The law in a certain state requires all hotels to provide devices to prevent a fire from spreading from one floor to another. A fire of undetermined origin started on the fifth floor of the Fenwick Hotel. Because of open stairways the fire spread quickly to the upper floors, and many guests lost their lives on the fifth, sixth, and seventh floors.

(a) If the hotel was not negligent in starting the fire, was it liable for the loss of life on the fifth floor?

(b) Was it liable for the loss of life on the sixth and the seventh floors?

7. Hawkins registered at a hotel and was assigned a room. During the night the hotel caught fire; neither the hotel nor its employees were negligent. When Hawkins was awakened, he could not leave by the stairway, so he sought the fire escape. Since there were no signs directing him to the fire escape, he could not find it. Seeing no other way out, he jumped from a second-floor window and was injured. All his baggage was destroyed. Hawkins brought suit against the hotel to collect for the value of his baggage and compensation for his injuries. Discuss the rights and obligations of the parties.

8. Rice, a traveling salesman, registered at the Unique Tavern and was assigned a room. Desiring to keep an appointment with a customer before going to his room, Rice had the clerk send his suitcase to his room, where it was stolen through no fault of Rice. What was the liability of the Unique Tavern for the loss of the suitcase?

9. Porter was a guest at the City Hotel. The hotel provided a safe for the deposit of jewels and other valuable articles. Proper notice of this service was posted on the door, according to the provisions of the law. Porter ignored this notice and retained possession of his valuables. They were stolen while he was a guest. He brought a suit for damages.

(a) Was the posting of the notice on the door sufficient, or must the hotelkeeper inform the guests of the protection provided?

(b) In your judgment was the hotelkeeper liable in this case?

10. The Standish Hotel served both transient and permanent roomers. McIntosh rented a room at a fixed rent by the month and occupied the room as a lodger rather than a transient. He was a resident of Portland where the hotel was located. While McIntosh was away for a few days, but still retaining possession of his room, a burglar entered the room and stole clothes and other articles valued in excess of $100. There was no evidence that the hotel was negligent in any way. McIntosh brought suit against the hotel for the value of the stolen property. Was he entitled to recover?

SUMMARY CASES

PART 4

1. Cerreta parked his automobile with the Kinney Corporation parking lot. On the back seat of the car were some valuable drawings and sporting equipment. The articles on the back seat were not visible from the outside of the car. When Cerreta returned to pick up the car, he discovered that the articles were missing. He sued the Kinney Corporation as a bailee. Decide. (Cerreta v. Kinney Corp., 50 N. J. S. 514, 142 A. 2d 917)

2. Wetmore stored two rugs in the warehouse of B. W. Hooker Co., Inc. There was no charge for this storage as it was done as a favor to Wetmore. Seven years later Wetmore asked for a return of the rugs, but the bailee could not locate one of them. The evidence showed that the Hooker Co. placed the rugs in the same space where it stored its own property. There was no way to account for the disappearance of the rug. Was the bailee liable for the value of the lost rug? (Wetmore v. B. W. Hooker Co., Inc., 111 Vt. 519, 18 A. 2d 181)

3. Tilson was a passenger on interstate railroad to Kansas City from St. Louis. She carried two handbags with her. She gave these handbags to a redcap in the station in St. Louis, and they were stolen. The luggage was later found and delivered to her in Kansas City, but jewelry valued at $2,885 had been taken from the luggage. The carrier operated under a rule approved by the Interstate Commerce Commission whereby a limit of $25 is set for the loss of any one piece of luggage or its contents unless a larger value is declared and an extra charge paid. She sued the carrier for $2,885. Was the carrier liable for the $2,885? (Tilson v. Terminal Railroad Association of St. Louis, 236 S. W. 2d 42)

4. Hamilton shipped two carloads of grapes to Schwalb, the consignee, in New York City. The grapes were packed in boxes so that the contents of the boxes could easily be inspected. A bill of lading was issued on which was this notation: "The property described below, in apparent good order, except as noted (contents of packages unknown)." When the grapes arrived in New York, they were badly damaged and in poor condition. The consignee sued the connecting railroad for the damages. It denied liability on the ground the bill of lading showed the condition of the contents could not be determined at the point of origin. Was the railroad liable? (Schwalb v. Erie Railroad Company, 293 N. Y. S. 842, 161 Misc. 743)

5. Featherstone became a guest at the Pacific Hotel. Some valuables were stolen from his room. The law required all hotelkeepers, if they wished to be relieved from the common-law liability as an insurer of the guest's property, to post three notices in conspicuous places in the hotel. The owners of the Pacific Hotel posted one notice on the wall of the elevator, one on the hotel register, and one in the private office of the manager of the hotel. Featherstone brought suit against the owners of the hotel to recover the value of the stolen articles. They denied liability on the ground that they had complied with the statute. Were the owners of the hotel liable? (Featherstone v. Victor and Louise Dessert, 173 Wash. 264, 22 P. 2d 1050)

6. Maher entered the back room at Chapin's Lunch Co. It was crowded, and he had to wait to get a table. The manager told him, "Hang your coat over there, and you will get a seat in a minute." Maher did so. When he finished and went to get his coat, it was gone. On the menu cards were printed statements that the restaurant would not be responsible for coats or other articles lost by its customers. Also, signs were posted to this effect on the wall. Was the restaurant liable? (Maher v. Chapin's Lunch Co., 119 Pa. Super. 213, 180 A. 739)

7. Bohan owned and operated an inn on the Island of Great Tybe. In addition to the inn, he owned and operated a bathhouse on the seashore. His guests and the public in general were encouraged to use this bathhouse. The charge for its use was the same for both the guests of the inn and the public. Mrs. Walpert was a guest at the inn. She became a patron of the bathhouse for a separate fee and while a patron, lost a valuable diamond ring. There was no evidence of negligence on the part of Bohan or his employees. Mrs. Walpert sued Bohan as innkeeper. Was he liable as an innkeeper? (Walpert v. Bohan, 126 Ga. 532, 55 S. E. 181)

8. The Salem Mills Company received a quantity of wheat from Savage. The wheat was stored with the Salem Mills Company's own wheat of the same grade. The contract with Savage provided that if the Company used the wheat for its own purposes, it would either return to Savage an equal quantity of wheat of the same grade and quality or pay for it at the market price. The wheat was destroyed under conditions that might impute negligence to the Salem Mills Company. Savage sued the company, not as a bailee, but as the purchaser of the wheat. Was this a bailment? (Savage v. Salem Mills Co., 48 Ore. 1, 85 P. 69)

9. Healy checked his traveling bag at the checkroom of the defendant railroad's station. On the back of the checking ticket he received was printed in small print the charges for checking and also a clause limiting the railroad's liability to $10 for the loss of any one parcel. This was not called to Healy's attention. Through an error, the baggage was delivered to the wrong person and never was located. Healy brought suit for the full value of the baggage. Was the railroad liable for the full value of the baggage? (Healy v. New York Central and Hudson Railroad, 138 N. Y. S. 287)

10. Gantt was a student at the Aircraft Sales and Service, a privately owned flight school. The school supplied the planes in which students did their flight training. On one flight with Gantt at the controls the plane went out of control and the pilot was unable to bring it under control. It crashed and Gantt was seriously injured. An investigation revealed that a mechanic for the school had left a screwdriver in the control mechanism. Gantt sued the school for his personal injuries. Was the bailor liable? (Aircraft Sales and Service v. Gantt, 52 So. 2d 388 Ala. 1951)

Part 5.

COMMERCIAL PAPER

Preview Cases for Part 5: Commercial Paper

- Massey made a note payable to Hess or order, and Hess indorsed the note to Frazier. Hess was a minor. When Massey refused to pay the note upon its due date, Frazier brought an action against him. Massey claimed that the minor was not competent to indorse the note and that Frazier could not sue and recover on the note. Should Frazier be allowed to recover?

- O'Kelly forged Cohen's name as drawer to a draft for $3,000 payable to Jones who presented it to Smith for acceptance. Jones then transferred the draft by indorsement to Berger. Later Smith learned that Cohen's signature was forged and refused to pay the draft when it became due. May he avoid payment?

- Hale drew a check payable to Shane in the amount of $500. Shane cleverly altered the check to $2,500 and negotiated it to McFain, an innocent purchaser who had no knowledge of the alteration. The bank refused to pay the check. From whom may McFain recover?

- Falk wrote out a check payable to Lytle. He later requested his bank to stop payment on it. The order was ignored and the check was paid. Falk sued the bank for the amount of the check. Will he recover?

- Heritage, a blind man, was expecting delivery of goods to his home by the Atlex Delivery Service. When the goods arrived, the deliverer requested Heritage to sign papers which he maintained were needed receipts for the delivery service. In fact, they were promissory notes made out to the delivery van driver. Will Heritage be liable on these notes?

These preview cases are designed to serve as a springboard for the study of this part. As you read through each chapter in this part, you will find the actual decisions for all these preview cases. Of course, there are many more such illustrative problems as well as case problems for decision at the end of each chapter. And there are also a number of even more challenging cases for review at the end of the part.

Chapter 20

NATURE OF COMMERCIAL PAPER

DEFINITION OF A NEGOTIABLE INSTRUMENT

A *negotiable instrument* is a written instrument drawn in a special form, which can be transferred from person to person as a substitute for money or as an instrument of credit. Such an instrument must meet certain definite requirements in regard to form and the manner in which it is transferred. Since a negotiable instrument is not money, a person is not required by law to accept one in payment of a debt due him unless he wishes to do so.

HISTORY AND DEVELOPMENT

In the days of sea pirates and land robbers the shipment of money in settlement of debts between traders was a risky business. The need for instruments of credit that would permit the settlement of claims between distant cities without the transfer of money has existed as long as trade has existed.

There were references to bills of exchange or instruments of credit as early as 50 B.C. Their widespread usage, however, began about 1200 A.D. as international trade began to flourish in the wake of the Crusades. At first these credit instruments were used only in international trade, but they gradually became common in domestic trade.

Prior to about 1400 A.D. all disputes between merchants were settled on the spot by special courts set up by the merchants. The rules applied by these courts became known as the *law merchant.* Later the common-law courts of England took over the adjudication of all disputes including those between merchants, but these common-law courts retained most of the customs developed by the merchants and incorporated the law merchant into the common law. Most, but by no means all, of the law merchant dealt with bills of exchange or credit instruments. The colonists brought these laws to America. After the Revolution each state developed the common law dealing with credit instruments in its own way so that by 1890 much confusion existed. In 1895 a commission was appointed by the American Bar Association and the American Bankers Association to draw up a Uniform Negotiable Instruments Law. The commission in 1896 proposed a Uniform Act. This act was adopted in all the states and thus became a truly national law, but has since been displaced by Article 3 of the Uniform Commercial Code.

TRANSFER OF NEGOTIABLE INSTRUMENTS

Negotiation is the act of transferring ownership of a negotiable instrument, such as a draft, a check, or a promissory note, to another party. A person who owns a negotiable instrument which is payable to him may negotiate it by merely writing his name on the back of it and delivering it to another party. When a person writes his name on the back of a negotiable instrument before delivery, he is said to *indorse* the instrument.

ORDER PAPER AND BEARER PAPER

Commercial paper is made payable either to the order of a named person, in which case it is called *order paper,* or to bearer, in which case it is called *bearer paper.* Order paper is negotiated to another person only by indorsement of the person to whom it is then payable and delivery of the paper by the indorser to the other person. In case of bearer paper, the transfer may be made merely by handing the paper to another person. Payment is made on a different basis with order paper than with bearer paper. Order paper may be paid only to the person to whom it is made payable on its face, the original payee, or the person to whom it has been properly indorsed. On the other hand, bearer paper may be paid to any person in possession of the paper.

■ Smithson owed Gregory $250. He gave Gregory a check payable to "bearer." Gregory had never seen bearer paper and insisted that Smithson needed to indorse it. Smithson claimed it would be illegal to indorse it. Although it is not necessary to indorse bearer paper, it is not illegal to do so.

When a negotiable instrument is transferred to one or more parties, these parties may acquire rights that are superior to those of the original owner. Parties who acquire rights superior to those of the original owner are known as holders in due course. It is mainly this feature of the transfer of superior rights that gives negotiable contracts a special classification all their own.

The law has clothed negotiable instruments with special advantages as a means to promote and to encourage commerce. How this is done will be more evident as the subject is developed.

CLASSIFICATION OF COMMERCIAL PAPER

The basic negotiable instruments may be classified as follows:

1. Drafts
2. Promissory notes

Inasmuch as these negotiable instruments are discussed in detail in succeeding chapters, a definition of each type will suffice at this time.

(1) **Drafts.** A *draft* or *bill of exchange* is "an unconditional order in writing addressed by one person to another, signed by the person giving it, requiring the person to whom it is addressed to pay on demand or at a particular time a sum certain in money to order or to bearer." The three main divisions of drafts are bills of exchange, trade acceptances, and checks.

(2) **Promissory Notes.** A *negotiable promissory note* is "an unconditional promise in writing made by one person to another, signed by the maker, engaging to pay on demand, or at a particular time, a sum certain in money to order or to bearer."

$450.00	Atlanta, Georgia ___ March 20, 19--	
Thirty days	AFTER DATE ___ I ___ PROMISE TO PAY TO	
THE ORDER OF ___ Johnson Furniture Company		
PAYABLE AT **Merchants Bank**		
Four hundred fifty no/100 _____ DOLLARS		
VALUE RECEIVED WITH INTEREST AT 5%		
No. 85 ___ DUE April 19, 19--	Fred H Hart	

Promissory Note

▪ Cramer delivered a note to Anderson in the amount of $1,000 which called for the payment of 10% of the amount of the note as attorney fee if default were made in the payment of the note and it was turned over to an attorney for collection. Anderson thought this provision made the note nonnegotiable since the sum would not be certain. It is negotiable since an attorney's fee, interest, and such additional payments alone do not prevent a note from being negotiable.

PARTIES TO NEGOTIABLE INSTRUMENTS

Each party to a negotiable instrument is designated by a certain term depending upon the type of instrument. Some of these terms are common to all types of negotiable instruments, while others are restricted to one type only. The same individual may be known by one term at one stage and may be designated by another term at a later stage through which the instrument passes before it is collected. These terms are payee, drawer, drawee, acceptor, maker, bearer, holder, indorser, and indorsee.

Payee. The party to whom any negotiable instrument is made payable is called the *payee.*

Drawer. The person who executes any draft, such as a bill of exchange, a trade acceptance, or a check, is called the *drawer.*

Drawee. The person who is ordered to pay a draft is called the *drawee.*

Acceptor. When the drawee accepts a bill of exchange, that is, indicates his willingness to assume responsibility for its payment, he is called the *acceptor.* Time drafts are accepted by writing upon the face of the instrument these or similar words: "Accepted John Daws." This indicates that John Daws is willing to perform the contract according to its terms. As a practical matter this transaction simply means that a creditor has previously extended credit to John Daws and is now willing to extend the credit period an additional period of time. The creditor and Daws could have used a promissory note to effect this extension of time. If the original creditor, however, owes someone himself, he may prefer to extend the time by drawing a time draft on Daws, sending it to the party he owes, and letting that party present the instrument to Daws for his acceptance.

```
$250.00                    WARREN, ILLINOIS  January 3      19--
   Three months after date                          PAY TO THE
ORDER OF            City National Bank
   Two hundred fifty 00/100 ————————————————DOLLARS
VALUE RECEIVED AND CHARGE TO ACCOUNT OF
TO  Clifford Reeder
No. 51  Columbus, Ohio  }  Walter B Adams
```

Draft

Maker. The person who executes a promissory note is called the *maker.* He is the one who contracts to pay the amount due on the note. His obligation is similar to that of the acceptor of a draft.

Bearer. Any negotiable instrument may be made payable to "bearer." The payee of such an instrument is the *bearer.* If the instrument is made payable to the order of "Myself," "Cash," or another similar name, these terms are equivalent to bearer.

Holder. Any person in possession of an instrument is the *holder* if it has been delivered to him and it is either bearer paper or it is payable to him as the payee or by indorsement. The payee is the original holder.

Indorser. When the payee of a draft, a check, or a note wishes to transfer the instrument to another party, he must indorse it. He is then called the *indorser.*

Indorsee. A person who becomes the holder of a negotiable instrument by an indorsement which names him as the person to whom the instrument is negotiated is called the indorsee.

 ▪ Belmont executed a note in favor of Webster. Webster indorsed it to Lewis and Lewis indorsed it to Norburn. Lewis was an indorsee after Webster indorsed the note and became an indorser when he indorsed it to Norburn.

NEGOTIATION AND ASSIGNMENT

In some respects negotiation and assignment are the same; in others they are different. In each case there are original parties. In a promissory note, for example, the original parties are the maker (the one who promises to pay) and the payee (the one to whom the money is to be paid). Between the original parties, both a nonnegotiable and a negotiable contract are equally enforceable. Also, the same defenses against fulfilling the terms of the contract may be set up. For example, in either case, if one party to the contract is a minor, he may set up his incapacity to contract as a defense against carrying out the agreement.

Although nonnegotiable and negotiable instruments are alike in the rights given to the original parties, they are different in the rights given to subsequent parties. When a nonnegotiable contract is transferred by assignment, the assignee receives only the rights of the assignor and no more. (See Chapter 10.) If one of the original parties to the contract has a defense that is valid against the assignor, it is also valid against the assignee. When an instrument is transferred by negotiation, however, the party who receives the instrument in good faith and for value will ordinarily have rights that are superior to the rights of the original holder. The nature of these rights and the conditions under which they are received are discussed in later chapters.

QUESTIONS

1. Explain the use of commercial paper as credit instruments and collection instruments.
2. What is generally a difference in the wording of "bearer" paper and "order" paper?
3. Can a negotiable contract ever be negotiated without an indorsement?
4. How does one indorse a negotiable instrument?
5. Who is the payee of a negotiable instrument?
6. What is the difference between the drawer and the drawee of a draft?
7. When the drawee accepts the bill of exchange, what is he called?
8. What does the maker of a promissory note contract to do?
9. Who is the indorser of a negotiable instrument? The indorsee?
10. How do assignment and negotiation differ?

CASE PROBLEMS

1. The Adams Company sold Huntley a hi-fi set for $400, and Huntley paid for it by giving a sixty-day nonnegotiable promissory note. Before the note became due, Huntley worked for the Adams Company and earned $350. When the note came due, Adams informed Huntley it had assigned

his note to the Comer National Bank, an innocent purchaser, and that he would have to pay the bearer. The Adams Company refused to pay the $350, and Huntley attempted to offset this $350 against the $400 when the bank demanded payment. Can he do so?

Would your answer be different if the note was so worded that it was negotiable and the note had been negotiated instead of assigned?

2. Gregory drew a check on the Dayton National Bank for $704.50, payable to "Bearer." Before the check was delivered, it was stolen by Davis and cashed at the bank. Gregory demanded that the bank restore the amount of the check to his checking account. Must the bank do this?

3. (a) Who is the payee in this trade acceptance?
(b) Identify the drawer and the drawee in this instrument.

T R A D E A C C E P T A N C E	No. 101 St. Louis_____ March 4, 19--
	To _Brown Store Company_____ Cleveland, Ohio ___
	On _June 2, 19--_ Pay to the order of___ Ourselves ___
	_Five hundred no/100--------------------------------Dollars, ($500.00 ____)
	The obligation of the acceptor hereof arises out of the purchase of goods from the drawer. The drawee may accept this bill payable at any bank, banker, or trust company in the United States which such drawee may designate.
	Accepted at *Cleveland* on *March 7* 19--
	Payable at *Second National* Bank Smith, McCord & Company
	Bank Location *Cleveland, Ohio*
	Buyers Signature *Brown Store Company*
	By Agent or Officer *D. C. Brown, Pres.* By *A. M. Smith, Treas.*

4. Strong of San Diego owed Lawson of Richmond, Virginia, $5,000. Bell of Richmond owed Strong $5,000. Show how by means of a draft, check, or other negotiable instrument Strong could pay Lawson the $5,000 he owes him and collect the $5,000 Bell owes him without sending any money across the country.

5. Smith borrowed $500 from Alexander and agreed to repay it in sixty days with 6 percent interest. When the sixty days were up, Smith tendered Alexander a check for the amount due. The check was payable to Smith and drawn by Lowe. Was Alexander obligated to accept this check?

Chapter 21

PROMISSORY NOTES

NATURE OF A PROMISSORY NOTE

Any written promise to pay money is a promissory note, but it may not be a negotiable instrument. To be negotiable, a note must contain the essential elements discussed in Chapter 25.

It is not necessary to use the word "promise" in a note, but the substitute word or words must literally mean "promise." Such expressions as "I will pay" and "I guarantee to pay" have been held to constitute a "promise to pay."

The two original parties to a promissory note are the maker, the one who signs the note and promises to pay, and the payee, the one to whom the promise is made. If the payee transfers the note, he becomes an indorser.

LIABILITY OF THE MAKER

The maker of a promissory note (1) expressly agrees that he will pay the note when it is due, (2) admits the existence of the payee, and (3) warrants that the payee is competent to transfer the instrument by indorsement.

- Massey made a note payable to Hess or order, and Hess indorsed the instrument to Frazier. Hess was a minor. When Massey refused to pay the note upon its due date, Frazier brought an action against him. Massey set up the defense that the minor was not competent to indorse the note to Frazier and therefore Frazier could not sue and recover on the note. The court held that Frazier could recover. Massey, by making the note payable to Hess, a minor, warranted the competency of Hess to negotiate the paper.

190

TYPES OF NEGOTIABLE NOTES

Any contract the wording of which corresponds to the definition of a note set out in the early part of this chapter is a negotiable note. Many types of notes are known by special names; thus one who deals with them must know what they are and what their special characteristics are. These classes are:

1. Bonds
2. Collateral notes
3. Real estate mortgage notes
4. Judgment notes
5. Debentures

(1) **Bonds.** A *bond* is a sealed written contract obligation, generally issued by a corporation, a municipality, or a government, which contains a promise to pay a sum certain in money at a fixed or determinable future time to order or to bearer. It will generally contain, in addition to the promise to pay, certain other conditions and stipulations. If it is issued by a corporation, it is generally secured by a deed of trust on the property of the corporation.

Bonds, which are more formal than ordinary promissory notes, may be classified as (a) registered bonds, and (b) coupon bonds.

A *registered bond* is a nonnegotiable bond payable to a named person and is recorded under his name by the organization issuing it to guard against its loss or destruction. When a registered bond is sold, a record of the transfer to the new bondholder must be made under the name of the new holder of the bond. In contrast with the registered bond, an ordinary bond may be payable to "bearer," in which case anyone in possession of the bond can require payment, and there is no registration of the name of the purchaser or any subsequent holder of the bond.

A *coupon bond* is so called because the interest payments which will become due on the bond are represented by individual coupons, which are detached as they become due and presented for payment. Coupon bonds and the individual coupons are usually payable to the bearer; as a result, they can be negotiated by delivery, and there is no registration of the original purchaser or any subsequent holder of the bond.

(2) **Collateral Notes.** A *collateral note* is a note secured by personal property. The collateral usually consists of stock, bonds, or

other written evidences of debt, or a security interest in tangible
personal property which is given by the debtor to the payee-creditor.
When the creditor is given possession of collateral, he must take
reasonable care of it and is liable to the debtor for any loss resulting
from his negligence. The transaction may vary in terms of whether
the creditor keeps possession of the property as long as the debt is
unpaid or whether, under some forms of security transactions, the
debtor is allowed to keep possession of the property until default.
Regardless of the form of the transaction, the debtor frees the property from the claim of the creditor if he pays the debt. If he does
not pay the debt, the creditor may sell the property in the manner
prescribed by law, returning to the debtor any excess of the sale
proceeds above the debt, interest, and cost, and holding the debtor
liable for any deficiency in this respect. If the creditor receives any
interest, dividend, or other income from the property which he holds
as collateral, he must credit such amount against the debt or return it
to the debtor.

(3) **Real Estate Mortgage Notes.** A *real estate mortgage note* is
given to evidence a debt which the maker-debtor secures by giving
to the payee a mortgage on real estate. As in the case of a modern
real estate mortgage generally, the mortgagor-debtor retains possession
of the property, but if he does not free the real estate by paying off
the debt, the holder may proceed on the mortgage or the mortgage
note to enforce the maker-mortgagor's liability as is more thoroughly
described in Chapter 46.

(4)ʼ **Judgment Notes.** In several states the law permits the use
of *judgment notes,* which include a confession of judgment clause.
This clause empowers the holder of the note to go into court and
obtain judgment in the event the note is in default. The maker need
not be summoned into court nor receive any notice. Except for this
confession of judgment clause, these notes are ordinary promissory
notes.

(5) **Debentures.** An unsecured bond or note issued by a business
firm is called a *debenture*. A debenture, like any other bond is nothing
more nor less than a promissory note under seal. It may be embellished
with gold-colored edges, but this adds not a penny to its value.
A debenture is usually negotiable in form, but like any other note,

it is the wording on the bond that determines whether or not it is negotiable, not its name.

CERTIFICATES OF DEPOSIT

The Uniform Commercial Code does not classify a certificate of deposit as a note. The Code defines a *certificate of deposit* as "an acknowledgment by a bank of a receipt of money with an engagement to repay it." A certificate has all the elements of a note except it does not contain the word "promise." A certificate of deposit cannot be considered a bill of exchange since it does not contain an order to pay. The Uniform Commercial Code changes the terminology slightly but not the law.

QUESTIONS

1. Must a promissory note contain the word "promise" to be enforceable?
2. Who is the payee of a note?
3. What are the obligations of the maker of a promissory note?
4. What is a bond and by whom are bonds usually issued?
5. What is the difference between a registered bond and a coupon bond?
6. How many coupons are there on a fifteen-year coupon bond if the interest is payable quarterly?
7. (a) What is a collateral note?
   (b) Of what does the collateral usually consist?
8. What is a judgment note?

CASE PROBLEMS

1. Dover borrowed $10,000 from Carlton and signed a collateral promissory note for the loan. The collateral consisted of "Bearer Coupon Bonds." Carlton's secretary filed the bonds and the note in a folder in the regular file cabinet instead of placing them in the safe. The bonds were stolen and cashed. Dover refuses to pay the note unless Carlton returns the bonds. Is he within his rights?

2. A bond salesman called on Mrs. Dale in an effort to sell her some 8 percent debenture bonds. The bonds were impressive looking with gold-colored edges and bore an impressive seal of the issuing corporation. Mr. and Mrs. Dale had $4,000 worth of government E bonds which paid only 3¾ percent. Mrs. Dale cashed them and bought the debenture bonds. Point out some factors that may make this a very unwise move.

3. Hart purchased $20,000 worth of registered bonds from Wirth. He put them in his safe deposit box and paid no more attention to them. After two years he became concerned because he had received no interest checks. Why had he not received interest checks?

4. Henderson borrowed $6,000 from Byrd. He deposited with Byrd six $1,000 coupon bonds as collateral for this loan. Before the loan was repaid, the semiannual coupons became due. Byrd detached them and deposited them in his personal bank account. When Henderson started to pay Byrd the $6,000 note, he demanded that he receive credit for the $150 in coupons. Byrd claims the coupons belonged to him. Who is correct?

5. Darter owned fifty $1,000 coupon bonds, the interest payable semi-annually. On one of the due dates of the interest coupons, Darter detached them, intending to cash them at the bank. Before he did so, they were stolen, and the thief cashed them at the Bank of Fargo. Darter sued the bank for reimbursement, claiming it should not have paid the coupons to the thief. Was Darter correct in his contention?

Chapter 22

DRAFTS

A bill of exchange is commonly called a draft. It is drawn or executed by the drawer in favor of the payee, who has the drawer's authority to collect the amount indicated on the instrument. It is addressed to the drawee, who is ordered by the drawer to pay the amount of the instrument when the amount is demanded by the payee or some other party to whom the payee has transferred the instrument by indorsement. The drawee, after he has accepted the instrument, that is, after he has agreed to pay it, becomes the acceptor.

An *inland bill of exchange* is one that shows on its face that it is both drawn and payable within the United States. If the draft shows on its face that it is drawn or payable outside of the United States, it is a *foreign draft.* All other drafts are *domestic* or *inland drafts.* In Chapter 24 the reason for making the distinction will be set forth fully.

FORMS OF DRAFTS

There are two principal classes of negotiable instruments—drafts and notes. This chapter deals with drafts. There are several forms of drafts, and employees who handle them must be able to recognize each one. The first step is to learn to recognize each of the three forms of drafts:

1. Bills of exchange
2. Trade acceptances
3. Checks (discussed separately in Chapter 23)

Sight and Time Drafts. There are two kinds of drafts to meet the different needs of business:

1. Sight drafts
2. Time drafts

Sight Drafts. A *sight draft* is a draft payable at sight or upon presentation by the payee or holder. By it the drawer demands payment at once.

$ 950.50	CLEVELAND, OHIO_____ February 11, ___19--

At sight--PAY TO THE

ORDER OF_____City National Bank, Gary, Indiana_____

Nine hundred fifty 50/100---DOLLARS

VALUE RECEIVED AND CHARGE TO ACCOUNT OF

GORDON ELECTRIC APPLIANCES

TO ___L. A. Britton_____

No.__167_____Gary, Indiana_____   BY *B. J. Carter*

Sight Draft

Time Drafts. A *time draft* has exactly the same form as a sight draft except that the drawee is ordered to pay the money a certain number of days or months after the date on the instrument or after sight rather than at sight.

The payee presents the draft to the drawee for acceptance. In the case of a time draft, the holder cannot require payment of the paper until it has matured. Whether or not the draft has been accepted does not affect the time when it matures.

If the drawee is ordered to pay the draft a specified number of days after sight, it must be presented for acceptance because the due date is calculated from the date of the acceptance, not from the date of the draft.

USE OF DRAFTS

Negotiable instruments are called instruments of credit and instruments of collection. If *A* sells *B* merchandise on sixty days' credit, the buyer may at the time of the sale execute a sixty-day negotiable note or time draft in payment of the merchandise. This note or draft then is an instrument of credit. But the time draft may also be used as a credit obligation of the drawee, in which case it is given the name of *trade acceptance.* The use of a trade acceptance is quite different from that of a negotiable note. The buyer fills out the note, signs it, and mails it to the seller. The seller fills out the trade acceptance and in most cases mails it to a bank in the buyer's hometown. The bank then presents it to the buyer for acceptance. The bank acts as agent of the seller. Both are instruments of credit.

If the seller in the transaction above is unwilling to extend the original credit at sixty days, he may draw a sight draft on the buyer, who then would be the drawee. The sight draft then is an instrument of collection. In this case, the drawer may make a bank the payee, the bank being a mere agent of the drawer. He may, however, make one of his creditors the payee so that he collects an account receivable and pays an account payable all in one transaction. If the buyer takes the initiative when the account receivable comes due, he will mail to the seller a check, which is a particular type of sight draft. The negotiable instruments law is very exacting in its demands on the drawing, the presenting, the indorsing, and the honoring of these instruments. Business firms must have an office force that clearly understands these laws to prevent serious losses. Failure to perform any one of the acts in the following paragraphs may cause a financial loss.

PRESENTMENT FOR ACCEPTANCE

All trade acceptances and all time drafts payable so many days after sight must be presented for acceptance by the payee to the drawee. In case of other kinds of drafts, presentment for acceptance is optional and is made merely to determine the intention of the drawee and to give the paper the additional credit strength of the acceptance.

(1) Place. The instrument should be presented at the drawee's place of business. If he has no place of business, it may be presented at his home or wherever he may be found.

(2) Party. It must be presented to the drawee or to someone authorized either by law or by contract to accept for him.

FORM OF ACCEPTANCE

The usual method of accepting a draft is to write on the face of it these words:

"Accepted

John Doe."

The word "accepted" and the drawee's name are all that is necessary to constitute a valid acceptance.

The drawee may use other words of acceptance, but the words used must indicate an intention to be bound by the terms of the contract and must be written on this instrument.

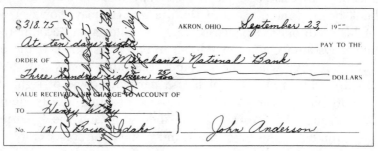

An Accepted Time Draft

If the drawee refuses to accept the draft or to accept it in a proper way, the holder of the draft has no claim against the drawee; but he can return the draft to the drawer. The payment made by the delivery of the draft is thereby canceled. If the draft is a trade acceptance, the refusal of the drawee to accept means that the buyer is refusing to go through with the financing terms of the transaction; and unless some other means of financing or payment is agreed upon, the transaction falls through.

> ▪ Arland proposed to pay Mike $500 which Arland owed him by drawing a draft in favor of Mike on Crawford. Before releasing the collateral securing the loan to Arland, Mike called Crawford on the telephone and asked if Crawford would accept the draft. Crawford said he would accept it. Mike then released the collateral to Arland. When he later presented the draft, Crawford refused to accept it. Can Mike force Crawford to pay the draft? No, since the drawee cannot accept by telephone.

PRESENTMENT FOR PAYMENT

All commercial paper must be presented to the primary party, that is the maker of the note or the acceptor of a draft, in order to get money for the paper. If, after presentment, the party to whom presentment was made fails to pay, it may be desirable to proceed against the drawer or indorsers. In such a case, the presentment must have been made subject to the rules set forth in Chapter 24.

OBLIGATION OF THE ACCEPTOR

When a draft is presented to a drawee for acceptance, he must either accept or return it. If he does not return it, he is treated as having stolen the paper from the holder. By accepting the instrument the drawee assumes the primary liability for the payment of the paper, which means that without any further demand or notice, and without going against any other party first, the debtor may proceed against him as the primary party. This liability of the primary party runs from the time that the paper is due until the statute of limitations bars the claim against him.

When the drawee accepts a draft, he makes two admissions concerning the drawer:

(1) That the signature of the drawer is genuine
(2) That the drawer has both the capacity and the authority to draw the draft

The drawee, by accepting a draft, also admits the payee's capacity to indorse, but not the genuineness of the payee's indorsement.

Having made these admissions, the acceptor cannot later deny them against a holder of the instrument.

■ O'Kelly forged Cohen's name as drawer to a draft for $3,000 payable to Jones who presented it to Smith for acceptance. Jones then transferred the draft by indorsement to Berger. Later Jones learned that Cohen's signature was forged and refused to pay the draft when it became due. He could not avoid payment because he admitted the genuineness of Cohen's signature when he accepted the draft. It was then too late to raise the defense of forgery against Berger. He could proceed, of course, against O'Kelly.

TRADE ACCEPTANCE

The *trade acceptance* is a time draft. Its use is confined to the sale of goods. It is a draft drawn by the seller on the purchaser of goods sold, and accepted by such purchaser. It is drawn at the time the goods are sold. The seller is the drawer, and the purchaser is the drawee.

ACCEPTANCE BY THE BUYER'S FINANCING AGENCY

Another financing technique employed in the sale of goods is "acceptance by the buyer's financing agency." As a variation of the pattern in which the buyer is the drawee of the trade acceptance, the buyer may arrange with his bank or finance company to accept the trade acceptance which the buyer will draw upon. When this is the case, the buyer will have worked out some loan or financing arrangements with the bank or finance company. The buyer will name the bank or finance company as drawee, and the bank or finance company will accept the draft. As in the case of any other kind of bank or finance company loan, the buyer may be required to furnish the bank or finance company with some form of security in order to induce it to make the loan and accept the instrument.

Whenever credit is extended in any transaction, it is lawful to extend credit without any particular document being executed. For example, the corner grocery store allowing its customer to run up a bill which is paid at the end of the month and the department store which puts the purchases on a monthly charge account are both extending credit without any document. In contrast with these simple transactions, the creditor may require the debtor to sign loan papers and some form of commercial paper. The execution of commercial paper has the advantage of giving written proof of the amount due and also of giving the creditor something which he can resell more readily than an open account receivable can be assigned. That is, the manufacturer can sell a trade acceptance to a bank more readily than he could sell the account receivable representing the purchase for which the trade acceptance is payment, for the reason that the holder of commercial paper is in a better legal position than the assignee of an account receivable. Moreover, greater flexibility is possible because the creditor can sell specific trade acceptances to a bank; whereas, it is difficult, if not impossible, to sell a portion of one's accounts receivable.

QUESTIONS

1. What is the difference between a domestic and a foreign draft?
2. Name three forms of drafts.

3. Name two types of drafts and indicate characteristics of each.

4. When the drawee accepts a draft, what admissions does he make concerning the drawer?

5. What is a trade acceptance?

6. Must a time draft payable thirty days after sight be presented for acceptance?

7. What should you write on a draft to indicate your acceptance?

8. Could a business concern more readily sell an account receivable or a trade acceptance to a bank?

CASE PROBLEMS

1. Scott wished to purchase $10,000 worth of merchandise from Dover on six months' credit. Dover needed the cash but did not wish to take a trade acceptance since he could not discount it at the bank without collateral, and he had no acceptable collateral. Explain in detail how Scott and Dover might complete this transaction satisfactorily.

2. Harold owed Jenkins $2,700. To pay it he drew a sixty-day time-sight (60 days after sight) draft on Henderson, one of his customers. When Jenkins received the draft, dated April 2, he filed it. On June 1, he presented the draft to Henderson for payment. Henderson refused to pay it, claiming he should merely accept it since it had never been presented for acceptance. Jenkins refused to let him accept it, and notified Harold the draft had been dishonored for nonpayment. Must Harold pay Jenkins?

3. Benson Brothers had an order from Holman of Cincinnati for $2,500. He wanted to purchase merchandise on sixty days' credit. Holman's credit was good, but he had the reputation of always denying that he received all the merchandise or claiming an error of some kind. Benson Brothers were willing to sell him the merchandise on credit but wanted to forestall any contention about the amount owed. Explain how they might accomplish this.

4. Dalton owed Harper and Son $3,200. When the account came due, he was unable to pay it. He drew a time draft on Turner for $3,200 and sent it to Harper and Son. Hand, the bookkeeper for Harper and Son, presented the draft to Turner for acceptance, and Turner wrote this on the draft: "The face of this draft is the correct amount I owe Harper and Son. A. Turner." Was this a proper acceptance?

5. Thomas J. Granger executed the following instrument:

Chicago, Ill., April 10, 19—

At sixty days sight pay to the order of Charles Hudson five hundred dollars ($500) and charge the same to the account of

To Albert W. Morris
St. Louis, Mo.   Thomas J. Granger

(a) Must this draft be presented for acceptance?

(b) To whom should it be presented?

(c) When should it be presented?

(d) If the drawee was out when it was presented and his secretary accepted it, would this be a proper acceptance?

(e) The drawee took the draft, and the next day returned it by mail with this memo stapled to it: "I will pay this draft when it comes due. A. W. Morris." Was this a valid acceptance?

(f) If the acceptance by Morris was not a valid acceptance, what may Hudson do to protect himself?

(g) When Hudson received the draft with the acceptance written on a separate paper, he notified Granger that this was unsatisfactory and demanded that Granger pay him. Granger did this. Two months later Morris paid Hudson and Hudson accepted the money but never remitted it to Granger. Must Morris pay Granger?

6. The following draft was sent to Milton V. Gray:

Denver, Colo., June 20, 19—

At sight pay to the order of Rocky Mountain National Bank for collection one thousand dollars ($1,000), and charge to the account of

To Milton V. Gray
   Billings, Mont.   R. W. Tate & Co.

(a) Who is the drawer of this draft?

(b) Who is to pay the draft?

(c) Must this draft be presented for acceptance?

7. (a) If the draft in the foregoing case read "At ten days sight," would it require presentment for acceptance? If it were accepted on June 25, when would it be due?

(b) If this draft read "Ten days after date pay . . . ," would an acceptance be necessary? If it were accepted on June 25, when would it be due?

Chapter 23

CHECKS

A *check* is a draft drawn on a bank and payable on demand. A check is basically a sight draft, the drawee being a bank instead of an individual or a business firm as is the case with a sight draft. There are, however, several differences between a check and a sight draft. A check is an order by a depositor, the *drawer,* upon his bank, the *drawee,* to pay a sum of money to the order of another person, the *payee.* A check is always drawn upon a bank as drawee and is almost always payable on demand.

CARLSON ADVERTISING, INC.	No. *78* 64-22/610
1112 Brookhaven Drive	

Atlanta, Georgia ___ *July 22* 19 --

PAY TO THE ORDER OF ___ *The Daily Mirror* ___ $ *110.53*

One hundred ten 53/100 ___ DOLLARS

Merchants Bank
ATLANTA , GEORGIA

J. L. Harvey
Treasurer, CARLSON ADVERTISING, INC.

⑆06 10⑈003 7⑈2 28 140⑈66 2⑈

Check

The numbers at the bottom of the above check are printed in magnetic ink which allows the specific account and the bank which holds the account to be identified and sorted by electronic data processing equipment. The Federal Reserve System requires that all checks passing through its clearinghouses be imprinted with such identifying magnetic ink. In most cases, however, the drawee bank will accept checks which do not carry the magnetic ink coding. In fact, the validity of a check is not affected by the material upon which it is written.

SPECIAL KINDS OF CHECKS

There are four special types of checks:

1. Certified checks
2. Cashier's checks
3. Bank drafts
4. Voucher checks

(1) **Certified Checks.** A *certified check* is an ordinary check which an official of the bank, the drawee, has accepted by writing across the face of the check the word "certified," or some similar word, and signed. Either the drawer or the holder may have a check certified. The certification of the check by the bank has the same effect as an acceptance, thereby making the bank primarily liable for the payment of the check and binding it by the warranties which are made by an acceptor.

The certification of a check may be obtained by the drawer or by any holder. If the certification is obtained by a holder, it releases the drawer from any liability on the theory that the holder has been willing to accept the obligation of the bank to pay rather than accept payment at the time, which payment, had it been made, would have discharged all other parties from all possible future liability. Having failed to free the other parties by accepting the certification in place of payment, the holder loses his right to proceed against the secondary parties.

> ■ Sherman Matney gave Garner a $10,000 check on a Grundy bank.
> Garner, not wishing to cash the check and carry the cash while traveling, had it certified. Before Garner arrived at his destination, the bank failed and its assets were insufficient to pay all its depositors. Garner received $4,000 from the bank upon liquidation and sued Matney for the remaining $6,000. Should Garner prevail? After certification, which party chose to keep the money in the bank which failed, thereby taking the risk?
> Had Matney been the one who had the check certified and mailed it to Garner, would Garner have been in a better position to recover against Matney?

(2) Cashier's Checks. A check that a bank draws on its own funds and that is signed by the cashier or some other responsible official of the bank is called a *cashier's check*. Such a check may be used by a bank in paying its own obligations, or it may be used by anyone else who wishes to remit in some form other than his own check.

(3) Bank Drafts. A *bank draft* is a check drawn by one bank on another bank. It is customary for banks to keep a portion of their funds on deposit with other banks. A bank, then, may draw a check on these funds as freely as any corporation may draw checks.

(4) Voucher Checks. A *voucher check* is one with a voucher attached. The voucher lists the items of an invoice for which the check is means of payment. It is customary, in business at least, for the drawer of the check to write on the check such words as "In full of account," "For invoice No. 1622," or similar notations. These notations make the checks excellent receipts when they are returned to the drawer. The voucher check is a check on which additional space is provided to make a notation for which the check is issued. When the payee indorses the voucher check, he agrees to the terms of the check which include the items specifically set forth in the voucher portion.

POSTDATED CHECKS

A check drawn on June 21, but dated July 1, is a *postdated check*. It is in effect a ten-day draft when so drawn. There is nothing unlawful about a postdated check, although as a practical matter the payee may refuse to accept it because he wants payment now rather than at a later date.

BAD CHECKS

If a check is drawn with intent to defraud the payee, not only is the drawer civilly liable, he is also subject to criminal prosecution in most states under so-called "bad check" laws. Usually these statutes state that if the check is not made good within a specific period, such as ten days, there is a presumption that the drawer originally issued the check with the intent to defraud.

PRESENTMENT OF A CHECK FOR PAYMENT

Generally, in the case of demand paper, presentment for payment must be made on any secondary party within a reasonable time after that party becomes liable on it. The nature of the instrument, existing commercial usage, and the particular facts of the case determine what a reasonable time is.

In the case of uncertified checks drawn and payable in the United States, 30 days after the date of the check or the date it was issued, whichever is later, is presumed as to the drawer to be a reasonable period in which to make presentment for payment. For an indorser, seven days after his indorsement is presumed to be reasonable.

LIABILITY OF THE BANK

The bank owes its customer, the depositor-drawer, the duty of maintaining secrecy regarding information acquired by the bank in connection with the depositor-bank relationship.

(1) **Refusal of Bank to Pay.** The bank is under a general contractual duty to its depositor to pay on demand all of his checks to the extent of the funds deposited to his credit. When the bank breaches this contract, it is liable to the drawer for damages. In the case of a draft, there is ordinarily no duty on the drawee to accept it or to make payment if he has not accepted it; and there is, therefore, no liability on his part to the drawer when he does not do so.

- Over a period of several months Thompson, a part-time employee of Fowler Construction Co., forged 24 checks in Fowler's name as drawer and cashed them. The construction company sued the bank for the amount of the checks. It was found that the bank was very careful to examine the signatures on the checks but the construction company also examined its monthly statements and had no reason to suspect a forgery. Therefore the bank was liable.

Even if he does not use the normal printed form supplied by the bank, the bank must pay a proper order by a depositor. Any written document which contains the substance of a normal printed check must be honored by the bank.

The liability of the drawee bank for improperly refusing to pay a check runs in favor only of the drawer. Even if the holder of the check or the payee may be harmed when the bank refuses to pay the check, he has no right to sue the bank. He may only proceed against the secondary parties on the instrument. However, he also has a right of action against the person from whom he received the check on the original obligation which was not discharged because the check was not paid.

A check which is presented more than six months after its date is commonly called a *stale check*, and a bank which acts in good faith may pay it; however, unless the check is certified, the bank is not required to pay it.

(2) **Stopping Payment.** The drawer has the power of stopping payment of a check. After the check is issued, he can notify the drawee bank not to pay it when it is presented for payment. This is a useful device when a check is lost or mislaid. A duplicate check can be written; and to make sure that the payee does not receive payment twice or that an improper person does not receive payment on the first check, payment on the first check can be stopped. Likewise, if payment is made by check and then the payee defaults on his contract so that the drawer would have a claim against him, payment on the check can be stopped, assuming that the payee has not cashed it.

A stop order may be written or oral. However, if it is oral, the bank is bound by it only for fourteen calendar days unless confirmed in writing within that time. A written order is effective for no more than six months unless renewed in writing.

Unless there is a valid limitation on the bank's liability, it is liable for the loss the depositor sustains when it makes payment on a check after receiving proper notice to stop payment. However, the depositor has the burden of proving the loss he sustained.

If the depositor stops payment without a valid reason, he is liable to the payee. He is also liable for stopping payment with respect to any holder in due course or other party having the rights of a holder in due course unless he stops payment for a reason that may be asserted against such a holder as a defense. The fact that the bank refuses to make payment because of the drawer's instruction does not make the case any different from any other instance in which the drawee refuses to pay, and the legal consequences of imposing liability upon the drawer are the same.

Usually it is only when the drawer has good cause with respect to the payee that payment is stopped. For example, the purchaser of goods may give the seller a check in advance payment for the goods.

The seller may then declare that he is not going to deliver the goods. The purchaser is within his lawful rights if he stops payment on the check since the seller has no right to the check if he does not perform his part of the sales contract. Thus the payee could not sue the drawer-purchaser for stopping payment on the check. If the check has been negotiated to a subsequent holder who is a holder in due course, the purchaser cannot assert this defense against such a holder. Accordingly, such a favored holder may hold the drawer liable on the dishonored check.

> ▪ Falk wrote out a check payable to Lytle. He later requested his bank to stop payment on it. The order was ignored and the check was paid. Falk sued the bank for the amount of the check. Falk did not recover because he was unable to show any damage as a result of the bank's payment of the check.

When the depositor makes use of a means of communication such as the telegraph to give a stop-payment notice, he cannot hold the bank liable if the notice is delayed in reaching the bank and the bank makes payment before receiving the notice. The depositor can, however, sue the telegraph company if negligence on its part can be shown.

A seller is always in a better position if he requires a certified check of the buyer or a cashier's check from the buyer's bank payable to him because neither the buyer nor the buyer's bank can stop payment to the seller on such checks.

(3) **Payment After Depositor's Death.** Usually a check is ineffective after the drawer dies. Thus, when a depositor dies, a bank usually cannot pay any checks drawn by him which it later receives. If the bank does make payment on such a check, it is liable to the depositor's estate. However, until the bank knows of the death and has had a reasonable opportunity to act, the bank's agency is not revoked; and the bank may even continue to pay or certify the depositor's checks for ten days unless a person claiming an interest in the estate orders it to stop.

QUESTIONS

1. Does the death of the drawer of a check revoke the bank's authority to pay it?

2. Is a check an assignment of the funds of the drawer to the drawee?

3. May a bank refuse to honor a check when presented for payment without giving any reason for its refusal?

4. What is a voucher check?

5. If the drawer's signature is forged to a check and the check is cashed, must the bank reimburse the depositor?

6. What is the difference between a check and a sight draft?

7. If the holder of a check has it certified, who is liable?

8. If one bank has some of its funds deposited in another bank and draws a check on these funds, what is this type of check called?

CASE PROBLEMS

1. Benton drew a check for $24,000 in favor of Aiken. The check was held by Aiken for one month before he presented it to the bank for payment. During the latter part of this month, the bank failed. The bank was insured by the Federal Deposit Insurance Corporation, and Aiken was able to collect only $20,000 on the check. May he look to Benton for the other $4,000?

2. Hartsfield owed Huff and Company $1,900. He wrote on a postcard these words:

The First National Bank
Pay to the order of Huff and Company $1,900
Cordially yours,
A. W. Hartsfield.

He put a stamp on this postcard and mailed it to Huff and Company. Since the owner of this company was on vacation, the bookkeeper held the postcard until his employer returned about four weeks later. In the meantime The First National Bank went into receivership, and the assets of the bank were sufficient to pay only $900 on the postcard. Who must bear the $1,000 loss, Hartsfield or Huff and Company?

3. Davison drew a check on June 7 payable to Lester Hardware Company. He dated the check June 12 and asked the Lester Hardware Company to hold the check until June 12 before cashing it, stating he would have the money to pay it in the bank at that time. The Lester Hardware Company deposited the check on June 8, and it was returned marked "Insufficient Funds." Davison was indicted for giving a bad check. Was he guilty?

4. Holston Tobacco Company received a check by indorsement from Davis, a customer. The check was misplaced by the auditor, and it was two weeks before it was located. The check was immediately deposited but was returned because the drawer had no money in the bank. Must Davis make this check good?

5. Donaldson had a check for $800 drawn by Harvey on the Acton Bank. Since Donaldson was leaving on an extended trip and did not care to carry $800 in cash with him, he had the check certified. The bookkeeper at the bank by error showed that Harvey's balance was $875, when in reality it was $185. Before the check was cashed, the bank auditor discovered the error and the bank refused to pay the check. Must the bank pay the full $800?

6. Dotson drew a check on the First National Bank for $375, payable to Adkins. At the time the check was drawn, Dotson had sufficient funds in the bank to cover the check.

(a) If Adkins held the check without presenting it for payment, would this delay justify Dotson's drawing the money out of the bank at the end of four months?

(b) If during the four months the bank became insolvent and a receiver was appointed, was Dotson released from liability?

Chapter 24

LIABILITIES OF THE PARTIES TO COMMERCIAL PAPER

The law of commercial paper imposes liability upon parties to negotiable instruments based upon the nature of the paper; the role of the individual as maker, acceptor, indorser, or transferor; and the satisfaction of certain requirements of conduct by the holder of the instrument. There are two basic categories of liability incidental to commercial paper: (1) the liability created by what is written on the face of the paper, and (2) the liability for certain warranties regarding the instrument which, unless such warranties are specifically excluded, the law of commercial paper automatically charges every transferor of commercial paper with making.

LIABILITY FOR THE FACE OF THE PAPER

Two types of liability exist regarding the order or promise written on the face of the instrument, primary liability and secondary liability. Parties whose signatures do not appear on the paper are not liable for its payment.

Primary Liability. A person who is primarily liable may be called upon to carry out the specific terms indicated on the paper. Of course, the paper must be due, but no other conditions need be met by the holder of commercial paper prior to the demand being made upon one who is primarily liable. Makers and drawees are the two parties who ordinarily have the potential of primary liability on commercial paper.

The maker of a note is primarily liable and may be called upon for payment. The maker has intended this by his unconditional promise to pay. Such a promise to pay contrasts sharply with the terms used by drawers of drafts who order drawees to pay. The drawer of a draft does not expect to be called upon for payment; he expects payment to be made by the drawee. However, it would be unreasonable to expect that the drawee could be made liable by a mere order of another party, the drawer. Understandably then, the drawee of a draft who has not signed the instrument originally has no liability on it. Only when a drawee accepts a draft by signing his name on it does he have any liability on the instrument at all. By acceptance the drawee says, "I promise to pay. . . ." This acceptance renders the drawee primarily liable just as the maker of a note is primarily liable.

Secondary Liability. Indorsers and drawers are the parties whose liability on commercial paper is ordinarily secondary. Generally, three conditions must be met in order for a party to be held secondarily liable:

1. The paper must be properly presented for payment.
2. The paper must be dishonored.
3. Notice of the dishonor must be given to the party who is to be held secondarily liable.

Presentment. In order for indorsers to remain secondarily liable, the instrument must be properly presented. Presentment of instruments on which there is a specified date for payment should be made on that date. Other instruments must be presented for payment within a reasonable time after a party becomes liable on the instrument. The Uniform Commercial Code specifies that in respect to the drawer of a check, a presentment within 30 days is presumed to be reasonable. As to indorsers, the Code does not give a holder the benefit of the legal presumption of reasonableness unless the presentment is made within seven days of the indorsement. The drawer of a draft other than a check, however, is only excused from his secondary liability for lack of proper presentment when the bank at which the draft was to have been presented fails subsequent to the time when presentment should have been made. The drawer, therefore, is asked to pay what would have been paid by the bank if the presentment had been timely.

- Reynolds was the holder of a note made by Agee in favor of
  Gerig. On the date the note came due, Reynolds failed to demand
  the funds from Agee. When he later requested the money, Agee
  was unable to pay. Reynolds then demanded the amount from
  Gerig who had endorsed the note to Reynolds. Gerig successfully
  defends against liability because Reynolds failed to make presentment to Agee on the due date.

  Later Agee inherits a large sum from his rich uncle. At this
  time Reynolds can again demand payment from Agee who as a
  primary party remains liable unless the statute of limitations has
  run.

When Presentment Is Not a Condition to Secondary Liability.
Proper presentment is not a condition of secondary liability on a note
when the maker has died or has been declared insolvent. In the case
of a draft, presentment is not required if it is the drawee or acceptor
who has died or gone into insolvency proceedings. Commercial paper
may contain terms specifying that the indorsers and the drawer agree
to waive their rights to the condition of presentment. Further, the
holder is excused from the requirement of presentment if, after
diligent effort, he has been unable to locate the drawee of a draft
or the maker of a note.

- Mr. and Mrs. Johnson executed a promissory note in favor of
  Smith who endorsed it to Collins. The note was delivered to
  Peterson for collection. The Johnsons had moved, leaving no
  address, so presentment for payment was not made. Notice of
  dishonor was given to Smith. Collins sued Smith for payment of
  the note. Smith is liable for payment because Peterson had exercised
  proper diligence in attempting to make presentment by going to
  the Johnsons' last known address and questioning neighbors as to
  the Johnsons' current address.

Finally, if the secondary party knows that the draft or note will
not be paid or has no reason to believe that the paper will be honored,
then presentment is excused.

Dishonor. The Uniform Commercial Code states that dishonor
occurs when a presentment is made and a due acceptance or payment
is refused or cannot be obtained within the prescribed time.

Notice of Dishonor. A holder desiring to press secondary liability
upon an indorser or drawer must inform that party of the dishonor.

Notice of dishonor must be conveyed promptly to parties who are secondarily liable. The Uniform Commercial Code provides that such notice shall be given by midnight of the third business day following the dishonor or receipt of notice of dishonor. This time limit applies to all holders except banks. The Code requires that banks give notice of dishonor to those they wish to hold liable by midnight of the next banking day following the day in which it receives notice of dishonor. In order to avoid unduly burdening holders, the Code provides that notice may be given by mail and that proof of mailing conclusively satisfies the requirement that notice be given.

Generally, notice of dishonor does not need to be in any special form. However, if the dishonored instrument is drawn or payable outside the United States of America, notice of dishonor must be certified by a public official authorized to do so. This requirement is known as *protest*.

Delay or failure to give notice of dishonor is excused in most cases where timely presentment would not have been required. Basically, this is when notice has been waived, when notice was attempted with due diligence but unsuccessful; or if the party to be notified had no reason to believe the instrument would be honored.

When the conditions of secondary liability, presentment, dishonor, and notice of dishonor have been met, a holder may require payment by any of the previous unqualified indorsers or by the drawer.

Qualified Indorsement. Obviously, indorsing an instrument puts a person in a position of potential liability. If a party is merely collecting payments for someone else, he may not wish to be liable on the instrument. In such a case an individual may make a qualified indorsement by specifying clearly that his indorsement is "without recourse." For example, writing "without recourse, John Doe" as an indorsement makes John Doe a qualified indorser. By doing this the individual escapes all liability on the instrument. It should be noted that unless a party is merely an agent and handling the instrument for someone else's convenience, few transferees would accept a document which is indorsed without recourse.

> ▪ Perkin, the attorney for Bruce, collected a debt owed Bruce. The check Perkin received was made out to him, so he indorsed it "without recourse, Perkin," and gave it to Bruce. Since Perkin was merely collecting the debt for Bruce, Bruce would not object to the "without recourse" indorsement and Perkin would not be liable on the check.

Liability of Agent. A negotiable instrument may be signed by an agent, and the principal will be bound if certain conditions are met. If the agent, authorized by his principal, signs the instrument, "John Smith, Principal, by James Doe, Agent," or more simply "John Smith by James Doe", the principal will be bound, but the agent will not be bound by the terms of the instrument.

There are three general types of situations in which the agent could carelessly sign the instrument. The result would be that the agent would be bound while the principal might not be bound.

(1) The agent could sign the instrument in such a way that the instrument did not name the principal, nor indicate that it was signed by an agent. For example, if the agent just signed, "James Doe," the principal would not be bound since his signature does not appear on the instrument. The agent would be bound since there was nothing to indicate that he did not sign in his own capacity.

(2) The agent could sign the instrument in such a way that the principal was named, but it was not shown that the agent was acting merely as an agent. If the agent signed, "John Smith and James Doe," the agent and the principal would both be bound. The agent would be bound because he did not indicate that he was an agent, and the other party to the instrument might have relied on the signature of the agent as an individual.

(3) The agent could sign the instrument in such a way that the principal was not named, but it would be clear that the agent signed as an agent and not for himself alone. Such a case would occur if the agent signed, "James Doe, Agent." In this situation, only the agent would be bound by the instrument since it would not be evident from the face of the instrument who the principal might be. However, in these last two examples, if the parties to the instrument knew that John Smith was the principal and James Doe was merely an agent, then only the principal would be bound to them.

In the case of a corporation or other organization, the authorized agent should sign his name below the corporation or organization's name and indicate what his office is after his signature. For example, Edward Rush, the president of Acme Industries should sign:

ACME INDUSTRIES
By Edward Rush, President.

If the instrument were signed this way, Acme Industries and not Edward Rush would be bound on it.

If an individual signs an instrument as an agent, "John Smith, Principal, by James Doe, Agent," but the agent is not authorized to sign for the principal, the principal would not be bound. It would be as if the agent, James Doe, had forged John Smith's signature. However, the agent who made the unauthorized signature would be bound. This result protects innocent parties to the instrument who would not be able to enforce their rights against anyone if the unauthorized agent was not bound.

Guarantors. Just as a party may diminish his liability by indorsing "without recourse," an individual may escalate his liability as an indorser to that of primary status by indorsing an instrument "Payment guaranteed." If the transferor indorses the instrument with the words "Collection guaranteed," he preserves his secondary liability. However, the contingencies which must be met by the holder in order to hold this guarantor liable are changed from presentment, dishonor, and notice of dishonor to obtaining a judgment against the maker or acceptor which cannot be satisfied by him.

> ▪ Williams executed a promissory note to the Merchants Bank and Gordon signed the note as a guarantor. Williams failed to make payment when the note was due, so Gordon paid it. Gordon then sued Williams for reimbursement of the amount he had paid. The court found that signing as a guarantor did not make Gordon primarily liable; therefore, when he paid the note he was not paying off his obligation but that of Williams. By paying the note Gordon succeeded to the bank's rights and could sue Williams on the note.

People usually act as guarantors in order to increase the security of commercial paper. Frequently, if someone else who is liable has a poor credit rating, he would not be able to negotiate the instrument without having an additional party sign as a guarantor of the instrument.

WARRANTIES OF THE TRANSFEROR OF COMMERCIAL PAPER

Every transferor of commercial paper warrants the existence of certain facts. It is significant to note that one's signature or even one's name does not have to appear on the instrument in order to be liable as a warrantor, for example, when a person negotiates bearer paper by delivery alone.

The Uniform Commercial Code specifies that each unqualified transferor warrants that:

1. He has good title to the instrument, authorization to obtain acceptance or payment on behalf of the rightful owner, and that the transfer is otherwise rightful
2. All signatures are genuine or authorized
3. The instrument has not been materially altered
4. No defense of any party is good against him
5. He has no knowledge of any insolvency proceedings instituted with respect to the maker or acceptor or the drawee of an unaccepted instrument

Qualified Transferors. Parties who transfer the paper bearing the notation "without recourse" in conjunction with their signature make all of the warranties above except item 4. Instead of warranting that no defense of any party is good against him, a qualified transferor of the instrument warrants that he has no knowledge of any defense against himself relating to the instrument.

> ▪ Kenner accepted a note from Simpson in payment of a debt even though he knew Simpson was insolvent. Kenner immediately indorsed it to Lincoln, "without recourse." When the note was not paid Lincoln sued Kenner who defended on the ground he was not liable because he had indorsed "without recourse." The court found for Lincoln since indorsing "without recourse" includes the warranty that the indorser has no knowledge of insolvency of the maker.

Selling agents or brokers who fail to disclose their agency make all of the warranties of an unqualified transferor unless the principal is fully disclosed. Full disclosure of the agency relationship makes the agent-transferor the warrantor of only his good faith and authority.

QUESTIONS

1. What is the difference between primary and secondary liability?
2. What two parties to commercial paper might be primarily liable?
3. What conditions must be met in order for a party to be held secondarily liable?
4. Under what circumstances is it unnecessary to make presentment?
5. What is *protest?*

6. What is a *qualified indorsement?*
7. What words should one use as an indorsement in order to make a qualified indorsement?
8. If someone signs a commercial paper as guarantor, what is the effect of this act
   (a) if he uses the words "Payment guaranteed"?
   (b) if he uses the words "Collection guaranteed"?
9. When does a dishonor occur?
10. To whom must notice of dishonor be given.

CASE PROBLEMS

1. Heitz held a note which was signed by Wyrick and indorsed by Prier. When the note came due Heitz immediately took the note to Prier and demanded payment. Must Prier pay?

2. Ashby, who was the agent of Bridges, signed a note "Bridges by Ashby, agent." When the note came due, Bridges was unable to pay. Is Ashby liable on the note?

3. Kelly, an attorney, accepted a check made to him as payee from Baker whom Kelly had sued in behalf of Winslow. Since Winslow was the party to whom the funds were to go, Kelly indorsed the check to Winslow, without recourse. When Baker fails to make the check good, can Winslow require Kelly to make it good?

4. Fritz wanted to buy some new furniture, but did not have an established credit rating. He and his uncle, Schmidt, decided that Fritz would execute a note for the price of the furniture in favor of Schmidt, who would then indorse it "collection guaranteed" to the furniture company. Fritz fails to pay the note. What must the furniture company do in order to make Schmidt pay the note?

Chapter 25

ESSENTIALS OF
NEGOTIABILITY

There are seven definite requirements as to form with which an instrument must comply in order to be negotiable. If any one of these requirements is lacking, the instrument is not negotiable even though it may be valid and enforceable as between the original parties to the instrument. These seven requirements are:

1. The instrument must be in writing and signed by the party executing it.

2. The instrument must contain either an order to pay or a promise to pay.

3. The order or the promise must be unconditional.

4. The instrument must provide for the payment of a sum certain in money.

5. The instrument must be payable either on demand or at a fixed or definite time.

6. The instrument must be payable to the order of a payee or bearer.

7. The payee (unless the instrument is payable to bearer) and the drawee must be designated with reasonable certainty.

(1) **A Signed Writing.** A negotiable instrument must be written. The law does not, however, require that the writing be in any particular form. The instrument may be written with pen and ink or with pencil; it may be typed or printed; or it may be partly printed and partly typed. If an instrument is executed with a lead pencil, it

meets the legal requirements of negotiability; but a person might hesitate to accept it because of the ease with which it could be altered without detection.

A signature must be placed on a negotiable instrument in order to indicate the intent of the promisor to be bound. The normal place for a signature is in the lower right-hand corner, but the location of the signature and its form are wholly immaterial if it is clear that a signature was intended. The signature may be written, typed, printed, or stamped. It may be a name, a symbol, a mark, or a trade name. The signature, however, must be on the instrument. It cannot be on a separate paper which is attached to the instrument.

The signature may be signed by another person who has been given authority to perform this act. When an agent signs for his principal or when an officer signs for his corporation, care must be taken to avoid making himself solely liable or jointly liable with his principal or corporation.

Below are some odd but valid signatures:

         His
(a) Richard ✕ Cooper
        Mark

(b) "I, Thomas Morley," written by Morley in the body of the note but signed on the typewriter in the usual place for the signature.

(c) "Snowwhite Cleaner," the trade name under which Glendon Sutton operates his business.

(2) **An Order or a Promise to Pay.** A draft, such as a bill of exchange, a trade acceptance, or a check, must contain an order to pay. If the request is imperative and unequivocal, it is an order even though the word "order" is not used.

A promissory note must contain a promise to pay. The word "promise" need not be used—any equivalent words will answer the purpose—but the language used must show that a promise is intended. Thus the words "This is to certify that we are bound to pay" were held to be sufficient to constitute a promise.

(3) **Unconditional.** The order or the promise must be absolute and unconditional. Neither must be contingent upon any other act or event. If Baron promises to pay Noffke $500 "in sixty days, or sooner if I sell my farm," the contract is negotiable because the

promise itself is unconditional. In any event he promises to pay the $500 in sixty days. The contingency pertains only to the time of payment, and that time cannot exceed sixty days. If the words "or sooner" were omitted, the promise would be conditional, and the note would be nonnegotiable. It is well to emphasize here again, however, that an instrument may be valid even though nonnegotiable.

If the order to pay is out of a particular fund or account, the instrument is nonnegotiable. For example, "Pay to the order of Leonard Cohen $5,000 out of my share of my father's estate" would be a conditional order to pay. The order or the promise must commit the entire credit of the one primarily liable for the payment of the instrument.

A reference to the consideration in a note that does not condition the promise does not destroy negotiability. The clause "This note is given in consideration of a typewriter purchased today" does not condition the maker's promise to pay. If the clause read, "This note is given in consideration for a typewriter guaranteed for ninety days, breach of warranty to constitute cancellation of the note," the instrument would not be negotiable. This promise to pay is not absolute, but conditional. Also, if the recital of the consideration is in such form as to make the instrument a part of another contract, the negotiability of the contract is destroyed.

> ▪ Mott inserted this statement in a note: "This note is a part of an agreement dated January 19, 1921." The court held that tying up the contract, which constituted the consideration for the note, with the note so that it all constituted one contract destroyed the negotiability of the note.

(4) A Sum Certain in Money. The instrument must call for the payment of money and money alone. It need not be American money, but it must be some national medium of exchange. It cannot be in scrip, gold bullion, bonds, or similar assets. Frequently, the instrument provides for the payment of either money or goods. If the choice lies with the holder, such a provision does not destroy its negotiability.

> ▪ Sixty days after date I promise to pay to the order of Ira Rasmussen $500 or 250 bushels of wheat at his option.
>
> Signed—*Frank Birchmore*

This note is negotiable because it is at the option of the payee, Rasmussen, or any subsequent holder of the instrument. If the words "his option" were changed to read, "my option," the note would not be negotiable.

The sum payable must be a certain amount that is not dependent upon other funds or upon future profits.

■ In consideration for recommending Varney for a certain construction job, Fulton received the following instrument: ". . . we hereby agree to pay you the sum of $1,059 ninety days from date; the amount to be paid out of our profits on the 3 East 40th Street job." The statement on the note that the money was to be paid out of a particular fund destroyed its negotiability.

Not only must the contract be payable in money to be negotiable, but the amount must be certain from the wording of the instrument itself. If a note for $5,000 provides that all taxes which may be levied upon a certain piece of real estate will be paid, it is nonnegotiable. The amount to be paid cannot be determined from the note itself. A provision providing for the payment of interest or exchange charges, however, does not destroy negotiability. Other terms which have been held not to destroy negotiability are provisions for cost of collection, a 10 percent attorney's fee if placed in the hands of an attorney for collection, and installment payments.

Frequently, through error of the party writing the negotiable instrument, the words on the instrument may call for the payment of one amount of money, while the figures call for the payment of another. The amount expressed in words prevails because one is less likely to err in writing this amount. Also, if anyone should attempt to raise the amount, it would be much simpler to alter the figures than it would be the words. By the same token, handwriting prevails over conflicting typewriting, and typewriting prevails over conflicting printing.

(5) **Payable on Demand or at a Definite Time.** An instrument meets the test of negotiability as to time if it is payable on demand (as in a demand note) or at sight (as in a sight draft) or when no time is specified (as in a check).

If the instrument provides for payment at some future time, the due date must be fixed.

■ Vaughn gave Marx an instrument containing the following provision: "I promise to pay Marx the sum of $450 when my son reaches the age of twenty-one." Such a condition rendered the instrument nonnegotiable because the time of payment was dependent upon a condition that might not happen. In other words, Vaughn's son might never reach the age of twenty-one.

- If Riggs promises to pay Burton $500 "sixty days after my marriage," the instrument is not payable at a fixed future time because the event is not certain to occur.

If an instrument is payable "30 days after my death," it is not negotiable even though the date is certain to arrive because the time is not definite.

In promissory notes there is often included either an acceleration clause or a prepayment clause. An acceleration clause is for the protection of the payee, and the prepayment clause is for the benefit of the party obligated to pay. A note or a draft is usually not a gift though we often incorrectly speak of "giving" a person a note. The instrument is usually executed and delivered in settlement of some contract that has just been consummated, such as an installment sale. A typical accelerating clause provides that in the event one installment is in default, the whole note shall become due and payable at once. This does not destroy its negotiability.

Most prepayment clauses give the maker or the drawee the right to prepay the instrument in order to save interest. This does not affect the negotiability of the instrument.

(6) **Payable to Order or Bearer.** The two most common words of negotiability are "order" and "bearer." The instrument is *payable to order* when some person is made the payee and the maker or drawer wishes to indicate that the instrument will be paid to the person designated or to anyone else to whom he may transfer the instrument by indorsement.

It is not necessary to use the word "order," but it is strongly recommended. A note payable to "Smith and assigns" was held to be nonnegotiable. If it had been payable to "Smith or assigns," it would have been negotiable. Also "Pay to the order of the holder" would be negotiable, but some people might hesitate to accept a check or other draft containing such wording. The law looks to the intention of the maker or the drawer. If the words used clearly show an intention to pay either the named payee or anyone else whom he designates, the contract is negotiable.

The other words of negotiability, *payable to bearer,* indicate that the maker or the acceptor of a draft is willing to pay the person who has possession of the instrument at maturity. The usual form in which these words appear is thus: "Pay to bearer" or "Pay to Lydia Lester or bearer." There are other types of wording that render a contract a bearer instrument. For example, "pay to the order of cash," and "pay to the order of bearer," or any other designation which does not refer to a natural person or a corporation is regarded as payable to bearer.

(7) **Payee and Drawee Designated with Reasonable Certainty.** When a negotiable instrument is payable "to order," the payee must be so named that the specific party can be identified with reasonable certainty. For example, a check which reads, "Pay to the order of the Treasurer of the Virginia Education Association" is not payable to a specific party, but that party can be ascertained with reasonable certainty; and the check is negotiable. If, on the other hand, the check is payable "to the order of the Treasurer of the Y.M.C.A." and there are three such organizations in the city, it would not be possible to ascertain with reasonable certainty who the payee is; and the check would not be negotiable.

The drawee of a draft must likewise be named or described with reasonable certainty so that the holder will know to whom he must go for an acceptance or payment.

EXECUTION AND DELIVERY

When a negotiable instrument is written by the drawer or maker, it does not have any effect until it is "issued" by him, which ordinarily means that he mails it or hands it over to the payee or does some other act which puts it out of his control and sends it on its way to the payee. When negotiation is made of order paper, there must be both an indorsement by the person to whom the paper is then payable and a delivery by him to the new holder. In the case of bearer paper no indorsement is required, and negotiation is effected by a physical transfer of the instrument alone.

Whenever delivery is made either in connection with the original issue or a subsequent negotiation, the delivery must be absolute, as contrasted with conditional. If it is conditional, the issuing of the instrument or the negotiation does not take effect until the condition is satisfied; although, as against a holder in due course, a defendant will be barred from showing that the condition was not satisfied.

DELIVERY OF AN INCOMPLETE INSTRUMENT

If a negotiable instrument is only partially filled out and signed before delivery, the maker or drawer is liable if the blanks are filled in according to instructions. If the holder fills in the blanks contrary to the authority given him, the maker or drawer is liable to the original payee or an ordinary holder for only the amount actually authorized. A holder in due course, however, can enforce the paper according to the actual terms filled in even though they were not authorized.

DATE AND PLACE

Various matters which are not of commercial significance do not affect the negotiable character of a negotiable instrument.

The instrument need not be dated. The negotiability of the instrument is not affected "by the fact it is undated, antedated, or postdated." The omission of a date may cause considerable inconvenience, but the date is not essential. The holder may fill in the correct date if the space for the date is left blank. If an instrument is due thirty days after date, and the date is omitted, the instrument is payable thirty days after it was issued or delivered. In case of dispute the date of issue may be proved.

The name of the place where the instrument was drawn or where it is payable need not be specified. For contracts in general, one's rights are governed by the law where the contract is made or where it is to be performed. This rule makes it advisable for a negotiable instrument to stipulate the place where it is drawn and where it is payable, but neither is essential for its negotiability.

QUESTIONS

1. If a negotiable contract is signed in pencil, is it negotiable?
2. Must the signature of the maker on a negotiable contract be in the lower right-hand corner?
3. Does an acceleration clause in a note destroy its negotiability?
4. If a check is signed but not filled out and is then stolen and completed, is the drawer liable on it?
5. Must a check be dated in order to be negotiable?
6. When must a negotiable instrument be payable?
7. Explain the difference between "payable to order" and "payable to bearer."
8. Why is it important to designate the payee and drawee with reasonable certainty?
9. Is negotiability of an instrument affected if the name of the place where the instrument was drawn is not specified?

CASE PROBLEMS

1. Claude Holmes signed a note that contained this clause: "This note is to be paid from the proceeds of the sale of my home." At the time the note was signed, Holmes had a contract to sell his home. Madison, the payee of the note, negotiated it for value before it was due to the Garret Auto Mart in payment of a car. Holmes never paid the note; the Garret Auto Mart sued Madison, the indorser. Is he liable?

2. An accepted time draft read as follows: "Sixty days after the presidential election, pay Adam Horton $2,700." This draft was negotiated soon after its acceptance to the Cates Land Company as a partial payment for some timberland. When the draft came due, the drawee was bankrupt, and the Cates Land Company sought to make the drawer pay the $2,700. Can it do so?

3. The sales manager of the Snead Motors, Inc., sold Henry Amos a new car for $3,800. Amos tendered in payment a check on which he was the payee. The check was not dated. The sales manager interpreted this to mean it was nonnegotiable. Amos contended it was negotiable. As a result Amos became angry and refused to buy the car. Who was right?

4. The Harbin Hosiery Mills, Inc., was a family-owned corporation. The president, James Harbin, borrowed $50,000 from the bank on a six-months note. He signed the note:

James Harbin, Owner
Harbin Hosiery Mills, Inc.

His intention was to commit the credit of the corporation for the loan, but not his personal estate. The corporation went into bankruptcy, and the note was unpaid. The bank sued, contending that James Harbin was personally liable on this note. Is he personally liable?

5. Is the following note negotiable?

Sixty days after Easter I obligate myself to pay Globe, Inc., or bearer, the sum of $5,000 out of the proceeds of the sale of my GMC stock.

Glen Tinsdale

---

6. (a) Is the following draft negotiable?

To Lennox, Inc.

At sixty days sight pay upon demand to John Ray $1,000 in gold bullion.

Henry Adams

(b) John Ray took this draft in payment of an account owed to him by Henry Adams. Lennox, Inc., accepted the draft on November 20, but never paid it. Ray now wishes to hold Adams liable. Can he do so?

7. Is the following instrument negotiable?

Sixty days after my death I bind my heirs to pay to the Treasurer of the Y.M.C.A., or to anyone else whom he may designate, the sum of $5,000 with interest from the date of my death.

Signed: Albert Sloan

---

8. Stanley was manager for the Anawalt Furniture Company. A customer selected furniture amounting to $700 and tendered in payment a check payable to the customer and drawn by A. W. Green. The check was for $750 in figures, but in words it stated: "Seven Hundred and No/100 dollars." The customer offered to indorse it and accept $700 as the correct figure. Stanley interpreted this discrepancy to mean the instrument was not complete and regular on its face and therefore it was not negotiable. He refused to accept it and lost the sale. Was Stanley correct in his interpretation?

Chapter 26

NEGOTIATION AND DISCHARGE

NEGOTIATION DEFINED

Negotiation is the transferring of a negotiable instrument in such a way as to constitute the transferee the holder of the instrument. Bearer instruments may be negotiated by delivery without any indorsement. This effectively invests ownership in the holder. In practice an indorsement is usually required even for bearer paper because this adds the liability of the new indorser to the paper and thus makes it a better credit risk. It also preserves a written chronological record of all negotiations. If the instrument is payable to "order," there can be a negotiation only by indorsement and delivery. By indorsing or transferring a negotiable instrument, certain liabilities are created depending upon the nature of the indorsement or transfer.

PLACE OF INDORSEMENT

The usual place to indorse a negotiable instrument is on the back of the form. If the indorser's signature appears elsewhere and it cannot be determined in what capacity he signed, he will be considered an indorser. In any event, the indorsement must be physically attached to the instrument. If one does not wish to assume the liabilities of an indorser even though the instrument is negotiable, he can assign it by writing out the assignment on a separate piece of paper.

Occasionally, the name of the payee or indorsee of an instrument is misspelled. If a paycheck intended for, and delivered to, John F. Smith is made out to "John K. Smith" through clerical error, John F. Smith may either ask his employer for a new check properly made out to him or he may keep the check and indorse in any of the following ways:

1. "John K. Smith"
2. "John F. Smith"
3. "John K. Smith, John F. Smith"

If he intends to receive value for the check, the person to whom it is negotiated may require him to sign both names.

However, if a check made payable to, and intended for, John K. Smith is obtained by John F. Smith, it would be illegal for the latter to indorse it and receive payment for it. Only when the check is actually intended for John F. Smith may he make a corrective indorsement.

It is not always necessary to correct an irregularity in the name of a party to an instrument, and this does not destroy its negotiability. Only if it is shown that different people were actually identified by the different names, as opposed to the different names standing for one person, must the irregularity be considered. It has been held that a note was correctly negotiated when indorsed "Greenlaw & Sons by George M. Greenlaw," although it was payable to "Greenlaw & Sons Roofing & Siding Co." There was nothing to indicate that the two enterprises were not the same firm.

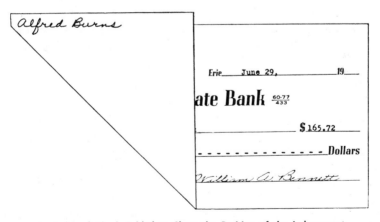

An Indorsed Check Folded to Show the Position of the Indorsement

KINDS OF INDORSEMENTS

There are five types of indorsements:

1. Blank indorsement
2. Special indorsement

3. Qualified indorsement
4. Restrictive indorsement
5. Conditional indorsement

(1) **Blank Indorsement.** As the name indicates, a *blank indorsement* is one having no words other than the name of the indorser. If the instrument is bearer paper, this type of indorsement preserves this status so that the new holder may pass good title to another holder without indorsing it. The one primarily liable on the instrument is bound to pay the person who presents it to him for payment on the date due. This may be a thief or other unauthorized party.

If the instrument is order paper, a blank indorsement converts it to bearer paper; but if it is thereafter indorsed specially, it becomes order paper. Risks involved in handling instruments originally payable to bearer or indorsed in blank can be minimized as shown in the following paragraph and in the section on special indorsements.

If the office force of a business firm is aware of these risks relative to bearer paper and paper indorsed in blank, the firm may be spared these risks in the following ways: (1) The drawer, if it is convenient, can be requested to make the instrument order paper from its inception; (2) If the firm becomes the indorsee by a blank indorsement, this indorsement may be converted to a special indorsement by writing over the

Indorsement in Blank

indorser's signature these words: "Pay to the order of Mays, Inc." This in no way alters the contract between the indorser and the indorsee. The instrument cannot now be negotiated except by indorsement and delivery.

(2) **Special Indorsement.** A *special indorsement* designates the particular person to whom payment is to be made. After such an indorsement is made, the paper is order paper, whether or not it was originally so payable or was originally payable to bearer. The holder must indorse it before he can further negotiate it. He may, of course, indorse the instrument in blank, which makes it bearer paper. Each holder has the power to decide to make either a blank or a special indorsement.

Special Indorsement

(3) Qualified Indorsement. A *qualified indorsement* has the effect of qualifying, that is, limiting the liability of the indorser. For example, if an agent receives checks in payment of his principal's claims which are made payable to the agent personally, the agent should and can elect to use a qualified indorsement. This is done merely by adding to either a blank or special type of indorsement the words "without recourse" immediately before the signature. This releases the indorser from liability for payment if the instrument is not paid because of insolvency or mere refusal to pay. The indorser still warrants that the instrument is genuine, that he has good title to it, that all prior parties had capacity to contract, and that the instrument to his knowledge is valid as was mentioned in Chapter 24. If the agent wishes to avoid these liabilities, he may do so by indorsing the instrument "without recourse or warranties."

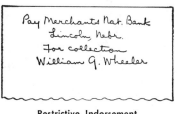

Pay to Rodman Harris
without recourse
David J. Hill

Qualified Indorsement

▪ Henderson was a special agent for the Cates Realty Company. One of his duties was to collect the rent from the occupants of rental properties handled by the Cates Realty Company. One of these tenants made a check for the rent payable to "John Henderson." When Henderson turned in his receipts at the end of the day, the accounting department asked him to indorse the check by special indorsement to the Cates Realty Company. This he did. The check was returned as the drawer had no funds in the bank to pay it. The Cates Realty Company demanded that Henderson make good on his special indorsement. This he must do. He should have indorsed this by a qualified indorsement.

(4) Restrictive Indorsement. A restrictive indorsement is just what its name implies. It is an indorsement which states that the indorsee holds the paper for a special purpose or as an agent or trustee for another. Such an indorsement does not affect the negotiability of the instrument or the ability to negotiate it further. As against a holder in due course, it is immaterial whether the restrictions have in fact been recognized by the indorsee.

Pay Merchants Nat. Bank
Lincoln, Nebr.
For collection
William G. Wheeler

Restrictive Indorsement

(5) Conditional Indorsement. The indorser by *conditional indorsement* may wish to impose a condition precedent to the payment.

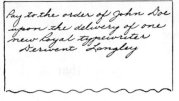

Pay to the order of John Doe upon the delivery of one new Royal typewriter Derwent Langley

Conditional Indorsement

In this event the indorsee may not receive full payment until the condition is met. The condition is binding upon the party to such indorsement. It may be ignored by other persons, and the failure to satisfy the condition is not a defense available to the indorser when the holder is a holder in due course.

LIABILITY OF INDORSER

(1) **Liability for Payment of Instrument.** By the fact of making his indorsement, an indorser, with the exception of a qualified indorser, agrees to pay any subsequent holder the face amount of the instrument. To obtain the benefit of this liability it is necessary that the holder present the instrument to the primary party when it is due and, if the primary party refuses to pay, give the indorser in question notice of such default. This notice may be given orally or by any other means but must be given before midnight of the third full business day after the day on which the default occurs.

(2) **Warranties of the Indorser.** Warranties of the indorser differ from liability for the face of the paper in that they are not subject to the requirements of presentment and notice. The distinction is also important for purposes of limiting liability; for an indorsement "without recourse" only destroys the liability of the indorser for the face of the instrument but does not affect warranties. An indorsement "without warranties" or a combined "without recourse or warranties" is required to exclude warranty liability. Some of these warranties include the following:

(a) *The indorser warrants that the instrument, whether a check, note, or draft, is genuine and in all respects what it purports to be.* If it purports to be a check for $500 drawn by Smith on the Bonner State Bank and payable to Danner, the indorser warrants that there has been no forgery, alteration, or other irregularity in the check. He warrants that it is exactly what it appears to be. If it is not as it is warranted to be, he can be sued by the holder for breach of warranty.

(b) *The indorser warrants that he has good title to the instrument.* This warranty is to provide the new holder with assurance that the person indorsing it to him did not steal the instrument, or find it, or come into possession of the instrument in any unlawful manner.

(c) The indorser warrants that all prior parties had capacity to contract. If a minor, an insane person, or other incompetent person draws a check, executes a note, or indorses any negotiable contract, he is no more liable for his act than he is on any other type of contract. He may plead his incapacity to contract as an absolute defense to the instrument. The indorser by this warranty assures the holder that all parties whose names appear on the instrument were competent to contract. If the maker of a note should avoid liability on the ground of drunkenness at the time he signed the note, for example, the indorser would have to reimburse the holder.

(d) The indorser warrants that at the time he indorses the instrument, it is a valid and binding contract. Many contracts prove defective and void. Sunday contracts, illegal contracts, contracts entered into by a mistake as to the existence of the subject matter of the contract, and many others are void. A negotiable instrument given in payment of a gambling debt is no more binding on the primary party than any other type of contract for a similar payment. Also, a negotiable instrument might be valid at the time it is accepted but subsequently become invalid. This warranty protects the holder against any of these infirmities in the contract.

OBLIGATION OF NEGOTIATOR OF BEARER PAPER

Bearer paper need not be indorsed when negotiated. Mere delivery passes title. One who negotiates a bearer instrument by delivery alone does not guarantee payment, but he is liable to his immediate purchaser only as a warrantor of the genuineness of the instrument, of his title to it, of the capacity of prior parties, and of its validity. These warranties are the same as those made by an unqualified indorser, except that the warranties of the unqualified indorser extend to all subsequent holders, not just to the immediate purchaser. But since negotiable instruments are not legal tender, no one is under any obligation to accept bearer paper without an indorsement. By requiring an indorsement even though not necessary to pass title, the holder protects himself by requiring the one who wishes to negotiate it to assume all the obligations of an indorser by indorsement.

■ Sands was the maker of a bearer negotiable note which he delivered to Holt. Subsequently, Burks became the holder with the note showing these indorsements:

Dorsey Harber
Wayne Finley

Holt had passed title to the note by mere delivery to Weston Dupree, and Dupree had delivered to Harber without indorsement. The maker was insolvent and unable to pay the note when it fell due. Burks can look only to Finley for payment and Finley can look to Harber. Harber, on the other hand, had received it from Dupree without indorsement, so he can look only to the maker.

DISCHARGE OF THE OBLIGATION

Negotiable instruments may be discharged by payment, by cancellation, or by alteration. Payment at or after the date of the maturity of the instrument by the party who is primarily liable constitutes proper payment. Cancellation consists of any act that indicates the intention to cancel the instrument. A cancellation is not effective, however, when it is made unintentionally or by mistake. A party to a negotiable instrument is discharged from liability if the instrument is materially altered without his consent. If such an instrument gets into the hands of a holder in due course, however, the holder in due course may collect according to the original terms of the instrument, and not according to its altered terms.

■ Hale drew a check payable to Shane in the amount of $500. Shane cleverly altered the check to $2,500 and negotiated it to McFain, an innocent purchaser who had no knowledge of the alteration. The bank refused to pay the check. McFain can recover $500 from Hale since this was the original amount of the check. He could then sue Shane for the $2,000.

The obligations of the parties may be discharged in other ways, just as in the case of a simple contract. For example, a party will be discharged from liability if he has been judicially declared bankrupt or if there has been the necessary lapse of time provided by a statute of limitations.

Frequently a negotiable instrument is lost or accidentally destroyed. This does not discharge the obligation. The party obligated to pay it has a right to demand the instrument's return if this is possible. If this cannot be done, then he has a right to demand security from the holder adequate to protect the payer from having to pay the instrument a second time. The security usually takes the form of an indemnity bond.

QUESTIONS

1. What is *negotiation*?
2. How may bearer instruments be negotiated?
3. Where should one indorse a negotiable instrument?
4. Name five kinds of indorsements and give an example of the proper use of each one.
5. Why is it usually undesirable to indorse a check in blank?
6. If an instrument that is payable to "bearer" is indorsed by special indorsement, what must the second holder do in order to pass title to it?
7. If a check is made payable to John Atkins, agent for the Branch Insurance Agency, when it should have been made payable to the agency, how should John indorse it when he delivers it to the agency? Why?
8. Give an illustration of the proper use of a qualified indorsement.
9. If one loses a negotiable instrument, is there any way he can collect it?
10. If bearer paper is indorsed by special indorsement, may the indorsee pass good title to it by delivery alone?

CASE PROBLEMS

1. Darrow was a collector for the Beusse Loan and Investment Company. One borrower paid his note of $502.84 by check made payable to Darrow. At the end of the day Darrow turned in his collections, and the bookkeeper discovered the check had been erroneously made payable to Darrow. He suggested that Darrow indorse it by special indorsement, and this Darrow did. The check proved to be a bad check, and Darrow was required to make the check good. What knowledge of law set out in this chapter would have helped Darrow avoid this loss?

2. Wood was the payee of a time draft for $3,200. He mailed the draft to James Hill for collection. Wood indorsed the draft as follows: "Pay to the order of James Hill only." Hill collected the draft and placed the $3,200 in his personal checking account and mailed his personal check to Wood. Hill owed the bank a note for $5,000 that was past due. It refused to honor any more checks on Hill's account and applied his balance to the note. Indicate specifically what errors Wood committed.

3. Richards owed Griffith $4,000. He executed a negotiable note as follows: "Ninety days after date I promise to pay to Bearer $4,000 with 6% interest from date.

Signed: E. J. Richards

This note was lost by Griffith. The finder transferred it by delivery alone to Hopkins. Griffith ordered Richards not to pay the note to Hopkins, but Richards ignored this order and paid it anyway. May Griffith compel Richards to pay him? What could Griffith have done to avoid this loss?

4. Fortson was the payee of a check for $802.63. He transferred it to Samuel for value and indorsed it as follows: "Pay to the order of A. Samuel without recourse."

Signed: Ben Fortson

The drawer of the check stopped payment on the check because he was a minor and wished to disaffirm his contract. Samuel demanded that Fortson reimburse him for the check. Must he do so?

5. Marsh purchased a hi-fi set from Comer and paid for it by giving Comer a ninety-day note for $400. When the note came due and Marsh wished to pay, Comer claimed he had accidentally burned it up but offered to give Marsh a written receipt certifying it had been paid in full. Marsh agreed to accept this receipt. The next day Stacy presented the note to Marsh and demanded payment. Marsh produced his receipt, but Stacy contended this receipt did not affect his right to collect. Was Stacy right in his contention?

6. Paul Chapman, as the administrator of his uncle's estate, was required to collect all debts due the estate. One of the estate's debtors paid his debt of $1,100 by check made payable to Paul Chapman. Chapman indorsed this check as follows: "Pay to the order of Paul Chapman, Administrator of John Chapman's Estate. Paul Chapman." This check was never paid because the drawer had insufficient funds in the bank. Later demand was made on Paul Chapman that he pay this $1,100 out of his personal funds because of his special indorsement. Was he personally liable for it?

7. McDonald was the payee of a note for $3,500, signed by Garrard. He entered into a contract with Bell which provided that Bell was to accept the note by assignment so that McDonald would not be liable as an indorser. This was agreeable to Bell, but they were uncertain how to make the assignment. They decided to write on the note these words: "I hereby assign all my rights and interest in this note to John Bell. (Signed) Alex Mc-Donald." Later Bell transferred the note by blank indorsement to Saye. The note was not paid by Garrard, and Saye sued McDonald as an indorser. He claimed he was only an assignor and therefore not liable under the warranties of an indorser. Was this contention correct?

8. Inez Katz owned and operated the Thrift Dress Shop, an exclusive dress shop. She sold an expensive gown to Mrs. Gene Shopen who paid for it by drawing a sight draft on Josiah Shopen for $1,100. Miss Katz sent this sight draft to Herman Shobelt, an attorney, for presentment for collection. She indorsed it as follows: "Pay to the order of Herman Shobelt. (Signed) Inez Katz." Shobelt collected the draft, but before he remitted the proceeds to Miss Katz, he was declared bankrupt. He had deposited the money in a special account, intending to remit by check from this special account. The question arose as to whether or not this $1,100 was a part of Shobelt's estate to be taken over by the receiver in bankruptcy. What do you think?

Chapter 27

HOLDERS IN DUE COURSE

Negotiable instruments would have no advantage over ordinary contracts if the remote parties could not be given immunity against many of the defenses which might be made against simple contracts. To enjoy this immunity, the holder of a negotiable instrument must be a *holder in due course*. The term "innocent purchaser" is also used to describe a person who is a holder in due course. Neither term can be used to describe anyone but the holder of a negotiable instrument who has obtained it under these conditions:

1. It must not be past due at the time of the negotiation.
2. The holder must take the instrument in good faith and for value.
3. At the time the instrument is negotiated, the holder had no notice of any defense against or adverse claim to the instrument.

(1) Instrument Not Past Due. One who takes an instrument that is past due cannot be an innocent purchaser. If it is due and unpaid, there must be a reason. It is the duty of the prospective purchaser to ascertain that reason. If he fails or neglects to do so, he forfeits the privileges of a holder in due course. If the note is dated and payable in a fixed number of days or months, the instrument itself indicates whether or not it is past due.

If the instrument is transferred on the date of maturity, it is not past due but would be overdue on the day following the due date. If it is payable on demand, it is due within a reasonable time after it is issued. What is a reasonable time "depends upon the nature of the instrument, the usage of trade or business with respect to such instruments, and the facts of the particular case." For example, if a demand note is given in temporary settlement for merchandise purchased for which the usual terms are 2/10, n/60, a reasonable time would be approximately sixty days.

(2) **For Value.** For obvious reasons the law of commercial paper is concerned only with persons who give something for the paper. Thus, to attain the specially favored status of being a holder in due course, it is necessary that the holder give value for the paper. Conversely, one who does not do so, as a nephew receiving a Christmas check from an uncle, cannot be a holder in due course. The requirement that value be given does not mean that one must pay full value for a negotiable instrument in order to be a holder in due course. Thus, one who purchases a negotiable contract at a discount can qualify as a holder in due course. The law states that he must take it "for value and in good faith." If the instrument is offered at an exorbitant discount, that fact may be evidence that the purchaser did not buy it in good faith. It is the lack of good faith that destroys one's status as a holder in due course, not the amount of the discount.

If the payee of a negotiable instrument for $3,000 offered to transfer it for a consideration of $2,700, and the purchaser had no other reason to suspect any infirmity in the instrument, he can qualify as a holder in due course. He took the instrument in good faith. If, on the other hand, the holder had offered to discount the note $1,000, the purchaser could not take it in good faith because he should suspect that there is some fatal infirmity in the contract because of the large discount.

As often occurs, the purchaser may pay for the instrument in cash and other property. The discount is concealed in the inflated value placed on the property taken in payment. The test always is: Were there any circumstances that should have warned a prudent man that the instrument was not genuine and in all respects what it purported to be? If there were, the purchaser did not take it in good faith.

▪ Smallwood executed a ninety-day note for $5,000 in favor of Greene. The note was in payment of a bookkeeping machine which Greene had guaranteed would save the services of one bookkeeper. This guarantee was absolutely false. Greene, knowing he could not collect because of this breach of warranty, sold the note before maturity to Hargrove for $3,000 cash and $2,000 worth of stock, par value, in a Canadian uranium mine. The stock at the time had no known market value and later proved to be absolutely worthless. When Hargrove demanded payment on the note, Smallwood refused to pay because of the breach of warranty. The sole question is whether or not Hargrove is an innocent purchaser, that is, did he take it for value and good faith? Yes. As the question is to be determined as of the time when he acquired the paper, the fact that the stock later proved worthless did not show that the purchaser knew or should have known that fact at the time of the transaction. As there was no existing market price by which to measure the value of the stock, it was not unreasonable for the parties to treat it as having some market value; and the fact that they were wrong in their estimate or prophecy does not show that the value given was so small as to be evidence of bad faith.

(3) **No Knowledge of Any Defense or Adverse Claim to the Instrument.** When one takes a negotiable instrument by negotiation, to obtain the rights of an innocent purchaser he must have no knowledge or reason to know of any defense against or claim adverse to the instrument. As between the original parties to a negotiable instrument, any act, such as fraud, duress, mistake, illegality, which would make any contract either void or voidable will have the same effect on a negotiable instrument. Many of these defenses, as will be seen in the next chapter, are eliminated as defenses if the instrument is negotiated to an innocent purchaser. To qualify as an innocent purchaser, one must have no knowledge either directly or indirectly that any of these defects in the contract exist. The following case illustrates this point:

> ▪ Sellers and Bell were engineers for an oil prospecting company. Their occupation was well known by Harley. Sellers told Harley they had discovered unmistakable signs of oil on a tract of land Sellers owned. He offered the land to Harley for $20,000. If there was no oil on it, its true value was $1,000. Bell knew Sellers was misrepresenting the facts to Harley although he took no part in the deal. Harley bought the land, giving Sellers $5,000 in cash and a 12-month negotiable note for $15,000. Sellers immediately sold the note to Bell for $14,000. The question is whether or not Bell can qualify as an innocent purchaser. He cannot because he knew at the time the note was negotiated to him that Harley, the maker, could raise the defense of fraud to his obligation to pay.

The first holder in due course brings into operation for the first time all the protections which the law has placed around negotiable instruments. When these protections once accrue, they are not easily lost. Consequently, a subsequent holder may avail himself of them even though he himself is not a holder in due course. Such a holder is known as a *holder through a holder in due course.* For example,

Adams, without consideration, gives Bryce a negotiable note due in sixty days. Before maturity Bryce indorses it to Cordell under conditions which make Cordell a holder in due course. Thereafter, Cordell transfers the note to Gray, but Gray is not a holder in due course since he did not give any consideration for the note. If Gray is not a party to any wrongdoing or illegality affecting this instrument, he acquires all the rights of a holder in due course. This is true because Cordell had these rights, and when Cordell sold the note to Gray, he sold all of his rights, which include the right to collect the amount due and the right to be free from the defense of no consideration.

DUTIES OF THE HOLDER

As has been pointed out before, the prime significance of negotiability is that the purchaser of a negotiable instrument may obtain rights greater than the payee had.

Stevens purchases an automobile from Griffin for $900 and gives in payment this note: "Sixty days after date I promise to pay Archibald Griffin or order $900. Harold Stevens." What are Griffin's rights? If there was no fraud in the transaction or other infirmity in the contract, Griffin's simple right is to collect $900 on the due date of the note. Like all property rights this one may be sold. If Griffin, the payee, sells his rights to Comer, a holder in due course, does Comer obtain rights superior to Griffin? If Griffin's rights were perfect, Comer could obtain no greater rights. If Griffin, in order to sell the car, had made fraudulent representations about it, his right to collect $900 is reduced by the amount of damages which Stevens sustained. In this case Comer does get greater rights than Griffin had because if he is a holder in due course this defense of fraudulent representation may not be raised against him.

Whether or not there is a defense between the original parties, Comer would obtain greater advantages than Griffin had. In order to collect the $900, Griffin could look only to Stevens. If Stevens is insolvent and unable to pay, Griffin's rights may prove to be worthless. Comer, however, has the right to look to both Stevens and Griffin for payment.

QUESTIONS

1. Who is a holder in due course?
2. The holder in due course of a negotiable instrument must have obtained it under what three conditions?
3. May a holder in due course obtain possession by receiving the instrument as a Christmas gift?
4. Explain how a future holder may benefit from the fact that an instrument was held in due course.
5. What is the prime significance of negotiability?
6. May value ever be something other than money?
7. When is an instrument past due?

CASE PROBLEMS

1. Leeburn obtained title to a note by indorsement from Terry. The time of the note had been clearly changed from 120 days to 60 days. Jones, the maker, had really made this change before he signed the note, but Leeburn did not know this at the time. The maker refused to pay the note on the due date because he had returned the merchandise for which the note had been given in payment. If Leeburn is a holder in due course, the maker could not deny liability to Leeburn for this reason. Was Leeburn a holder in due course?

2. Tillman was the indorsee of a draft for $3,264.80 drawn by Stafford and payable to Kent. Tillman purchased the draft from Kent ten days before it was due for $2,800. Kent claimed he was desperate for cash and for that reason was offering Tillman a bargain. The drawee had already paid Kent the full amount of the draft. After receiving payment Kent did not surrender the draft. When Tillman presented the draft, Stafford refused to pay him. For Tillman to be able to collect this draft from the drawee, he must qualify as a holder in due course because Stafford already paid Kent. Can he?

3. Charles was the payee on a note made by Benjamin. Charles indorsed the note to his attorney Lawrence for the purpose of having Lawrence available for legal services in the event Charles would need services in the future. Benjamin defaulted on the note claiming that the goods which had been given in exchange for the note were defective and failed to conform to the promises given by Charles. Lawrence claims to be a holder in due course. Benjamin says he gave no value for the note. Who will prevail?

4. Super Discount Carpets sold wall-to-wall carpeting to Rogain. Rogain executed a note in return for the carpet. The note was in the amount of

$1,600 but Rogain was assured in a separate agreement that his home would be used as a model home and a $50 credit against the $1,600 for each visitor who would agree to hear a sales presentation regarding the carpet. Super Discount Carpets negotiated the note to First City Bank and then vanished, leaving Rogain with no way of gaining his $50 credits. Rogain refused to pay the note. Can the bank recover?

5. Bennet promised to mow the lawn for Amos, who was a holder in due course of a note made by Norton. In return for Bennet's promise, Amos negotiates the note to Bennet who is refused payment when he presents the note. Norton says since Bennet only gave a promise for the note, he cannot have the rights of a holder in due course. Bennet says that he is a holder through a holder in due course and, therefore, he has holder in due course rights. Who should prevail?

6. Paulston negotiates a past due note to Marks. Marks was skeptical about the note being overdue, but Paulston assures Marks that it is overdue because Paulston has been ill and simply hasn't had the time to present it to Clark for payment. When Marks presents the note to Clark for payment, Clark reveals that he had refused to pay because he was sold defective goods when he made the note. Does Marks qualify as a holder in due course?

Chapter 28

DEFENSES

WHO MAY MAKE A DEFENSE?

When the holder is refused payment, he may bring a lawsuit. In an earlier chapter it has been seen which parties are liable for the payment of the face of the paper. What defense can be raised by the defendant who is being sued? This, of course, is a question which does not arise until it has been first determined that the plaintiff is the holder of the paper and that the defendant is a person who would ordinarily have liability for payment of the face of the paper. Assuming that those two questions have been decided in favor of the plaintiff, the remaining question is whether this defendant has a particular defense which he may raise.

CLASSIFICATION OF DEFENSES

(1) **Defenses of the Defendant Against the Plaintiff.** In every case, the defendant may raise against the plaintiff any defense which he has against him.

- Randolf was the maker of a $400 note made out with Burton as payee. Burton had negotiated the note for value to Mallory who owed Randolf $450. When Mallory sues Randolf for the note, Randolf attempts to assert that Mallory owes him $450 and refuses to pay on that basis. Which party will prevail?

(2) **Defenses of Defendant Against Person with Whom He Dealt.** Assume that instead of the holder suing his indorser, we have the situation in which there are four successive indorsers and the holder who comes at the end of these four indorsers sues the first

indorser. Can the first indorser raise against the holder a defense which the first indorser has against the second indorser, for example, that the first indorser was induced by fraud to make the indorsement? More commonly the situation will arise in which the remote holder sues the drawer of a check who defends on the ground that the check had been given in payment for goods or services and that the drawer never got what he paid for, or it did not work, or was not satisfactory. Can the drawer now raise against the remote holder the defense that he has against the payee of the check, namely, the defense of failure of consideration? The answer to this depends on the nature of the defendant's defense against the person with whom he dealt and the character of the holder. If the defense is a limited defense and the remote holder is a holder in due course, the defendant cannot raise such a defense. If the defense is a universal defense or the holder is an ordinary holder, the defendant may raise that defense.

(a) Plaintiff an Ordinary Holder. If the plaintiff is an ordinary holder, he has the same standing as an assignee of an ordinary contract and is subject to all defenses which the defendant possesses against the person with whom he dealt. Specifically, if the holder in the check case above is an ordinary holder, the drawer will not have to make good on his check if he can show that he never got the proper goods or services from the payee.

(b) Limited Defenses. There are defenses which are limited to being raised against an ordinary holder and cannot be raised against a holder in due course. Common examples of limited defense include:

1. Absence or failure of consideration
2. Fraud which induced the execution of the instrument
3. Conditional delivery
4. Improper completion
5. Payment or part payment
6. Illegality

(c) Universal Defenses. These are defenses which can be universally raised regardless of who is being sued or who is suing. Thus, they can be raised against the holder in due course as well as an ordinary holder. The more common universal defenses are:

1. Minority
2. Forgery
3. Fraud as to the nature of the instrument or its material terms

LIMITED DEFENSES

(1) **Absence or Failure of Consideration.** In general the defenses available in a dispute over a contract may be raised only against holders who do not qualify as holders in due course. Accordingly, if the instrument is held by a holder in due course, the defense of failure of consideration is not effective when raised by the maker who alleges that he received no consideration for the paper. In an action on an ordinary contract, the promisor may defend on the ground that there was no consideration for his promise; or that if there was consideration in the form of a counterpromise, the promise was never performed; or that the consideration was illegal. Thus, if Smith agrees to paint Jones' house, but does not do it properly, Jones would have a right of action against Smith for breach of contract; or he could refuse to pay Smith the price agreed upon. If Smith were to assign his right to payment, Jones would be able to raise against the assignee the defenses he has against Smith.

However, if Jones were to pay Smith by check before the work was completed, and the check were negotiated to a holder in due course, Jones could not defend on the ground of failure of consideration. He would have to pay the check. Jones's only right of action would be against Smith for his loss.

(2) **Fraud Which Induced the Execution of the Instrument.** When a person knows that he is executing a commercial paper and knows its essential terms but is persuaded or induced to execute it because of false representations or statements, this is not a defense as against a holder in due course. For example, if Drucker is persuaded to buy a car from Randolph because of false statements made by Randolph about the car and he gives Randolph a note for it which is later negotiated to a holder in due course, Drucker cannot defend on the ground that Randolph lied to him about the car. Drucker will have to pay the note and seek any recovery from Randolph.

> ▪ Morgan and his wife agreed to have vinyl siding installed on their home and to pay for it in installments pursuant to a note They signed made out to Last Ever Aluminum Company. Meany, the representative of the siding company, assured the Morgans that the siding would reduce their heating costs by 80%. Last Ever and Meany negotiated the note to County Finance. The siding not only failed to cut heating bills, but Morgan learned that it was not vinyl but cardboard. County Finance sues to enforce the note and the Morgans claim that they were fraudulently induced to sign the note by false statements about the siding. This defense would prevail

against the claim of an ordinary holder. However, if County Finance is a holder in due course, the Morgans must pay!

(3) **Conditional Delivery.** As against a holder in due course, an individual who would be liable on the instrument cannot show that the instrument, absolute on its face, was delivered subject to an unperformed condition or that it was delivered for a specific purpose but was not used for it. If Sims makes out a check for Byers and delivers it to Richter and tells him not to deliver it until Byers delivers certain goods, but Richter delivers it to Byers who then negotiates it to a holder in due course, Sims will have to pay on the check.

(4) **Improper Completion.** If any term in a commercial paper is left blank, e.g., the payee or the amount, and the drawer then delivers the instrument to another to complete it, the drawer cannot raise the defense of improper completion against a holder in due course. The holder in due course may require payment from the drawer.

(5) **Payment or Part Payment.** Upon payment of commercial paper the party making the payment should demand the surrender of the instrument. If the instrument is not surrendered, it may be further negotiated; and a later holder in due course would be able to demand payment successfully. A receipt is not adequate as proof of payment because the subsequent holder in due course would have no notice of the receipt; whereas, surrender of the instrument would clearly prevent further negotiation.

If partial payment is made, the holder will be unlikely to surrender the instrument. In such a case the person making the payment should note the payment on the instrument, thereby giving notice to any subsequent transferee of the partial payment.

(6) **Illegality.** The fact that the law makes certain transactions illegal gives rise to a defense against an ordinary holder. Such a defense would be unavailable against a holder in due course unless the law making the transaction illegal also specifies that instruments based upon such transactions are unenforceable.

UNIVERSAL DEFENSES

(1) **Minority.** The fact that the defendant is a minor capable of avoiding his agreements under contract law is a defense that may be raised against any holder.

(2) Forgery. Except in cases where forgery was made possible by the negligence of the defendant, forgery may be raised successfully against any holder.

(3) Fraud as to the Nature of the Instrument or Its Material Terms. The defense that one was induced to sign an instrument when one did not know that it was in fact commercial paper is available against any holder. For example, an illiterate man who is told that a note is a receipt and thereby is induced to sign it may successfully raise this defense against any holder. This defense is not available, however, to competent individuals who have negligently failed to give reasonable attention to the details of the documents they sign.

> ■ Heritage, a blind man, was expecting delivery of goods to his home by the Atlex Delivery Service. When the goods arrived the deliverer requested Heritage to sign papers which he maintained were needed receipts for the delivery service. In fact, they were promissory notes made out to the delivery van driver. Will Heritage be liable on these notes? No, fraud as to the nature of the instrument is a universal defense.

ALTERATION

Alteration is a peculiar defense which does not exactly fit into the classifications above. If an instrument is altered, the instrument has no effect if the plaintiff is an ordinary holder. If the plaintiff is a holder in due course, the instrument can be sued upon according to its terms before it was altered. An "alteration" exists only if (1) a party to the instrument (2) fraudulently made (3) a material change. If any one of these elements is lacking, the modification of the instrument is not called an alteration and has no legal effect. As a practical matter, however, there may be some difficulty in proving just what the instrument said before it was modified.

MISCELLANEOUS MATTERS

In addition to the defenses described above, it must be remembered that every lawsuit presents certain standard problems so that a defendant, assuming the facts support his position, can always raise the defense that the suit is not brought in the proper court; that he was not served with process; or that the statute of limitations has run and bars suing him. Any defendant in a suit on commercial paper

I IS THE INSTRUMENT NEGOTIABLE?	II IS THE PARTY A HOLDER IN DUE COURSE?	III WHAT IS THE NATURE OF THE DEFENSE?
The instrument must: 1. Be in writing and signed by the party executing it. 2. Contain either an order or a promise to pay. 3. Make the order or the promise unconditional. 4. Provide for the payment of a sum certain in money. 5. Be payable on demand or at a fixed future time. 6. Be payable to the order of a payee or to the bearer of the instrument. 7. Designate the payee and the drawee with reasonable certainty.	1. It must not be past due at the time of the negotiation. 2. The holder must take the instrument in good faith and for value. 3. The holder must have no notice of any defense against or adverse claim to the instrument.	Limited Defenses: 1. Absence or failure of consideration. 2. Fraud which induced the execution of the instrument. 3. Conditional delivery. 4. Improper completion. 5. Payment or part payment. 6. Illegality. Universal Defenses: 1. Minority. 2. Forgery. 3. Fraud as to the nature of the instrument or its material terms.

Important Features of the Law of Negotiable Instruments

can claim that the instrument is not negotiable; that the plaintiff is not the holder; and that the defendant is not a party liable for payment of the paper. If the holder claims that the defendant is secondarily liable for the payment of the face of the paper, the defendant may also show that the paper had not been properly presented to the primary party and that proper notice of his default had not been given to the secondary party.

■ Crane offered to sell Yardley his car for $500 and stated that the car just recently had a complete overhauling of the engine and transmission. Yardley, relying upon this false statement, accepted the offer to his detriment. Crane suggested that Yardley sign a memorandum of the agreement pending final consummation of the sale. Crane, by trickery, substituted a negotiable note for $1,000 which Yardley signed.

There was fraud in the sale which preceded the signing of the instrument. This type of fraud is a personal defense and is of no avail against a holder in due course.

■ Mitchell was the drawee of a ninety-day draft for $2,000, payable to Aldredge. Mitchell sold Aldredge a trailer truck for $7,200, but allowed him credit for the $2,000 even though the draft was not yet due for thirty days. Aldredge said, "I'll mail the draft to you in a day or two." Aldredge had actually negotiated the draft to Brown, an innocent purchaser. When Brown presented it for payment on the due date, Mitchell denied liability because he had already paid it through a credit allowance. The defense that part payment had been made was a limited defense and could not be used against an innocent purchaser.

QUESTIONS

1. Name the primary parties in (a) a note, (b) a time draft, (c) a check.
2. State in one sentence the chief advantage of being the holder in due course of commercial paper.
3. Is it any advantage being the holder of a negotiable instrument even though one is not a holder in due course?
4. What is the difference between limited defenses and universal defenses?
5. Name and explain three limited defenses.
6. Name and explain three universal defenses.
7. Name and explain three miscellaneous defenses.
8. What is the effect upon a holder in due course if the instrument was not completed nor delivered by the maker thereof although it had been subsequently filled in naming an inappropriate party as payee and specifying an unduly large sum?

CASE PROBLEMS

1. Caroline Debbs was a private secretary to General Neal W. Butter. One of her duties was to reconcile his personal bank account each month. One month three checks had been clearly altered, but she delayed reconciling his statement. She was not exactly sure how to make a reconciliation and had not been able to make one for the two preceding months. She did not report them for 95 days and would not have discovered them then had it not been for the fact that General Butter gave a check in payment of his country club dues that was returned as a bad check. This mortified General Butter, and he threatened to sue the bank. Must the bank or General Butter bear the loss of the amount of the forged checks?

2. Dobbs gave his favorite daughter, Peggy, a note for $10,000, due and payable on April 1, 1974, her 21st birthday. Peggy was only sixteen at the time. She immediately negotiated the note in full payment of a sports car. When the note came due, her father refused to pay it, claiming lack of consideration. The cost of the car was $6,500. May Dobbs set up the defense of lack of consideration against the holder?

3. Landry accepted a ninety-day time draft payable to Case and drawn by Holt. Landry accepted the draft as part payment for the purchase of the D & E Cafeteria. Holt, when he sold the cafeteria to Landry, showed him his receipts averaging $30,000 a month. These records had been padded so that they materially overstated the profit prospects from the operation of the cafeteria. Case sold the draft to Bagget, an innocent purchaser. Landry refused to pay the draft, pleading fraud. Is this defense good?

4. Dewey of Salem, Oregon, purchased a boat from Morse. At the time the contract was made the boat was supposedly in a boathouse on a lake in Idaho. Dewey gave a check for $3,500 in payment of the boat. Morse indorsed the check immediately to Wayne. A few hours after the sale, Morse received a wire informing him that the boathouse and the boat were destroyed in a fire the day before the sale. When he learned of this, Dewey stopped payment on the check. Wayne sued both Morse as indorser and Dewey as the drawer. Is either or both liable?

5. Garrett gave Brooks the following note:

Date _____

Six months after date I promise to pay E. Brooks or order, $1,572.84 with _____% interest from date in payment of one lot purchased by deed of even date and his promises to clear the lot of debris.

A. Garrett

Brooks induced Garrett to give him this note through fraudulent statements as to the value of the land. He sold the note to Smith, an innocent purchaser. Smith, in turn, sold it to Jones who knew of the fraudulent nature of the transaction. Jones sued Garrett for the note, and Garrett attempted to plead fraud as a defense. Would the court permit him to offer this defense?

6. Davis filled out a note payable to Mullins. It was complete in every respect except that the amount was omitted, pending a determination of the exact amount. Through a mistake, Davis' secretary mailed the note to Mullins who, although he knew the proper amount was between $300 and $400, filled in the amount spaces for $1,000, and then sold it to Fortune, an innocent purchaser. Could Fortune collect the note from Davis?

What would your answer be if it had been completed before Mullins obtained possession of it?

SUMMARY CASES

PART 5

1. The following instrument was signed by Bushred Buek:

"For value received I promise to pay John Peron, or bearer, five hundred seventy-five dollars and fifty cents, it being for property I purchased of him in value at this date, as being payable as soon as can be realized of the above amount for the said property I have this date purchased of said Peron, which is to be paid in the course of the season now coming." The sole question to be determined was: Is this instrument negotiable in form? (Cota v. Buek, 7 Metc. [Mass.] 588)

2. The following note was on a printed form but with the parts underscored being in the handwriting of Cecelia W. Donohoe:

"I, Cecelia W. Donohoe, after date, August 30th, promise to pay to the order of Richard Donohoe, Thirteen Thousand and Seventy Dollars and 86/100 Dollars without defalcation, value received, with interest at 6%. Witness my hand and seal."

Hester Johnson,
Notary Public

There was no signature in the space normally reserved for the signature of the maker. The sole question to be decided here is: Was this instrument properly signed as a negotiable instrument? (Donohoe's Estate, 271, Pa. 554)

3. Haskin drew a check payable to himself and then indorsed it as follows: "Pay to the order of Mrs. Mary Hook for the benefit of her son." The drawer died, and the executor of his estate refused to honor the check, claiming that there was no consideration to induce the indorsement. The sole question to be decided was whether or not this indorsement must be supported by a consideration. (Hook v. Pratt, 78 N. Y. Court of Appeals 498)

4. A check was drawn by the Havana Canning Company for $125, payable to George Wells. The check was regular in every detail except that in the lower left-hand corner were these words: "For berries to be delivered to us June 8th." This check was indorsed by George Wells to an innocent purchaser. The drawer wished to raise a defense to the payment of a breach of warranty, which being a failure of consideration was a limited defense. In order to raise this defense, he had to establish the fact that this check was nonnegotiable because of this notation. Did this notation make the order to pay conditional? (First National Bank of Marianna v. Havana Canning Company, 195 So. 118, 142 Fla. 554)

5. Berry executed a promissory note payable to William C. Stepp. The note was in perfect order. Stepp indorsed the note before maturity as follows: "I hereby transfer my right to this note over to W. E. McCullough. (signed) William C. Stepp." The maker failed to pay the note, and McCullough brought suit against Stepp, the indorser. His defense was that the indorsement was a qualified indorsement and, therefore, he was not liable since the maker's only reason for not paying was insolvency. Was this a qualified indorsement? (McCullough v. Stepp, 91 Ga. App. 103, 85 S. E. 2d 159)

6. Producers Consolidated Oil drew the following bill of exchange:

$260.06   Mexico, Mo.
                                                      April 1, 1921

One hundred and eighty days from date hereof, pay to the order of The Producers Consolidated Oil Company, $250 at office of Savings Bank of Mexico, Mo., for petroleum products sold to drawee. With interest hereon at the rate of 8 percent from date.

                           The Producers Consolidated Oil Company

On April 1 this instrument was duly and properly accepted by Ralph Dobyns and A. L. Hendrix as joint acceptors. The payee negotiated the instrument to Clay and Funkhouser Banking Company for value and before maturity. There were two questions to be decided in this case: (a) Was the instrument negotiable in form? (b) Was the Clay and Funkhouser Banking Company a holder in due course? (Clay and Funkhouser Banking Company v. Dobyns, 255 S. W. 946)

7. A check was drawn by Fellsway Motors, Inc., on October 25, made payable to Therrien. Therrien then drew a line through the "5" in "25" to make it look like Oct. 28. The line was in a different color of ink from the rest of the check, and the change in the number was perfectly evident. On October 29 Therrien indorsed the check to Manuel Medeiros for value and in good faith. Before the check was paid, payment was stopped by the drawer. The key question to be decided in the case was whether or not Medeiros was a holder in due course. (Medeiros v. Fellsway Motors, Inc., 96 N. E. 2d 170)

8. In August, 1949, Hier executed a negotiable note for $1,075, payable to the Washington Fixtures and Equipment Company. The note was to be paid in installments, the first installment to be due December 1, 1949, with a provision that if any installment was not paid on time, the entire balance should become due and payable at once. The first installment was not paid. On December 23, the payee indorsed the note to the Federal Glass Company, Inc. for value. When Hier was sued by the holder, he wished to plead fraud and a breach of warranty. The holder claimed he was not required to defend himself against such a defense. What fundamental error did some employee for the Federal Glass Company commit in this case? (Hier v. Federal Glass Co., Inc., Mun. Ct. App. D. C. 102, A. 2d 840)

9. The Washington Motor Company, a corporation, executed a note in favor of W. A. Sinkey. The note before delivery was indorsed in blank by Herman Steffens and some other directors of the corporation. Some time after the note became due, Steffens died. Up to the time of Steffens' death, Sinkey had made no presentment of the note for payment to the Washington Motor Company nor had any notice of dishonor ever been given to him prior to Steffens' death. Sinkey brought suit against Dorthea Steffens, the executrix of Herman Steffens' estate, and the other indorsers. Judgment for whom? (Steffens v. Sinkey, 43 Ohio App. 355, 183 N. E. 288)

10. J. M. Carver executed a negotiable note in favor of J. W. Crafton. The note was in payment of a gambling debt. Crafton indorsed the note by blank indorsement to the Wachovia Bank and Trust Company. Carver denied liability on the note when it came due because it was for a gambling debt. The holder immediately made demand upon Crafton for payment under his indorsement. Was either Carver or Crafton liable to the holder for this note? (Wachovia Bank and Trust Company v. Crafton, 181 N. C. 404, 107 S. E. 316)

11. The Jonesboro Rice Milling Company drew a draft on McGill Brothers Rice Mill Co. The draft was duly accepted by the drawee. The draft was then discounted by indorsement by the Jonesboro Milling Company, the payee. The indorsement of the payee was made by Franklin W. Cohen and Harry E. Bovay, the owners. The draft was properly presented on the due date and was dishonored, but no notice of dishonor was ever received by Bovay. The notice of dishonor was addressed to: "Jonesboro Rice Mill Co., Jonesboro, Ark., Attention Mr. Bovay." Mr. Bovay claims he never received the notice. Was the notice of dishonor properly addressed to Bovay? (Harry E. Bovay v. Fuller, Circuit Court of Appeals, Eighth Circuit 63 F. 2d 280)

12. Brewer made a note payable to the Murphy Motor Company. There was a provision in the note that it was payable at the Planters' Bank of Clarksdale. The note was negotiable in form. Cutrer indorsed this note as an accommodation to Brewer. The Murphy Motor Company negotiated the note before maturity to the Automobile Sales Company. When the note came due, the holder took it to Brewer's office and presented it for payment, and payment was refused. This was on the due date. The next day the holder notified each indorser that the note had been presented at Brewer's office and payment was refused. The holder then sued the indorsers for payment. (a) Was there a proper presentment for payment? (b) Was there a proper notice of dishonor? (c) If you were the employee of the Automobile Sales Company whose job it was to handle this transaction, what

statutory provision would you need to know in order to perform your duty satisfactorily? (Brewer et al. v. Automobile Sales Company, 147 Miss. 603)

13. Yates and Gray were makers of a negotiable note which was negotiated several times before maturity. The first indorsement was by Horton. Linn, the last holder, presented the note for payment to Yates and Gray, and payment was refused. Linn, the holder, immediately notified the last indorser of the dishonor. In the notice of dishonor to the last indorser were included notices of dishonor for all the other indorsers, including Horton, the first one. As he received the notices of dishonor each indorser mailed them to the next preceding indorser. For some reason Horton never received his notice. Which indorsers, if any, were properly notified? (Linn v. Horton, 7 Wis. 157)

14. Stanton purchased a color television set and gave in payment a $512.60 ninety-day negotiable note. Johnson, the payee, indorsed the note by a qualified indorsement before maturity to Butler Brothers in part payment of a piano. The salesman for Butler Brothers knew Stanton well and was aware he was only eighteen years old. When the note came due, it was properly presented to Stanton for payment, and he refused on the grounds he was a minor. Johnson claims he is not liable because of his qualified indorsement. Is either Stanton or Johnson bound to pay Butler Brothers?

Part 6.

AGENCY AND
EMPLOYMENT

Preview Cases for Part 6: Agency and Employment

- The owner of a radio shop employed Devaney to sell radios and instructed him to sell for cash only. If he disregarded this instruction and sold a radio on credit at reasonable terms of payment, would the contract have been binding on the owner of the radio shop?

- Slaughter had a checking account with the Citizens Bank. The Bank was not authorized to honor any checks except those with Slaughter's signature. Over a period of six months Mrs. Slaughter signed her husband's name on dozens of checks and signed them: "by Mrs. Slaughter." Mr. Slaughter notified the bank to stop honoring his wife's checks and demanded that the bank restore to his account all checks drawn by her. Should the bank be so required?

- Hawkins was the manager of the Three Bar Ranch. The owner went on a world tour and left Hawkins in complete charge. Hawkins used the proceeds from the sale of cattle to buy and sell cattle at the public sales barns. His gross profits from these speculations amounted to $3,800 and his losses to $1,400, leaving a net profit of $2,400. When the principal returned and learned of these speculations, he demanded the $3,800 in profits. Is he entitled to recover this amount?

- The Cheyney Hardware Company owed Hanson $4,200. Hanson was appointed the agent for the Cheyney Company to collect certain accounts receivable with instructions to keep the first $4,200 and remit the balance to Cheyney. After Hanson had collected $1,000, Cheyney attempted to discharge him. Did the Cheyney Company have the right to do so?

- Dexter was employed as a welder in the Safe Machine Shop. Space was inadequate, making it necessary to pile sheet steel and I-Beams on the floor. Dexter tripped over some of this material, and the flame from the welding machine touched his face, causing him to lose sight in one eye. Is the employer liable for Dexter's injury?

These preview cases are designed to serve as a springboard for the study of this part. As you read through each chapter in this part, you will find the actual decisions for all these preview cases. Of course, there are many more such illustrative problems as well as case problems for decision at the end of each chapter. And there are also a number of even more challenging cases for review at the end of the part.

Chapter 29

CREATION OF AN AGENCY

NATURE OF AGENCY

When one party, known as a *principal,* appoints another party, known as an *agent,* to enter into contracts with third parties in the name of the principal, a contract of *agency* is formed. By this definition at least three parties are involved in every contract which an agent negotiates, the principal, the agent, and the third party. It is this making of a contract with a third person on behalf of his principal which distinguishes an agency from other employment relationships. The principal, the agent, or the third party may be a person, a partnership, or a corporation.

IMPORTANCE OF AGENCY

Because of the magnitude and the complexity of our modern industry, many of the important details pertaining to business transactions must be delegated by the owners of businesses to agents for performance. The relation creating this delegation of powers is governed by the general principles of law pertaining to contracts.

The underlying principles of partnerships are dependent upon an application of the law of agency, and the business of a corporation can be carried on only through agents. Much of the business of banks, manufacturing enterprises, and similar businesses is carried out by agents.

Even in the performance of ordinary routine matters by individuals, agents are necessary in order to bring one person into a business contractual relationship with other persons. Thus a farmer who sends an employee to town to have a piece of machinery repaired gives the latter the authority to enter into a contract that binds the farmer to the agreement. This case is an application of the maxim that "whatever a person does through another, he does himself."

WHAT POWERS MAY BE DELEGATED TO AN AGENT?

As a general rule, all those things that one has the right to do personally he may do through an agent. There are, however, certain acts which are of such a personal nature that the courts will not permit them to be delegated to others. The law insists that if these acts are performed at all, they must be performed by the one who, because of the personal nature of such acts, should do them. Some of the acts that are considered personal and that may not be performed by an agent are voting in a public election, executing a will, or serving on a jury.

What one may not lawfully do himself may not be done through another. Thus no person can authorize an agent to commit a crime, to publish a libelous statement, to perpetrate a fraud, or to do any other act that is illegal, immoral, or opposed to the welfare of society.

OTHER TYPES OF EMPLOYMENT RELATIONSHIPS

There are two other types of employment relationships:

1. Independent contractor
2. Employer and employee, originally referred to in law as master and servant

(1) Independent Contractor. An *independent contractor* is one who contracts to perform some tasks for a fixed fee but is independent of the control of the other contracting party as to the means by which he performs the contract except to the extent that the contract sets forth specifications and requirements to be followed. He is merely held responsible for the proper performance of the contract. The contract does not create either a principal-agent relationship or an employer-employee relationship. The most usual type of independent contractor relationship is in the building trades.

> ▪ Pope entered into a contract with Bruce to build a house for Bruce for $20,000, the house to conform to prescribed blueprints and to be completed within three months from date. Bruce has no control over Pope during the construction. His only rights are to insist it conform to the blueprints and be finished within three months. This is a typical independent contractor relationship.

There are many reasons why one must not confuse a contract of employment with a contract of independent contractor. In the first place, an employer may be held liable for any injuries his employees negligently cause to third parties. This is not true of independent contractors. In the second place, there are several laws an employer must comply with relative to his employees. He must withhold social security taxes on their wages, pay a payroll tax for unemployment compensation, withhold federal income taxes, bargain with his employees collectively when properly demanded, and many others. None of these laws apply when one contracts with an independent contractor. He is the employer of those employed by him to perform the contract.

(2) **Employer and Employee.** An employee performs work for an employer and is under his control both as to the work to be done and as to the manner in which it is to be done. The main difference between an employee and an agent is that an employee does not have the power to bind his employer on a contract while an agent does have that power.

The main difference between an employee and an independent contractor is that the employer has constant power to control the doing of the work by the employee, whereas one contracting with an independent contractor does not have such control.

CLASSIFICATION OF AGENTS

Agents may be classified as follows:

1. General agents
2. Special agents

(1) **General Agents.** A *general agent* is one who is authorized to carry out all of his principal's business of a particular kind, or all of his principal's business at a particular place even though it is not all of one kind. A purchasing agent and a bank cashier are examples of general agents who perform all of the principal's business of a particular kind. A manager who is in full charge of one branch of a chain of shoe stores is a general agent who transacts all of his principal's business at a particular place. In this capacity he buys and sells merchandise, employs help, pays bills, collects accounts, and performs all other duties. He has a wide scope of authority and the power to act on his own initiative.

A general agent has considerable authority beyond that expressly stated in his contract of employment. He has in addition to his express authority that authority which one in his position customarily has. This is sometimes called *customary authority*. If in fact the express authority of the agent is less than such an agent would customarily have, a third person who knows the actual extent of the agent's contractual authority cannot rely upon customary authority.

(2) **Special Agents.** A *special agent* is one who is authorized by his principal to transact some specific act or acts. He has only limited powers which he may use only for a specific purpose. The authorization may cover just one act, such as buying a house; or it may cover a series of acts which are mere repetitions, such as selling admission tickets to a movie.

SPECIAL TYPES OF AGENTS

There are several special types of agents. In general these are special agents, but because of the nature of their duties, their powers may exceed those of the ordinary special agent:

1. Factors
2. Factors del credere
3. Brokers
4. Attorneys in fact

(1) **Factors.** A *factor* is one who receives possession of another's property for sale on commission. The commission merchant is the largest class of factors. He may sell in the name of his principal, but the usual practice is for him to sell in his own name. When he collects, he deducts his commission or factorage and remits the balance to the principal. The third party as a rule is aware that he is dealing with an agent by the nature of the business or by the name of the business. The words "Commission Merchant" usually appear on all stationery. He has the power to bind the principal for the customary terms of sale for the type of business he is doing. In this regard his powers are slightly greater than those of the ordinary special agent.

(2) **Factors Del Credere.** A *factor del credere* is a commission merchant who sells on credit and guarantees to the principal that the purchase price will be paid by the purchaser or by the factor.

This is a form of contract of guaranty, but the contract need not be in writing as required by the Statute of Frauds since the agreement is a primary obligation of the factor.

(3) Brokers. A *broker* is a special agent whose task is to bring the two contracting parties together. Unlike the factor, he does not have possession of the merchandise. In real estate and insurance he generally is the agent of the buyer rather than the seller. If his duty is merely to find a buyer, or sometimes a seller, he has no authority to bind the principal on any contract.

(4) Attorneys in Fact. An *attorney in fact* is a general agent who has been appointed by a sealed authorization.

EXTENT OF AUTHORITY

As a general rule, a general agent has authority to transact two classes of acts: those clearly within the scope of his actual or contractual authority, and those outside of this scope which appear to third parties to be apparently within the scope of the agent's authority. Appearance of authority may arise when by custom such agents ordinarily possess such powers. In addition, without regard to custom, the principal may have made statements to the third person which caused him to believe that the agent has the authority. To illustrate the latter situation, the Smith Insurance Company might advertise "For all your insurance problems see your local Smith Insurance man." This would give the local Smith Insurance Company men apparent authority to arrange any insurance matters even though actually they did not have such authority or had been told that certain kinds of cases had to be referred to the home office.

As to innocent third parties, the powers of a general agent may be far more extensive than those granted to him by his principal. Limitations upon an agent's authority are not binding upon a third party who has no knowledge of them; but if the third party knows of them, he is bound by them.

> ▪ The owner of a radio shop employed Devaney to sell radios and instructed him to sell for cash only. If he disregarded this instruction and sold a radio on credit at reasonable terms of payment, the contract would have been binding upon the principal. Since it is the custom of radio shops in general to sell on credit, the purchaser had a right to presume that Devaney had authority to sell on credit. This is frequently called *customary authority.*

If Devaney had taken a car in payment of the radio and had agreed to pay the purchaser $150 for the difference in value, the shop owner would not have been bound. This would clearly have been beyond even the apparent scope of the agent's authority, and the purchaser would have had no right to assume that the agent had such authority.

In every case the person who would benefit by the existence of authority on the part of the alleged agent has the burden of proving the existence of authority. If a man represents himself to be the agent of another for the purpose of selling the car of that other person, the prospective purchaser must seek assurance from the principal as to the agent's authority.

Once the third party has learned the actual scope of an agent's authority from the principal, it is clear that the agent has no greater authority than the principal's statements indicate, together with such customary authority as would attach to the express authority given by the principal.

WHO MAY APPOINT AN AGENT?

Every person who is legally competent to act for himself may act through an agent. This rule is based upon the principle that whatever a person may do for himself, he may do through another. Hence corporations, partnerships, unincorporated clubs and societies, as well as individuals, may appoint agents.

The contract by which a minor appoints an agent to act for him is voidable. Some states hold that a minor's appointment of an attorney to act for him is void.

WHO MAY ACT AS AN AGENT?

Ordinarily, any person may be appointed to act as an agent, provided he has sufficient intelligence to carry out his principal's orders. The latter is not a legal requirement but is a practical consideration of whether the principal is going to have the particular person act as his agent. Corporations and partnerships may act as agents also.

There are some types of transactions which cannot be performed by an agent unless he meets certain requirements. For example, in many states a real-estate agent must possess certain definite qualifications and must, in addition, secure a license to act in this capacity. Unless he does this, he is disqualified to act as an agent in performing the duties of a real-estate agent. Where the law imposes limitations on the right to act as an agent, it does so for the purpose of protecting the public from loss at the hands of dishonest or untrained "agents."

CREATION OF AN AGENCY

There are several ways in which the relationship of agency may be created. They are usually created by:

1. Appointment
2. Ratification
3. Estoppel
4. Necessity

(1) **Appointment.** The usual way of creating an agency is by appointment. The contract may be oral or written, formal or informal. There are some instances, however, where the appointment must be made in a particular form. The contract appointing an agent must be in writing if the agency is created to transfer title to real estate. Also, if an agent's authority is to extend beyond one year from the date of the contract, the contract is required by the Statute of Frauds to be in writing. If an agent is appointed to execute a formal contract, such as a bond or sealed contract, the contract of appointment must be formal.

A sealed written instrument indicating the appointment of an agent is known as a *warrant* or *power of attorney*. If a power of attorney is to be recorded, it must also be acknowledged before a notary public or other officer authorized to take acknowledgments. An ordinary form of power of attorney is shown on the following page.

(2) **Ratification.** The approval by one person of an act previously done by another in the former's name without authority is known as *ratification*. The unauthorized act may have been done by an assumed agent who purported to act as an agent without real or apparent authority, or it may have been done by a real agent who exceeded his apparent authority. The supposed principal in such a case is not bound by the act unless and until he ratifies it. The effect of the ratification is that the ratification relates back to the date of the act done by the assumed agent; hence the assumed agent is put in the same position as if he had had authority to do the act at the time the act was done by him.

𝔓𝔬𝔴𝔢𝔯 𝔬𝔣 𝔄𝔱𝔱𝔬𝔯𝔫𝔢𝔶

𝔎𝔫𝔬𝔴 𝔄𝔩𝔩 𝔐𝔢𝔫 𝔅𝔶 𝔗𝔥𝔢𝔰𝔢 𝔓𝔯𝔢𝔰𝔢𝔫𝔱𝔰: *that* I , Gene Dorsey of Boise, Idaho

ha ve made, constituted and appointed and by these presents do make, constitute and appoint

James Turner

my   *true and lawful attorney for* me   *and in* my   *name, place and stead to*

represent me in the operation of my lumber mill in the State of Idaho

Hereby giving and granting unto my   *said attorney*   *full and whole power and authority in and*

about the premises; and generally to do all and every act and acts, thing and things, device and devices, in the law what-

soever needful and necessary to be done in and about the premises, for me   *and in* my   *name to do, execute*

and perform as large and amply, to all intents and purposes, as I   *might or could do, if personally present;*

and an attorney or attorneys under him   *for the purpose aforesaid, to make and substitute, and the same to*

remove and revoke at his   *pleasure, hereby ratifying and confirming as good and effectual, in law and in equity,*

all that my   *said attorney or* his   *substitute shall lawfully and legally do by virtue hereof.*

𝔍𝔫 𝔚𝔦𝔱𝔫𝔢𝔰𝔰 𝔚𝔥𝔢𝔯𝔢𝔬𝔣, I   *have hereunto set* my   *hand and seal the* tenth

day of March   *in the year of our Lord one thousand nine hundred and*

𝔖𝔢𝔞𝔩𝔢𝔡 𝔞𝔫𝔡 𝔇𝔢𝔩𝔦𝔳𝔢𝔯𝔢𝔡 𝔦𝔫 𝔓𝔯𝔢𝔰𝔢𝔫𝔠𝔢 𝔬𝔣 }   *Gene Dorsey*   (SEAL)

Glenn Gordon   (SEAL)

Frances Taylor

A Power of Attorney

The essential elements of a valid ratification are:

(a) The one who assumed the authority of an agent must have made it known to the third person that he was acting on behalf of the party who attempts to ratify the act.

(b) The one attempting to ratify must have been capable of authorizing the act at the time the act was done. Thus an act of a promoter cannot be ratified by a corporation that is formed subsequently. Since the effect of the ratification is that the ratification is thrown back to the day the act was done, the corporation cannot ratify the act of the promoter because it was not in existence at the time of the act.

(c) The one attempting to ratify must be capable of authorizing the act at the time he gives his approval of the act.

(d) The one attempting to ratify must have knowledge of all material facts.

(e) The one attempting to ratify must approve the entire act.

(f) The act that is ratified must be legal, although a forgery on commercial paper may be ratified by the person whose name has been forged.

(g) The ratification must be made before the third party has withdrawn from the transaction.

(3) **Estoppel.** *Agency by estoppel* arises when a person by words or conduct leads another person to believe that a third party is his agent or has the authority to do particular acts. The principal is bound to the extent of his representations for the purpose of preventing an injustice to parties who have been misled by the acts or the conduct of the principal.

> ▪ Slaughter had a checking account with the Citizen's Bank. The bank was not authorized to honor any checks except those with Slaughter's signature. Over a period of six months Mrs. Slaughter signed her husband's name on dozens of checks and signed them: "by Mrs. Slaughter." Mr. Slaughter notified the bank to stop honoring his wife's checks and demanded that the bank restore to his account all checks drawn by her. The court held that because he allowed six months to pass without protesting, he was estopped to deny she had the authority to sign his name to checks. Had he protested as soon as he learned of the act, the bank would have had to make good the checks so drawn.

(4) **Necessity.** The relationship of agency may be created by necessity. A husband is bound to support his wife and minor children. If he fails to provide them with necessaries, the wife may pledge the husband's credit, even against his will. Agency by necessity may also arise from some unforeseen emergency. Thus the driver of a bus operating between distant cities may pledge the owner's credit in order to have needed repairs made and may have the cost charged to the owner.

QUESTIONS

1. What is an agency?
2. Name the parties who are involved in a contract which an agent negotiates.
3. Why are most business transactions carried on by agents?
4. What acts can never be delegated to an agent?
5. How does an independent contractor differ from an agent?

6. What is the difference between an employee and an agent?

7. What is a general agent?

8. What is customary authority?

9. Name two reasons why it is most important to distinguish between an agent and a broker.

10. May corporations act as agents?

11. Is a wife always the agent of her husband?

12. In order for a principal to ratify an unauthorized contract of an agent, must the agent have pretended to act for the principal?

CASE PROBLEMS

1. McDowell was business manager for the WTUW radio station. Philips, representing himself as the agent of the Hartsfield Oil Company, presented to McDowell an advertising program to run for two weeks over the station. The charge agreed upon was $800. After the program was completed, McDowell sent a bill to the Hartsfield Oil Company. The company denied liability on the ground that Philips did not have the authority to place advertising contracts with the station. The facts showed that Philips' actual authority was to call on stations selling the Hartsfield products, to recruit new agents for the company, and to build goodwill for the oil company whenever possible. Was this authority broad enough to empower him to contract for advertising campaigns?

2. The Kinsey Machine Tool Company shipped by its own truck a truck load of machine tools from its plant in New Jersey to Jacksonville, Florida. On the way the truck driver had several flat tires, and one tire blew out because the truck was overloaded. He stopped in Richmond and purchased twelve new heavy duty tires and tubes, a complete set for the truck, and had the tire company install them. He charged the tires to the Kinsey Machine Tool Company. When the bill was received, the company refused to pay it, claiming the truck driver was only an employee, not an agent. Was the purchaser liable for the tires?

3. Hinton entered into a contract with Barnett whereby Barnett was to paint a building Hinton owned for $1,100, Barnett to furnish all materials and to pay for all labor. The work was to be completed within 30 days; otherwise, Barnett was free to work as he pleased. Barnett hired Dinkler to assist with the painting. A ladder on which Dinkler was standing broke; he fell to the sidewalk and was seriously injured. The ladder was clearly not safe to use. Is Hinton liable to Dinkler for damages?

4. Denny was employed by a mimeograph manufacturing company to sell new mimeograph machines. The company's usual selling terms provided for trading in old mimeograph machines. Denny sold the Comet Letter Service two new machines and agreed to take six secondhand typewriters as a part of the purchase price. The company refused to abide by the contract. Must it do so?

5. Paulson employed Darwin to sell an automobile repair shop and filling station he owned. Darwin was specifically instructed to sell for cash only, with possession to be given to the buyer within sixty days. Darwin entered into a contract with Laster to buy the business for one-third cash and the balance to be paid in three equal installments with possession to be given in ten days. Paulson refused to sell on these terms. Is he bound on the contract the agent made for him?

6. Courts was a stock salesman for a proposed new corporation. Courts sold Carlton 1,000 shares of stock for $50,000 and agreed to take in payment Carlton's small firm in bulk and make Carlton a director in the new corporation. Through its board of directors the corporation ratified Court's action. After the corporation was formed, Carlton refused to go through with the transaction, claiming Courts had no authority to make such a contract. Does this ratification make the contract valid?

7. Gutherie was the manager of a drugstore owned by Mrs. Fowler. Gutherie entered into a contract with Comstock to sell the drugstore in bulk for $18,000, claiming he was the owner. After the contract was written and signed, Comstock learned that Mrs. Fowler was the owner. She had not authorized Gutherie to make the contract, but she ratified the agreement. Is Comstock bound on the contract after it is ratified?

8. Knowles delivered two valuable antiques to Harbin, a licensed factor for antiques. Harbin sold the two items to Mrs. Fort for $1,400. Knowles was dissatisfied with the price received and attempted to recover the items from Mrs. Fort, claiming Knowles could not transfer title to them since he was clearly not the owner. Is this contention sound?

9. Mary had an invitation to attend the Magnolia Ball, the leading social event on the college campus. She purchased a gown for the occasion from a department store for $510 and charged it to her father. Her father refused to pay for it on the basis that his daughter had no right to make the contract in his name. The department store contended Mary was her father's agent by necessity. Was she?

Chapter 30

OPERATION AND TERMINATION OF AN AGENCY

OPERATION OF AGENCY

In a contract of agency, the law imposes upon the agent certain duties even though they are not set out in the contract. Likewise, the relationship of agency creates specific duties and obligations which the principal owes to his agent even though these are not specifically enumerated in the contract. In turn, the same relationship imposes upon both principal and agent certain duties and obligations to third parties. An examination of these duties and obligations will reveal the importance of the relationship of agent and principal as well as the necessity for each party in the relationship to be fully cognizant of both his rights and his duties.

AGENT'S DUTIES TO HIS PRINCIPAL

An agent owes the following important duties to his principal:

1. Loyalty and good faith
2. Obedience
3. Reasonable skill and diligence
4. Accounting
5. Information

(1) **Loyalty and Good Faith.** The relationship of principal and agent is fiduciary in nature; that is, the principal must trust the agent to perform his duties according to contract. The relationship of agent

and principal calls for a higher degree of faith and trust than do most contractual relationships. For this reason the law imposes upon the agent the duty of loyalty and good faith, and deprives him of his right to compensation, reimbursement, and indemnification when he proves disloyal to his principal or acts in bad faith. The interests of the principal must be promoted by the agent to the utmost of his ability.

Loyalty and good faith are abstract terms that give the courts wide latitude in interpreting what acts constitute bad faith or a breach of loyalty. Such acts as secretly owning an interest in a firm that competes with the principal, disclosing confidential information, selling to or buying from himself without the knowledge of the principal, and acting simultaneously as the agent of a competitor are acts which the courts have held to be a breach of good faith. If the agent acts in bad faith, not only may he be discharged, but the principal may recover any damages which he has sustained. Also, the principal may recover any profits the agent has made while acting in bad faith even though the principal was not damaged by the act.

> ■ Hawkins was the manager of the Three Bar Ranch. The owner went on a world tour and left Hawkins in complete charge. Hawkins used the proceeds from the sale of cattle to buy and sell cattle at the public sales barns. His gross profits from these speculations amounted to $3,800 and his losses to $1,400, leaving a net profit of $2,400. When the principal returned and learned of these speculations, he demanded the $3,800 in profits. Hawkins was required to turn over $3,800 to the principal. He could not offset his losses against the profits. This is the penalty for a breach of good faith.

(2) **Obedience.** An agent may have two types of instructions from his principal: one is routine and the other is discretionary. In all routine instructions the agent must carry them out to the letter. An illustration is an instruction not to accept any payments made by check. The agent is liable for any losses incurred by reason of disobeying instructions. He is not justified in disobeying such instructions under any conditions.

If the instruction is a discretionary one, the agent must use the best judgment of which he is capable. For example, if the agent is instructed to accept checks, he is not liable for a bad check when in his judgment the drawer of the check was solvent and reliable. If he accepts a check, however, which he has reason to believe is bad, he will be liable for any loss which the principal sustains by reason of this act.

(3) Reasonable Skill and Diligence. One who acts as an agent must possess the skill required to perform his duties and must be diligent in performing the skill. There is an implied warranty that the agent has such skill and will exercise such diligence. Any breach of this warranty subjects the agent to a liability for damages for the loss by reason of the breach.

As a general rule, an agent may not delegate any of his authority or appoint subagents unless such delegation is recognized as a necessary incident to the performance of his duties as agent. As a rule, an agent is appointed because of his own peculiar skill to perform the duties of an agent. If he delegates any of these duties or appoints subagents, the principal may be forced to accept the services of unskilled people. In addition to making contracts for his principal, an agent may have certain clerical duties to perform, such as record keeping. These duties can be delegated. In many types of businesses, such as real estate and insurance, it is customary for agents to employ subagents. It is assumed the principal agrees to this practice when it is customary. Also, the contract may specifically provide for subagents. In any case, the agent must use skill and diligence in appointing competent subagents and remains liable to the principal for their breach of good faith or lack of skill.

(4) Accounting. The duties of an agent include the keeping of a record of all money transactions pertaining to the agency. He must account to the principal for any money and property of the latter that may come into his possession. Money should be deposited in a bank in the name of the principal, preferably in a bank other than that in which the agent keeps his own personal funds. If the deposit is made in the name of the agent, any loss that may be caused by the failure of the bank will fall on the agent. The agent must keep personal property belonging to the principal separate from that belonging to him.

(5) Information. It is the duty of an agent to keep the principal informed of all facts pertinent to the agency that may enable the principal to protect his interests. In consequence, a principal's promise to pay a bonus to his agent for information secured by the agent in the performance of his duties is unenforceable on the ground that the principal was entitled to the information anyway. The promise was therefore not supported by consideration.

PRINCIPAL'S DUTIES TO HIS AGENT

The principal has four important duties in respect to his agent:

1. Compensation
2. Reimbursement
3. Indemnification
4. Abide by the terms of the contract

(1) **Compensation.** The compensation due the agent is determined by the contract of employment. As in most other contracts, this provision may be either express or implied. If the amount is clearly and expressly stated, disputes seldom arise. If one is asked to serve as an agent but no amount of compensation is stated, the agent is entitled to reasonable or customary compensation for his services. This is especially true when one acts as an attorney or an accountant. If there are no customary rates of compensation, a reasonable rate will be fixed by the court according to the character of the services rendered. Frequently, the compensation is on a contingent basis, such as a percentage of the selling price, provided a sale is made. In such a case, no matter how much time is expended by the agent, he cannot collect compensation from his principal unless a sale is made.

> ■ The Devon Motor Company promised Fletcher a reasonable commission on all sales of cars which Fletcher might make. Fletcher sold one for $2,400 and then demanded a 33⅓ percent commission. It was shown that the customary commission in the community was 20 percent. It was clear that the company expected to pay some commission; and as it had not specified any particular amount, a promise to pay "reasonable" commissions would be construed as calling for the payment of commissions customary in that community for that kind of selling.

(2) **Reimbursement.** Any expenses incurred or disbursements made by the agent from his personal funds as a necessary part of the agency are the liability of the principal. The agent is entitled to reimbursement. If, for example, the agent had to pay from his personal funds a $100 truck repair bill before he could continue his mission, he would be entitled to reimbursement. If, on the other hand, he had to pay a $50 fine for speeding, the principal would not be required to reimburse him. Any expense incurred as a result of an unlawful act must be borne by the agent.

(3) Indemnification. A contractual payment made by the agent for the principal is an expense of the principal. If the payment is made by the agent, not by reason of a contract but as a result of a loss or damage due to an accident, the principal must indemnify the agent. He reimburses him for expenses and indemnifies him for losses and damages. If the principal directs the agent to sell goods in the stock room which already belong to the principal's customer, that customer can sue both the principal and the agent. If the agent is required to pay the customer damages, the agent can in turn sue the principal for giving the instructions which caused him loss.

(4) Abide by the Terms of the Contract. The principal must abide by the terms of the contract in all respects. Thus, he must employ the agent for the period stated in the contract unless there is justification for terminating the contract at an earlier date. If the cooperation or participation of the principal is required in order to enable the agent to perform his duties, the principal must cooperate or participate to the extent required by the contract. For example, if the agent is to sell by sample and be paid a commission on all sales, he must be furnished samples. He must be given the opportunity to earn his fee or commission. In real estate agencies this creates peculiar problems. If the owner of land merely lists his land with the agent, either the owner or any other real estate agent may sell the property. In this case the first agent has no complaint. If the owner makes the first agent his exclusive agent for selling the land, the owner cannot list the property with another agent, for that would deprive the exclusive agent of his contractual opportunity to earn his commission. The owner, however, may sell the land himself. A third variant of this type of agency is the "exclusive sale" agency. In this case neither another agent nor the owner can sell the property while the agency remains in effect.

AGENT'S LIABILITIES TO THIRD PARTIES

Ordinarily, whenever an agent performs his duties, he thereby binds the principal but not himself. In his relations with third parties, however, an agent may make himself personally liable on contracts and for wrongs in several ways:

(1) If an agent contracts in his own name and does not disclose the name of the principal, he becomes liable to the same extent as though he were the principal.

(2) An agent may make himself personally liable to the third party by an express agreement to be responsible.

(3) If a person assumes to act for another without authority, or if one exceeds or materially departs from the authority that he was given, he is personally liable to those with whom he does business. The latter situation may arise when an agent is overzealous in effecting what he may think is a desirable contract.

(4) If an agent signs a contract in his own name, he will be held liable. The proper way for an agent to sign so as to bind only his principal is to sign "principal, by agent." A signing of the principal's name alone will likewise protect the agent although the third person may require the agent to put his name under the name of the principal so that at a later date it can be determined which agent had obtained the contract.

(5) An agent is personally liable for fraud or any other wrongdoing, whether it was caused by disobedience, carelessness, or malice, or whether it was committed on the order of the principal.

PRINCIPAL'S DUTIES AND LIABILITIES TO THIRD PARTIES

The principal is ordinarily liable to third parties for contracts made within the actual or the apparent scope of the agent's authority. When the agent enters into an unauthorized contract that is not within the apparent scope of his authority, the principal is not bound unless he subsequently ratifies the contract.

The test of whether there is apparent authority is whether on the basis of the conduct of the principal a reasonable man would believe that the agent had the authority to make the particular contract. If the answer is in the affirmative, the principal is bound by the contract. For example, if the manager of a furniture store sells a suite of furniture on credit contrary to the authority granted to him, the principal is bound to fulfill the contract with the third party, provided the latter did not know of the limitation upon the agent's authority. The agent is then liable to the principal for any loss sustained.

The principal, as well as the agent, is liable for an injury to the person or the property of a third party that was caused by the negligence or the wrongful act of the agent in the course of his employment. When the agent steps aside from the business of his principal and commits a wrong or injury of his own to another, the principal is not liable unless he ratifies the act.

TERMINATION BY ACTS OF THE PARTIES

Agencies may be terminated by acts of the parties or by operation of law.

An agency may be terminated by acts of the parties by:

1. Original agreement
2. Subsequent agreement
3. Revocation
4. Renunciation by the agent

(1) **Original Agreement.** The contract creating the agency may specify a date for the termination of the agency. In that event, the agency is automatically terminated on that date. Most special agencies, such as a special agency to sell an automobile, are terminated because their purpose has been accomplished.

(2) **Subsequent Agreement.** An agency may be terminated at any time by a mutual agreement between the principal and the agent.

(3) **Revocation.** The principal may revoke the agent's authority at any time, thereby terminating the agency. One must distinguish between the right to terminate the agency and the power to do so. The principal has the right to terminate the agency any time the agent breaches any material part of the contract of employment. If the agent, for example, fails to account for all money collected for the principal, the agent may be discharged; and the principal incurs no liability for breach of contract. The principal, on the other hand, has the power, with one exception, to revoke the agent's authority at any time. Under these circumstances, however, the principal becomes liable to the agent for the damages which he sustains by reason of the unjustifiable discharge. This is the agent's sole remedy because he cannot insist upon the right to continue to act as an agent even though he has done nothing to justify a termination before the end of the contract period. The only exception to this rule is an agency coupled with an interest.

Interest may take one of two forms: (1) interest in the authority, and (2) interest in the subject matter. An agent has interest in the authority when he is authorized to act as an agent in collecting funds for the principal with an agreement that the agent is not to remit the collections to the principal but to apply them on the debt owed to the agent by the principal. In the second case, the agent has a lien on the property of the principal as security for a debt and is appointed as agent to sell the property and apply the proceeds on the debt.

> ■ The Cheyney Hardware Company owed Hanson $4,200. Hanson was appointed the agent for the Cheyney Hardware Company to collect certain accounts receivable for the principal with instructions to keep the first $4,200 and remit the balance to the principal. After Hanson had collected $1,000, the principal attempted to discharge him. The principal cannot terminate this agency until Hanson has collected at least $4,200.

(4) Renunciation. Like the principal, the agent has the power to renounce the agency at any time. If the agent abandons the agency without cause before the contract is fulfilled, he is liable to the principal for all losses due to the unjustified abandonment.

TERMINATION BY OPERATION OF LAW

An agency may be terminated by operation of law. This may occur because of:

1. Subsequent illegality
2. Death or incapacity
3. Destruction
4. Bankruptcy
5. Dissolution
6. War

(1) Subsequent Illegality. Subsequent illegality of the subject matter of the agency terminates the agency.

(2) Death or Incapacity. Death or incapacity of either the principal or agent terminates the agency. For example, if the agent permanently loses his power of speech so that he cannot perform his principal's business, the agency is automatically terminated.

(3) Destruction. Destruction of the subject matter, such as the destruction of a house by fire that was to be sold by the agent, terminates the agency.

(4) Bankruptcy. Bankruptcy of the principal terminates the agency. In most cases bankruptcy of the agent does not terminate the agency.

(5) **Dissolution.** Dissolution of a corporation terminates an agency. This is equivalent to death since a dissolution of a corporation is a legal death.

(6) **War.** When the country of the principal and that of the agent are at war against each other, the agent's authority is usually terminated or at least suspended until peace is restored. When war makes performance impossible, the agency is terminated.

NOTICE OF TERMINATION

When an agency is terminated by the act of the principal, he must give notice to third parties with whom the agent has previously transacted business and who would be likely to deal with him as an agent.

When an agency is terminated by the operation of law, notice need not be given either to the agent or to third parties.

QUESTIONS

1. What duties does an agent owe his principal?
2. What two types of instructions may a principal give his agent?
3. What does an agent warrant when he accepts his job?
4. How should an agent deposit his principal's money in a bank?
5. If the agent and the principal do not set the amount of the agent's compensation at the time the contract is performed, on what basis is the amount determined if the agent and the principal cannot agree?
6. If an agent must pay agency expenses out of his personal funds in order to complete his mission, what is the liability of the principal?
7. If an agent exceeds his authority when contracting with a third party, who is held liable on the contract?
8. If an agent commits a fraudulent act on the instructions of the principal, who is liable to the third party for damages?
9. What is the principal's liability in regard to third parties for injuries caused by the negligent acts of his agents?
10. How may an agency be terminated?

CASE PROBLEMS

1. Heckman was an agent to sell Porter's country manor for $60,000. Johnson contacted Heckman and asked him to find him a property of certain descriptions and agreed to pay him 5 percent of the purchase price if he found a desirable place. Without disclosing to Johnson that he also was the agent to sell Porter's property, Heckman persuaded Johnson to buy the Porter mansion. After the sale was consummated, Johnson learned of Heckman's status as an agent for both parties and refused to pay Heckman his 5 percent commission. Must he pay?

2. The Scott Investment Company owned a housing project consisting of about 200 private dwellings. Langdon was the manager for this project. One of his duties was to keep each property properly insured. He was a secret partner in an insurance agency with his mother-in-law. He placed all insurance with this agency. There was no evidence that he purchased any more insurance than was necessary nor was there any excessive charge of any kind. When the principal learned of Langdon's ownership of the agency, it demanded his share of the profits on all policies placed on the 200 private dwellings. Was the Scott Investment Company entitled to these profits?

3. Bursham was a sales agent and representative for a jewelry manufacturer. In calling on retailers he carried several thousand dollars' worth of samples at all times. He was dismissed but refused to return the samples. He sold them for $1,000 above the manufacturer's selling price and kept all the money. (a) Must he remit to the principal any or all of the proceeds? (b) Does the $1,000 profit belong to the principal or to the agent?

4. Tolbert was a sales agent for a vacuum cleaner distributor. Among other instructions he was told not to accept checks in payment of a machine "unless in your opinion the check is good." Tolbert sold one machine for $85 and was paid by check. The check was dishonored and the principal demanded that Tolbert make good the loss. Tolbert contended that since the man "looked honest," he was justified in thinking the check was good. Did Tolbert obey instructions?

5. Watson was employed by Whitworth as his agent at a salary of $12,000 a year plus expenses while traveling. Watson worked the first month and during that time he filed an expense account of $75 for each day he worked, although some days he did not leave town. Whitworth discharged him and refused to pay him any salary or reimburse him for expenses. Watson sued for one year's salary plus one month's travel expense. Discuss their rights.

6. Wright was employed by Tucker as his agent. One of his duties was to present drafts for acceptance and payment. One draft for $1,284.72 was "payable at the Cross Keys National Bank." The draft was accepted on June 7 and payable ninety days after that date. On September 6, Wright went to the office of the drawee and presented it for payment. Payment was refused and four days later Wright notified the drawer of the dishonor. Did Wright have the skill necessary to perform correctly the duties for which he was employed?

7. Drake acted in the capacity of a general agent for the D & E Grocery Company. One of Drake's duties was to collect each week from the company's charge customers. Drake was discharged. Without the knowledge of the company, he made several collections after his discharge and failed to account for the money. The D & E Grocery Company demanded that its customers pay a second time. Must they pay again if they had already paid Drake?

Chapter 31

EMPLOYER AND EMPLOYEE

NATURE OF THE EMPLOYMENT CONTRACT

Over a period of many decades the common law developed many rules governing the relationship between an employer and his employee, frequently called the master and servant relationship. Not only have the terms "master" and "servant" been largely abandoned, but the laws governing their relationship have also been greatly modified. In every state there remain remnants of the common law which still apply to the employer-employee relationship. Many of its features dealing with safe working conditions and other aspects of the employment contract have been retained in modern labor legislation. These new laws do not cover all employees. In every state there is a small number of employees who still have their rights and duties determined largely by the common law master-servant concept. The common law was slanted heavily in favor of the employer. This chapter will deal primarily with the common law as it relates to employers and employees.

CREATION OF EMPLOYER AND EMPLOYEE RELATIONSHIP

The relationship of employer and employee arises from the contract of employment, either express or implied. As a rule, the relationship arises only from an express contract. The common law was jealous of the right of the employer to hire whom he pleased and of the right of the employee to choose freely his employer. The relationship of employer and employee could not be imposed upon anyone without his assent. Thus, if one voluntarily performs the duties of a servant, he cannot by that act subject the employer or householder to assume the liability of a master. But if a man accepts the proffered services of another in such a way as to imply a willingness to hire him, he will be bound as an employer even though the contract is implied.

In the event an employee is discharged without cause, the employer must pay him up to the end of the contract period. Seldom is the length of the contract period mentioned when the employer-employee relationship is created. It is usually implied by the terms of compensation. If the employee is paid by the hour, he may be discharged without liability at the end of any hour. If he is paid by the week or by the month, as is usually the case with secretaries, stenographers, and many other office employees, the term of employment is one week or one month as the case may be. With the monthly paid employees, the term of employment may depend upon the way the compensation is specified. If the quoted salary is $7,500 a year, the term of employment is one year even though the employee is paid once a month.

The terms of the employer-employee contract, other than the compensation, are seldom stated. They are determined by law, custom, and union contracts.

UNION CONTRACTS

As indicated previously, the employer-employee relationship can come into existence only as the result of a contract, express or implied. Formerly the employer contracted individually with each employee. Under this condition two employees doing the same kind of work might receive radically different rates of pay. The contract of employment came into existence by an offer and an acceptance. Theoretically it was a personal matter with each employee whether he was willing to work for less money than a fellow employee doing the same work. Men with large families and great responsibilities tended to be meek in direct ratio to their responsibilities. This generally tended to hold wages down. Out of this and other economic factors grew the union movement and collective bargaining or contracting in many industries. Under this method, an agent of the employees speaks and contracts for all the employees collectively. As a general rule, a contract is still made individually with each employee, but the union contract binds the employer to recognize certain scales of union wages, hours of work, job classifications, and related matters.

DUTIES AND LIABILITIES OF THE EMPLOYER

The employer under the common law had five well-defined duties

1. Duty to exercise care
2. Duty to provide a reasonably safe place to work
3. Duty to provide safe tools and appliances
4. Duty to provide competent and sufficient employees for the task
5. Duty to instruct employees with reference to the dangerous nature of employment

(1) **Duty to Exercise Care.** The employer under the common law is not an insurer of the employee's safety. He is liable if his negligence causes harm to an employee. He must exercise that degree of care which the nature of the employment demands. He is not liable, however, for injuries resulting from the hazardous nature of the employment when he is not guilty of any breach of duty to the employee. The test whether the employer has exercised proper care is whether he has done what a reasonable man would have done under the circumstances to avoid harm. If the nature of the business is highly hazardous, then the employer must exercise a high degree of diligence to prevent accidents to his employees. The employer is not under a duty to make the employment "accident-proof." The fact that an employee is injured does not prove that he is negligent.

(2) **Duty to Provide a Reasonably Safe Place to Work.** The employer is required to furnish every employee with a reasonably safe place to work. What is a safe place depends upon the nature of the work. A coal mine is a dangerous place; but if it is made as safe as the nature of coal mining permits, the employer is not liable for accidents under the common law. Most states have statutes modifying the common law for hazardous industries. When one of these statutes and the common law conflict, the statute prevails.

> ▪ Dexter was employed as a welder in the Safe Machine Shop. Space was inadequate, making it necessary to pile sheet steel and I-beams on the floor. Dexter tripped over some of this material, and the flame from the welding machine touched his face, causing him to lose sight in one eye. The court held the employer liable in this case since the accident was directly caused by the failure of the employer to provide safe working conditions.

The safe place to work includes not only the particular spot where the worker performs his duties but the whole premises which the employee may use in the course of his employment.

(3) **Duty to Provide Safe Tools and Appliances.** The tools furnished the employees by the employer must be reasonably safe. This

rule applies also to the machinery and appliances. "Reasonably safe" does not mean, of course, free from all danger or accident-proof. Some types of machinery and appliances are dangerous even under the best working conditions possible. The employer is required to use only ordinary care, relative to the nature of the work, in providing safe tools and machinery. He is not bound to discard old tools in order to install the latest and safest devices. If experience has shown that certain appliances or devices are dangerous and that newer devices have eliminated or greatly minimized the hazardous nature of the tool or device, then an employer must provide the safer method.

(4) **Duty to Provide Competent and Sufficient Employees for the Task.** Both the number of employees and their skill and experience affect the hazardous nature of many jobs. A task which is safe when performed by four men may be highly hazardous when only three men attempt it. Furthermore, the task may be safely performed by three men who are competent, but the same task may be very hazardous when one of the men is inexperienced. The employer is liable for all injuries to employees when the direct cause is due either to an insufficient number of workers or to the lack of skill of some of the workers. The employer is required to know the safe number of men required for each task. He also must have knowledge of the skill required to perform the task in a safe manner and make sure that each employee actually possesses that skill.

> ▪ The Baxter Lumber Company was engaged in buying saw logs and cutting them into lumber. To get to the saw, the logs had to be stacked on a machine and then rolled onto the saw carriage for cutting. Baxter hired Burton to roll the logs onto the carriage. The job was exceptionally hazardous unless performed by an experienced man. Burton was totally inexperienced in this work. As a direct result of his inexperience, a pile of logs was loosened and rolled violently against the saw carriage, knocking the saw operator against the moving saw. He lost both legs. The Baxter Lumber Company was held liable for his injury since the cause was the inexperience of Burton.

(5) **Duty to Instruct New Employees.** In all positions where machinery, chemicals, electric appliances, and other modern production instruments are used, there are many hazards of various degrees. The dangerous nature of these instruments may be perfectly evident to an experienced worker but not to an inexperienced worker. A machine that is perfectly safe to operate when the operator is skilled may be very hazardous when operated by one who is new at the job.

One need not be told that a buzzing saw is dangerous if touched. How much instruction, then, if any, must be given to a new employee depends upon his experience, the nature of the machinery or chemical, and the degree to which the danger is self-evident to even an inexperienced employee. The law requires the employer to give that degree of instruction which a reasonable man would exercise under the circumstances to avoid reasonably forseeable harm which could result from a failure to give instructions.

LIABILITIES OF THE EMPLOYER TO THIRD PARTIES

The employer is liable under certain circumstances for injuries to third parties which are caused by his employees. To be liable, the employee must have committed the injury in the course of his employment. If the employee, on his own initiative, injures a third party, and the injury was not a result of his work on his job, then the employee is personally liable, but the employer is not. The employer will be liable, however, if he ordered the act which caused the injury, or if he had knowledge of the act and assented to it. Finally, the employer is liable for the torts of his employees when these torts are due to his own negligence in not enforcing safe working procedures, or providing safe equipment, such as trucks, or in not employing competent employees.

> ▪ The Benten Wrecking Company instructed its employees not to throw timbers from the roof of the building it was wrecking unless one employee was on the ground to see that no one was in danger. The employees ignored this instruction and threw a large timber from the roof, injuring a man walking along beside the building. The company was liable for this injury even though the employees ignored their instructions.

EMPLOYEE'S DUTY TO HIS EMPLOYER

The employee owes certain duties to his employer. He must perform his duties faithfully and honestly. In skilled positions the worker must perform the task with ordinary skill. He must not reveal trade secrets or confidential information. In the event an employee breaches any of these duties, the employer's only practical remedy is to discharge the employee.

In the absence of an express or implied agreement to the contrary, the inventions of an employee belong to him, even though he used the time and property of the employer in their discovery, provided that he was not employed for the express purpose of inventing the things or the processes which he has discovered.

If the invention is discovered during working hours and with the employer's material and equipment, the employer has the right to use the invention without charge in the operation of his business. If the employee has obtained a patent for the invention, he must grant the employer a nonexclusive license to use the invention without the payment of royalty. This *shop right* of the employer does not give him the right to make and sell machines that embody the employee's invention; it only entitles him to use the invention in the operation of his plant.

When the employee is employed in order to secure certain results from experiments to be conducted by him, the courts hold that the inventions equitably belong to the employer on the ground either that there is a trust relation or that there is an implied agreement to make an assignment.

In any case an employee may expressly agree that his inventions made during his employment will be the property of the employer. If such contracts are not clear and specific, the courts are inclined to rule against the employer. The employee may also agree to assign to the employer inventions made after the term of employment.

COMMON-LAW DEFENSES OF THE EMPLOYER

Even when the employer has violated his duty to his employee, the employer is still not liable if he can show that the nonfatal injury of the employee was caused by one of the following:

1. The employee's contributory negligence
2. The act of a fellow servant
3. A risk assumed by the employee

In addition, the employer is not liable for damages in any case where the employee dies as a result of his injuries. This is not based on any employment law principle but on the general rule of the common law that a cause of action or a claim for injuries dies with the victim.

(1) Contributory Negligence Rule. Under the common law if a worker sustains an injury on the job, he can sue his employer for damages. To establish liability, he must prove breach of duty on the part of the employer, namely that he failed to provide safe working conditions, or one of the other duties set out on page 281. The employer can escape liability for this breach of duty if he can establish the fact that the employee's own negligence contributed to the accident. If the employee could have avoided the injury by the exercise of due diligence, he is not entitled to collect damages from the employer.

(2) **The Fellow-Servant Rule.** If an employee is injured on the job and he himself was in no way negligent, the employer may still avoid being held liable by proving that the injury was caused by a fellow servant. A *fellow servant* is an employee who has the same status as the injured worker and is working with him. A foreman is not a fellow servant, nor is an employee in a different department even though he has the same status as the injured worker. The justification of this rule is that the employees assume this risk when they accept employment.

(3) **Assumption-of-the-Risk Rule.** Every type of employment in industry has some normal risks. Employees assume these normal risks by voluntarily accepting employment. This does not excuse the employer from the duty of providing safe working conditions; but even after this is done, many types of jobs, such as coal mining, are hazardous. If the injury is due to the hazardous nature of the job, the employer cannot be held liable. Even when the employer fails to provide the safe tools or safe conditions of employment, the employer is not liable if the employee could easily see the hazardous condition and did not protest. He is assumed to have waived his right to demand safe working conditions.

The defenses described above have been abolished as discussed in the next section. The rule that a claim dies with the victim has been abolished by statutes applicable to all kinds of claims, and workmen's compensation statutes make express provisions for compensation for death claims.

EMPLOYER'S LIABILITY FOR EMPLOYEE'S INJURIES

For most kinds of employment, workmen's compensation statutes govern. They provide that the injured employee is entitled to compensation as long as the accident occurred in the course of his employment from a risk involved in that employment.

In some employment situations common-law principles apply. Under them the employer is not an insurer of the employee's safety. It is necessary, therefore, to consider the duties and defenses of an employer apart from statute.

Common-Law Status of Employer. An employer has certain duties and is entitled to set up certain defenses.

(1) Duties. The employer is under the duty to furnish an employee with a reasonably safe place in which to work, reasonably safe tools and appliances, and a sufficient number of competent fellow employees for the work involved; and to warn the employee of any unusual dangers peculiar to the employer's business.

(2) Defenses. The employer at common law is not liable to an injured employee, regardless of his own negligence, if the employee was guilty of contributory negligence, or if he was harmed by the act of a fellow servant, or if he was harmed by an ordinary hazard of the work, as he is deemed to assume such risks.

Statutory Changes. The rising incidence of industrial accidents, due to the increasing use of more powerful machinery and the growth of the industrial labor population, led to a demand for statutory modification of the common-law rules relating to the liability of employers for industrial accidents.

(1) Modification of Common-Law Defenses. One type of change was to modify by statute the defenses which an employer could assert when sued by an employee for damages. Under such statutes as the Federal Employers' Liability Act and the Federal Safety Appliance Act, which apply to common carriers engaged in interstate commerce, the plaintiff must still bring an action in a court and prove the negligence of the employer or of his employees, but the burden of proving his case is made lighter by limitations on the employer's defenses.

In many states the common-law defenses of employers whose employees are engaged in hazardous types of work have also been modified by statute.

(2) Workmen's Compensation. A more sweeping development has been made by the adoption of workmen's compensation statutes

in every state. With respect to certain industries or businesses, these statutes provide that an employee, or certain relatives of a deceased employee, are entitled to recover damages for the injury or death of the employee whenever the injury arose within the course of the employee's work from a risk involved in that work. In such a case compensation is paid without regard to whether the employer or the employee was negligent, although generally no compensation is allowed for a willfully self-inflicted injury or a harm sustained while intoxicated.

There has been a gradual widening of the workmen's compensation statutes, either by amendment or by the adoption of special statutes, so that compensation today is generally recoverable for accident-inflicted injuries and occupational diseases. In some states compensation for occupational diseases is limited to those specified in the statute by name, such as silicosis, lead poisoning, or injury to health from radioactivity. In other states any disease arising from the occupation is compensable.

Workmen's compensation proceedings differ from the common-law action for damages or an action for damages under an employer's liability statute in that the latter actions are brought in a court of law, whereas workmen's compensation proceedings are brought before a special administrative agency or workmen's compensation board.

Workmen's compensation statutes do not bar an employee from suing another employee for the injury caused him.

QUESTIONS

1. In what important respect are employees distinguished from agents?
2. Are contracts of employment ever required to be in writing? If so, when?
3. How has collective bargaining affected the employer-employee relationship?
4. If a mine owner fails to brace the slate roof of the mine properly and, as a direct result of this failure, a miner is injured, who is liable for the injury?
5. What is the duty in regard to the safety of the tools the employer furnishes?
6. What is the employer's liability concerning the number of competent employees he must provide for each task?
7. Must an employer provide all the very latest safety devices?
8. May an employer sue an employee for lack of loyalty and good faith?
9. If an employee invents some device on the employer's time, does he have exclusive right to it?

10. What are the basic provisions of workmen's compensation statutes with regard to injury or death of an employee resulting in the course of the employee's work from a risk involved in that work?

11. Have the state workmen's compensation laws repealed the common law of employer liability for injuries for all workers?

12. Under the Federal Employers' Liability Act, does contributory negligence on the injured employee's part bar recovery?

CASE PROBLEMS

1. Hawthorne was employed by Combs to help float a raft of sawlogs down the Levisa river to the Ohio river. The river was in flood stage and contained several dangerous rapids. Hawthorne was aware of these conditions, as he had rafted logs on the river before. The raft was broken apart on one rapid and Hawthorne was seriously injured. There was evidence that the raft was not secured by the best method of constructing rafts. Was Combs liable to Hawthorne for damages?

2. Cheney was a chauffeur for Carter. While taking Carter to the airport to catch a plane, Cheney had a collision with a truck and was seriously injured. Carter was late and during the drive to the airport kept urging Cheney to drive faster. The collision was caused by a combination of too much speed, faulty brakes which Cheney was supposed to keep in good order, and Cheney's attempt to pass a car without adequate view of oncoming traffic. Is Carter liable to Cheney for damages?

3. Keller was color blind. He was employed by Koner to operate a crane. The foreman had a red light signal to notify the crane operator when to stop and a green light to tell him to proceed with the operation. While the red light was flashing, Keller continued to operate the crane and as a direct result of this, House was injured. Is Koner liable for this injury?

4. Lawson was injured by the moving parts of a piece of machinery. The injury could not have happened had a guard been placed over the moving part. It developed that a guard had been provided but that it had been removed by the previous operator of the machine. Lawson was not aware a guard had ever been on the machine. Is Lawson entitled to damages under the common law?

5. Kline was employed by the Keller Machine Shop. As a direct result of his particular job, he invented a machine that was a vast improvement over the one he was using. He worked on his new machine occasionally on company time and with company materials although his job was to operate the machine, not invent a new one. Kline patented his machine and then attempted to prevent the Keller Machine Shop from using it unless he was paid a royalty on the machine. (a) Must the Keller Machine Shop pay Kline to use one of the new machines? (b) Can the Keller Machine Shop manufacture the new machine and license other shops to use it? (c) Can Kline be prevented from patenting the new machine and marketing it in any way he sees fit?

Chapter 32

LABOR LEGISLATION

INTRODUCTION

Since 1930 more laws dealing with industrial relations have been passed by the federal government than had been passed during the entire history of the Republic. Although these laws together with the court interpretations of them are for the most part beyond the scope of a course in business law, some basic knowledge of them is valuable.

THE FAIR LABOR STANDARDS ACT

The Fair Labor Standards Act had two major objectives. The first objective was to place a floor under wages so that all employees engaged in interstate commerce would be paid a minimum wage regardless of economic conditions. The second objective was to discourage a long work week and thus spread employment. The first objective was accomplished directly by setting a minimum wage, which by successive amendments has increased to a rate of $1.60 per hour. The second objective was achieved not by fixing the maximum number of hours to be worked each week but by requiring the employers to pay time and a half for all hours over 40 hours. An employer may work his employees, other than women and children, any number of hours a week if he is willing to pay the overtime wage.

EXCLUSIONS FROM THE ACT

Not all workers are covered by the provisions of the Fair Labor Standards Act. There are various classes of exclusions; the following are examples:

1. Employees working for firms engaged in intrastate commerce are not covered by the Act. This is not a specific exclusion in the Act but is the result of the constitutional provision giving Congress power to regulate interstate commerce, not intrastate commerce.
2. A large number of employees who are engaged in interstate commerce are not covered by the Act since certain businesses are specifically excluded. These exclusions are rather numerous. Other exclusions apply to the type of position rather than the nature of the industry. An example of the first type of exclusion is agricultural processing, such as canning, processing, or ginning. Examples of the second type of exclusion are executives, administrators, and outside salesmen.
3. The maximum hours provisions only do not apply to employees in that part of the transportation industry over which the Interstate Commerce Commission has control, to any employee engaged in the canning of fish, and to persons employed as outside buyers of poultry, eggs, cream, or milk in their natural state.

CHILD LABOR PROVISIONS OF THE FAIR LABOR STANDARDS ACT

The Act forbids "oppressive child labor." The employment of children under 16 years of age is for the most part prohibited. This rule does not apply to parents or guardians employing their children or wards, to newspaper delivery boys, or to certain types of employment specified by the Secretary of Labor as being excepted by the regulations. Those between the ages of 16 and 18 are not permitted to work in industries declared by the Secretary of Labor to be particularly hazardous to health.

CONTINGENT WAGES

Many types of employment call for the payment of wages on a commission basis or on a piece-rate basis. Many salespeople receive a commission on sales made rather than a salary. If the commissions earned in any one week are less than the minimum wages for the hours worked, then the employer must add to the commission enough to bring the total earnings to the minimum wage. The same is true for those on a piece-rate basis. These types of incentive wages are not prohibited, but they cannot be used to evade the minimum wage provisions of the Act.

THE LABOR MANAGEMENT RELATIONS ACT

The federal Labor Relations Act of 1937, expanded by the federal Labor Management Relations Act of 1947, was aimed at creating bargaining equality between employers and employees by requiring that the employer recognize the representative, typically a union, selected by the employees as a representative and bargain with such representative (collective bargaining). It also sought to eliminate certain forms of conduct from the scene of labor negotiations and employment by condemning them as unfair practices.

The Act applies to all employers engaged in interstate commerce with the following specific exceptions:

1. The railroad industry, which is under the Railway Labor Act of 1947
2. Agricultural laborers
3. Domestic servants
4. Supervisory employees who are considered a part of management
5. Government employees

MAJOR PROVISIONS OF THE ACT

There are five major provisions of the Labor Management Relations Act. These five provisions are:

1. The National Labor Relations Board
2. A declaration as to the rights of employees
3. A declaration as to the rights of employers
4. A prohibition of employers' unfair labor practices
5. A prohibition of unfair union practices

(1) **The National Labor Relations Board.** The Labor Management Relations Act provides for a National Labor Relations Board of five members appointed by the President. This board hears complaints of unfair labor practices of employers and also complaints made by both employers and employees of unfair union practices. If the board finds that an unfair practice exists, it has the power to seek an injunction to enjoin the practice. In addition to the powers of the National Labor Relations Board, the President, when a strike threatens national health or safety, may appoint a five-man board of inquiry and then upon the basis of their findings apply to the federal court, if he so desires, for an injunction which will postpone the strike for

eighty days. The board conducts investigations of complaints of unfair labor practices and supervises elections to determine the bargaining representative for the employees within each bargaining unit. In case of dispute, it determines the size and nature of the bargaining unit. In addition to the board's function, a general counsel is appointed by the President. This general counsel is entirely independent of the board in prosecuting complaint cases, but in most other matters he acts as the chief legal advisor to the board.

(2) A Declaration as to the Rights of Employees. The Labor Management Relations Act sets forth the following list of rights which the employees have:

(a) To organize

(b) To bargain collectively through their own chosen agents

(c) To engage in concerted action; that is, strike, for their mutual aid and protection

(d) Of an individual employee to join or not to join a union as he wishes unless a majority of all workers vote for a union shop and the employer agrees thereto.

(3) A Declaration as to the Rights of Employers. The Labor Managements Relations Act gives the employer many important rights:

(a) To petition for an investigation when he questions the union's right to speak for the employees

(b) To refuse to bargain collectively with foremen and other supervisory employees

(c) To institute charges before the board of unfair labor practices by the unions

(d) To sue unions for breaches of the union contract whether the breach is done in the name of the union or as an individual union member

(e) To plead with his workers to refrain from joining the union, provided no threats are used.

(4) A Prohibition of Unfair Labor Practices by Employers. The chief acts which are declared to be unfair practices by employers are:

(a) Interfering in the exercise of the rights granted employees

(b) Refusing to bargain collectively with employees when they have legally selected a representative

(c) Dominating any labor organization or contributing financial support to it

(d) Discriminating against or favoring an employee in any way because of his membership or lack of membership in the union, although an employee may be fired for nonmembership in a union when there is a valid union shop contract

(e) Discriminating against an employee because he has filed a complaint against his employer

When the National Labor Relations Board finds the employer guilty of any of these acts, it usually issues a "cease and desist order." If the cease and desist order is not effective, an injunction may be obtained.

(5) A Prohibition of Unfair Union Practices. The federal statute lists seven specific acts which unions and their leaders may not engage in:

(a) Coercion or restraint of workers in the exercise of their legally expressed rights

(b) Interference with the employer in his selection of a bargaining agent

(c) Refusal to bargain collectively with the employer

(d) Charging excessive initiation fees and discriminatory dues and fees of any kind

(e) Barring a worker from the union for any reason except the nonpayment of dues

(f) Secondary boycotts or strikes in violation of law or the contract, although certain exceptions are made in the construction and garment industries

(g) Attempts to exact payment for services not rendered

FEDERAL SOCIAL SECURITY ACT

The Federal Social Security Act has four major provisions:

1. Old Age and Survivors Insurance
2. Old Age Assistance
3. Unemployment Compensation
4. Taxation to finance the act

(1) **Old Age and Survivors Insurance.** In Chapter 40 on life insurance, both life insurance and annuity insurance are defined and illustrated. The first provision of the Social Security Act provides for the payment by the Social Security Board of decreasing term life insurance to the dependents of a covered worker who dies before the age of retirement. This is called Survivors Benefits. If the worker lives to a specified age and retires, then he and his wife draw a retirement annuity known as a Joint and Last Survivor Annuity as described in Chapter 40. This is the old age part of the provision. Both parts of the first provision are properly called insurance because they shift risks that life insurance companies will assume for a fee. The survivors insurance covers the risk of the breadwinner's dying, leaving those who depend on him without a source of income. The old age benefits cover the risk of outliving one's savings after retirement. These are exactly the same risks assumed by life insurance and annuity insurance contracts.

Who Is Covered? The Social Security Act was passed in 1935 and has been amended at almost every session of Congress since then. Today practically everyone is covered by the life and annuity insurance provisions of the Act. Employees in state and local governments, including public school teachers, may be brought under the coverage of the Act by means of agreements between the state and the federal government. Before these workers can be covered by this agreement, a majority of the eligible employees must vote in favor of the coverage.

Farmers, professional people, such as lawyers, and self-employed business people are for the most part covered by this provision of the Act. Self-employed people who net less than $400 a year are excluded. Also specifically excluded are certain types of work of close relatives, such as a parent for a child, work by a child under 21 for his parents, employment of a wife by her husband, but the Act covers self employment by a wife.

Eligibility for Retirement Benefits. To be eligible for retirement benefits, one must meet these requirements:

(a) Be fully insured at the time of retirement
(b) Be 62 years of age or older
(c) After reaching the age of retirement have applied for retirement benefits. If one elects to start drawing benefits at age 62, there is a penalty in the form of a reduction in benefits depending on how

many months one is short of age 65. To be entitled to the maximum retirement benefits, one must wait until age 65 to apply for the benefits.

Eligibility for Survivors Benefits. When a worker dies before he achieves a fully insured status, his family is entitled to survivors benefits if he was currently insured at the time of his death. One is currently insured if at the time of his death he has a specified number of quarters of coverage ending with the quarter in which he dies or the quarter in which he becomes entitled to old-age insurance benefits.

(2) **Old-Age Assistance.** Since many people for various reasons are not covered by the insurance feature of the Social Security Act, other means of assistance are provided for people over 65. Each state was left to adopt its own pension system, and the federal government agreed to match any state pension up to 75 percent of the first $20 and 50 percent of the remainder. This is a noncontributory system. Need is the only test, whereas with the old-age insurance need is not considered.

(3) **Unemployment Compensation.** In handling unemployment compensation, the federal government cooperates with the states, which set up their own rules for the payment of unemployment benefits. Payments of unemployment compensation are made by the states and not by the federal government.

Federal Law. Every employer of four or more persons (except employers of the exempted classes) must pay a federal tax on his payrolls. No tax is levied on the employee.

Under the provisions of the federal act, no payment of benefits can be made to any individual with regard to unemployment that occurs within two years after the beginning of the time when contributions were required by the state in which he lived.

State Laws. The unemployment compensation laws of the various states differ in many respects, although they tend to follow a common pattern. They are alike, however, in providing for raising funds by levies upon employers.

The state unemployment compensation laws apply in general to workers in commerce and industry. Agricultural workers, domestic servants, governmental employees, and the employees of nonprofit organizations formed and operated exclusively for religious, charitable, literary, educational, scientific, or humane purposes are generally not included under the laws.

In order to be eligible for benefits, a worker generally must meet the following requirements:

(a) He must be available for work and registered at an unemployment office

(b) He must have been employed for a certain length of time within a specified period in an employment covered by the state law

(c) He must be capable of working

(d) He must not have refused employment for which he is reasonably fitted

(e) He must not be self-employed

(f) He must not be out of work because of a strike or a lockout still in progress

(g) He must have served the required waiting period

(4) Taxation to Finance the Plan. To pay the life insurance and the annuity insurance benefits of the Social Security Act, both the employer and the employee are taxed an equal percentage of all income earned in any one year up to a specified maximum. Since both the maximum income and the rate may be changed at any session of Congress, one needs to check current regulations. The unemployment compensation part of the Act is financed by a payroll tax of a maximum of 3 percent. In most states this tax is borne entirely by the employer. The Old Age Assistance part of the Act is paid for by general taxation. No specific tax is levied to meet these payments.

QUESTIONS

1. What was the chief purpose of the Labor Management Relations Act?
2. What Act prohibited "oppressive child labor"?
3. Are all workers covered by the Fair Labor Standards Act?
4. Under the National Labor Management Relations Act of 1947, what power does the President have in a strike affecting the national health and safety?
5. (a) If an employer refuses to bargain collectively with his employees, is this an unfair labor practice?
   (b) Name some unfair labor practices by employers.

6. What are the unions' rights in regard to initiation fees and dues?

7. What workers or income recipients in America are not covered under the old-age retirement part of the Social Security Act?

8. Who may benefit if the insured dies before reaching 65?

9. How can local government employees gain coverage under the Social Security Act?

10. What are the general requirements for a person to be eligible for unemployment benefits under typical state laws governing unemployment compensation?

CASE PROBLEMS

1. John was employed by the Ritz Hotel for $20 a week plus his tips. Tips amounted on the average to $40 a week. After John had worked six months, he demanded that the hotel pay him the minimum wage, exclusive of tips, for the six months he had been working. Must the hotel pay?

2. The Fenton Model Airplane Company made kits for model airplanes, boats, and cars. It sold some finished products. To make the finished products ready for sale, it contracted with high school and business college boys to make the kits into finished products. Each boy would take a given number of kits home, and when he returned them all finished, he was paid a fixed sum for each item. After several months John became dissatisfied with the amount he was earning and demanded that he be paid the minimum wage for the number of hours he worked on the models. The company insisted he was an independent contractor and, therefore, not entitled to minimum wages. Is the company's contention correct?

3. The Independent Carpenters Union was a local union made up of all the employees of the Grace Sheet Metal Company who worked in any way with wood. The president of the company contributed $500 a month to the union so it would not have to charge its members dues. Some of the members who wanted to be represented by the National Carpenters' Union, a dues-paying union, filed a complaint with the National Labor Relations Board charging the company with an unfair labor practice. Is this an unfair labor practice?

4. The teachers of Clarke County wish to be covered by social security. The County School Board refuses to consider placing them under social security. What act, if any, can the teachers take to obtain coverage?

5. The Walton Wax Company employed about 400 workers at the peak of its business load. When business became slack, instead of shutting down, it went on a two-day week for everyone. The workers insisted that the company shut down completely until business picked up so that the workers would be eligible for unemployment compensation. May they compel the company to do this?

6. Crawford owned a cotton gin and cotton storage company. At the peak of the cotton picking season he employed twenty or more workers,

but only four employees had full-time work. Often when there was a long line of trucks waiting to have the cotton ginned, he would keep running until midnight. Some of the workers would work fourteen hours a day. They brought suit to compel Crawford to pay them minimum wages and time and a half for overtime. Are they entitled to this relief?

SUMMARY CASES

PART 6

1. J. F. Powell was an agent for the Continental Oil Company. The job was to call on local dealers to explain the company's advertising program, to call on them to get new business, and to increase the old business. His territory covered about 12 counties. He placed an advertising program with C. C. Baxter, owner of radio station KFPL. This program consisted of 26 electrical transcriptions called the "Conoco Listeners' Hour." The company refused to pay for the advertising and Baxter sued. Was the company bound on this contract? (Continental Oil Company v. Baxter, 59 S. W. 2d 463)

2. Samuel Leviten, a commission merchant in New York City engaged the brokerage firm of Bickley, Mandeville and Wimple, Inc. of Chicago to make short sales for him on the Chicago Merchants' Exchange. These brokers at one time covered some short sales by making purchases for Leviten without his knowledge or consent. Leviten was later notified of their act but made no protest for several days. He later brought suit for damages against the brokers alleging that they violated their contract with him. Did Leviten's silence constitute a ratification? (Leviten v. Bickley, Mandeville and Wimple, Inc., 35 F. 2d 825)

3. Alfred S. Dale was the owner of an apartment building in Bismarck. He ordered some beds from Sears, Roebuck and Company. When the beds arrived, he contracted with Nelson to install one of them in one of the apartments. Claude Newman rented the apartment. The bed collapsed and Newman was seriously injured. Nelson had not followed instructions in installing the bed. He used wood screws instead of the lag screws which the seller had recommended for the installation. This was the direct cause of the collapse. Was Nelson an employee of Dale or an independent contractor? (Newman v. Sears Roebuck Co. and Dale, 43 N. W. 2d 411)

4. Raymond was the agent of Davies in the management and operation of Davies' farm. He brought suit to collect for his unpaid salary of $2,187.35 and $439.99 for money he advanced from his personal funds. Davies denied all the liability on the grounds of breach of good faith. Raymond was secretly a stockholder in Farmers' Cooperative Exchange. He purchased many farm supplies from this corporation for the principal and at one time received a bonus for these purchases in the form of 7 shares of stock. He did not reveal this fact to Davies. Was this act a breach of good faith? (Raymond v. Davies, 293 Mass. 117, 199 N. E. 321)

5. Moore was a real estate broker in Fargo. He approached Olsen, owner of some real estate, relative to selling the real estate. Olsen agreed to pay him 5 percent commission if he would sell it. Moore introduced one Flatt as a prospective purchaser who wished to use the property as a summer resort. The sale was finally consummated to Flatt for $15,000. Olsen then learned that the true purchaser was Pettibone who also owned and operated a summer resort on the same lake where the Olsen property was located. Moore was secretly Pettibone's agent. Upon learning these facts, Olsen brought suit to rescind the contract. May Olsen rescind this contract? (Olsen v. Pettibone, 168 Minn. 414, 210 N. W. 149)

6. McDonnell was the general agent of the Seaboard Air Line Railway at Savannah, Georgia. Among his other duties McDonnell was to issue bills of lading and to notify consignees when freight had arrived. McDonnell fraudulently forged several bills of lading purporting to have originated in Charleston, S. C. He notified Gleason, a cotton factor in Savannah, that cotton consigned to him had arrived. He then induced Gleason to pay him a large sum of money for this nonexistent cotton. Gleason, upon learning of the forged documents, brought suit against the principal to recover the amount of his loss. Was the principal liable for the fraudulent act of its agent? (Gleason v. Seaboard Air Line Railway, 278 U. S. 349, 49 S. Ct. 161)

7. The International Seaman's Union had a contract with the Peninsular and Occidental Steamship Company. At the time this contract was signed, there was no other union claiming to represent the seamen. Later the National Maritime Union began organizing the crew and obtained a majority of the crew as members. A strike resulted over the issue as to which union should represent the crew. About 150 members of the crew who engaged in sitdown strikes and threatened to sabotage the ship were dismissed. The dismissed members of the crew filed a complaint with the National Labor Relations Board, alleging the shipowners had engaged in an unfair labor practice by dismissing them for union activity. The board found the steamship company guilty and ordered the dismissed crew members restored to their jobs with back pay. The shipowners alleged that the crew members were dismissed for their mutiny and threatened sabotage, not for their union activity. Did the steamship company commit an unfair labor practice? (The Peninsular and Occidental Steamship Co. v. National Labor Relations Board, C. C. A. 5, 98 F. 2d 411)

8. Curtis applied to the Phelps Dodge Corporation for employment. His application was turned down because he was a member of a labor union. After vainly seeking work for some time, he brought an action before the National Labor Relations Board, alleging an unfair labor practice. The board found the company guilty and ordered the company to employ Curtis and pay him for the wages he would have earned had he been employed. The company appealed this ruling in the U. S. Circuit Court. The question to be answered in this case is: If "firing" a man for union activity is an unfair labor practice, should refusing to hire a man for the same activity be an unfair labor practice? (Phelps Dodge Corp. v. National Labor Relations Board, 313 U. S. 177)

9. Eleanor Beard conducted a business whereby she supplied materials to women from which they made comforters and quilts. Before delivery the material was stamped with special designs. The women were to take the material home and do the work at their leisure. When the quilts were completed, they were returned, and payment was made according to the contract price. The Collector of Internal Revenue classified these workers as employees and compelled Beard to pay social security taxes on their earnings. Beard appealed to the Federal Court to recover these taxes on the ground these parties were independent contractors, not employees. Were they employees? (Glenn, Collector of Internal Revenue v. Beard, 141 F. 2d 376).

10. John P. Finnegan was the driver of a truck for the New York Tribune, Inc. On his way to deliver a truckload of paper, he collided with a bus driven by Sauter. When Sauter got out of the bus, an argument ensued between Sauter and Finnegan. Finnegan became very angry and kicked Sauter in the face, causing a very painful injury. Sauter then sued the employer of Finnegan, the New York Tribune, Inc., for damages for this unprovoked assault. Was the employer liable for this act of its employee? (Sauter v. New York Tribune, Inc. et al, 305 N. Y. 442, 113 N. E. 790)

11. A telegraph operator in a railway station was asleep when a freight train passed by his station. Because of this, the operator did not hear the train. Later he was called by another operator to inquire if the freight train had passed his station and he assured the operator that it had not. On the basis of this assurance, a train was dispatched over a single track line, heading toward the station the train had passed. The two trains later had a head-on collision causing the death of Dixon, the fireman. Dixon's estate sued the railroad for damages because of Dixon's death. Was the railroad company liable? (Northern Pacific Railroad Company vs. Dixon, 194 U. S. 338)

Part 7.

PARTNERSHIPS

Preview Cases for Part 7: Partnerships

▪ Brinkley was a retired merchant. While he was in business, he had bought vast quantities of merchandise from a particular wholesaler. His credit with the wholesaler was excellent. Hartman, in the presence of the credit manager of the wholesale firm, said, "Mr. Brinkley and I have formed a partnership and will be ordering some merchandise from your firm soon." Brinkley did not deny this statement. Soon thereafter Hartman sent in an order amounting to more than $5,000 on 90 days' credit. The account was never paid and the wholesaler sued Brinkley. Is Brinkley liable?

▪ Reed was a partner in the engineering firm of Reed and Dudley. Because of carelessness, as well as incompetency, Reed miscalculated the dimensions of steel piers for a bridge. As a result of this lack of care and skill, the firm was held liable for a $30,000 loss. May the firm hold Reed liable?

▪ The net profit after paying partners' salaries of the partnership of Carlton, Gutherie, and Knowles was $40,000. Knowles and Gutherie insist that the $40,000 be retained in the business for expansion to meet competition. Gutherie insists upon withdrawing his share of the profits. Does he have the right to do so?

▪ The widow Jones left some bearer bonds and other valuables with the partnership firm of Flannagan and Boyd for safekeeping. Boyd cashed some of the bonds and used the money for his personal benefit. Is the firm liable to Mrs. Jones? Is Boyd liable to the firm?

▪ O'Day and Ferber own a patent on a new piece of farm machinery. They form a partnership to continue for five years to manufacture and market the machinery. After two years they sold only ten pieces of machinery, and the purchasers of these were highly dissatisfied. O'Day wished to liquidate and call an end to the undertaking while they could still avoid bankruptcy, but Ferber insisted on continued operation until the end of the partnership agreement. What legal steps may O'Day take to end the partnership?

These preview cases are designed to serve as a springboard for the study of this part. As you read through each chapter in this part, you will find the actual decisions for all these preview cases. Of course, there are many more such illustrative problems as well as case problems for decision at the end of each chapter. And there are also a number of even more challenging cases for review at the end of the part.

Chapter 33

FORMATION OF A PARTNERSHIP

WHAT IS A PARTNERSHIP?

A *partnership* is an association of two or more persons who have combined their money, property, or labor and skill, or some or all of them, for the purpose of carrying on as co-owners some lawful business for their joint profit.

The partnership must be formed for the purpose of operating a lawful business. If the business is unlawful, the attempt to form a partnership to operate such a business is void. Furthermore, a partnership may not be formed for the purpose of conducting a lawful business in an illegal manner.

Since the purpose of a partnership must be to conduct a trade, business, or profession for profit, a hunting club, a sewing circle, a trade union, a chamber of commerce, or other nonprofit association cannot be treated as a partnership.

ADVANTAGES OF THE PARTNERSHIP

By the operation of a partnership, capital and skill may be increased, competition may be lessened, labor may be made more efficient, the ratio of expenses per dollar of business may be reduced, and management may be improved. It is not certain that all these advantages will accrue to every partnership, but the prospect of greater profits by reason of them is the incentive which leads to the formation of a partnership.

DISADVANTAGES OF THE PARTNERSHIP

The most important disadvantages are:

(1) The unlimited liability of each partner for the debts of the partnership

(2) The relative instability of the business because of the danger of dissolution by reason of the death or withdrawal of one of the partners

(3) The divided authority among the partners, which may lead to disharmony

CLASSIFICATION OF PARTNERSHIPS

Partnerships may be classified as follows:

1. Ordinary or general partnerships
2. Limited partnerships
3. Trading and nontrading partnerships

(1) **Ordinary or General Partnerships.** When two or more persons voluntarily contract to pool their capital and skill to conduct some business undertaking for profit, with no limitations upon their rights and duties, an *ordinary partnership* or *general partnership* is created. This is the oldest type of business combination and is still widely used today. This type of business organization is governed by the common law except in those states which have adopted the Uniform Partnership Act.* The purpose of this act is to bring about uniformity in the partnership laws of the states.

(2) **Limited Partnerships.** A *limited partnership* is one in which one or more partners have their liability for the firm's debts limited to the amount of their investment. This type of partnership cannot operate under either the common law or the Uniform Partnership Act.** Such a partnership cannot be formed without a specific state statute prescribing the conditions under which it can operate. If the limited partnership does not comply strictly with the enabling statute, the courts hold it to be an ordinary partnership.

---

* The Uniform Partnership Act has been adopted in Guam and all states except Alabama, Florida, Georgia, Hawaii, Iowa, Kansas, Louisiana, Maine, Mississippi, and New Hampshire.

** A Uniform Limited Partnership Act has been adopted in all states except Alabama, Delaware, Kansas, Kentucky, Louisiana, Maine, Oregon, and Wyoming.

(3) **Trading and Nontrading Partnerships.** A *trading partnership* is one engaged in buying and selling merchandise. A *nontrading partnership* is one devoted to services, such as accounting, medicine, dentistry, law, and similar professional services. The chief reason for making the distinction is that the members in a nontrading partnership usually have considerably less apparent authority than the partners in a trading partnership. For example, one partner in a nontrading partnership cannot borrow money in the name of the firm and bind the firm. One dealing with a nontrading partnership is charged with considerably more responsibility in ascertaining the actual authority of the partners to bind the firm than is a person dealing with a trading partnership.

WHO MAY BE PARTNERS?

Since a partnership is based upon a contract, any person who is competent to make a contract is competent to be a partner. A minor may become a partner to the same extent to which he may contract about any other matter. His contracts are voidable by him; but since he is the agent of the other partner or partners, he can bind the partnership on contracts within the scope of the partnership business. A minor partner is subject to the liabilities of the partnership as long as he is a partner. If he withdraws from the partnership, there is a conflict of authority as to whether he can withdraw the entire contribution which he originally made or whether his share of the losses must first be deducted.

KINDS OF PARTNERS

The members of a partnership may be classified as follows:

1. General partner
2. Silent partner
3. Secret partner
4. Dormant partner
5. Nominal partner

(1) **General Partner.** A *general partner* is one who is actively and openly engaged in the business and is held out to everyone as a partner. He has unlimited liability in respect to the partnership debts. He holds himself out to the public as a full-fledged partner, assumes

all the risks of the partnership, and limits none of his rights. This is the usual type of partner.

(2) **Silent Partner.** A *silent partner* is one who, though he may be known to the public as a partner, takes no active part in the management of the business. He limits his rights as a partner to the sharing of the profits in the ratio agreed upon. As a general rule, the other partners offer him two inducements to invest his money but to take no active part in the management. The inducements are limited liability and no share of the losses.

(3) **Secret Partner.** A *secret partner* is an active partner who attempts to keep his status as a partner concealed from the public. His motives are to escape the unlimited liability of a general partner and at the same time to take an active part in the management of the business. Should his relationship to the firm become known to the public, however, he would not escape unlimited liability. He differs from the silent partner in two respects: (1) he is unknown to the public; and (2) he takes an active part in the management of the business. He may feign the status of an employee or he may work elsewhere; but he meets frequently with the other partners to discuss management problems.

(4) **Dormant Partner.** A *dormant partner* (sometimes referred to as a *sleeping partner*) usually combines the characteristics of both the secret and the silent partner. He is usually unknown to the public as a partner, and he takes no part in the management of the business of the firm. When he becomes known to the public as a partner, he is liable for the debts of the firm to the same extent as a general partner. He foregoes his right to participate in the management of the firm. In return he receives a limitation on his liability so far as the other partners are able to effect it. He may, in addition, agree to limit his income to a reasonable return on his investment, since he contributes no services.

(5) **Nominal Partner.** A *nominal partner* holds himself out as a partner or permits others to hold him out as such. In fact, however, he is not a partner since he does not share in the management of the business nor in the profits; but in some instances he may be held liable as a partner.

CREATION OF A PARTNERSHIP

A partnership is the result of a contract, express or implied, just as all other business commitments result from a contract. The partnership contract must meet the five tests of a valid contract as set out in Chapter 3. A partnership may also be created by law when two or more parties act in such a way as to lead third parties to believe that a partnership exists. This manner of formation is treated more fully under "Implied Partnership Agreements" and "Partnerships by Estoppel" later in this chapter.

ARTICLES OF PARTNERSHIP

In the absence of a statute to the contrary, a written contract providing for the formation of a partnership need not be in a particular form. The written agreement is commonly known as *articles of partnership*. Partnership articles may vary according to the needs of the particular situation involved, but ordinarily they should contain the following:

(1) Date
(2) Names of the partners
(3) Nature and the duration of the business
(4) Name and the location of the business
(5) Individual contributions of the partners
(6) Sharing of profits, losses, and responsibilities
(7) Keeping of accounts
(8) Duties of the partners
(9) Amounts of withdrawals of money
(10) Unusual restraints upon the partners
(11) Provisions for dissolution and division of assets
(12) Signatures of partners

IMPLIED PARTNERSHIP AGREEMENTS

A partnership arises whenever the persons in question enter into an agreement which satisfies the definition of a partnership. Thus there is a partnership when three persons agree to contribute property and money to the running of a business as co-owners for the purpose of making a profit, even though they do not in fact call themselves partners. Conversely, the mere fact that persons say "we are partners now" does not establish a partnership if the elements of the definition of a partnership are not satisfied.

In many instances, it is not possible to prove exactly what happened because of the death of witnesses or the destruction of records. Because of this, it is provided by the Uniform Partnership Act that proof that a person received a share of profits is *prima facie* evidence of a partnership. This means that in the absence of other evidence, it should be held that there was a partnership; but this *prima facie* evidence can be overcome, and the conclusion then reached that there was no partnership, by showing that the share of profits was received as wages or as payment of rent or the purchase price of goods.

PARTNERSHIP BY ESTOPPEL

The conduct of persons who in fact are not partners could be such as to mislead persons into thinking that they are partners. The situation is then the same as when a person misleads others into thinking that someone is his authorized agent. In a case of a false impression of a partnership, the law will frequently hold that the apparent partners are estopped from denying that a partnership exists; otherwise third persons will be harmed by their conduct.

> ▪ Brinkley was a retired merchant. While he was in business, he had bought vast quantities of merchandise from a particular wholesaler. His credit with the wholesaler was excellent. Hartman, in the presence of the credit manager of the wholesale firm, said, "Mr. Brinkley and I have formed a partnership and will be ordering some merchandise from your firm soon." Brinkley did not deny this statement. Soon thereafter Hartman sent in an order amounting to more than $5,000 on 90 days' credit. The account was never paid and the wholesaler sued Brinkley. He is liable since his silence estops him from denying that a partnership exists.

PARTNERSHIP FIRM NAME

A firm name is not a legal necessity or requirement for a partnership, but it is useful as a matter of convenience and for the purpose of identification. Any name that does not violate the rights of others or that is not contrary to law may be adopted by the firm and may be changed at will by agreement. In some states it is not permissible to use the name of a person who is not a member of the firm, or to use the words "and Company" unless the term indicates partnership. Many of the states permit the use of fictitious or trade names, but require the firm to register its name, address, purpose, and the names and addresses of the partners.

At common law a partnership cannot bring a suit at law or be sued in the name of the firm, but by statute or court rule a partnership may sue or be sued either in the firm name or in the names of the partners. Under the common law, real property may be held only in the names of the partners, but under the Uniform Partnership Act any property, whether real or personal, may be owned either in the names of the partners or in the name of the firm.

PARTNER'S INTEREST IN PARTNERSHIP PROPERTY

There are three classes of joint ownership of property. *Joint ownership* exists when the survivors of joint owners get full title to all the property upon the death of one. In *common ownership* and upon the death of one party, the surviving co-owners do not get title to the deceased owner's part as in joint ownership. His share passes under his will, or if there is no will, to his heirs. In both the joint and common ownerships, each owner can sell or give away his fractional share without the consent of the other owner or owners. A partner is a *tenant* or *owner in partnership.* This type of ownership differs fundamentally from the other two types. A surviving partner does not get full ownership upon the death of the other partner as is the case in joint ownership. One partner is not as free to sell his interest in partnership property as is the case with both the joint and common ownership. The personal creditors of one partner cannot sell specific pieces of property of the partnership to satisfy personal debts, nor can they sell a fractional part of specific assets. The personal creditors of one partner can sell only his pro rata interest in the partnership, not specific assets. Each partner owns, and can sell, only a pro rata interest in the partnership as an entity. The purchaser of one partner's share cannot demand that the other partners accept him as a partner. The purchaser acquires only the right to receive the share of profits the partner would receive.

JOINT-STOCK COMPANIES

A *joint-stock company* is in some respects similar to a partnership, but the ownership is indicated by shares of stock, as in a corporation.

The ownership of these shares may be transferred without dissolving the association, thus overcoming one of the chief disadvantages of the general partnership. The joint stockholders are still liable, jointly and severally, for the debts of the firm while they are members, and for this reason, joint-stock companies do not offer the safeguards of a corporation. These joint-stock companies are permitted to operate in some states by special statutes authorizing them, or in some states, without statute, as a common-law association.

JOINT VENTURES

A *joint venture* is a relationship in which two or more persons combine their labor or property for a single undertaking and share profits and losses equally or as otherwise agreed. For example, two friends enter into an agreement to get the rights to cut timber from a certain area and market the lumber. A joint venture is similar in many respects to a partnership, the primary difference being that a joint venture is for a single transaction, even though its completion may take several years. A partnership, on the other hand, is generally a continuing business.

QUESTIONS

1. For what purpose may a partnership be formed?
2. (a) What are the advantages of a partnership?
   (b) What are the disadvantages of a partnership?
3. What are the different classes of partnerships?
4. Are partnerships in your state governed by the common law or by the Uniform Partnership Act?
5. (a) Who may be a partner?
   (b) May a minor be held to his partnership agreement?
6. (a) What are the classifications of partners?
   (b) How is a partnership formed?
7. How might two or more parties be held to have formed a partnership when they had no intention to form one?
8. Are partners liable for the negligent acts of the other partners committed in the course of the performance of their partnership duties?
9. If there are three members of a partnership, may two of them "fire" the third one and still keep his investment in the firm?
10. Does every partner have an equal right to work for the firm?

CASE PROBLEMS

1. Goldberg in applying for credit states that he is a partner in the firm of Goldberg and Rowan. Credit was extended to him on the basis of this assertion. It developed that two months prior to this transaction, Goldberg had sold his interest in the firm to Rowan, but Rowan had retained Goldberg's name in the firm. Is Rowan liable on this debt after Goldberg defaults because of insolvency?

2. Mathis and Lyons were employed by the Twin Bar Ranch to manage the ranch for the owner and to receive as compensation two thirds of the net profits plus living quarters. The Dale Feed Company knew of their receipt of a share of the profits and sold feed to the Ranch on the assumption that Mathis and Lyons were partners. Were they?

3. Grider and Greene were partners in a CPA firm. One of their largest clients was in a tight financial situation. Grider offered to buy some stock the client owned by paying him one third cash and giving him a twelve-month note for the balance. The note was signed:

Grider & Greene
By Grider

The stock became worthless, and Greene refused to pay any part of the note. Grider claims it is a partnership debt since he made the deal to build goodwill for the firm. Must Greene pay his share of the note?

4. Gordon was urged by McLain and Meyer to form a partnership. Gordon was profitably employed and did not wish to undertake a new enterprise. McLain and Meyer proposed that if he would invest $15,000 in the firm, they would make him a full-fledged member, guarantee him 2 percent on his investment before they received any profits, and would not reveal to the public that he was a member of the firm. McLain and Meyer were to manage the business. The partnership was organized along the lines mentioned. The firm went bankrupt. A creditor learned of Gordon's relationship with McLain and Meyer and sued him as a partner. Is he liable?

5. Dennison and Morse were partners operating a road construction business. They owned several expensive road scrapers, dirt movers, and other machinery incident to road construction. When Dennison became personally insolvent, his personal creditors attempted to sell some specific pieces of machinery belonging to the partnership to satisfy Dennison's personal debts. May they do so?

6. Perry, store manager for one of a chain of supermarkets, secretly entered into a partnership with Allen to operate an independent supermarket. He invested half the capital but took no part in the management of the firm. He was to receive 8 percent on his investment guaranteed, and one fourth of any additional profits. The firm became insolvent, and the creditors learned of Perry's status. Perry claimed he was a limited partner, while the creditors contended he was a dormant partner. What was the significance of making this distinction?

7. Dince, Strahorn, and Gilbert operated an ordinary partnership. Gilbert died leaving a wife but no children. The two surviving partners agreed to employ Mrs. Gilbert at $200 a month and to give her the share of profits which Mr. Gilbert would have received had he lived. At the end of five years, the firm was to belong solely to Dince and Strahorn. During this five years, Mrs. Gilbert was to have all the powers of a partner, and the name Dince, Strahorn, and Gilbert Clothiers was to remain unchanged. At the end of two years, the firm was insolvent. The creditors sued Mrs. Gilbert personally for the debts of the firm. Was she liable?

8. Taffell and Taylor jointly own a building that rents for $800 a month. They pay all expenses and divide the balance evenly. Taylor has an automobile wreck in which two people are killed. Suit is brought against him and Taffell for $100,000, alleging that a partnership existed. Was this a partnership?

9. Watford owned, as a sole proprietor, a hardware store. He had three sons who had helped him in the business when they were not in school. After they finished school, they devoted full time to the business. No salaries were ever paid, but each one was permitted to withdraw a stipulated amount each week. This arrangement continued for five years, and then the sons sued in a court of equity for an accounting and a dissolution of the partnership. Other than the use of the three sons as helpers, no change in the operation or management of the business was ever made. Was this a partnership?

10. Rich operated the Home Radio Shop and employed Smith as a clerk. A salesman for the Plymouth Radio Manufacturers took the shop's order for $1,500 worth of radios. Rich, in an effort to boost his credit standing, introduced Smith as his partner in the business. The seller had previously sold goods to Smith and knew his credit was good. Smith did not deny the statement of Rich that they were partners. The Home Radio Shop became bankrupt, and the seller sued Smith for the $1,500. Were Rich and Smith partners?

Chapter 34

OPERATION OF A PARTNERSHIP

The law imposes upon each partner the utmost fidelity in all his relationships with his fellow partners. If any partner is remiss in his duty, the other partners have ample legal recourse to redress the wrong.

The five most common duties which the partner owes to the others are:

1. Duty to exercise loyalty and good faith
2. Duty to use reasonable care and skill
3. Duty to conform to the partnership contract
4. Duty to keep records
5. Duty to inform

(1) **Duty to Exercise Loyalty and Good Faith.** Partners owe each other and the firm the utmost loyalty and good faith. Since each partner is the agent of the firm, the relationship of principal and agent prevails. This relationship is a fiduciary one, so that strict fidelity to the interests of the firm must be observed at all times. No partner may take advantage of his copartners. Any personal profits earned directly as a result of one's connection with the partnership must be considered profits of the firm. If the personal interest or advantage of the partner conflicts with the advantage of the partnership, it is the duty of the partner to put the firm's interest above his personal advantage.

313

■ Rucker owned a bakery. He formed a partnership with Dillon to
    open a cafeteria, Dillon to be a secret partner. Rucker purchased
from his own bakery all the pastries used in the cafeteria and charged
the regular prices. Dillon did not know of Rucker's ownership of the
bakery. Rucker had to account to the partnership for all profits he
made on the sale of pastries to the cafeteria. Keeping his ownership
of the bakery secret was not an act of good faith.

(2) **Duty to Use Reasonable Care and Skill.** Each partner must
use reasonable care and skill in conducting the firm's business. Any
loss resulting to the firm because of a partner's failure to use adequate
care and skill in transacting business must be borne by that partner.
If the partnership supplies expert services, such as accounting services
or engineering services, then each partner must perform these services
in a manner that will free the firm from liability for damages for
improper services. However, honest mistakes and errors of judgment
do not render a partner liable individually nor the partnership liable
collectively.

■ Reed was a partner in the engineering firm of Reed and Dudley.
    Because of carelessness, as well as incompetency, Reed miscalcu-
lated the dimensions of steel piers for a bridge. As a result of this
lack of care and skill, the firm was held liable for a $30,000 loss. Reed
in turn was personally liable to the firm for the loss.

(3) **Duty to Conform to the Partnership Contract.** Anyone who
enters into a contractual relationship with another has a duty to
abide by the terms of the contract. The partnership contract must be
observed scrupulously because of the fiduciary status of the partnership type of business organization. Each partner has the power to do
irreparable damage to his copartners should he choose to betray
their trust in him. For this reason, the law holds each partner to the
utmost fidelity to the partnership agreement. Any violation of this
agreement gives the other partners at least two rights: First, they can
sue the offending partner for any loss resulting from his failure to
abide by the partnership agreement; second, they may elect also to
ask the court to decree a dissolution of the partnership. A trivial
breach of the partnership agreement will not justify a dissolution,
however.

■ Hanks, Haley, and Friddle formed a partnership to conduct a
    jewelry store. The partnership agreement stipulated that Hanks
was to have the exclusive right to do all the buying for the firm. Contrary to this agreement, Haley purchased $20,000 worth of jewelry for

the firm. Hanks had previously bought an adequate stock of merchandise. Because of a rapid drop in prices, the firm lost $5,000 on the merchandise that Haley purchased. Haley was liable to the partnership for this loss.

(4) **Duty to Keep Records.** Each partner must keep such records of partnership transactions as are required for an adequate accounting. If the partnership agreement provides for the type of records to be kept, a partner's duty is fulfilled when he keeps such records, even though they may not be fully adequate. Since each partner must account to the partnership for all his transactions for purchases, sales, commission payments, receipts, and all other business transactions, this accounting should be based upon written records.

(5) **Duty to Inform.** Each partner has the duty to inform the partnership of matters relating to the partnership. He must render on demand true and full information of all things affecting the partnership to any partner or the legal representative of any deceased partner or partner under legal disability.

RIGHTS OF PARTNERS

Every partner, in the absence of an agreement to the contrary, has five well-defined rights:

1. Participate in management
2. Inspect the books at all times
3. Contribution
4. Withdraw advances
5. Withdraw profits

(1) **Right to Participate in Management.** In the absence of a contract limiting his rights, each partner has the right by law to participate equally with the others in the management of the partnership business. Because the exercise of this right often leads to disharmony, it is considered one of the basic disadvantages of the partnership type of business organization; but it deserves to stand as a prime advantage because the investor maintains control over his investment, even though his control may often be exercised in a foolish manner. The right of each partner to a voice in management does not mean a dominant voice. With respect to most management decisions, regardless of importance, the majority vote of the individual partners

is controlling. If the decision involves a basic change in the character of the enterprise, or the partnership agreement so requires, the unanimous consent of the partners is required.

> ▪ Meeks, Harold, and West pooled their money and formed a heating and air conditioning business. Meeks was an advertising expert but knew nothing about air conditioning. Harold was an automobile salesman, and West had years of experience in the heating and air conditioning business. The partnership agreement did not state how the work was to be shared. Meeks and Harold wanted to buy a building, but West insisted on renting. Meeks and Harold claimed that since they constituted a majority voice, West's ideas could be ignored. This contention was correct. The partnership agreement was silent on the matter, which did not involve a change in the basic character of the enterprise.

(2) **Right to Inspect the Books.** Each partner must keep a clear record of all transactions he performs for the firm; the firm's books must be available to all partners and each partner must explain on request the significance of any record he makes that is not clear. All checks written must show the purpose for which they are written. There must be no business secrets among the partners.

(3) **Right of Contribution.** If one partner pays a firm debt or liability from his personal funds, he has a right to contribution from each of the other partners.

The Uniform Partnership Act states that "the partnership must indemnify every partner in respect of payments made and personal liabilities reasonably incurred by him in the ordinary and proper conduct of its business or for the preservation of its business or property." The partner has no right, however, to indemnity or reimbursement when he (a) acts in bad faith, (b) negligently causes the necessity for payment, or (c) has previously agreed to bear the expense alone.

(4) **Right to Withdraw Advances.** No partner is entitled to withdraw any part of his original investment without the consent of the other partners. If one partner, however, makes additional advances in the form of a loan, he has a right to withdraw this loan at any time after the due date. Also, he is entitled to interest on this loan unless there is an agreement to the contrary. A partner is not entitled to interest on his capital account. It is, therefore, desirable to keep each partner's capital account separate from his loan account.

(5) **Right to Withdraw Profits.** Each partner has the right to withdraw his share of the profits from the partnership at such time as is specified by the partnership agreement or by express authorization by vote of the majority of the partners in the absence of a controlling provision in the partnership agreement.

- The net profit after partners' salaries of the partnership of Carlton, Gutherie, and Knowles was $40,000. Knowles and Gutherie insist that the $40,000 be retained in the business for expansion to meet competition. Carlton insists upon withdrawing his share. The partnership agreement is silent on such a matter; therefore, the majority vote of Knowles and Gutherie would control.

LIABILITIES OF PARTNERS

A partner's liabilities are of two kinds:

1. Liability for contracts
2. Liability for torts

(1) **Liability for Contracts.** Every member of a general partnership is unlimitedly liable individually for the debts of the firm. If one partner incurs a liability in the name of the firm that is beyond both his actual and apparent authority, he is personally liable for the breach of an implied warranty of his authority, as in the case of an unauthorized agent; but the firm is not. The firm also is not liable for illegal contracts made by any member of the firm since everyone is charged with knowledge of what is illegal. Thus, if a partner in a wholesale liquor firm contracted to sell an individual a case of whiskey, the contract would not be binding on the firm in a state where individual sales are illegal for wholesalers.

(2) **Liability for Torts.** The partnership is liable for all torts committed by each partner if the tort is committed in the course of his services to the partnership. If the liability arises because of the fault of the partner, he can be required to indemnify the partnership and any partners for loss caused them.

- The widow Jones left some bearer bonds and other valuables with the partnership firm of Flannagan and Boyd for safekeeping. Boyd cashed some of the bonds and used the money for his personal benefit. The partnership was liable to Jones for the injury even though Boyd in turn would be liable to indemnify the partnership for the loss it sustains because of his conduct.

NATURE OF PARTNERSHIP LIABILITIES

The partners are jointly liable on all partnership contractual liabilities unless the contract stipulates otherwise. They are jointly and severally liable on all tort liabilities. For joint liabilities the partners must be sued jointly. If the firm's assets are inadequate to pay the debts or liabilities of the firm, the partners are, of course, liable individually for the full amount of debts or liabilities. If all the partners but one are insolvent, the remaining solvent partner must pay all the debts even though the judgment is against all of them. The partner who pays the debt has a right of contribution from the other partners, but as a practical matter may be unable to collect from the other partners.

Withdrawing partners are liable for all partnership debts incurred up to the time they withdraw unless these partners are expressly released from liability by the creditors. New partners admitted to the firm under the common law are liable only for the debts incurred after admission unless they agreed otherwise. Under the Uniform Partnership Act, each incoming partner is liable for all debts as fully as if he had been a partner when the debt was incurred, except that this liability for old debts is limited to his investment in the partnership. Withdrawing partners may contract with incoming partners to pay all old debts, but this is not binding on creditors.

POWERS OF A PARTNER

A partner has any authority which is expressly given by the partnership agreement or by the action of the partnership. In addition he has all powers which it is customary for partners to exercise in that kind of business in that particular community. As in the case of an agent, any limitation on the authority the partner would customarily possess is not binding upon a third person unless made known to him, although the firm is entitled to indemnity from the partner who causes the firm loss through his violation of the limitation placed on his authority. Each partner in an ordinary trading partnership has the following customary or implied authority:

(1) To compromise and release a claim against a third party

(2) To receive payments and to give receipts in the name of the firm

(3) To employ agents and employees whose services are needed in the transaction of the partnership business, or to discharge them

(4) To draw and indorse checks, to make notes, and to accept drafts

(5) To insure the property of the partnership, to cancel insurance policies, or to give proof of loss and to collect the proceeds

(6) To buy goods on credit or to sell goods in the regular course of business

POWERS NOT IMPLIED

Among the acts that a partner does not have the implied power to do and for which he must obtain express authorization are the following:

(1) To assign the assets of the firm for the benefit of creditors

(2) To indorse a negotiable instrument as an accommodation

(3) To submit a partnership controversy for arbitration

(4) To discharge a personal debt by agreeing that it will be set off against one due the firm

(5) To dispose of the goodwill of the business, or to do any other act that would make impossible the continuance of the business

SHARING OF PROFITS AND LOSSES

The partnership agreement usually specifies the basis upon which the profits and the losses are to be shared. This proportion cannot be changed by a majority of the members of the firm. If the partnership agreement does not fix the ratio of sharing the profits and the losses, they will be shared equally and not in proportion to the contribution to the capital. In the absence of a provision in the partnership agreement to the contrary, the majority of the partners may order a division of the profits at any time.

QUESTIONS

1. What duties does each partner owe his copartner?
2. If one partner, as a result of his membership in the firm, is able to make a personal profit, must he share this profit with the other partners?

3. If *A* and *B* form a partnership for the purpose of operating a public accounting office, who is personally liable if *A*, through his ignorance of accounting principles, loses $1,000 of the firm's money?

4. What records must a partner keep of the transactions he performs for the partnership?

5. Is the right of each partner to participate in management equally with the other partners an advantage or disadvantage of the partnership type of business?

6. Does a partner have the right to inspect firm records at all times?

7. If one partner makes a loan to the firm, when may he withdraw this money without the consent of the other partners?

8. What are a partner's liabilities?

9. What are the implied powers of a partner in a trading partnership?

10. If the partnership contract does not set out the method of dividing profits and sharing losses, how are these distributed?

CASE PROBLEMS

1. Hacket, Hammond, and Harper each invested $15,000 in an insurance agency. Each one was to handle a specified function of the business. Salaries of $500 each were to be drawn at the end of each month. After the partnership had operated for two years, during which time the net profits after salaries were $15,000, Hacket and Hammond wanted to retain all profits in the business and add a real estate agency. They would then enter into an ambitious suburban real estate development program. Hacket and Hammond were to handle these added duties and receive an additional $500 a month salary. Harper was to receive no increase. Harper refused to agree to these proposals. Hacket and Hammond insisted that the majority should rule and attempted to ignore Harper's objections. Could these changes be undertaken without Harper's consent?

2. Day, Dolwin, and Farmer operate a partnership engaged in the laundry and dry cleaning business. Each one has $40,000 invested in the business. In addition Day has loaned the business $10,000. At the end of the year the net profits are $25,000. Day and Farmer want to use the profits to install new machinery although the machinery they now have is good. The new machinery has a few modern gadgets which they think will tend to improve their profits. Cash equal to their reserve for depreciation account has been invested in common stock of various corporations. Dolwin insists this stock should be sold and used to purchase new machinery when necessary. He claims he needs his share of the profits to send his four sons to school and insists upon withdrawing his profits. Does he have the right to do so?

3. Albright was a dormant partner in the firm of Town Talk Cleaners. The other two partners managed the firm and kept all records. Albright wanted to inspect the books because he suspected that the other partners were defrauding him. They refused to permit Albright to inspect the books since he had only suspicion, not proof, that something was wrong. Was this a justification for refusing to permit a dormant partner to inspect the books?

4. Anthony and Bill were partners in a tax consultant enterprise. Anthony had a few clients whom he served on Saturdays and at night. The fees they paid him were not turned over to the partnership bookkeeper. Anthony contended that any income he had for services performed on his own time after working hours was his personal income. Was this contention sound?

5. Langford and Palmer were partners in a neon sign installation service. One of their best customers, the Sunset Drive-In Theater, needed credit to build a new drive-in theater in an adjoining town. Langford, without Palmer's knowledge or consent, indorsed in the name of the partnership as an accommodation indorser a note to the Citizens Bank for $15,000 with the owner of the Sunset Drive-In Theater as the maker. The note was never paid; the bank sued the partnership on the indorsement. Is the partnership liable?

6. Pressman and Jordan own and operate an insurance agency as a general partnership. Neal, an experienced underwriter for a large insurance company, is approached by Pressman to purchase the agency since Jordan is sick and unable to work. Pressman without Jordan's knowledge or consent enters into a contract with Neal to sell the agency in bulk for $40,000. Neal paid one half down and agreed to pay the balance by turning over to Pressman and Jordan 10 percent of the commissions earned until the balance was paid. Neal resigns his position and operates the agency one month before Jordan learns of the sale. He repudiates the contract and demands that Neal restore control and management to the partnership. Discuss the rights of the parties.

7. Fargo, Denton, and Howell were the three owners of a partnership selling and servicing boats. Over a period of two years there were many bitter disputes over management policies. Usually Fargo was a minority of one against Denton and Howell. Howell read in a law book that one of the disadvantages of a partnership was disharmony among the partners due to the rule of unanimity. Howell and Denton propose that the partnership incorporate. Fargo asks your advice. What would you tell him?

8. Pringle and Whyte were partners in a drug business. The partnership agreement provided that each partner might draw $50 each week as his share of the profits of the business. Pringle became seriously ill, and as a result Whyte was compelled to work overtime to take care of the business. Because of the extra work he performed, Whyte drew a larger amount of money each week.

(a) Did Whyte have the right to draw a larger sum?

(b) If Whyte found it necessary to employ another person, would the wages of this person be considered an expense of the firm or would they be deducted from the amount Pringle drew?

(c) While Pringle was ill, was he entitled to as much of the profits as though he had worked all the time?

9. Gotesky and Grant were partners in a public accounting firm. Gotesky audited a firm's books in such a careless and negligent manner that the firm lost $4,000 by relying on the inaccurate audit. The partnership was required to pay damages of $4,000. Was Gotesky required to reimburse Grant?

10. Collins and Conwell were partners in a men's clothing store. Each invested $12,000. At the end of the first year the profits were $10,000 and each partner drew out $3,600. The balance of the profits were distributed equally to their capital accounts. The following year Collins wished to draw out the remaining $1,400 of his profits plus $1,100 of his original investment. Was he able to do this without Conwell's consent?

Chapter 35

DISSOLUTION OF A PARTNERSHIP

DISSOLUTION AND TERMINATION OF A PARTNERSHIP

If one member of a going partnership withdraws for any reason, the partnership relation is dissolved, and cannot thereafter do any new business. The partnership continues to exist for the limited purpose of winding up or cleaning up its outstanding obligations and business affairs and distributing its remaining assets to creditors and partners. After all this has been completed, the partnership is deemed terminated and goes out of existence.

DISSOLUTION BY ACTS OF THE PARTIES

A partnership is dissolved by act of the partners in the following ways:

1. Agreement
2. Withdrawal or alienation
3. Expulsion

(1) **Agreement.** At the time the partnership agreement is formed, the partners may fix the time when the partnership relation will cease. Unless the agreement is renewed or amended, the partnership is dissolved on the agreed date. If no date for the dissolution is fixed at the time the partnership is formed, the partners may by mutual agreement dissolve the partnership at any time. Even when a definite date is fixed in the original agreement, the partners may dissolve the

323

partnership prior to that time. In this case the agreement is not binding as an agreement unless all the partners consent to the termination.

Sometimes no date is fixed for terminating the partnership, but the agreement sets forth the purpose of the partnership, such as the construction of a building. In this event the partnership is terminated as soon as the purpose has been achieved.

(2) **Withdrawal or Alienation.** The withdrawal of one partner at any time and for any reason dissolves the partnership. In a partnership for a definite term, any partner has the power to withdraw at any time, but he does not have the right to withdraw. He is liable for any loss sustained by the other partners because of his withdrawal. If no termination date is fixed in the partnership agreement, a partner may withdraw at will without liability. After creditors are paid, in any other dissolution and winding up of a partnership, the withdrawing partner is entitled to receive his capital, undistributed profits, and any loan upon his withdrawal.

If a termination date is fixed in the partnership agreement or by subsequent agreement, the withdrawing partner breaches his contract by withdrawing prior to the agreed date. When a partner withdraws in violation of agreement, the damages which he causes the firm may be deducted from his distributive share of the assets of the partnership.

Closely related to the withdrawal of a partner is the alienation of his interest either by a voluntary sale or an involuntary sale to satisfy personal creditors. The sale does not of itself dissolve the partnership. But the purchaser does not become a partner by purchase since the remaining partners cannot be compelled to accept as a partner anyone who might be "persona non grata" to them. The buying partner has a right to the capital and profits of the withdrawing partner, but he does not have the right to participate in the management.

(3) **Expulsion.** The partnership agreement may and should contain a clause providing for the expulsion of a member, especially if there are more than two members. This clause should spell out clearly the acts for which a member may be expelled and the method of settlement for his interest. The partnership agreement should also set forth that the remaining partners agree to continue the business if that be the case; otherwise, it will be necessary to wind up the partnership business and distribute all the assets to the creditors and partners, thereby terminating the partnership existence.

DISSOLUTION BY COURT DECREE

Under certain circumstances the court may issue a decree dissolving a partnership. The chief reasons justifying such a decree are:

1. Insanity
2. Incapacity
3. Misconduct
4. Futility

(1) Insanity of a Partner. A partner may obtain a decree of dissolution when his partner has been judicially declared a lunatic or when it is shown that he is of unsound mind.

(2) Incapacity of a Partner. If a partner develops an incapacity which makes it impossible for the partner to perform the services to the partnership which the original partnership agreement contemplated, a petition may be filed to terminate the partnership on that ground. A member of an accounting firm who loses his eyesight would probably be incapacitated for his work to the extent of justifying a dissolution. The court, not the partners, must be the judge in each case as to whether or not the partnership should be dissolved.

The incapacity as a rule must be permanent, not temporary. A temporary inability of one partner to perform his duties is one of the risks which the other partners assumed when they formed the partnership and does not justify a court decree in dissolving the partnership.

(3) Misconduct. If one member of a partnership is guilty of misconduct that is prejudicial to the successful continuance of the business, the court may, upon proper application, decree a dissolution of the partnership. Typical illustrations of such misconduct are habitual drunkenness, dishonesty, persistent violation of the partnership agreement, irreconcilable discord among the partners as to major matters, and abandonment of the business by a partner.

■ Gann and Saye were partners in a dry cleaning business. The partnership had three more years to run as provided by the partnership agreement. Every weekend Saye would become intoxicated but was always sober by Monday morning. There was no evidence that his addiction to drink had any adverse effect on the business. Gann was a teetotaler and wanted to dissolve the partnership. Saye would not agree to a voluntary dissolution, and Gann petitioned the court to decree a dissolution. The court refused, since Saye's drinking was always on his own time and did not harm the business.

(4) Futility. All business partnerships are conducted for the purpose of making a profit. When it is clear that this objective cannot be achieved, the court may decree a dissolution. One partner cannot compel the other members to assume continued losses after the success of the business becomes highly improbable and further operation appears futile. A temporarily unprofitable operation does not justify a dissolution. It is only when the objective reasonably appears impossible to attain that the court will issue a decree of dissolution.

> ▪ O'Day and Ferber own a patent on a new piece of farm machinery.
> They form a partnership to continue for five years to manufacture and market the machinery. After two years they sold only ten pieces of machinery, and the purchasers of these were highly dissatisfied. O'Day wished to liquidate and call an end to the undertaking while they could still avoid bankruptcy, but Ferber insisted on continued operation until the end of the partnership agreement. O'Day petitioned the court to decree an immediate dissolution. This the court did on the ground the patented article had no market and the undertaking was probably futile.

DISSOLUTION BY OPERATION OF LAW

Under certain well-defined circumstances, a partnership will be dissolved by operation of law; that is to say, it will be dissolved immediately upon the happening of the specified event. No decree of the court is necessary to dissolve the partnership. The most common examples are:

1. Death or insanity of a partner
2. Bankruptcy
3. Illegality

(1) Death or Insanity of a Partner. The death of one member of a partnership automatically dissolves the partnership. A representative of the deceased may act to protect the interest of the heirs, but he cannot act as a partner. This is true even when the partnership agreement provides that the partnership is not to be dissolved by the death of a member. A dead man cannot be a partner, nor can he appoint an agent to act for him because death also terminates the relationship of principal and agent.

The partnership agreement can provide for an orderly process of dissolution upon the death of a member. Thus, a provision that the surviving partners shall have twelve months in which to liquidate the firm and pay over the deceased partner's share to the heirs is binding. This is not, however, a continuation of the partnership.

Likewise, upon the permanent insanity of a partner, a representative (commonly called a guardian or committee) will be appointed by a court to protect his interests generally and in the liquidation of the partnership which then takes place.

(2) **Bankruptcy.** When an individual is declared a bankrupt, he is discharged from most of his debts, including those connected with the partnership. Thus, the unlimited liability of the partner which would otherwise exist is in effect destroyed, and the partner is not a good credit risk. Because of this, the law regards bankruptcy of a partner as automatically terminating the partnership. The trustee in bankruptcy has the right to assume control of the bankrupt partner's share of the partnership business, but the trustee is not a partner. The trustee merely stands in the place of the partner to see that the creditors' interests are protected.

The bankruptcy of the partnership also terminates the partnership as it is impossible for the partnership to continue doing business when in the course of the bankruptcy proceeding all of its assets have been distributed to pay its creditors.

(3) **Illegality.** Many types of business are legal when undertaken, but because of a change in the law, they may later become illegal. This is particularly true in the alcoholic beverage field. If a partnership is formed to conduct a lawful business and later this type of business is declared illegal, then the partnership is automatically dissolved. If a partnership is formed for the purpose of operating an insurance underwriting business, the partnership is dissolved by a law restricting this type of business to corporations.

- ■ Smith and Combs formed a partnership to operate a tavern. Subsequent to the formation of the partnership, the county in which it was located voted in a local option election to prohibit the sale of alcoholic beverages within the county where the partnership business was located. Since the business is now illegal, the partnership was dissolved by operation of law.

EFFECTS OF DISSOLUTION OF A PARTNERSHIP

Dissolution terminates the right of the partnership to exist and must be followed by the liquidation of the business. Existing contracts may be performed. New contracts cannot be made, except for minor contracts that are reasonably necessary for completion of existing contracts in a commercially reasonable manner. If a part of the assets of the firm are goods in process and additional raw materials must be purchased before the goods in process can be converted into finished goods, these raw materials may be purchased.

After dissolution, a third person making a contract with the partnership stands in much the same position as a person dealing with an agent whose authority has been revoked by the principal. If the transaction relates to winding up, the transaction is authorized and binds the partnership and all partners just as though there had not been a dissolution. If the contract constitutes new business, it is not authorized; and the liability of the partnership and of the individual partner so acting depends upon whether notice of dissolution has been properly given.

NOTICE OF DISSOLUTION

When a partnership is dissolved, the change may not become known to creditors and other third parties who have done business with the old firm. For the protection of these third parties, the law requires that in certain cases they must be given actual notice of the dissolution. If notice is not given, every member of the old firm may be held liable for the acts of the former partners that are committed within the scope of the new business.

Notice is usually given to customers and creditors by mail. It is sufficient to give the general public notice by publication. When a new partnership or corporation has been organized to continue the business after dissolution and termination of the original partnership, the notice of dissolution will also set forth this information as a matter of advertising. If the name of the dissolved partnership included the name of the withdrawing partner, he should, of course, have his name removed from the firm name on all stationery so that he may avoid further liability with regard to the business.

In the following instances notice is usually not deemed necessary:

(1) To those who were partners
(2) When the partnership was dissolved by the operation of law
(3) When the partnership was dissolved by a judicial decree
(4) When a dormant or a secret partner retired

DISTRIBUTION OF ASSETS

After the termination of a partnership, the partners are entitled to participate in the assets remaining after the debts are paid to creditors. The distribution of the remaining assets among the partners is usually as follows:

(1) Partners who have advanced money to the firm or have incurred liabilities in its behalf are entitled to reimbursement.

(2) Each partner is next entitled to the return of the capital that he contributed to the partnership.

(3) Any assets remaining are distributed equally, unless there is an agreement in the partnership contract that provides for an unequal distribution.

When a firm sustains a loss, the loss will be shared equally by the partners, unless there is an agreement to the contrary.

QUESTIONS

1. Must a partnership business dissolve every time there is a change in ownership?
2. If a partnership is to run five years, may one partner withdraw at the end of two years without incurring any liability to the other partners?
3. What are the rights of a person who buys a partner's interest in the firm?
4. In the absence of a specific provision in the partnership contract, may one partner be expelled by the other members?
5. If one member of a firm becomes ill and cannot perform his share of the work, what recourse do the other partners have?
6. What is the remedy for the innocent partners if one of their members conducts himself in such a way that the good name of the business is seriously damaged?
7. When one member of a partnership dies, what effect does this have on the partnership?
8. If a partner is declared personally bankrupt, what effect has this upon the partnership?
9. After the termination of a partnership, how are the assets divided?

CASE PROBLEMS

1. Randolph and Holcomb formed a partnership to operate a private school for girls. The Tug River Wholesale Grocery Company extended

credit to the firm over a period of two years. The partnership was subsequently incorporated, but no notice of this fact was ever given to the creditors except on the letterhead of the school's purchase orders and other papers. The school became insolvent, owing the Tug River Wholesale Company $26,000. The company sued Randolph and Holcomb personally on the debt. The bookkeeper admitted he knew the school had incorporated, but the evidence showed that the owner of the wholesale firm did not. Are Randolph and Holcomb personally liable for this debt?

2. Mize and Duvall formed a partnership to prospect for uranium. The partnership was dissolved at the end of one year by agreement, and due notice was given of the dissolution. Mize borrowed $2,000 from Lawson and executed the firm's note for this loan since the money was to be used to facilitate the liquidation of the partnership. May Duvall deny all liability on the note?

3. Burson and Barber form a partnership to run for 10 years. There is a provision in the partnership agreement stating that in the event one partner dies, the surviving partner shall continue operation of the partnership for one year. Barber died and Burson, pursuant to this provision, operated the firm for one year during which time the firm lost $30,000. Must Barber's estate bear one half of this loss?

4. Smith, Combs, and Dennis were partners in a law firm. Smith was appointed judge of the Superior Court. There was a state law stating that it is illegal for an attorney who is also a judge to be a member of a law firm. The Stacy Furniture Company sold some office furniture and office equipment in the sum of $1,584.75 to the firm of "Smith, Combs, and Dennis," upon Combs' order. The debt was never paid, and the Stacy Furniture Company attempted to hold the partners personally liable, alleging no notice of termination was ever received. Are Smith and Dennis, either or both, personally liable for this account?

5. Andrews and Averitt operated a shoe store as a partnership. Andrews became seriously ill, and the court decreed a dissolution and a liquidation. The Snow Shoe Company sold $3,000 worth of shoes to the firm upon Averitt's order even though its manager, Henry Griffith, had notice of the dissolution. The account was never paid, and the Snow Shoe Company insisted upon the right of sharing in the firm assets along with other partnership creditors. Was it entitled to do so?

6. Kelley, Love, and Marler form a partnership to operate a men's clothing store. The firm operates several years and is very profitable. Marler becomes insane and appears to be beyond hope of recovery. Mrs. Marler enters into a contract with Kelley and Love to dissolve the partnership. Kelley and Love pay her Marler's share of the partnership assets. Kelley and Love operate the new partnership for three years during which time their net profits are $36,000. Marler, having regained his sanity, now demands one third of these profits. Is he entitled to them?

7. Adams and Diehl conducted a printing establishment as a partnership under the name of The Economy Print Shop. Diehl withdrew, and Miss Haley, the secretary-bookkeeper, was instructed to send notices of dissolution to all creditors. She did so but overlooked one paper company from which the partnership had in the past bought a considerable quantity of paper on credit. About two weeks after the dissolution, Adams ordered $1,000 worth of paper from the paper mill that had not received notice of dissolution. The order was made on a new type of order blank from which Diehl's name had been removed. Other than this, there was nothing to indicate any change in the business. The purchase price was never paid. Is Diehl liable for the bill?

SUMMARY CASES

PART 7

1. J. Morris conducted a business under the name of J. Morris and Co. After his death, his two sons, Irving Morris and Jacob Morris continued the business under the same name and at the same place. Jacob Morris signed all checks, and Irving Morris did the selling. Both at various times purchased merchandise on credit from the Sunset Broom and Brush Co. This latter company assigned its accounts receivable to Bedell. J. Morris & Co. failed to pay its account and Bedell sued Irving Morris and Jacob Morris as partners. Jacob Morris denied liability on the ground that he was never a partner. There was little or no evidence that he ever expressly agreed to become a partner. Was Jacob Morris liable as a partner? (Bedell v. Morris, 63 Calif. A. 453, 218 P. 769)

2. Cornell and Sagouspe were partners in a ranch and livestock enterprise. The partnership agreement stipulated that each partner was to withdraw profits from time to time but that the withdrawals were to be equal. No mention was made of salaries. Cornell brought suit to have the partnership dissolved and to have an accounting. Sagouspe claimed accrued salary over a nine-year period of $16,475 for himself and $8,237.50 for his wife. Cornell and his wife were to be allowed only $3,522.50 for the two of them. This disparity of salaries was due to the fact that Sagouspe lived at the ranch and devoted much more time to it than did Cornell and his wife. Decide. (Cornell v. Sagouspe, 53 Nev. 145, 295 P. 443)

3. Beals sold a large tract of timber to Bennett on the following terms: $4 per thousand board feet plus ⅓ of the sales receipts over $21 per thousand. This ⅓ was referred to as ⅓ of the profits, but the profits were arbitrarily fixed at the excess of sales over $21 per thousand board feet. The Worden Company extended considerable credit to Bennett during the logging operations. These debts were never paid. The Worden Company sued Beals as a partner. Did this agreement constitute Beals a partner? (Worden Co. v. Beals, et al., 120 Ore. 66, 250 P. 375)

4. Askew was a partner in the Austin Company. Mrs. Silman was a customer of the Austin Company during the time Askew was a partner but was never a creditor. Askew withdrew from the partnership and gave notice to the public of this withdrawal by a newspaper advertisement. Mrs. Silman never saw the advertisement. Over two years after Askew's withdrawal, Mrs. Silman extended credit to the partnership, thinking Askew was still a partner. She brought suit against Askew since the debt was never paid. Is Askew liable to Silman for this debt? (Askew v. Silman, 95 Ga. 678, 22 S. E. 573)

5. The L. Katz and Company was a partnership consisting of Katz and Brewington. Katz kept control of the books and refused to allow Brewington to inspect them. He also insisted upon managing the business, and refused to permit Brewington to have access to the business or have a voice in its management. Katz did this because he supplied all the capital, even though profits were to be divided equally. Brewington brought an action to compel Katz to give him access to the books. Was Brewington entitled to inspect the books? (Katz v. Brewington, 71 Md. 70)

6. Yost, Campbell, and Sewell formed a partnership operating under the name of the Independent Lumber Company. Freeman purchased Campbell's interest in the firm. At the time of the purchase there were many debts outstanding. Freeman knew of these debts but did not agree to become liable for them. New debts were incurred after the date of purchase. Freeman denied liability for both the old debts and the new debts on the ground that he never intended to become a partner, but intended to make an investment. Was Freeman liable for both the old and the new debts? (Freeman v. Hutting Sash & Door Company, 105 Texas 560)

Part 8.

CORPORATIONS

Preview Cases for Part 8: Corporations

- The charter of the Well Pump and Supply Company set forth that the corporation was "to engage in the boring of wells, installing pumps, selling pumps and supplies, and the servicing of these pumps." The board of directors planned to enter a contract with the Board of Supervisors of Buchanan County to hard surface three miles of county roads. May a stockholder apply to the court for an injunction to prohibit the corporation from fulfilling the contract?

- Bluegate Gardens made a contract to sell nursery supplies and insisted on making the contract out to Evergreen Nurseries, Inc., even though Bluegate Gardens knew the corporation was not yet formed. Simmons signed as president of Evergreen. The corporation was never formed, so Bluegate sued Simmons and the other promoters. Will Bluegate be able to recover from the promoters?

- Wildcat Oil, Inc. engaged in the development of petroleum resources. One of the speculative drillings showed dramatic evidence of the discovery of a vast reserve of natural gas. Martin, the president of the company, while maintaining the discovery as confidential information among the directors of the corporation, purchased many additional shares from stockholders who knew nothing of the new discovery. Martin then announced the discovery and the value of the stock rose sharply. Kelly and Dalton, stockholders who had sold to Martin before the announcement, demand the return of their stock. Will they prevail?

- At a meeting of the board of directors of the Sac River Mining Co., the board voted to loan $20,000 to Parsons, one of the board members. Allen, another board member, dissented vigorously and his dissent was recorded in the minutes of the board. Parsons failed to pay back the loan. In an action by the stockholders against the members of the board, will Allen be liable?

These preview cases are designed to serve as a springboard for the study of this part. As you read through each chapter in this part, you will find the actual decisions for all these preview cases. Of course, there are many more such illustrative problems as well as case problems for decision at the end of each chapter. And there are also a number of even more challenging cases for review at the end of the part.

Chapter 36

NATURE OF A
CORPORATION

WHAT IS A CORPORATION?

A *corporation* is "an association of individuals united for some common purpose, and permitted by law to use a common name and to change its members without dissolution of the association." This definition was given in an early decision by the Supreme Court of the United States and is still considered a satisfactory definition of the term "corporation." Unlike a partnership, a corporation need not be organized for the purpose of making and sharing profits. It may be organized for any lawful purpose, whether that purpose is for pleasure or profit.

A corporation is known in law as an "entity," that is, something that has a distinct existence separate and apart from the existence of its individual members. Chief Justice Marshall defined a corporation as "an artificial being, invisible, intangible, and existing only in contemplation of law." Under certain circumstances, the courts may disregard the entity concept of the corporation and determine the case as though the individuals running the corporation and not the corporation were involved.

A corporation is considered an artificial person that has been substituted for the natural persons who are responsible for its formation and who manage and control its affairs. Hence, when a corporation makes a contract, the contract is made by and in the name of this legal entity, the corporation, and not by and in the name of the individual members. It has all the rights and powers of an individual. It can sue and be sued, it can be fined for violating the law, it has recourse to the constitution to protect its liberties, and in most respects it enjoys the same rights as an individual.

IMPORTANCE OF CORPORATIONS

Corporations have been in existence for a long time, but essentially they are the product of the modern era. The rapid expansion of industry from small shops to giant enterprises required large amounts of capital. Few men had enough money of their own to build a railroad or a great steel mill, and men hesitated to form partnerships with any but trusted acquaintances. In addition, even though four or five men did form a partnership, insufficient capital was still a major problem. The need was for hundreds or even thousands of men, each with a few hundred or a few thousand dollars, to pool their capital for concerted undertakings. The corporate form of business was well adapted to meet this need. It not only provided the necessary capital but also freed the investors from the risks and restraints of partnerships by specifically limiting each investor's liability to his original investment.

It is evident that our mass-production enterprises could not have expanded to their present size except through corporate financing. Small enterprises still offer opportunities; but experience has demonstrated that certain businesses that require much capital, such as a steel mill, an automobile manufacturer, or a railroad, can best be operated by a corporation.

Within the last few decades, incorporation has become attractive to small businesses as a means of obtaining limited liability as will be later discussed. Thus, many businesses that formerly would have been organized as a partnership are today corporations with the "partners" each owning an equal number of shares of the stock of the corporation. In many instances, the single proprietor of the small business has incorporated and owns all the stock of the corporation or virtually all, so that in effect he is a one-man corporation.

DIFFERENCES BETWEEN PARTNERSHIPS AND CORPORATIONS

There are many differences between the law governing partnerships and that governing corporations. For the investor particularly, these differences are extremely important. For example, three men with $20,000 each can form a partnership with a capital of $60,000. We saw, however, in the chapters on partnership, how each partner risks losing not only this $20,000 but also almost everything else he may own since he is personally liable for all partnership debts. If a corporation is formed and each investor contributes $20,000, this amount is the maximum he can lose since he is not liable for the corporate debts beyond his investment.

This advantage of the corporation over the partnership is offset by at least one important disadvantage. In a partnership each partner has an equal voice in the management of the business. Furthermore, he is the sole judge as to whether or not his share of the profits should be withdrawn or left in the business. In a corporation the men who own or control a majority of the common stock have not merely a dominant voice in management but the sole voice. If there are fifteen stockholders but one owns 51 percent of the common stock, he is free to run the corporation as he sees fit by his ability to dominate the board of directors and the corporate officers. The person who invests his savings in a business in the hope of becoming "his own boss" may not find the corporate type of business organization the most desirable unless he can be certain that he controls a majority of the voting stock.

PUBLIC CORPORATIONS

Corporations may be classified as public and private. A *public corporation* is one formed to carry out some governmental function, such as a city, a state university, or a public hospital. The powers and functions of public corporations are not comparable with private corporations conducted for profit. Public corporations are created by the state primarily for the purpose of facilitating the administration of governmental functions.

Some public bodies, such as school boards, boards of county commissioners, and similar bodies are not true public corporations but have many similar powers, such as the right to sue and be sued, own, buy, and sell property, and to sign other contracts as an entity. They are called *quasi corporations*, quasi having the meaning "as if" or "in the nature of."

In recent years the custom has arisen of referring to a corporation as "public" when its stock may be bought by the public at large as distinguished from what is a "private" or "closed" corporation, the stock of which is held by a small group and not sold to outsiders. This use of the terms "public" and "private" is inconsistent with the technical definitions above given for the reason that in fact the corporation is merely a private corporation and remains such even though its stock can be purchased by the public.

PRIVATE CORPORATIONS

Private corporations are those formed by private individuals to perform some nongovernmental function. They in turn are classified as:

1. Charitable corporations
2. Profit corporations

(1) **Charitable Corporations.** A *charitable corporation* is one formed by private individuals for the purpose of conducting some charitable, educational, religious, social, or fraternal service. These corporations are not organized for profit, nor is membership in them evidenced by stock ownership. There is no stock issued. The corporation, however, is a legal entity like any other corporation, and can sue and be sued as a corporation, can buy and sell property, and otherwise operate as any other corporation. Membership in these corporations is acquired by agreement between the charter members in the beginning and between the present members and new members thereafter.

(2) **Profit Corporations.** In terms of number and importance, stock corporations organized for profit constitute the chief type discussed in this text. Membership in a *stock corporation* is represented by shares of stock. The extent of one's rights and liabilities is determined by the number of shares of stock owned and by the charter and the bylaws of the corporation.

OTHER CLASSES OF CORPORATIONS

Corporations may be classified in other ways depending on the purpose of the classification. Thus we may need to classify them as domestic or foreign corporations. A corporation is a *domestic corporation* in the state where it received its initial charter; it is a *foreign corporation* in all other states. If it is incorporated in another country, it may be referred to as an *alien corporation*.

FORMATION OF A CORPORATION

The initial step of forming a corporation is usually taken by one who acts as the promoter. A lot of preliminary work must be done before the corporation comes into existence. The incorporation papers must be prepared, a prospectus drawn up and approved by the Securities and Exchange Commission and by the appropriate state officials, the stock must be sold, and many contracts entered into for the benefit of the proposed corporation. Approval by the Commission is not required in the case of smaller corporations. The corporation can be organized in any state the promoter chooses and then operate in any other state it chooses as a foreign corporation so long as it complies with the registration requirements and any other requirements of the other states.

Minor defects in the formation of a corporation may generally be ignored. In some instances the defect is of a sufficiently serious character that the attorney general of the state which approved the articles of incorporation of the corporation may obtain the cancellation or revocation of such articles. In some instances, the formation of the corporation is so defective that the existence of a corporation is ignored and the persons organizing the corporation are held liable as partners or joint venturers.

LIABILITY ON PROMOTER'S CONTRACTS

The corporation does not automatically become a party to contracts made by the promoter. After the corporation is organized it will ordinarily, expressly or by its conduct, approve or adopt the contracts made by the promoter, after which it is deemed bound by such contracts and entitled to sue thereon.

The promoter may avoid personal liability on contracts made for the benefit of the corporation by including a provision in the contract that he is not to be held personally liable after the corporation adopts the contract. In the absence of such a provision, it is a question of the wording of the contract whether the promoter is bound by the contract either pending the formation of the corporation or after it has come into existence.

 ▪ Bluegate Gardens made a contract to sell nursery supplies and insisted on making the contract out to Evergreen Nurseries, Inc., even though Bluegate Gardens knew the corporation was not yet formed. Simmons signed as president of Evergreen. The corporation was never formed, so Bluegate sued Simmons and the other promoters. Bluegate lost since the contract was made on behalf of the corporation and the other party had agreed to look to the corporation and not to the promoters for payment.

ADOPTION OF EXPENSES

Along with the adoption of the promoter's contracts, the corporation may or may not adopt the expenses of the promoter in organization of the corporation. It is customary for the corporation after it comes into existence to reimburse the promoter for all necessary expenses in forming the corporation. This may be done by a resolution passed by the board of directors.

ISSUE OF STOCK

When a new corporation is about to be formed its stock will generally be sold in advance of its actual incorporation. In such case the purchase of or subscription to stock by a prospective stockholder or investor is merely an offer to buy. This offer may be revoked anytime prior to acceptance in most jurisdictions. The corporation is the offeree, and it cannot accept the subscription until the stock is sold and the charter accepted. If the stock is sold in a corporation already in existence, it can accept all subscriptions immediately and make them binding contracts. If the promoter is to receive a stock option for his services, the corporation can make such a contract with him before the services are performed. Most state laws provide that a minimum amount of stock must be sold and paid for before the corporation can begin operations.

> ▪ Rogers and Talmadge wish to incorporate an enterprise to market a new catalytic muffler to reduce the pollutant emissions from automobiles. They know that unless the corporation can assemble capital resources of at least $375,000 their enterprise cannot be launched. In order not to commit any resources until they have assurance of the money, they can contract on behalf of the corporation for the money in exchange for stock through the subscription agreement.

ARTICLES OF INCORPORATION

The *articles of incorporation* is a written document setting forth the facts prescribed by law for the issuance of a charter and asserting that the corporation has complied with these legal requirements. The articles are the base on which rests all the authority of the corporation. It is a contract between the corporation and the state. So long as the corporation complies with the terms of the contract, the state cannot alter the articles in any material way without obtaining the consent of the stockholders.

When the incorporators meet, elect a board of directors, and begin business, acceptance of the charter is presumed, and all parties are bound by it.

POWERS OF A CORPORATION

A corporation has powers expressly granted to it and powers which are deemed implied from or incidental to the powers which are expressly granted to it or which are essential to its existence as a corporation. The express powers are generally found in the statute or code under which the corporation is formed and to a lesser degree in the corporation's articles. In a few instances, powers of a corporation are set forth in the state constitution.

Incidental Powers. Certain powers that are always incidental to a corporate existence are:

1. To have a corporate name
2. To have a continuous existence
3. To buy, sell, and hold property
4. To make bylaws and regulations
5. To sue and be sued in the corporate name
6. To have and use a corporate seal

(1) Corporate Name. A corporation must have a corporate name. The members may select any name they wish, provided it is not contrary to the statutes or is not already used by another firm or corporation within the state. Many of the states have statutes regulating corporate names, for example, by requiring the name to end with "Company," or to be followed by the word "Incorporated" or an abbreviation thereof.

(2) Continuous Existence. The existence of the corporation is continuous for the period for which the charter is granted. This is one of the features of a corporation that makes this form of organization valuable. The death of a member does not dissolve the organization. Sometimes this characteristic is referred to as perpetual or continuous succession.

(3) Property Rights. A corporation has the right to buy, sell, and hold property that is necessary in its functioning as a corporation and that is not foreign to the purpose for which it was created.

(4) Bylaws and Regulations. Rules and regulations are necessary to govern and to determine the future conduct of the organization. They must conform to the statutes and must not be contrary to public policy.

(5) Legal Actions. Another power that has long been considered incidental to corporate existence is the power to sue in the corporate name. Since a corporation may be composed of hundreds or thousands of stockholders, it would be a very cumbersome task, if not an impossible one, to secure the consent of all the stockholders each time a suit was to be brought by a corporation. A corporation may likewise be sued in the corporate name.

(6) Corporate Seal. A corporation has the incidental power to have and to own a seal. Under the common law the corporation was required to use its seal in most of its transactions. The rule now is that a corporation need not use a seal except (a) in executing deeds and other written instruments that require the use of a seal when executed by natural individuals, or (b) in carrying out transactions where the use of the seal is required by special statutory requirements.

Implied Powers in General. In addition to the powers that are incidental to or expressly conferred upon all corporations, a corporation has also the implied power to do all acts that are reasonably necessary for carrying out the purpose for which the corporation was formed. A corporation may borrow money and contract debts if such acts are necessary for the transaction of the corporate business. It may make, indorse, and accept negotiable instruments. It has the power to acquire and convey property, and to mortgage or lease its property in case such transactions are necessary for carrying on its business. Modern corporation codes as a rule expressly list the various implied powers above described so that they are express powers.

ULTRA VIRES CONTRACTS

Any contract entered into by a corporation that goes beyond its powers is called an *ultra vires contract.* As between the parties to the contract, that is, the corporation and the third person, the contract is generally regarded as being binding. However, a stockholder may bring an action to prevent the corporation from entering into such a contract or to recover damages from the directors or officers who have caused loss to the corporation by such acts. In extreme cases, the attorney general may obtain a court order revoking the articles of incorporation of the corporation if the improper acts are so frequent or so serious as to make it proper to impose such an extreme penalty.

> ▪ The charter of the Well Pump and Supply Company set forth that the corporation was "to engage in the boring of wells, installing pumps, selling pumps and supplies, and the servicing of these pumps." The board of directors planned to enter into a contract with the Board of Supervisors of Buchanan County to hard surface three miles of county roads. The court upon application by a stockholder issued an injunction prohibiting the board from fulfilling this contract as it was an executory ultra vires contract.

QUESTIONS

1. What is the main difference between a corporation and a partnership?
2. Is the entity concept of a corporation ever ignored by the court?
3. If one wishes to go into business for himself so he can "be his own boss," is he more likely to achieve his objective as a partner or as a stockholder in a corporation? Explain.
4. What is meant by adoption of a promoter's contracts?
5. What are the rights of the stockholders who control a majority of the common stock in a corporation?
6. If one person owns 49 percent of the stock in a corporation, does this fact automatically give him a right to work for the corporation?
7. What kinds of powers does a corporation have other than those expressly set out in its charter?
8. What action may the state take if a corporation engages in an ultra vires act?

CASE PROBLEMS

1. Perdue was the promoter for the formation of an auto finance corporation. The plan of incorporation called for the sale of $1,000,000 worth of common stock. Perdue leased for five years a building to be used for the company's main place of business. The lease was in the name of Perdue,

but the lessor understood the purpose of the lease since he had subscribed for 100 shares of stock. The rent amounted to $900 a month. After the corporation was formed, the board of directors refused to abide by the lease and leased instead another building. (a) Is the corporation bound on the lease made by the promoter? (b) Is the promoter personally bound on this lease?

2. Mr. and Mrs. Land and their son John proceed to organize a family corporation to be known as The Right Way Laundry. The business began operating with all three parties actively engaged in carrying on the business while the incorporation papers were being drawn up. Neither the charter nor the certificate of incorporation was ever issued by the state, and no stockholders' meeting was ever held. Mr. Land borrowed $10,000 from the bank and signed the note:

> Right Way Laundry
> By Henry Land, President

The note was never paid, and the bank sued Mrs. Land as a partner. Was this a partnership?

3. The Hudson Truck Lines, a corporation, leased ten trailer trucks instead of buying trucks. The corporate charter provided that the scope of the corporation's business was to own and operate an interstate truck freight business. A stockholder brought a suit to prohibit the corporation from leasing the trucks, claiming the contract was an ultra vires act. Do you agree?

4. Bisher and Furman formed a corporation to manufacture and market athletic equipment. They employed a stockbroker to obtain subscriptions to the $100,000 authorized capital stock. After all the stock had been fully subscribed, Bisher as copromoter, made contracts in the name of the corporation amounting to $11,000. Over half of the subscribers canceled their subscriptions. Since additional subscribers could not be found, the enterprise fell through. What serious blunder did Bisher and Furman commit in this undertaking?

5. Ten stockholders owned all of the stock in the Frost Tire Company, a company specializing in recapping tires. The company was only modestly successful. At a special stockholders' meeting, nine of the stockholders vote to sell all the assets of the tire recapping business and use the proceeds to start manufacturing "camel backs," the strip of rubber used to recap tires. The tenth stockholder brought suit to enjoin the corporation from engaging in this new enterprise. Is this procedure followed by the objecting stockholder proper?

6. Donaldson, who owned two large farms devoted to the production of livestock, had two sons, John and Henry. He wanted to take them into business with him in such a way that he would keep one of the farms exclusively for himself and operate the other one as a partnership or corporation. He was told that under a partnership arrangement both farms could still be subjected to liability for the debts of the partnership. To avoid this, the three of them drew up a corporation type of contract, pro-

viding for shares of stock, a board of directors, and all the other requirements of a corporation. They did not obtain a charter, however, nor did
they attempt to comply with the state corporation laws. They did file a
federal and state corporation income tax return each year. The firm, due
to the bad management of the two sons, became heavily indebted, and
the creditors brought suit to collect. The firm's assets were wholly inadequate to pay the firm's debts. The creditors then sought to hold the father
personally liable for these debts. Was he liable?

7. A group of fifty dairy farmers formed a corporation for the purpose
of marketing milk and other dairy products. The charter stipulated that it
was authorized to bottle and market whole milk in the city of Auburn.
Soon the question arose as to whether or not the corporation could do any
of these acts: (a) buy milk from farmers other than the fifty members;
(b) make and sell ice cream; (c) make and sell butter and cheese; (d) buy
and operate a freezer locker plant in conjunction with its milk plant; (e)
buy a dairy farm in the name of the corporation to produce milk for sale
by the corporation; (f) operate a feed store for the convenience of the
stockholders in purchasing dairy feed; (g) own and operate the Dairy
Queen, a restaurant, selling only dairy products, such as ice cream, milk
shakes, and other dishes consisting mainly of milk or milk products.
Which of these powers were (1) express, (2) incidental or implied, or
(3) not possessed by the corporation?

8. The Blue Stone Coal Company, a corporation, voted through its board
of directors to use its surplus to construct a hotel to be operated for a profit.
After the hotel was completed and in operation, a stockholder brought an
action to compel the board of directors to sell the hotel. Is this procedure
brought by the stockholder proper?

9. The Big Ben Railroad, a corporation, signed a contract with the
Hodgsen Fertilizer Corporation to run an experimental farm to test the
various types of fertilizer manufactured by Hodgsen. The Hodgsen Corporation sued the railroad for $10,000, the amount owed for fertilizer bought
for the experiments. The railroad claims it is not liable because the contract
was an ultra vires act. Was this defense valid?

10. A corporation organized in New Jersey was authorized by its articles
of incorporation to engage in highway construction. Soon after the corporation's organization, it was lowest bidder on a state road construction job
and the contract was duly let to the corporation. Later the state attempted
to avoid the contract, claiming a corporation was not entitled to the protection of the Federal Constitution protecting individual citizens against the
abridgement of their contractual rights. Do corporations enjoy the same constitutional protections as individual citizens?

11. Childs, Clyatt, and Collins formed a partnership dealing in antiques.
Each invested $20,000 in the business. It was a very profitable enterprise but
was endangered by the constant bickering among the three partners. As a
solution to their problem, they incorporated, each taking $20,000 worth of
stock in the corporation. In addition, the corporation was authorized to sell
an additional $21,000 worth of stock, $7,000 worth for each stockholder.

When Clyatt and Collins refused to buy any more stock, Child's mother-in-law bought the other shares. In electing a board of directors each of the original stockholders put up a separate slate. Child's slate won all places. The board of directors discharged Clyatt and Collins from their jobs and denied them all access to the business. From Clyatt's and Collins' point of view, did the corporate type of business organization overcome the so-called weaknesses of the partnership type?

12. A corporation was formed for the purpose of manufacturing and selling jewelry. It owned its own building. The directors found that they had more space than was needed for their business, and they decided to rent one of the floors for office purposes. One of the stockholders opposed the idea, contending that such an act would be ultra vires. Was the stockholder right in his contention in this case? Why?

Chapter 37

MEMBERSHIP IN A CORPORATION

CAPITAL STOCK

The *capital stock* of the corporation is the amount authorized by the charter and the articles of incorporation. This stock is subscribed and paid for by the members. It generally is not necessary that all the capital stock of a corporation be subscribed and paid for before the corporation begins operation. The amount of capital stock authorized in the charter cannot be altered without the consent of the state and the stockholders.

The capital stock is divided into units called *shares*. These shares may have a set or par value of one dollar, ten dollars, or one hundred dollars.

MEMBERSHIP

Membership in a stock corporation is acquired by the ownership of one or more shares of stock. The members are known as *shareholders* or *stockholders*. The shares of stock may be obtained by subscription either before or after the corporation is organized, or they may be obtained by gift or purchase from another shareholder.

STOCK CERTIFICATE

The amount of ownership, that is, the number of shares owned, is evidenced by a stock certificate. It shows on its face the number of shares represented, the par value of each share if there is a par value, and the signatures of the officers.

KINDS OF STOCK

Stock is divided into many classes. The classes are determined by the laws under which the corporation is organized. The two principal classes of stock are:

1. Common stock
2. Preferred stock

(1) **Common Stock.** *Common stock* is the simplest form of stock issued. If a corporation has issued 5,000 shares of common stock, the owner of 100 shares is entitled to 1/50 of the profits that are made available to the common stockholders. Unlike the partners in a partnership, the owners cannot receive the profits until they have been made available in the form of a dividend declared by the board of directors.

The common stockholders generally have full right to manage and operate the corporation, but they cannot perform this function as individual stockholders or as a group. They must elect directors, who in turn appoint the managers. Unless a stockholder happens to be selected as a director or appointed as an officer, he has no voice in the running of the corporation beyond his annual vote for the board of directors.

(2) **Preferred Stock.** *Preferred stock* differs from common stock in that some sort of preference is granted to the holder of this stock. The preference may pertain to the division of dividends, to the division of assets upon dissolution, or to both of these preferences. The more valuable preference is the preference as to dividends.

The fact that particular stock is called preferred stock does not tell much about what preference the holder really has. It may be preferred as to assets only, which gives the holder no advantage except in the event of liquidation. It may be preferred as to dividends only, but not as to assets in the event of liquidation. The most common type is that which gives preference both as to dividends and assets; but even here the stock may be either first preferred, second preferred, or third preferred. In this event the first preferred is given preference in the payment of dividends before the second preferred is entitled to anything. Likewise, the second preferred must be paid before the third preferred is entitled to receive a dividend.

- The Glenrock Mining Corporation issued two classes of stock, common and preferred. The preference granted gave the preferred stockholders a prior right to the assets of the corporation on dissolution. The par value of the outstanding preferred stock totaled $300,000. The corporation assets on dissolution after payment of debts amounted to $425,000. How should the $425,000 be allocated between the stockholders? The preferred stockholders should get the first $300,000 to be disbursed, leaving $125,000 to be divided among the owners of common stock.

The two rights usually given up by the preferred stockholders are the right to vote in stockholders' meetings and the right to participate in profits beyond the percentage fixed in the stock certificate.

When the stock is preferred as to dividends, this right may be cumulative or noncumulative. This fact is significant if the corporation operates at a loss in any given year or group of years. For example, a corporation that has $1,000,000 outstanding common stock and $1,000,000 outstanding 7 percent preferred stock operates at a loss for two years, and then earns 21 percent net profit the third year. If *noncumulative preferred stock* has been issued, it is entitled to only one dividend of 7 percent; and the common stock is entitled to the remaining 14 percent. If *cumulative preferred stock* has been issued, it is entitled to three preferences of 7 percent, or 21 percent in all, before the common stock is entitled to any dividend. Or if the company earns a net profit each year equal to only 7 percent on the preferred stock, the directors could, if the preferred stock is noncumulative, pass the dividend the first year and declare a 7 percent dividend on both the common and the preferred stock for the second year. Since the directors are elected by the common stockholders, the common stockholders could easily defraud the preferred stockholders. For that reason the law is that preferred stock is cumulative unless specifically stated to be noncumulative. This is true, however, only when the corporation earns a profit but fails to declare a dividend. Unless the stock certificate expressly states that it is cumulative, the preference does not cumulate in the years during which the corporation operated at a loss.

Preferred stock may also be participating or nonparticipating. Thus 7 percent *participating preferred stock* may pay considerably more than 7 percent annually; but if it is *nonparticipating preferred stock*, 7 percent annually would be the maximum to which the preferred stockholders would be entitled no matter how much the corporation earned. If the preferred stock is participating, it is entitled to share equally with the common stock in any further distribution of dividends made after the common shareholders have received dividends equal to those which the preferred shareholders have received by virtue of their stated preference. If the preferred stock is to participate, this right must be expressly stated in the stock certificate or articles of incorporation. The law presumes it is nonparticipating in the absence of a contract to the contrary. If it does participate, it can do so only according to the terms of the contract. The contract may provide that the preferred stock shall participate equally with the common stock, or it may provide that the preferred stock is entitled to an additional 1 percent for each additional 5 percent the common stock receives.

THE PROSPECTUS

Every new corporation and every old corporation offering to the public a new issue of stock equal to $100,000 or more must provide every subscriber a prospectus. Before the stock is sold, a copy of the prospectus must be submitted to the Federal Securities and Exchange Commission and to appropriate state officials. The *prospectus* must set forth the nature of the corporation, the type or types of stock to be issued, the selling price, and other pertinent information. If the promoter of a new corporation is to receive any stock options or other compensation in stock, this information must be set forth in the prospectus.

TIE-IN STOCK SUBSCRIPTIONS

In recent years a new type of stock arrangement has been quite common. Two classes of stock are issued, one voting common stock and one nonvoting common stock. The nonvoting common stock usually has most of the features of preferred stock. It is preferred as to dividends and is participating but usually not cumulative. The one feature that distinguishes nonvoting common stock from preferred stock is that the stock subscriber must purchase both classes, usually in units of 100 shares of A nonvoting stock, and then 80 shares of B voting stock are donated to the subscriber. For this reason the B voting stock must have a very low par value, usually one cent or even one-tenth of one cent a share. Ostensibly this arrangement overcomes the objection preferred stockholders have of giving up their voting rights. If one buys 100 shares of A nonvoting stock, he cannot vote this stock, but he receives a right to vote through the gift of 80 shares. The public is never permitted to buy just voting B stock; but unless the prospectus sets forth otherwise, there is nothing to keep the promoter or promoters from buying only voting stock. With an investment of $100 it would be possible to buy a majority of the voting stock in a $1,000,000 corporation.

PAR-VALUE STOCK AND NO-PAR-VALUE STOCK

Stock to which a face value, such as $25, $50, or $100, has been assigned is *par-value stock*. Stock to which no face value has been assigned is *no-par-value stock*. Preferred stock usually has a par value, but common stock may be either par-value or no-par-value stock. The law requires that par-value stock be issued in return for payment in money, property, or services equal in value to the full par value. This relates only to the price at which the corporation may issue the stock to an original subscriber and has no effect upon the price which is paid as between a shareholder and a buyer thereafter, the price ordinarily being the same as the market price which may be more or less than the par value. No-par-value stock may be issued at any price, although some states do set a minimum price, such as $5, for which it can be issued.

If par-value stock is sold by the corporation at a discount, the purchaser is liable to subsequent creditors for the amount of the discount.

TREASURY STOCK

If a corporation purchases stock that it has sold, this stock is referred to as *treasury stock*. When stock is first offered for sale, there may be less sales resistance encountered if the prospective purchaser can be assured that the corporation will repurchase the stock upon request. Treasury stock may also be reacquired by gift. The corporation then sells the stock and places the proceeds in a donated surplus account. This may be done when the corporation is in financial difficulties and the stockholders agree to this plan of building up the working capital.

Treasury stock can be purchased only out of surplus. If the corporation resells it, the directors may fix any price which they deem feasible. Until it is resold, no dividends can be paid on it nor can it be voted.

 ▪ The stock of the Mill Valley Corp. is owned equally by Sampson and Lawrence. Each owns 10,000 common shares. They have an agreement that if either one dies the corporation will buy his stock from his heirs for $5 per share. The corporation carries $50,000 in life insurance on each stockholder. Lawrence dies and the corporation uses its $50,000 in life insurance proceeds to purchase Lawrence's stock. This stock is now treasury stock.

WATERED STOCK

When par-value stock is issued as fully paid up but the purchase price is paid with property of inflated values, it is said to be *watered stock*. If real estate actually worth $10,000 is paid for in stock having a par value of $100,000, it is watered to the extent of $90,000. In most instances, watering stock is not prohibited outright, but it cannot be used to defraud creditors. In the event of insolvency, the creditors may sue the owners of watered stock for the difference between the par value and the actual purchase price. This is not true, of course, if the creditors knew the stock was watered or if the holder of the stock purchased it without knowledge of its being watered from the one to whom it was originally issued. Except for creditors, most state statutes do not prohibit the watering of stock by corporations other than public utility companies.

If the payment for stock is in overvalued real estate, the extent of the watering can be determined with reasonable accuracy. If the payment is in the form of patents, trademarks, blueprints, or other similar assets, it may be difficult to fix the extent of the watering.

TRANSFER OF STOCK

A stock certificate indicates the manner in which the stock may be transferred to another party. On the back of the certificate is a blank form which the owner may use in executing an assignment. The signature of the previous owner gives to the new holder full possession and the right to exchange the certificate for another made out to himself by the corporation. The new owner should have the certificate exchanged for a new one in his own name so that he will be registered as a stockholder on the books of the corporation. Unless he is so registered, he is not entitled to the rights and privileges of a stock-holder, and he will not receive any dividends when they are declared.

STOCK OPTIONS

A *stock option* is a contract entered into between the corporation and an individual, giving the individual the option for a stated period of time to purchase a prescribed number of shares of stock in the corporation at a given price. If the stock in a new corporation is sold to the public at $2 a share, the individual having the option must also pay $2, but he may be given, two, five, or even ten years in which to exercise the option. If the corporation succeeds and the price of the stock goes up, the individual will of course want to exercise the option, for he can buy at the low option price and then resell at the higher market price. If the corporation fails, he does not have to buy stock. Existing corporations may give officials of the corporation in lieu of a salary increase an option to purchase a given number of shares of authorized but unissued common stock at a price substantially below the current market price. This type of option is usually for a short period of six to twelve months. If the market price of the stock does not fall, an official may make a capital gain by buying the stock, holding it six months, and selling it. The income tax on a capital gain is considerably less than that on a normal income. This type of compensation may be more attractive to top management officials than a straight increase in salary, enabling a corporation to retain their services at a lower cost than a salary increase.

DIVIDENDS

The profits of a corporation belong to the corporation until the directors set them aside for distribution as *dividends*. Dividends may be paid in cash, stock, or other property.

A cash dividend usually can be paid out of earned surplus only, but there are two exceptions. A cash dividend may be paid out of donated or paid-in surplus. Also, for corporations with depleting assets, such as coal mines, oil companies, lumber companies, and similar industries, cash dividends may be paid out of capital.

Stock dividends are usually paid out of earned surplus, but they may usually be paid out of any surplus account. A stock dividend cannot be declared if there is no surplus of any kind, for this would result in stock watering. Dividends also may be paid in the form of property which the corporation manufactures, but this is seldom done.

The right to declare a dividend on either common or preferred stock depends entirely upon the discretion of the directors. The directors, however, must act reasonably and in good faith.

Once a cash dividend is declared, it cannot later be rescinded. It becomes a liability of the corporation the minute it is declared. A stock dividend on the other hand may be rescinded at any time prior to the issuance and delivery of the stock.

BLUE-SKY LAWS

The purpose of the so-called *blue-sky laws* is to prevent fraud through the sale of worthless stocks and bonds.

These security laws vary from state to state. Some prescribe criminal penalties for engaging in prohibited transactions, and others require that dealers be licensed and that a state commission approve sales of securities before they are offered to the public.

FEDERAL SECURITIES ACT, 1933

Because the state blue-sky laws apply only to intrastate sales of securities, in 1933 the Congress passed the Federal Securities Act to regulate the sale of securities in interstate commerce. Any corporation offering a new issue of securities for sale to the public must register them with the Securities and Exchange Commission and issue a prospectus containing specified information. This act does not apply to the issuance of securities under $100,000 nor does the act regulate the sale or purchase of securities after they have been issued by the corporation.

In addition to the registration and the information contained in it, the proposed prospectus must be filed and approved by the Securities and Exchange Commission before the securities can be offered for sale. Full information must be given relative to the financial structure of the corporation. Information filed must also include the types of securities outstanding, if any, the terms of the sale, bonus and profit-sharing arrangements, options to be created in regard to the securities, and any other data which the Securities and Exchange Commission may deem as required.

■ Wildcat Oil Inc. engaged in the development of petroleum resources. One of the speculative drillings showed dramatic evidence of the discovery of a vast reserve of natural gas. Martin, the
president of the company, while maintaining the discovery as confidential information among the directors of the corporation, purchased
many additional shares from stockholders who knew nothing of the
discovery. Martin then announced the discovery and the value of the
stock rose sharply. Kelly and Dalton, stockholders who had sold to
Martin before the announcement, demand the return of their stock.
Will they prevail? Insiders are not allowed to use information
regarding the condition of the company to the disadvantage of other
stockholders to whom the critical information is unavailable.

The registration statement must be signed by the company, its
principal officers, and a majority of the board of directors. If either
the registration statement or the prospectus contains misstatements or
omissions, the Commission will not permit the securities to be offered
for sale. If they are sold before the falsity of the information is ascertained, an investor may rescind his contract and sue any individual
who signed the registration statement for damages he has sustained.
Any failure to comply with the law also subjects the responsible
corporate officials to criminal prosecution.

FEDERAL SECURITIES EXCHANGE ACT, 1934

The chief markets for the sale of securities are the security exchanges and over-the-counter markets. In 1934 Congress passed the
Securities Exchange Act to regulate such transactions. The Act declares
it unlawful for any broker, dealer, or exchange to use the mails for the
purpose of using the exchange facilities in making a sale unless the
exchange is registered with the Securities and Exchange Commission.

All the securities exchanges must declare definite rules for the
regulation of members of the exchange. The bylaws of every security
exchange must provide for the expulsion or disciplining of any member
who violates the rules of the exchange or who engages in conduct
contrary to the rules of the trade. No exchange can sell securities
until it is registered with the Commission, and this registration may be
withdrawn if the exchange violates the requirements of the statute.
Individuals making misleading statements or contracts in violation of
the Act may be punished by a fine and imprisonment.

QUESTIONS

1. Must all of the authorized stock of a corporation be sold before the corporation can begin business?
2. What evidence does one have that he owns stock in a corporation?
3. What are the two principal classes of stock?
4. How do the stockholders of a corporation manage the corporation?
5. Explain the difference between par-value stock and no-par-value stock.
6. What is a prospectus?
7. May dividends be paid in property of a corporation?
8. What is the purpose of *blue-sky laws?*

CASE PROBLEMS

1. Mrs. Dixon used the proceeds of her deceased husband's life insurance policies to purchase $50,000 worth of noncumulative 7 percent preferred stock in the belief that the $3,500 annual income from this investment would be adequate to support her. Over a ten-year period the corporation averaged 14 percent on its preferred stock, but during four years it earned no net profits and paid no dividends. Mrs. Dixon sued the corporation to compel it to pay these dividends. Was she entitled to dividends for the four years when the corporation operated at a loss?

2. Parrish, Mosteller, and Garrard operated a very profitable partnership in the wholesale meat business. Garrard died. Parrish and Mosteller persuaded Mrs. Garrard, who was the bookkeeper for the firm, to enter the partnership as a general partner. She accepted their offer, and her share of the profits in addition to her salary as bookkeeper gave her a very nice income. Parrish and Mosteller proposed that the partnership incorporate. Soon after the corporation was formed, Parrish and Mosteller decided not to pay any dividends and to use them instead to open up a new plant in another city. Mrs. Garrard protested so vehemently that they voted to discharge her as bookkeeper. She was then without any source of income. She brought suit to compel the directors to declare a dividend and also to restore her to her position as bookkeeper for the firm. Was she entitled to these remedies?

3. Smith was the promoter in forming the Life Insurance Stock Holding Company. The prospectus states the corporation has an authorized capital stock of 500,000 shares of nonvoting A stock, par value $5, and 500,000 shares of voting B stock, par value one cent. It further states the stock is to be sold in units of 100 shares of A and 40 shares of B stock at $5 a share for the A stock with the B stock as a bonus. Point out how Smith legally ends up owning a controlling interest in this corporation with an investment of only $3,000.

4. Malcolm, Blair, and Mattox are the three promoters for a new corporation to operate a discount house. The authorized capital stock is 500,000 shares with a par value of $1. The prospectus states that 100,000 shares are reserved for options. The other 400,000 shares are sold for the par value, and the company begins operations and is very successful. After ten years, the book value of the stock is $5 a share. Malcolm, Blair, and Mattox then take up their options on the 100,000 shares at $1 a share. Show how this affects the book value of the 400,000 shares.

5. The capital stock outstanding of the Mattox Corporation is $1,000,000; the earned surplus is $800,000. No dividends have ever been paid. Grantham is a retired accountant for this firm. During his twenty years with the firm, he had been a member of an employee group who monthly purchased stock in the Mattox Corporation. When Grantham retired, he had 1,500 shares with a book value of $30,000. He had banked on his dividends from this stock to supplement his social security income. He brought suit to compel the board of directors to declare a dividend. Will he succeed?

6. Konter was the owner of 1,000 shares of stock for which he had paid only about 10 percent of their true value at the time the stock was issued. Later he sold 500 shares to Raul who paid full value for the stock. The corporation became insolvent, and the creditors sued Raul, claiming that since his stock was 90 percent watered, he was personally liable. Was this correct?

7. The profits and surplus of a corporation are equal to the capital stock. The corporation is ten years old and has never paid a dividend. The board of directors decide again this year not to pay a dividend but to use 80 percent of the accumulated profits to build an extension to the factory. A stockholder owning 20 percent of the stock brings suit to compel the directors to declare a dividend. Who will win the suit?

Chapter 38

MANAGEMENT AND DISSOLUTION OF A CORPORATION

NATURE OF CORPORATE MANAGEMENT

Since a corporation is an artificial being, existing only in contemplation of law, it can perform business transactions only through actual persons, acting as agents. The directors as a group are both trustees and agents. To the corporation, they are trustees and are chargeable for breaches of trust. To third parties, directors as a group are agents of the corporation.

The board of directors elects the chief agents of the corporation, such as the president, the vice-president, the treasurer, and other officers, who perform the managerial functions. The board of directors is primarily a policy-making body. The chief executives in turn appoint subagents for all the administrative functions of the corporation. These subagents are agents of the corporation, however, not of the appointing executives.

The directors and officers manage the corporation. The stockholders indirectly control the board of directors, but neither the individual directors nor a stockholder merely by reason of membership in the corporation, can act as an agent or exercise any managerial function.

Even if a stockholder owned 49 percent of the common stock of a corporation, he would have no more right to work or take a direct part in running the corporation than a stranger would have. Under the partnership law, if a man owns even 1 percent of the partnership, he has just as much right to work for the partnership and to participate in its management as any other partner. In a corporation the only way one can be sure that he can have employment with his own company is to own 51 percent of the stock.

THE CINCINNATI SHOE COMPANY
Notice of Annual Meeting of Shareholders
MARCH 22

The annual meeting of the shareholders of The Cincinnati Shoe Company will be held at the Main Office of the Company, 170 East Main Street, Cincinnati, Ohio, on Thursday, March 22, at 10:00 o'clock A. M., Eastern Standard Time, for the purpose of electing directors, receiving reports of officers, and transacting such other business as may properly come before the meeting.

The Board of Directors has fixed the close of business, February 15, as the record date for determining shareholders entitled to notice of the meeting and to vote.

Proxy Statement accompanies this Notice.

T. L. LAWSON, Secretary.

By Order of the Board of Directors.
February 22.

You are requested to sign and return, as soon as possible, the attached Proxy.

A Notice of a Stockholders' Meeting

STOCKHOLDERS' MEETINGS

In order to make the will of the majority binding, the stockholders must act at a duly convened and properly conducted stockholders' meeting.

A regular meetng is usually held at the place and time specified in the articles of incorporation or in the bylaws; notice of the meeting is ordinarily not required. A special meeting may be called by the directors of the corporation or in some instances by a particular officer or a specified number of stockholders. Notice specifying the subjects to be discussed is always required for a special meeting.

These meetings of the stockholders are theoretically a check upon the board of directors. If the directors do not carry out the will of the stockholders, a new board can be elected that will be amenable to the stockholders' wishes. This procedure is, in the absence of fraud or bad faith on the part of the directors, the only legal means by which the investors can exercise any control over their investment.

QUORUM

A stockholders' meeting, in order to be valid, requires the presence of a quorum. At common law a *quorum* consisted of the stockholders actually assembled at a properly convened meeting. A majority of the votes cast by those present expressed the will of the stockholders. It is now ordinarily required by statutes, bylaws, or by the articles of incorporation that a majority of the outstanding stock be represented at the stockholders' meeting in order to constitute a quorum. This representation may be either in person or by proxy as described later in this chapter.

▪ At the annual meeting of the Gillespe Paper Corporation 23,954 votes were cast in favor of a resolution and 17,821 were cast against it. Smedley, who was a stockholder against the resolution attempted to get an injunction to prevent the action. Since there were 82,000 outstanding shares, 23,954 did not constitute a majority of the outstanding shares and he claimed that a majority of the total shares was necessary to pass any resolution. As long as a quorum, in this case more than 41,000 shares, were represented at the meeting, only a majority of the shares at the meeting were necessary to pass a resolution.

VOTING

The right of a stockholder to vote is his most important right because this is the only way in which he can exercise any control over his investment. The right to vote is limited to the stockholders, as shown by the stockholders' record book. An owner of stock purchased from an individual does not have the right to vote until the transfer has been made on the books of the corporation. Subscribers who have not fully paid for their stock are not as a rule permitted to vote.

The right to vote is controlled by the state corporation laws. There may be issued, if the law permits, voting and nonvoting common stock.

There are two major classes of elections in which the stockholders vote: the annual election of directors, and the elections to approve or disapprove some corporate policy which only the stockholders can authorize. Examples of some of these acts are consolidating with another corporation, dissolving, increasing the capital stock, and changing the number of directors.

METHODS OF VOTING

Each stockholder has one vote for each share of stock that he holds. In the election of a board of directors, the candidates receiving a majority of the stock actually voting win. In corporations with 500,000 stockholders, control of 10 percent of the stock is often sufficient to control the election. In all cases the owners of 51 percent of the stock can elect all the directors. This leaves the minority stockholders without any representation on the board of directors. To alleviate this situation, two legal devices are in existence which may give the minority stockholders a voice, but not a controlling voice, on the board of directors:

1. Cumulative voting
2. Voting trusts

(1) **Cumulative Voting.** In some states the statutes provide that in the election of directors a stockholder may cast as many votes in the aggregate as are equal to the number of shares held by him multiplied by the number of directors to be elected. This method of voting is called *cumulative voting.* Thus, if a stockholder owns ten shares and ten directors are to be elected, he can cast ten votes for each of the ten directors or one hundred votes for one director. As a result, under this plan of voting the minority stockholders may have some representation on the board of directors, although it is a minority.

(2) **Voting Trusts.** Under a voting trust stockholders give up their voting privileges by transferring their stock to the trustee and receiving in return *voting trust certificates.* This is not primarily a device to give the minority stockholders a voice on the board of directors; but it does do that, and often in large corporations it gives them a controlling voice. Twenty percent of the stock always voted as a unit is more effective than individual voting. State laws frequently impose limitations on voting trusts, as by limiting the number of years that they can run.

PROXIES

Under the common law a stockholder was not permitted to vote unless he was present in person. Under the statutory law, the articles

A Proxy

of incorporation or the bylaws, a member who does not wish to attend a meeting and vote in person may authorize another to vote his stock for him. This right is called *voting by proxy;* the person who is authorized to vote for another is known as a *proxy.* The written authorization to vote is also called a proxy.

If a stockholder should sign more than one proxy for the same stockholders' meeting, the proxy having the later date would be effective. A proxy is good in most states for no more than six months. If the stockholder attends the stockholders' meeting in person, this acts as a revocation of the proxy.

- Robinson was a stockholder in the Southwest Smelting Corp.
  Six weeks before the annual meeting he received a notice of the upcoming meeting and a proxy in favor of the president of the company. Robinson signed the proxy and mailed it back. Forgetting about the proxy he went to the meeting and attempted to vote. He was allowed to vote in person since his appearance constituted a revocation of the proxy.

PROXY WARS

If the stockholders are dissatisfied with the policies of the present board of directors, a new board may be elected. To elect a new board is often a difficult or impossible task. If one or even several men own a majority of the voting stock, there is no way the objecting stockholders can obtain a majority of the voting stock to insure success. If the voting stock is widely held and no group owns a majority of the voting stock, then the objecting stockholders at least have a chance to elect a new board. To do this a majority of the stock represented at a stockholders' meeting must be controlled by this dissatisfied group. To insure this success, the leaders of the group will obtain proxies from stockholders who cannot attend the stockholders' meeting in person. The current board members will also attempt to secure proxies. This is known as a proxy war. The present board of directors is permitted in most instances to pay the cost of this solicitation from corporate funds. The "outsiders" must bear the cost of the proxy war out of their personal funds. If there are 1,000,000 shareholders, the cost of soliciting their proxies is enormous. For this reason proxy wars are seldom undertaken and seldom won when they are undertaken.

RIGHTS OF STOCKHOLDERS

The stockholders of a corporation enjoy several important rights and privileges. Three of these rights have been discussed. They are:

(1) A stockholder has the right to receive a properly executed certificate as evidence of his ownership of shares of stock.

(2) He has the right to attend corporate meetings and to vote unless this right is denied him by express agreement, the articles of incorporation, or statutory provisions.

(3) He has the right to receive a proportionate share of the profits when profits are distributed as dividends.

In addition, each stockholder has the following rights:

(4) He has the right to sell and transfer his shares of stock.

(5) He may have the right, when new stock is issued by the corporation, to subscribe for new shares in proportion to the shares that he owns. For example, if a stockholder owns 10 percent of the original capital stock, he has a right to buy 10 percent of the shares added to the stock. If this were not true, stockholders could be deprived of their proportionate share in the accumulated surplus of the company. Only stockholders have the right to vote to increase the capital stock.

(6) He has the right to inspect the corporate books. He also has the right to have the corporate books inspected by an attorney or an accountant. This right is not absolute since most states have laws restricting the right. The tendency is for these laws to be drawn to

protect the corporation from indiscriminate inspection, not to hamper a stockholder in his right.

(7) He has the right, when the corporation is dissolved, to share pro rata in the assets that remain after all the obligations of the company have been paid. In the case of certain preferred stock, the shareholders may have a preference in the distribution of the corporate assets upon liquidation.

DIRECTORS

Every corporation is managed by a board of directors elected by the stockholders. The law requires every board to consist of at least three members; but if the number is in excess of three, the number, together with qualifications and manner of election, is fixed by the articles of incorporation and the bylaws of the corporation.

The directors, unlike the stockholders, cannot vote by proxy. Nor can they make corporate decisions as individual directors. All decisions must be made collectively and in a called meeting of the board.

The functions of the directors can be classified as:

1. Powers
2. Duties
3. Liabilities

(1) **Powers.** The powers of the board of directors are limited by law, by the articles of incorporation, and by the bylaws. The directors have the power to manage the corporation. They may do any legal act reasonably necessary to achieve the purpose of the corporation so long as this power is not expressly limited. They may appoint agents to act for the corporation or delegate authority to any number of its members to so act. If a director obtains knowledge of something while he is acting in the course of his employment and in the scope of his authority, the corporation is charged with this knowledge.

(2) **Duties.** The directors are charged with the duty of establishing policies that will achieve the function of the corporation, selecting executives to carry out these policies, and supervising these executives to see that the policies are efficiently executed. They must act in person in exercising all discretionary power. The directors may delegate ministerial and routine duties to subagents, but the

duty of determining all major corporate policies, except those reserved to the stockholders, must be assumed by the board of directors.

(3) **Liabilities.** As trustees of the corporation, the directors are liable for bad faith and for negligence. They are not liable for losses when they act with due diligence and reasonably sound judgment. Countless errors of judgment are made annually by directors in operating a complex business organization. Only when these errors result from negligence or a breach of good faith can a director be held personally liable.

The test of whether the directors failed to exercise due care depends upon whether they exercised the care which a reasonably prudent man would have exercised under the circumstances. If they did that, they were not negligent and are not liable for the loss which follows. The test of whether they acted in bad faith is whether they acted in a way which conflicted with the interests of the corporation. As in the case of agents and partners, the corporate directors are under a similar duty of loyalty to the corporation.

Directors may be held liable for some acts without evidence of negligence or bad faith either because the act is illegal or bad faith is presumed. Paying dividends out of capital and ultra vires acts are illustrations of acts that are illegal. Loaning corporate funds to officers and directors is an act to which the court will impute bad faith.

The members of the board of directors are subject to civil and criminal liability in their corporate actions. That is to say, the fact that a person is a director does not give him any immunity or protection from the legal consequences of his conduct. Because of this, the individual director who does not agree with the action taken by the other directors must be careful to protect himself by having the minutes of the meeting of the directors show that he dissented from their action. Otherwise stated, every director who is present at a board meeting is conclusively presumed to have assented to the action taken unless he takes positive action to overcome this presumption. If the directors who are present and dissent have a record of their dissent entered in the minutes of the meeting, then they cannot be held liable for the acts of the majority.

> ▪ At a meeting of the board of directors of the Sac River Mining Co., the Board voted to loan $20,000 to Parsons, one of the board members. Allen, another board member dissented vigorously

and his dissent was recorded in the minutes of the board. Parsons failed to pay back the loan. In an action by the stockholders against the members of the board Allen was not liable because of his dissent to the loan.

DISSOLUTION

A corporation may terminate its existence by paying all its debts, distributing all remaining assets to the stockholders, and surrendering its articles of incorporation. The corporation then ceases to exist, and its dissolution is complete. This action may be voluntary on the part of the stockholders, or it may be involuntary by action of the court or state. The state may ask for a dissolution for any one of the following reasons: (1) forfeiture or abuse of the corporate charter, (2) violation of the state laws, (3) fraud in the procurement of the charter, and in some states (4) failure to pay specified taxes for a specified number of years.

When a corporation dissolves, it is legally dead. It is then incapable of suing, owning property, or forming contracts except for the purpose of converting its assets into cash and distributing the cash to the creditors and stockholders.

In the event that there are not enough assets to pay all creditors, the stockholders are not held personally liable. This is one of the chief advantages of a corporation over a sole proprietorship or partnership. It is an advantage from the stockholder's standpoint, but a disadvantage from the creditors' standpoint.

QUESTIONS

1. What is the only way that a corporation can perform business transactions?
2. What is the function of the board of directors?
3. How many stockholders must be present at a stockholders' meeting to constitute a quorum?
4. How does the corporation determine who is qualified to vote at a stockholders' meeting?
5. How many votes does each stockholder have?
6. What is cumulative voting?
7. If a stockholder cannot attend a stockholders' meeting, how may he vote?

8. Does every stockholder have the right to vote?

9. When are directors liable to the stockholders for errors of judgment that result in financial loss?

10. (a) Under what conditions may the state order a dissolution of a corporation against the stockholders' objection?

    (b) In the event of the dissolution of a corporation, how are the corporate assets distributed?

CASE PROBLEMS

1. The directors of the Lime Products Corporation declared a stock dividend of 10 percent to all common stock. When the bookkeeper began calculating the size of each stockholder's dividend, he discovered there was not enough unissued common stock to pay the dividend in full. He realized that it was illegal to issue stock that had not been authorized. He brought this to the attention of the board of directors, and they attempted to rescind the declaration of the dividend. A stockholder brought suit to compel the issuance of his dividend stock, alleging the board could not rescind its act of declaring a dividend. Is the allegation correct?

2. Rooney was the president of the Frozen Food Lockers, Inc. The three-man board of directors loaned Rooney $15,000 from the corporate funds. Later Rooney became bankrupt, and the corporation lost the entire loan. The stockholders brought suit against the board members personally for the loss. Were they liable?

3. Dawson, who owned 10 shares of common stock in a corporation, was very much dissatisfied with the management because of its failure to pay dividends. There was a movement to line up proxies to elect a new board of directors. Dawson received a letter from Carlton James who expressed great dissatisfaction also and asked Dawson to send him a proxy so that he could vote Dawson's shares. Dawson did this. After the election, he learned that James was the corporation's attorney and had used this ruse to inveigle Dawson to send a proxy actually to be voted in favor of the present board. Dawson brought suit to have the election of the board of directors nullified and a new election held. Was he entitled to this relief?

4. O'Malley was the chief accountant for the Quitman Corporation, which has capital stock outstanding of $100,000 and an earned surplus of $3,500. The board of directors declared a 2.5 percent dividend and instructed O'Malley to calculate the amount due and mail each stockholder a check. O'Malley, through an error, calculated the dividend at 25 percent instead of 2.5 percent. This resulted in a payment of dividend out of capital. Later the judgment creditors sued the directors personally for the amount of the dividend in excess of earned surplus. Were they liable?

5. Hanson, Dupree, and Rice are directors in a bank. The board votes to use a part of the bank's surplus to start an auto finance company under a trade name to conceal the bank's identity with the finance company. Rice dissented vehemently on the ground the act was clearly ultra vires. He was outvoted. To avoid future liability what might Rice do to protect himself?

6. Meeks was a stockholder in a corporation of 15,000 stockholders. The outstanding capital stock was $50,000,000; the earned surplus was $40,000,000. Meeks was dissatisfied with the operating policy of the corporation in retaining all profits for expansion instead of paying dividends. He started a proxy war to line up other stockholders who agreed with him. The board of directors retaliated by soliciting proxies at the corporation's expense. Meeks sought through legal action to enjoin the directors from spending corporate funds to solicit proxies. Will he succeed?

7. Henderson was a director on the board of directors of the Watson Corporation. Henderson also was a large stockholder in a competing firm. In a board of directors' meeting Henderson voted for a measure that was highly detrimental to the Watson Corporation but highly profitable for the competing firm. A stockholder in the Watson Corporation sought to make Henderson personally liable for the loss incurred by paying $50,000 for items worth only $10,000. Was he liable?

SUMMARY CASES

PART 8

1. Kirkup was one of the incorporators of the Anaconda Amusement Co. He had a contract with the other promoters whereby he was to sell the corporation's stock and receive a commission of ten percent for its sale. He sold 770 shares, but the corporation never assumed this contract either expressly or impliedly. He brought suit against the corporation to compel it to carry out the terms of his contract with the promoters. Is the corporation liable on this contract? (Kirkup v. Anaconda Amusement Company, 59 Mont. 469, 197 P. 1005)

2. The Kentucky State Bank loaned R. M. Jones $3,500 and received as collateral security 750 shares of stock in the Millner Construction Company, a corporation. The stockholders subsequently voted to liquidate the corporation. The assets of the corporation were converted into cash, and the cash was distributed to the stockholders without requiring the stockholders to surrender their shares of stock. The bank could not and did not register the 750 shares in its name. Consequently, when the cash was distributed, Jones, not the bank, received the cash represented by the 750 shares. Jones did not use the cash to liquidate his loan to the bank. The bank sued Bogardus, the officer of the corporation in charge of the liquidation for the loss sustained. (a) Was the bank entitled to any part of the cash distribution which represented a share of the profits? (b) Was the bank entitled to the cash that represented a return of capital? (Bogardus v. Kentucky State Bank, 281 S. W. 2d 904)

3. Harold Baker, Laura Baker, and Theodore Sweetland undertook to organize a corporation known as the Congress Square Men's Shop, Inc. The organizers failed to do two specific and important acts to become a corporation: (1) record the certificate of incorporation in the registry of deeds as required by law, and (2) file a copy thereof with the secretary of state. There were other minor failures to comply with the law. Stock was issued, bylaws were adopted, and a board of directors was elected. Harold Baker was the major stockholder and manager. Sweetland and Laura Baker held minor positions in the business but took no major part in management. Harold Baker incurred debts in the name of the corporation with the Bates-Street Shirt Co. and others. These creditors sued the three stockholders as partners, alleging there was never a corporation and that, therefore, it must be a partnership. Was this a partnership? (Baker et al. v. Bates-Street Shirt Co. et al., 6 F. 2d 854)

4. Margaret Morrison was a stockholder in the State Bank of Wheatland, a corporation. The corporation had never paid a dividend, although its reserves were about 600 percent of the capital stock. Morrison brought suit to compel the directors to declare at least $600 a share on the outstanding stock. She alleged but did not prove that the failure to pay a dividend was for a capricious purpose. Must the directors declare a dividend? (Morrison v. State Bank of Wheatland, et al., 58 Wyo. 138, 126 P. 2d 793)

5. The Tennessee and Kentucky Tobacco Co. was incorporated with R. T. Bohannon, H. T. Stratton, and R. F. Long, and R. F. Long, Trustee for E. B. Long, subscribing for $9,000 worth of stock each, the entire issue. The stock was issued but never paid for. The corporation borrowed money by the stockholders' lending their credit, but none of them ever sustained any loss on these loans. The profits were substantial, but no dividends were ever paid. Due to a heavy fire loss, the corporation became insolvent, owing S. R. Russell and others $1,063.33. After the fire, there were no corporate assets with which to pay the debts. Russell and others brought suit against the four stockholders to collect their subscriptions. Did the lending of credit by the stockholders and the foregoing of dividends equivalent in value to the subscription price of the stock constitute payment for the stock? (Russell et al. v. Tennessee and Kentucky Tobacco Company, 65 S.W. 2d 256, 16 Tenn. App. 561)

6. Charles Hammond owned $19\frac{2}{7}$ percent of the outstanding stock of the Edison Illuminating Company. The stockholders voted in a regular stockholders' meeting to increase the outstanding stock of the corporation. Since Hammond owned 140 shares of the stock before the increase, he contended that he was entitled to purchase an additional 27 shares so as to keep his ownership at $19\frac{2}{7}$ percent of the outstanding stock. Is he entitled to purchase the 27 shares? (Hammond v. Edison Illuminating Company, 131 Mich. 79, 90 N. W. 1040)

7. The Zale Jewelry Company was a Kansas Corporation organized to engage in the jewelry business. It leased to Dr. Marks, a licensed optome-

trist, and to the Douglas Optical Company, owned by Carp, a portion of its premises. Both leases provided that the Zale Jewelry Company should handle the business and financial affairs of the lessees. All charges for services and optical supplies were carried on the Zale Jewelry Co.'s books. If Marks and Carp are employees, then the Zale Jewelry Company is practicing optometry, an illegal act. Is the corporation illegally practicing optometry? (State v. Zale Jewelry Co. of Wichita, Inc., 179 Kan. 628, 298 P. 2d 283)

8. The Mutual Bank and Trust Company, a corporation, entered into a unique savings plan with a life insurance company. The plan called for the depositors to undertake a systematic savings plan of $2,000 with the bank, the depositor to make monthly deposits to the account. If the depositor died before the savings account plus accrued interest reached $2,000, the life insurance company paid into his account enough to make it equal $2,000. The bank paid the premiums as a group rate. An action was brought to determine whether or not this was an ultra vires act. Was this an ultra vires act? (Mutual Bank and Trust Co. et al. v. Shaffner et al., 1952 [Mo.], 2485 S. W. 2d 585)

Part 9.

RISK-BEARING DEVICES

Preview Cases for Part 9: Risk-Bearing Devices

■ Thompson owned a fishing vessel. The ship and its crew left port on a ten-day fishing expedition. A day or two later a raging storm was reported in the area where the ship was supposed to be. Thompson could not contact the ship after the storm. He placed a marine hull policy on the ship and its rig but did not tell the agent about his concern for the safety of the ship. The ship and its crew were never heard from again, although there was no proof the ship had sunk when the policy was actually placed. The insurance company refused to pay. Is it obligated to pay?

■ Crutchfield applied for a life insurance policy. On the application for insurance, the question was asked: "What is your occupation?" Crutchfield answered: "Airplane pilot." The insurance policy had a clause which stated that the company would not pay if the insured was an airplane pilot. The company issued the policy. One year later Crutchfield died of a heart attack, and the company refused to pay. Is the company obligated to pay?

■ Raines was a bomber pilot. He had a $10,000 life insurance policy with a war clause. While over open water in the Pacific, he radioed his home base that he was being attacked by Japanese fighter planes. He was never heard from again, nor was any trace of his plane ever found. Should the insurance company have been required to pay?

■ Graham had an automobile liability policy covering both bodily injury and property damage to others. In a collision with another car, the driver of the other car was seriously injured and his car wrecked. Graham's policy provided for coverage up to $15,000 for bodily injury and $5,000 for property damage. The injured driver offered to settle the claim out of court for $14,000. The insurance company rejected the offer and defended the claim in court. The court gave judgment against Graham for $30,000. How much is Graham obligated to pay? How much is the insurance company obligated to pay?

■ A creditor insured the life of a debtor for the amount due him. Before the death of the insured, the debt was paid in full. The company refused to pay. Would it be required to pay?

These preview cases are designed to serve as a springboard for the study of this part. As you read through each chapter in this part, you will find the actual decisions for all these preview cases. Of course, there are many more such illustrative problems as well as case problems for decision at the end of each chapter. And there are also a number of even more challenging cases for review at the end of the part.

Chapter 39

NATURE OF INSURANCE

It is the function of insurance to provide a fund of money when a loss covered by the policy is sustained. Life is full of unfavorable contingencies. The possibility of any one of these contingencies happening is ever present. A homeowner is faced with the constant possibility that his home will burn with a large loss to him. By accepting an absolutely certain annual loss in the form of a fire insurance premium, he can shift the possible large loss to the insurance company. Not every peril in life can be shifted by insurance, but many of the most common perils can be shifted, or at least the financial burden can be shifted. *Insurance* is a contract whereby a party transfers a risk of financial loss for a fee to the risk bearer, the insurance company.

Every insurance contract specifies the particular risk being transferred. The name by which the policy is described is not controlling as to the coverage or protection of the policy. For example, a particular contract may carry the name "Personal Accident Insurance Policy," but this name may not clearly indicate the risk being assumed by the insurance company. A reading of the contract may reveal that the company will pay only if the accident occurs while the insured is in actual attendance in a public school. In such case, the premium paid covers only this much protection against a financial loss due to an accident, not the loss due to any accident in spite of the broad title of the policy.

TERMS USED IN INSURANCE

The company agreeing to make good a certain loss is known as the *insurer*, or sometimes as the *underwriter;* the person protected against the loss is known as the *insured*, or the *policyholder*. In life insurance the person who is to receive the benefits or the proceeds thereof is known as the *beneficiary*.

Whenever a person takes any kind of insurance, he enters into a contract with the insurance company, just as in the case of other business agreements. The written contract is commonly called a *policy*. The amount that the insurer agrees to pay in case of a loss is known as the *face* of the policy, and the consideration the insured pays for the protection is called the *premium*. The danger of a loss of, or injury to, property, life, or anything else, is called a *risk* or *peril;* when that danger may be covered by insurance, it is known as the *insurable risk*. The factors, such as fire, floods, and sleet, that contribute to the uncertainty are called *hazards*.

TYPES OF INSURANCE COMPANIES

There are two major types of insurance companies:

1. Stock companies
2. Mutual companies

(1) **Stock Companies.** A *stock insurance company* is a corporation organized for the purpose of making a profit. As in all other corporations, the stockholders elect the board of directors and receive the profits as dividends. The original capital is raised through the sale of stock, either common or common and preferred. Unlike other corporations, insurance companies must place a major portion of their original capital in a reserve account. As the volume of business increases, the reserve must be increased by setting aside a part of the premiums.

(2) **Mutual Companies.** In a *mutual insurance company* the policyholders are the members and owners and correspond to the stockholders in a stock company. In these companies the policyholders are both the insurer and the insured, but the corporation is a separate legal entity. If a person takes a $10,000 fire insurance policy in a mutual company that has $100,000,000 insurance in force, he owns

1/10,000 of the company and is entitled to share the profits in this ratio. He also may have to share losses in the same ratio if it is an assessment mutual. In a stock company he never shares the losses.

In a nonassessment mutual insurance company, the policyholder's liability is limited to the amount of premium which he contracts to pay. If his pro rata share of the losses for any year exceeds his premium, he cannot be assessed for the excess. In this case the insured is as fully protected as a stockholder in a stock company. In an assessment mutual insurance company, however, the insured is liable for his pro rata share of the losses of the corporation without reference to the premium he agrees to pay. If this premium is inadequate to pay all losses, the insured can be assessed for his pro rata share of the losses in excess of his premium.

WHO MAY BE INSURED

To become an insured, one must first of all have an insurable interest. The insurance contract is in its entirety an agreement to assume a specified risk. If the insured has no interest to protect, there can be no assumption of risk, and hence no insurance. The law covering insurable interest is different for life insurance and for property insurance. Consequently, this law will be treated fully in the chapters dealing with these types of insurance.

To become an insured, one must also be competent to contract. Insurance is not a necessary; thus, a minor is not bound on his insurance contracts if he wishes to disaffirm them. A minor who disaffirms a contract may demand the return of his money. Since insurance contracts provide protection only, this cannot be returned. Some states hold that because of this a minor cannot demand a refund of his insurance premium except the unearned premium for the unexpired portion of the policy.

SOME LEGAL ASPECTS OF THE INSURANCE CONTRACT

The laws applicable to contracts in general apply to insurance contracts. There are five principles, however, that have special significance for insurance contracts:

1. Concealment
2. Representation

3. Warranty
4. Subrogation
5. Estoppel

(1) **Concealment.** The nature of insurance is such that the insurer must rely upon the information supplied by the insured. This places upon the insured the responsibility of supplying all pertinent information. A willful failure to disclose this pertinent information is known as *concealment*. The concealed facts must be material; that is, they must relate to matters which would affect the insurer in reaching the decision whether to insure the insured and the premium rate to fix for him. Also, the concealment must be willful. The willful concealment of material fact renders the contract voidable.

■ Thompson owned a fishing vessel. The ship and its crew left port on a ten-day fishing expedition. A day or two later a raging storm was reported in the area where the ship was supposed to be. Thompson could not contact the ship after the storm. He placed a marine hull policy on the ship and its rig but did not tell the agent about his concern for the safety of the ship. The ship and its crew were never heard from again, although there was no proof the ship had sunk when the policy was actually placed. The insurance company refused to pay. It was justified. The owner concealed a material fact, a fact which he knew would cause the insurance company to refuse the coverage if he had revealed it.

The rule of concealment does not apply with equal stringency to all types of insurance contracts. In fire insurance where the agent has an opportunity to inspect the property, the court may consider the concealed hazard as waived. In ocean marine insurance the concealed hazard is never waived, and the concealment need not be willful.

(2) **Representation.** An oral or written misstatement of a material fact is called a *false representation*. If the insured makes a false representation, the insurer may avoid the contract of insurance. This is true whether or not the insured made the misstatement purposely.

It is now usual for insurance policies to provide that if the insured misstates his age, the policy will not be voided; however, the sum paid on the policy "shall be that sum which the premium paid would have provided for had the age been correctly stated."

■ Gilmer owned a paper mill. He insured it as a paper mill against loss by fire in the amount of $100,000. At the time he took out the policy, Gilmer was not using the building as a paper mill and had installed some stone burrs and was using the mill to grind wheat and corn into flour and cornmeal on the shares for farmers. This use was temporary while the paper business was depressed. While the mill was being used as a grist mill, it was totally destroyed by fire. The company refused to pay on the ground of misrepresentation. The court held this was not misrepresentation since the mill was still a paper mill even though it was being used temporarily as a grist mill. Furthermore, the misrepresentation was not material since a grist mill is less likely to burn than a paper mill and is a superior risk.

(3) **Warranty.** It is customary for the insurer to require an applicant to agree in the policy that the applicant's statements of facts and promises shall be *warranties*. If the warranties are not true or the promises are not fulfilled, the insurer may declare the policy void.

There are several differences between warranties and representations. Warranties are included in the actual contract of insurance or are incorporated in it by reference, while representations are merely collateral or independent matter, such as oral statements or written statements appearing in his application for insurance or other writing separate from the actual contract of insurance.

Also, in order to avoid the contract of insurance, the representations must concern a material fact, while the warranties may concern any fact or be any promise. A representation need only be substantially correct, while a warranty must be absolutely true or strictly performed.

Several states have enacted legislation which eliminates any distinction between warranties and representations and without a showing that the warranty is material or the insured intended to defraud. A breached warranty does not void the policy. Even in states without such statutes, the courts are reluctant to find policies invalid and will construe warranties as representations whenever possible and will in any case interpret warranties strictly against the insurer so as to favor the insured.

(4) **Subrogation.** In insurance, *subrogation* is the right of the insurer under certain circumstances to "step into the shoes" of the insured. Subrogation is particularly applicable to some types of automobile insurance. If the insurer pays a claim to the insured, under the law of subrogation the insurer is entitled to any claims which the insured had because of the loss. For example, A has a collision insurance policy on his car. B negligently damages A's car. The insurance company will pay A but then has the right to sue B for indemnity.

(5) **Estoppel.** Either party to an insurance contract may not be allowed to claim the benefit of a violation of the contract by the other party. Such a party is said to be *estopped* from claiming the benefit of such violation. An estoppel arises whenever the insurer, by statements or actions, leads the insured to a conclusion which he relies upon and from which he would be harmed if the insurer were allowed to show that the conclusion is not true. For example, if the insurer gives the insured a premium receipt, the insurer would be estopped from later asserting that the premium was not paid in accordance with the terms of the policy.

> ■ Crutchfield applied for a life insurance policy. On the application for insurance, the question was asked: "What is your occupation?" Crutchfield answered: "Airplane pilot." The insurance policy had a clause which stated that the company would not pay if the insured was an airplane pilot. The company issued the policy. One year later Crutchfield died of a heart attack, and the company refused to pay. The court held the company had waived this provision regarding airplane pilots.

QUESTIONS

1. Define *insurance.*

2. Which is more fatal to an insurance policy, a breach of warranty or a misrepresentation?

3. What is the effect of the insured's concealing material facts in applying for insurance?

4. What is *estoppel* as applied to insurance contracts?

5. Give an illustration of subrogation as applied to insurance contracts.

6. Does an "accident insurance policy" cover loss due to all accidents?

7. How does a mutual fire insurance company differ from a stock fire insurance company?

CASE PROBLEMS

1. Thomas owned and operated a storage business and carried fire insurance to cover about 50 percent of its value. Someone called him and told him that smoke was coming from the gable end of the building and that he believed it was on fire. Before going to the building, Thomas saw his insurance agent and placed another $50,000 fire policy on it but made no mention of the smoke and possible fire. It developed that there was no fire. About two weeks later, however, the building was destroyed by fire, and the

company refused to pay on the second policy because it had learned of the circumstances under which it was purchased. Was the insurance company liable on this policy?

2. A fire insurance policy contained a clause that no provision of the policy could be waived by the agent except in writing and attached to the policy. One provision in the policy stated that manuscripts were not covered unless specifically named in the policy. Mitchell, an author, had a manuscript almost completed for a novel which he felt would be a best seller. He called his agent and asked that the manuscript be named in his household effects policy. The agent said that was not necessary and that the policy covered it. A fire destroyed Mitchell's home and the manuscript was burned up. The company refused to pay for it. Was Mitchell entitled to collect for the value of the manuscript?

3. Hipps, the bookkeeper for the Concrete Block Corporation, was charged with the responsibility of keeping the insurable risks of the company fully covered. He placed a theft policy on the company's valuable papers. He was asked, "Where are the papers kept?" He replied, "In an iron safe in the office." The papers actually were seldom kept in the safe. About $5,000 worth of notes receivable were stolen from the drawer of a steel desk. Must the company pay for this loss?

4. In an application for comprehensive coverage of the Johnson Construction Company's equipment, it was stated the trucks were kept in "a garage at night at 1480 Stockbridge Road." The trucks were actually kept parked on an open parking lot next to the main building and were seldom placed in the garage. One truck caught fire while being driven on the highway and was destroyed. The company refused to pay. Must it?

5. Hendrix has a $20,000 fire insurance policy in an assessment mutual fire insurance company. The company has $200,000,000 worth of insurance in force. A fire results in a loss of $80,000. How much of this must Hendrix pay?

6. Savage applied for a disability income policy whereby the insurance company obligated itself to pay the insured $200 a month if he became so disabled that he could not continue his profession as a typesetter. At the time Savage took out the policy he knew he was going blind and would be totally blind within two or three years. He did not tell the insurance company about this condition. When the company refused to pay off on the policy, Savage claimed he did not reveal this fact because he did not think the company wanted the information. Must the company pay Savage disability compensation after he became blind?

7. Chandler had a fire insurance policy on his stock of merchandise and building for $20,000, approximately half of the actual value. A competitor set fire to the building and destroyed it and its contents. Chandler accidentally learned that the fire was set by his competitor. He made a secret deal with the arsonist that he would not reveal the information as to his guilt if he would agree to pay all the loss not covered by insurance. When the insurance company learned of this agreement, it refused to pay off on the fire policy. Must it do so?

8. Durwood's home was completely destroyed by fire caused by a spark from the smokestack of an engine belonging to the Big Sandy and Cumberland Railroad. The law required all railroad companies to keep spark arresters on all smokestacks. This was not done in this case. Durwood carried full fire insurance on his home, so he elected to collect from the insurance company. Can the insurance company compel him to sue the railroad?

9. Pennington carried fire insurance on his store building and merchandise. A clause in the policy stipulates that no act shall be committed that increases the hazard. The store was heated with a coal stove. The brick flue collapsed. Pennington, not wishing to build another, ran the stovepipe thru the window with the pipe jutting out about one foot from the outside wall. He asked the insurance company's agent if that would affect his policy and was assured it would not. A spark from the stovepipe ignited a wooden eave, and the building and contents were destroyed. Must the company pay for the loss?

10. Morrison, who owned three houses, asked his secretary to call the insurance agent and place a fire insurance policy on the one at 256 Cloverhurst. The agent asked her, "Is the house brick or frame?" She was not sure but thinking it made no difference, replied, "It is a brick building." It was in fact a frame building. The house was destroyed by fire, and the company refused to pay for the loss. Was Morrison entitled to collect?

11. A fire insurance policy on a sawmill contained this clause: "The insured warrants that a watchman will be on duty at all times while the mill is not operating." The mill caught fire during the day and was completely destroyed. The previous night the night watchman was ill and could not work. He called Brewer, the superintendent, and informed him that he could not report for work. Brewer did not get anyone to take the watchman's place and the mill was without a watchman for that one night only, but the fire was in no way related to this fact. The insurance company refused to pay for the loss. Could the owner of the mill collect on this policy?

12. Schools, a minor, insured his house against loss by fire, and his automobile and jewelry against loss by either fire or theft. Eleven months later he demanded a return of his entire premium. Was he entitled to a refund?

Chapter 40

LIFE AND ANNUITY INSURANCE

DEFINITION OF LIFE INSURANCE

Life insurance is a contract by which the insurer pays a specified sum or sums of money to a beneficiary upon the death of the insured. While it is generally obtained to protect the beneficiary from financial hardship resulting from the death of the insured, neither economic loss nor dependency upon the insured is essential to the death mission of life insurance.

TYPES OF LIFE INSURANCE CONTRACTS

There are many different types of life insurance policies and annuity contracts, but the following are the most important:

1. Term insurance
2. Endowment insurance
3. Whole life insurance
4. Combinations, and other types

(1) **Term Insurance.** As the name indicates, *term life insurance* contracts are those whereby the company assumes for a specified term the risk of the death of the insured. In this sense it is similar to a term fire insurance policy, or a term automobile insurance policy. This term may be for only one year; or it may be for five, ten, or even fifty years. The term must be stated in the policy. There are many variations of the term policies. In short-term policies, such as five years, the insured may, if the policy so provides, have the option of renewing it for another equal term without a physical examination. The cost is

higher for each renewal period. This is called *renewable term insurance*. It is designed to enable young married people to buy a lot of life insurance when their needs are usually the greatest and their ability to pay low. In nonrenewable term insurance the insured does not have the legal right to renew it unless the company consents to the renewal.

Term policies also may be either level term or reducing term. In level term, the face of the policy is written in units of $1,000. The amount remains at this sum during the entire term of the policy. In reducing term contracts, the policy is generally written in multiples of $10 a month income. For example, a young man aged 20 could purchase a reducing term policy covering a period of 600 months or 50 years for ten units, that is $100 a month. If he dies the first month after purchasing the policy, his beneficiary would draw $100 a month for 600 months, or $60,000 ultimately.

All term policies have one thing in common—they are pure life insurance. They shift the specific risk of loss as a result of death—and nothing more—just as a fire insurance policy shifts the risk of loss of property by fire, and nothing more.

(2) **Endowment Insurance.** An *endowment insurance policy* is reducing term insurance plus a savings account. The sum of the insurance plus the savings always equals the face of the policy. For example, if a twenty-year endowment policy for $10,000 costs a young man aged 20 about $450 a year, approximately $60 of this compensates the insurance company for the risk of death during the term of twenty years. The other $390 is a savings account that with accrued interest equals $10,000 at the end of twenty years. If the insured dies during the twenty years, his beneficiary will collect the $10,000. If the insured is still living at the end of the term, he will collect the $10,000 unless he has designated some beneficiary to receive the amount. All endowment policies then are really two contracts in one. One is a risk transfer; the other sets up a debtor-creditor relationship.

(3) **Whole Life Insurance.** In reality all life insurance contracts are either term insurance or endowment insurance. A whole life insurance policy is one that continues, assuming the premium is paid, until age 100 or death, whichever occurs first. If the insured is still living at age 100, he collects the face of the policy as an endowment. A whole life policy might correctly be defined as endowment insurance at age 100. As with all endowment policies, a whole life

policy is reducing term insurance plus a savings account. Whole life policies consist of several classes. A straight life policy is a whole life policy calling for the payment of the premium till death or age 100, whichever occurs first. For a young man twenty years of age, this would be an eighty-pay eighty-year endowment. If he wants the same contract but wishes to limit the premiums to twenty years, the policy would be a twenty-pay whole life policy, or a twenty-pay eighty-year endowment. Either term accurately describes the contract.

(4) **Combination and Other Types of Policies.** The three basic life insurance contracts, term, endowment, and whole life, can be combined in almost an endless variety of combinations to create slightly different contracts. The Family Income Policy, for example, is merely a straight life policy with a twenty-year reducing term policy attached as a rider. A *rider* on an insurance policy is a clause or even a whole contract added to another contract to modify, extend, or limit the base contract. In addition to the reducing term insurance, there are several other riders frequently found in life insurance policies. The disability income rider may be attached to any policy and pays the insured an income if he becomes disabled. Other riders are waiver of premium rider, which waives the annual premiums if the insured becomes disabled, and the double indemnity rider. By paying an additional premium, the insured can generally obtain a policy requiring the insurer to make a greater payment when death is caused by accidental means. This greater payment is customarily twice the ordinary amount of the policy and is hence described as "double indemnity."

ANNUITY INSURANCE

An annuity insurance contract pays the insured a monthly income from named age, generally age 65, until death. It is a risk entirely unrelated to the risk assumed in a life insurance contract even though both contracts are sold by life insurance companies. Someone has defined life insurance as shifting the risk of dying too soon and annuity insurance as shifting the risk of living too long, that is, outliving one's savings. Annuity insurance provides for a systematic liquidation of one's savings and at the same time guarantees the insured an income for life even if he lives to be 110. If the annuity contract calls for the monthly payments to continue until the second of two insureds dies, it is called a *joint and survivor annuity*. This type of annuity is

suitable for a man and wife who wish to extend their savings as long
as either one is still living.

LIMITATION ON RISKS IN LIFE INSURANCE CONTRACTS

Policies of life insurance place various limitations upon the risk
covered by the policy. The two most common limitations are:
(1) suicide, and (2) death from war activity.

Suicide. The typical suicide clause found in most life insurance
contracts stipulates that the company will not pay if death occurs by
suicide, whether sane or insane, within two years from the date of
the policy. If death is caused by suicide after the two-year period
lapses, the company must pay.

Death from War Activity. The so-called "war clause" provides
that if the insured dies as a consequence of war activity the company
will not pay. If a member of the armed forces dies a natural death,
the company must pay. The insurance company has the burden of
proving that death was caused by war activity; and if it cannot prove
that such was the case, the insurer must pay the amount of the
insurance.

> ▪ Raines was a bomber pilot. He had a $10,000 life insurance policy
> with a war clause. While over open water in the Pacific, he radioed
> his home base that he was being attacked by Japanese fighter planes.
> He was never heard from again, nor was any trace of his plane ever
> found. The court held that the insurance company had to pay since
> the company could not prove he died as a result of war activity. The
> court pointed out the pilot could have reached an island and died
> a normal death.

PAYMENT OF PREMIUMS

The premiums must be paid within the time specified by the
policy. If they are not paid when due, the policy will lapse either
automatically or may be declared forfeited at the option of the insurer.
The policy or a statute of the state may provide that after a certain
number of premiums have been paid, the policy will be extended for
a specified time in case of the nonpayment of a premium. Under such
a condition a paid-up policy is sometimes issued for the term of the
insurance but for a smaller amount. Sickness is no legal excuse for
the nonpayments of premiums. In such a case the company may, if

it so elects, extend the time of payment or take a promissory note for the amount of the premium. However, by the payment of an additional premium the insured may generally obtain a policy containing a waiver of premiums which becomes effective when the insured is disabled, with the result that if he is disabled, he does not have to pay premiums for the period of time during which the disability exists.

GRACE PERIOD

All life insurance companies are required by law to provide a grace period of generally 30 or 31 days in every life insurance policy. This grace period gives the insured 30 or 31 days from the due date of the premium in which to pay it without the policy's lapsing. This provision is extremely important in life insurance contracts. If the insured through an oversight is one day late in paying his premium, the policy either lapses or may be forfeited by the insured. If it is forfeited or lapsed, the insured may obtain a reinstatement of the policy, but he may sometimes be required to pass a new physical examination. If he wants to buy another policy, he must pass a physical examination and also pay the higher rate for his then attained age.

INCONTESTABILITY

Life insurance policies are made incontestable, either by statute or by the policies themselves, after a certain period of time, usually one year. After the expiration of the period of contestability, the insurance company usually cannot contest the validity of a claim on any ground except nonpayment of premiums.

INSURABLE INTEREST

In most states every person can take out a life insurance policy on his own life and make any person he pleases the beneficiary. The beneficiary need not have an insurable interest in the insured's life.

When one person insures another's life, however, and makes himself or someone else whom he selects beneficiary, he must have an insurable interest in the life of the insured at the time the policy is taken out.

A person has an insurable interest in the life of another when such a relationship exists between them that a direct pecuniary benefit will be derived from the continued existence of the other person. The relationships most frequently giving rise to an insurable interest are parents and children, husband and wife, partner and copartner, and a creditor in the life of the debtor to the extent of his debt. This list is not exhaustive, as there are numerous other relationships which give rise to an insurable interest. A sister may have such an interest in her brother if she has a reasonable expectation that he will support her.

The insurable interest must exist at the time when the policy of insurance is obtained. The fact that it does not exist at the time of the death of the insured is immaterial. Hence a policy naming the insured's wife as beneficiary is valid even though prior to the insured's death the wife obtained a divorce from him.

■ A creditor insured the life of a debtor for the amount due him.
Before the death of the insured, the debt was paid in full. The court held that the insurable interest which existed at the time the policy was taken out supported an action to recover against the insurance company after the death of the insured.

CHANGE OF BENEFICIARY

The modern form of life insurance policy reserves to the insured the right to change the beneficiary. Under such a policy, he may change the beneficiary as he pleases, and this power of the insured is not affected by the fact that the beneficiary had paid the premiums on the policy.

The modern insurance policy permits the insured to name successive beneficiaries so that if the first beneficiary should die before the insured, the proceeds would pass to the second named or contingent beneficiary.

ASSIGNMENT OF THE POLICY

The policy of insurance may be assigned by the insured, either absolutely or as collateral security for a loan which the insured obtains from the assignee, such as a bank. The assignment does not affect the validity of the policy since the hazard involved, namely the life of the insured, is not changed by the assignment. In many instances, the problem of assigning to a creditor is avoided by the insured's obtaining a loan directly from the insurer. The right to make such a loan is expressly reserved in the modern contract of insurance and no assignment of the policy is made in such case.

Distinct from an assignment by the insured is an assignment made by the beneficiary. If made before the death of the insured, the assignment by a beneficiary under a typical policy reserving to the insured the right to change the beneficiary is merely the transfer of the possibility that the beneficiary may receive the insurance proceeds in the event that the insured dies without changing beneficiaries. Under the basic principle that the rights of the assignee rise no higher than those of the assignor, the assignee of the beneficiary is subject to the same disadvantage as the named beneficiary that the insured may change beneficiaries. If the assignment is made after the insured has died, then the assignment is an ordinary assignment of an existing money claim; and, barring some defense, the beneficiary's assignee is then entitled to payment of the face amount of the policy.

OTHER TYPES OF INSURANCE

There are several other types of insurance closely related to life insurance. They are health and accident insurance, hospitalization insurance, and group medical insurance. These types of insurance differ from life insurance in a number of particulars. In the first place, the beneficiary is always the insured. The purpose is to protect the insured against loss or impairment of earning power or burdensome expenses rather than to protect someone who depends upon the insured for support.

QUESTIONS

1. Define *life insurance.*
2. Define *annuity insurance.*
3. What is *decreasing term life insurance?* How does it differ from level-premium insurance?
4. Why is an endowment life insurance policy two contracts in one?
5. What is a *rider* on a life insurance contract?
6. What are some limitations on risks that a life insurance company may provide?
7. What is the nature of the incontestability clause in a life insurance contract?
8. When does a person have an insurable interest in the life of another?
9. Under what circumstances may the insured change the beneficiary of a policy?
10. Name other types of insurance closely related to life insurance.

CASE PROBLEMS

1. Stewart had carried a 40-year reducing term life insurance policy on himself for ten years. When the premium came due on March 21, he wrote the company he wanted to cancel the policy. Ten days later he died, and his wife immediately mailed the premium to the company and then demanded that she be paid the face amount due on the policy. This amounted to 300 monthly payments of $200 each. The company denied liability because Stewart had canceled the policy even though the grace period had twenty more days to run. Must the company pay?

2. Mason, age 26, and his wife have three children all under the age of six. He earns $450 a month. He has the choice of purchasing a twenty-pay life policy, face amount of $10,000, for an annual premium of $290 a year or a reducing term policy for $85,000 for $260 a year. The twenty-pay life policy will build a substantial cash value in a few years; the term policy has no cash value. Which would you recommend that he buy?

3. Goff was treated over a period of three years by Dr. Richardson for serious stomach ulcers. He applied for a life insurance policy and on the application was this question: "Have you been treated by a doctor for any illness during the past five years?" Goff answered "No." Three years after the policy was issued the insurance company learned of the false statement and brought suit to have the policy nullified. Will the company succeed?

4. Donovan carried a $300-a-month reducing term policy on himself with his wife the beneficiary. The war clause in the policy stated, "The company will not be liable under this policy if the insured dies while engaged in military activities." Donovan was killed in an automobile accident on his way home on a furlough. Must the company pay?

5. Mr. Latture reached age 65 and retired. His only retirement income was $150 a month from Social Security plus $55 a month interest on their bank savings of $22,000. Mr. Latture feels he and Mrs. Latture must have at least $250 a month to live on so long as both of them are alive. He has two ways to obtain this sum. One is to withdraw a part of his principal each month so that the bank interest plus the withdrawn savings will always equal $100 a month. This, when added to his Social Security income, will provide the desired $250. The other way is to purchase a joint and last survivor annuity policy for $100 a month for a single premium of $18,000. Which method would you recommend?

6. Hawkins purchased a $10,000 Family Income Policy with a twenty-year reducing term rider for $100 a month. In addition he had a waiver of premium rider and a double indemnity rider. Three years later he died in an automobile accident. How much will Mrs. Hawkins collect?

7. Matthew purchased a $200-a-month decreasing term life insurance policy for the protection of Mrs. Matthew and his four small children. He was 23 when he purchased it for an annual premium of $225.80. He carried this policy until age 35 but through an oversight forgot to pay the premium on the due date. Three weeks later he learned of the oversight. The rate for this same policy at age 35 was $497.20. May he still keep the $225.80 rate if he pays his premium immediately?

Chapter 41

PROPERTY INSURANCE

Property insurance is a contract whereby the insurer, in return for a compensation, agrees to reimburse the insured for loss or damage to specified property that is caused by the hazard covered. A contract of property insurance is one of indemnity that protects the policyholder from actual loss.

If a building actually worth $10,000 is insured for $15,000, the extra premiums which were paid for the last $5,000 worth of coverage do not provide any benefit for the insured since $10,000, the actual value, is the maximum that can be collected in case of total loss. On the other hand, if the building is insured for only $8,000 and it is totally destroyed, the insurance company must pay only $8,000. It will be seen from this that the maximum amount to be paid is fixed by the policy when the insurance is less than the value of the property. If the property is fully insured, the value of the property fixes the maximum.

FIRE INSURANCE

Fire is the greatest source of loss to property. Originally this was the only risk covered by insurance. As the additional types of property insurance developed, the same laws were applied to them that had been applied to fire insurance. Consequently, a thorough understanding of the laws of fire insurance is essential to understanding the basic laws governing all types of property insurance.

LOSSES RELATED TO FIRE

Fire insurance covers damage to property caused only by what are known as hostile fires. A *hostile fire* is defined as one out of its normal place, while a *friendly fire* is one contained in the place where it is intended to be. Scorching, searing, singeing, smoke, and similar damages from a friendly fire are not covered under the fire policy. In order to be covered by the fire policy, there must be an actual fire. Loss from heat without fire is not covered. In one case several thousand bales of cotton were under water during a flood. After the flood receded, heat in the bales of cotton was so intense smoke poured forth for days, but no flame was ever detected. The court held there was no fire.

Fire insurance also does not cover economic loss which results from a fire. A hostile fire may cause many losses other than to the property insured, yet the fire policy on the building and contents alone will not cover these losses. An example is the loss of profits while the building is being restored. This loss can be covered by a special policy called *business interruption insurance*. If one leases property on a long-term, favorable lease and the lease is canceled because of a fire damage to the building, the tenant may have to pay a higher rent in new quarters. This increased rent loss can be covered by a *leasehold interest insurance policy* but not by a fire policy.

The typical fire policy may also cover the risks of loss by windstorm, explosion, smoke damage from a friendly fire, falling aircraft, water damage, riot and civil commotion, and many others. Each one of these additional risks must be added to the fire policy by means of riders or extra clauses. This is commonly known as *extended coverage*.

INSURABLE INTEREST

One must have an insurable interest in the property at the time of the loss to be able to collect on a fire insurance policy. Ownership is, of course, the clearest type of insurable interest; but there are many other types of insurable interest. Insurable interest occurs when the insured would suffer a money loss by the destruction of the property. The most common types of insurable interest other than ownership are:

(1) The mortgagee has an insurable interest in the property mortgaged to the extent of his mortgage.

(2) When property is sold on the installment plan and the seller retains a security interest in it as security for the unpaid purchase price, the seller has an insurable interest in the property.

(3) The bailee has an insurable interest in the property bailed to the extent of his possible loss. The bailee's loss is from two sources. He will lose his compensation as provided for in the contract of bailment. Secondly, he may be held legally liable to the owner if the loss is due to the bailee's negligence or to the negligence of his employees.

(4) A partner has an insurable interest in the property owned by his firm to the extent of his possible loss.

A change in title or possession of the insured property may destroy the insurable interest, which in turn may void the contract because insurable interest must exist at the time of the loss.

THE FIRE INSURANCE POLICY

The fire insurance policy will state a maximum amount which will be paid by the insurer. When only a maximum is stated, the policy is called an *open policy* and in the event of partial or total loss, the insured must prove the actual loss which he has sustained. The policy may be a *valued policy*, in which case, instead of stating a maximum amount, it fixes a value on the property, which the insurer pays once a covered total destruction of the property is shown. If there is only a partial loss, the insured under a valued policy must still prove the amount of his loss, which amount cannot exceed the stated value.

> ▪ Dudley owned the Anderson Antique Shop. He carried the regular fire policy on his stock of antiques for $100,000. A fire destroyed about half the stock. After an extensive and expensive appraisal to ascertain the value of the items destroyed, he was able to collect $50,000. Had he carried a valued policy, he could have collected $50,000 without an appraisal.

Insurance policies also may be specific, blanket, or floating. A *specific policy* applies to one item only, such as one house. A *blanket policy* covers many items of the same kind in different places or different kinds of property in the same place, such as a building, fixtures, and merchandise in a single location. *Floating policies* are used for trucks, theatrical costumes, circus paraphernalia, and similar items which are not kept in a fixed location. A floater policy is also desirable for items that may be sent out for cleaning, such as rugs or clothes. Articles of jewelry and clothes that may be worn while traveling are also covered in a floater policy. A fire insurance policy on household effects covers for loss only at the named location. The purpose of the floater policy is to cover the loss no matter where the property is located at the time of the loss.

Another type of fire insurance policy of particular interest to merchants is the Reporting Form for Merchandise inventory. This policy permits the merchant to report periodically, usually once a month, the amount of inventory on hand. This enables him to carry full coverage at all times and still not be grossly over-insured during periods when his inventory is low.

DESCRIPTION OF THE PROPERTY

Both personal and real property must be described with reasonable accuracy in order to identify the property and to inform the insurer of the nature of the risk involved. This description applies both to the nature of the property and its location. A description of a house as brick when it is actually asphalt brick siding is a misrepresentation. Personal property should be so described that in the event of loss, its value can be determined. One "piano" does not indicate the value of the piano. Also, the general description "living room furniture" may make it difficult to establish the value and the number of items. A complete inventory should be kept. In this event, such description as "household furniture" is adequate.

The location of the property is important because the location affects the risk. If personal property used in a brick house on a broad paved street is moved to a frame house on an out-of-the-way dirt road, the risk may be increased considerably. Express permission must always be obtained when property is moved except under a "floating" policy. Most fire policies sold today have a clause continuing the coverage at the new location for five days together with coverage during the moving trip. If a loss occurs during the five-day period, the company must pay even though no notice has been given of the changed location. When property is by its nature not used at a fixed place, such as an automobile, coverage will be provided in terms of use within a specified area, as within a radius of 50 miles from the home of the insured.

▪ Jordan carried fire insurance on his household effects at 1327 Ellis Street, a two-story frame building. He moved to 237 Beechwood Hills, a one-story stone building. He did not give notice of the move within the five days required. A fire damaged the furniture to the extent of $1,000. The company did not have to pay even though the new location carried a lower rate than the old.

RISK AND HAZARD

The insurance company assumes the risks caused by normal hazards. The insured must not commit any act which increases the risk. Negligence by the insured is a normal hazard unless so gross as to indicate a criminal intent. When a fire occurs, the insured must use all due diligence to minimize the loss. He is not held responsible for an increased risk over which he has no control or knowledge. The insured must remove household effects from the building if this can safely be done. The owner must do everything possible to minimize the loss by protecting the property from further damage from the elements. Any expense involved in doing this is recoverable as a part of the loss.

- Mullin's house was on fire. Both the house and the furniture were insured. Part of the furniture was damaged while it was being removed; and while the furniture was piled in the street, a part of it was stolen and sparks damaged a part of it. The insurance company was liable for the breakage, the damage caused by sparks, and for the loss due to theft. If the insured had not removed the property, he would have increased the risk to the company and thus rendered the policy voidable.

COINSURANCE

Under the principle of *coinsurance* the insured recovers on a loss in the same ratio as his insurance bears to the amount of insurance which the company requires. Many policies contain an 80 percent coinsurance clause. This clause means that the insured may carry any amount of insurance he wishes up to the value of the property, but that the company will not pay the full amount of a partial loss unless he carries insurance for at least 80 percent of the value of the property. If a building is worth $20,000 and the insured buys a policy for $8,000, the company under the 80 percent coinsurance clause will pay only half of the damage and never more than $8,000. The 80 percent clause requires the insured to carry $16,000, or 80 percent of $20,000, to be fully protected. Since he carries only half of this amount, he can collect only half of the damage.

The coinsurance clause may be some percentage other than 80 percent. In burglary insurance it may be as low as 5 percent or 10 percent and on rare occasions as high as 100 percent in fire insurance.

REPAIRS AND REPLACEMENTS

Most insurance contracts give the insurer the option of paying the amount of loss or repairing or replacing the property. If the property is repaired or replaced, materials of like kind and quality must be used. The work must be completed within a reasonable time. The option to replace is seldom exercised by the insurer. He may also have the option of taking the property at an agreed valuation and then paying the insured the full value of the damaged property.

If the insurer pays a sum equal to the damage and the insured restores the property to its original status, new insurance must be obtained to cover the replaced part, unless there is an automatic restoration clause in the contract. Such a clause is frequently provided in insurance policies covering residential property where the loss is limited to a relatively small amount. Policies covering large industrial plants, motels, apartment buildings, and similar structures seldom contain a restoration clause.

CANCELLATION AND TERMINATION OF THE POLICY

Fire insurance policies permit each party to cancel by giving the other party notice. If a policy is canceled by the insured, a refund is made of the unearned premiums in excess of the short-term rate at which premiums would have been charged had the original contract of insurance been for such short term only. If at the end of six months the insured cancels a three-year policy costing $600, he is not entitled to a refund of $500. The short-term rate for six months is considerably higher than one-sixth of a thirty-six month policy.

QUESTIONS

1. What is meant by the statement that a property insurance contract is one of indemnity?
2. If one insures a fur coat for $2,000 against theft when its actual value is only $800, how much may the owner collect if the coat is stolen?

3. When must one have an insurable interest before he can collect under a fire insurance policy?

4. A delivers a deed to a house to B and is paid in full. At the time of the sale A has a $20,000 fire insurance policy on the house. What effect does the sale have on the insurance policy?

5. What is the difference between a valued fire insurance policy and an open policy?

6. What is the purpose of a floating insurance policy?

7. How must one identify his household furniture when he purchases household effects fire insurance?

8. When one insures property located at 256 Hope Street, what is the effect on the policy if the owner moves to a new location without notifying the insurance company?

CASE PROBLEMS

1. John, the bookkeeper for the Anderson Department Store, had the responsibility for placing all the needed insurance to protect the firm from the major hazards. The firm's merchandise inventory fluctuated from $40,000 during the dull season to $120,000 at the peak of the rush season. The average was about $70,000. In order to be fully covered, John carried a fire policy for $120,000 at the rate of 30 cents per hundred dollars. What insurance knowledge would enable John to reduce the cost of this policy?

2. In the above case the Anderson Department Store sold several thousand dollars worth of television sets, suites of furniture, and other items on the installment plan with the seller retaining title until the merchandise was paid for. John placed no insurance on this merchandise. One customer owed the company $1,100 for furniture when his home was destroyed by fire. He carried no fire insurance on his household effects. How could the Anderson Department Store avoid similar losses in the future?

3. Anderson Department Store's building was valued at $100,000. John calculated that the odds the building would be totally destroyed by fire were almost zero. To save money he placed a $50,000 fire and extended coverage policy on it. The policy contained an 80 percent coinsurance clause, but John did not understand what this clause meant. The building sustained a loss by fire amounting to $12,000. How much of this loss will be paid for by the insurance company?

4. The Anderson Department Store carries a line of moderately priced pianos. In an attempt to sell one to Halstead for $1,400, it permitted Halstead to buy on a "sale on approval" contract. Before Halstead indicated his approval or disapproval of the piano, his home and all its contents were destroyed by fire due to no negligence on Halstead's part. Did the company's merchandise inventory fire policy cover this loss?

5. Hunt owned a factory building. It was rented to Sevede Dressmakers, Inc. for $1,000 a month. A fire caused a $12,000 loss to one section of the building. This section was immediately restored, but soon thereafter the entire building was destroyed by fire. Hunt carried a $100,000 fire insurance policy on the building, its full value. How much can he collect on this policy?

6. Donald purchased a home for $20,000, giving a mortgage to Tillman for $18,000. Tillman purchased an $18,000 fire policy on the house and paid the premium himself. The house was destroyed by fire. Since Tillman did not own the house, can he collect on the policy?

7. John gave his young bride, Josephine, a fur coat as an anniversary present. The cost of the coat was $2,500. John and Josephine had a fire insurance policy on their household effects in the amount of $2,000. Realizing that this amount was too low, especially since the value of their effects had been increased by $2,500, they increased the face of their policy to $5,000 and paid the additional premium. While visiting relatives, the relatives' home was destroyed by fire and the fur coat was burned up. Could Josephine collect for this loss on her insurance contract?

Chapter 42

AUTOMOBILE INSURANCE

The laws dealing with automobile insurance can be understood best by discussing the major classes of insurance and their risks. These two classes of insurance are physical damage insurance, including fire, theft, and collision, and public liability, including bodily injury and property damage. To understand the law one must know what specific risk is assumed by the insurance carrier and the terms of the policy covering that specific risk. The term "automobile insurance" is loosely used to refer to insurance which the insured obtains to cover his own car and the injuries which he and other members of his family may sustain and also liability insurance which protects the insured from claims that third persons may make for injuries caused them or damage to their property caused by the insured.

PHYSICAL DAMAGE INSURANCE

As the name implies, *physical damage insurance* covers the risks of injury or damage to the car itself. It includes:

1. Fire insurance
2. Theft insurance
3. Collision insurance
4. Comprehensive coverage

(1) **Fire Insurance.** Much of the law of fire insurance discussed in the preceding chapter applies to automobile insurance. If the car is damaged or destroyed by the collision, sinking, stranding, or burning of any conveyance upon which the car is being transported, such as a barge, boat, or train, the fire policy covers this loss.

(2) Theft Insurance. *Theft* is defined as taking another's property by stealth. Automobile theft insurance either by law or by contract covers a wider range of losses than those by stealth. Obtaining possession of a car lawfully but converting it to one's own use is known as *conversion*. Taking another's car by force is known as robbery. In some states the automobile theft policy is required by law to cover all these losses. The policy itself may define theft broadly enough to cover theft, conversion, larceny after trust, and robbery. Unless the policy is broadened either by law or by the wording of the policy, a theft policy covers only the taking of the car by stealth.

Automobile theft insurance usually covers pilferage of any parts of the car but not articles or clothes left in the car. It also covers any damage done to the car either by theft or attempted theft. It does not cover loss of use of the car unless the policy specifically provides for this loss.

> ▪ Mrs. Snowden purchased a new car from Seagraves and paid for it by check. The check was not paid by the bank, for Mrs. Snowden had no money on deposit. The car was never recovered. Seagraves was able to collect on his theft insurance policy as it contained a "larceny by trick or device clause" designed specifically to cover this type of loss.

(3) Collision Insurance. The standard collision policy covers all damage to the car caused by a collision or upset. There is a collision whenever an object strikes the insured car or the car strikes an object. It is not required that both objects be automobiles nor that both be moving. A rolling rock that crashed into the car while it was parked was held to be a collision. Likewise, there was a collision when a horse kicked the door of the insured automobile. It is generally held that there is no collision when the colliding object is a natural phenomenon, such as rain or hail.

Practically all collision policies provide that the policy is either void or suspended if a trailer is attached to the car unless insurance of the same kind carried on the car is placed on the trailer. The question of interpretation then arises as to what constitutes a "trailer." A small boat trailer and a small two-wheel trailer generally are not considered trailers, but horse or cattle trailers must be covered if they are attached.

If collision insurance but not fire is carried on the car, the policy will, in most states, pay both the fire loss and the collision loss, both occurring in the same wreck, so long as the fire ensues after collision and as a direct cause of the collision. A few states hold that even if the collision is the direct and proximate cause of the fire, the collision policy will not cover both losses. This is a minority view, however.

Most collision insurance policies have a deductible clause. It is possible to buy policies without any deductible clause, but the rates are higher. It is cheaper for one to assume some of this risk.

If the insurance company pays the insured a claim for collision damage, under the law of subrogation the company has the right to sue the other party to the collision if he was at fault.

(4) Comprehensive Coverage. Insurance companies will write automobile insurance covering almost every conceivable risk to a car such as: windstorm, earthquake, flood, strike, spray from trees, malicious mischief, submersion in water, acid from battery, riot, glass breakage, hail, and falling aircraft. All companies today write what is called a *comprehensive policy* which may include all of these risks plus fire and theft. A comprehensive policy covers only the hazards enumerated in the policy.

PUBLIC LIABILITY INSURANCE

The second major division of automobile insurance is designed to protect third persons from bodily injury and property damage.

(1) Bodily Injury Insurance. Insurance covering the risk of bodily injury to the insured's passengers, pedestrians, or the occupants of another car is designated public liability insurance. The insurance company obligates itself to pay any sum not exceeding the limit fixed in the policy for which the insured may be personally liable. If he is not liable for damages, the insurance company has no liability except the duty of defending the insured in court actions brought by injured persons. This type of insurance does not cover any injury to either the person or the property of the insured. Such loss is covered by other policies.

The coverage under the automobile liability policy is usually written as 5/10/1, 25/50/5, 100/300/10, or similar combinations. The first number indicates that the company will pay $5,000, $25,000, or $100,000, respectively, to any one person for bodily injury in any one accident. The middle number fixes the maximum amount the company will pay for bodily injury in any one accident. The third figure sets the limit the company will pay for property damage. This usually is the damage to the other person's car but may include damage to any property belonging to another not under control of the driver.

Under the "defense clause" the insurer agrees to defend the insured against any claim for damages. The insurer reserves the right to accept or reject any proffered settlement out of court.

> ▪ Graham had an automobile liability policy covering both bodily injury and property injury to others. In a collision with another car, the driver of the other car was seriously injured and his car wrecked. Graham's policy provided for coverage up to $15,000 for bodily injury and $5,000 for property damage. The injured driver offered to settle the claim out of court for $14,000. The insurance company rejected the offer and defended the claim in court. The court gave judgment against Graham for $30,000. Graham had to pay all over and above his insurance. Had the insurance company settled out of court, Graham would not have had to pay anything. The insured has unlimited liability, but the insurer's liability is limited to the amount stated in the policy.

A bodily injury insurance policy does not cover accidents occurring while the car is being driven by a person who is under the age designated by state law. It does not cover accidents occurring while the car is rented or leased unless specifically covered, as in the case of cars leased from a car rental agency, while the car is used to carry passengers for a consideration, while the car is used for any purpose other than that named in the policy, or while it is used outside the United States and Canada. Some policies exclude accidents while the car is being used for towing a trailer or any other vehicle used as a trailer. These are the ordinary exclusions. Some policies may have additional exclusions of various kinds.

The insured is not permitted to settle claims or to incur expenses other than those for immediate medical help. In the event that the insurance company pays a loss, it is entitled to be subrogated to any rights that the insured may have against others because of such losses.

(2) **Property Damage Insurance.** In automobile property damage insurance the insurer agrees to pay, on behalf of the insured, all sums that the insured may be legally obligated to pay by reason of the liability imposed upon him by law for damages because of injury to or the destruction of property, caused by accident and arising out of the ownership, the maintenance, or the use of the automobile. The liability of the insurer, however, is limited as stated in the policy.

The policy usually provides that the insurer will not be liable in the event that the car is being operated, maintained, or used by any person in violation of any state or federal law as to age or occupation. The insurer is not liable for damage to property owned by, leased to, transported by, or in charge of the insured.

NOTICE TO THE INSURER

In the event of an accident, it is the duty of the policyholder to give the insurer written notice regarding the damages resulting from the accident. The notice must identify the insured and give the names and addresses of the injured persons, the owner of the damaged property, and those of any available witnesses. It is also necessary to give information relative to the time, the place, and to the detailed circumstances of the accident.

If a claim is made or a suit is brought against the insured, he must immediately forward to the insurance company every demand, notice, or summons received in order that the insurer may be able to make the proper legal defense. The insured must help secure any necessary information, evidence, and the presence of witnesses. In short, he must cooperate to the fullest extent with the insurer.

LAST CLEAR CHANCE RULE

In the public liability coverage of automobile insurance, the injured party must prove the driver of the car was at fault before the insured becomes liable. As often happens, both drivers are negligent. Formerly, the driver bringing suit had to come into court with clean hands. If his own negligence contributed even slightly to the accident, he could not recover. This harsh rule has been replaced in most states by the *last clear chance* rule. This rule simply states that if one driver is negligent but the other driver had one last clear chance to avoid hitting the negligent driver, but did not take it, then he is the one liable.

In a number of states the harshness of the common-law rule as to contributory negligence has also been modified by statutes which provide that the contributory negligence of the plaintiff reduces his recovery but does not completely bar him from recovering from the defendant. That is to say, the negligence of each party is balanced against that of the other.

FINANCIAL RESPONSIBILITY LAWS

A few states have compulsory automobile liability insurance laws, and most states have financial responsibility laws. These latter laws do not require one to have any insurance until he has his first accident. If he then cannot prove he is financially able to pay any claims against him up to the amount fixed by law, usually $10,000, then he must buy insurance for this amount, that is 5/10/1 coverage. If one is required to carry insurance in order to be permitted to drive but no insurance company will sell him a policy, then in many states the state insurance commissioner will assign this driver to an insurance company. The company must issue the policy under the "assigned risk" rule.

QUESTIONS

1. What are the two main classes of automobile insurance?
2. If John, the owner of a car, and four other young men drive to Jacksonville to attend a football game and each is to pay one fifth of the cost of the trip, is the insurer liable if the car is destroyed by fire during the trip?
3. What is covered by theft automobile insurance?
4. What effect does attaching a trailer to an automobile have on collision insurance?
5. Why do most automobile collision insurance policies have a deductible clause?
6. Name several causes of damage that may be covered by comprehensive insurance.
7. What two kinds of losses are covered by public liability insurance?
8. Who is liable for property damage if the owner is not driving the car?
9. What must one do with reference to his insurance when he has an accident?
10. If A has in his possession a watch worth $100 belonging to B and as a direct result of an automobile accident the watch is destroyed, who must pay for the loss?

CASE PROBLEMS

1. A car owned and driven by John collided with a car owned and driven by Henry. The damage to John's car was $1,100 and that to Henry's car was $800. Henry carried collision and public liability insurance, but John carried no insurance. The collision was clearly the result of John's negligence. John

and Henry were fraternity brothers, and Henry agreed to admit it was his fault. Miss Vaughn, secretary to the agent who serviced Henry's insurance policy, overheard the agreement between John and Henry and reported it to her employer. As a result, the insurance company refused to pay for the damage to either John's car or Henry's car. Was the company within its rights?

2. John and Janet Kettle hooked their car to their house trailer and set out to tour the country. They carried full insurance on the car but none on the trailer. While crossing a mountain in West Virginia, John lost control of the car and it plunged over the mountainside, completely demolishing both the car and the trailer. The insurance company refused to pay the damage for either the car or the trailer. Must it pay for the car?

3. Bennett, a truck driver for the Beck Bakery, struck a child. The child was not hurt, and the police exonerated Bennett for the accident. Consequently Beck did not notify the insurance company of the accident. Six months later the boy's father sued the bakery for $10,000, alleging the boy suffered internal injuries. It cost Beck $800 to defend the suit even though he won it. Was the insurance company liable for the $800?

4. Kemp negligently ran into Benton's car causing Benton to lose control of his car and collide with a car owned and driven by Spooner. The damage to Benton's car was $1,400 and to Spooner's car, $900. In addition to this property damage, Benton received a bodily injury for which he was awarded damages of $8,000; Spooner was awarded $9,000 for bodily injury. Kemp carried 5/10/1 coverage on his car for any one accident. The question arose as to whether this was one accident or two accidents. How much will the insurance company pay?

5. Henderson came to a highway crossing at which there was a stop sign. Henderson did not stop. Fulcher approached from the right on the other highway at a speed of 60 miles an hour, the maximum speed limit. He struck Henderson's car on the rear fender and demolished it and injured Henderson. Fulcher had a clear view of the crossing and admitted he never applied his brakes. Had Fulcher slowed down so as to delay his arrival at the crossing one or two seconds, Henderson would have been in the clear. Who is liable for the loss in this case?

6. Seabolt carried a 5/10/1 liability policy on his car. He negligently injured a child who was playing in the street. The father of the child offered to settle the claim for $9,000. Seabolt insisted the insurance company accept the offer, but the company refused. The father sued Seabolt and obtained judgment for $12,000. How much will the insurance company pay?

7. Cullison carried full automobile coverage on his car. The policy contained this clause: "This policy shall not apply while the automobile is used as a public or livery conveyance." On a trip Cullison took three riders who agreed to share the cost of the trip. They agreed to figure the cost at seven cents a mile and each one would pay one fourth the cost. On the trip Cullison collided with another car and suffered $420 damage to his car. Must his insurance company pay for the damage to his car under the collision policy?

8. Colbert was accident prone. He had been in four serious car wrecks for which he had been held liable in each case. He was such a poor risk no company would sell him a policy. He did not have enough property to qualify for a driver's license under the state financial responsibility law. Is there any way he can be permitted to drive?

Chapter 43

GUARANTY AND
SURETYSHIP

NATURE OF THE CONTRACT

The contract of guaranty or suretyship is a contract to ensure or guarantee that someone else will perform his contract. It is an agreement whereby one party promises that he will be responsible for the debt, default, or obligation of another. Such contracts generally arise when one person assumes responsibility for the extension of credit to another, as in buying merchandise on credit or in borrowing money from a bank.

A person who is entrusted with money of another, such as a cashier, a bank teller, or a county treasurer, may be required to have someone guarantee the faithful performance of his duties. This, too, is a contract of suretyship, although it is commonly referred to as a *fidelity bond.*

PARTIES

There are three parties to a contract of guaranty or of suretyship. The party who undertakes to be responsible for another is the *guarantor* or the *surety*; and the party to whom the guaranty is given is the *creditor*; and the party who is primarily liable is the *principal debtor*, or simply the *principal.*

DISTINCTIONS

The words "surety" and "guaranty" are often used interchangeably. Sometimes such usage is correct, and sometimes it is incorrect. In a contract of suretyship the liability of the insurer is coextensive with that of the principal debtor. The surety renders himself directly and primarily responsible for the debt or obligation as though he were the primary debtor himself. His obligation, then, is identical with the one for whom he assumes the responsibility.

A guarantor's obligation is collateral to that of the principal debtor. He promises to pay only in the event that the principal defaults. The guarantor's obligation does not arise simultaneously with the principal's. His obligation is contingent upon the happening of another event, namely, the failure of the principal to pay.

Charlotte, N. C., Jan. 10, 19--

Mr. Jack E. Smith
Blue Pine, North Carolina

Dear Sir:

In consideration of the letting of the premises located at 861 South Street, this city, to Mr. William H. Prost for a period of two years from date, I hereby guarantee the punctual payment of the rent and the faithful performance of the covenants of the lease.

Very truly yours,

Herbert Hanason

A Letter of Guaranty

For the most part, however, the law of suretyship and guaranty applies with equal force to both paid sureties and accommodation sureties. In some instances, however, the contract is interpreted strictly as to a paid surety. Thus, in the case of acts claimed to discharge the surety, it is sometimes held that the paid surety must prove that it has actually been harmed by the conduct of the principal.

IMPORTANCE OF MAKING A DISTINCTION

Three reasons why it is important to distinguish between a contract of guaranty and a contract of suretyship pertain to:

1. Form
2. Notice of default
3. Remedy

(1) Form. Contracts of guaranty and suretyship have many similarities, but the dissimilarities particularly need to be recognized. All the essential elements of a contract must be present in both. If the nature of the contract is such that it falls within the description of a contract of guaranty, it must be in writing; most contracts of suretyship may be oral.

The Statute of Frauds provides: "The promise to answer for the debt, default, or obligation of another must be in writing and be signed by the party to be charged, or by his authorized agent." This provision applies only to a promise that creates a secondary obligation, that is, an obligation of guaranty, not to a promise that creates a primary obligation, that is, suretyship. One must first classify the obligation as primary or secondary before he knows whether or not the contract must be in writing.

(2) Notice of Default. Since the surety is primarily liable for the debt, it is not necessary to notify him if the debt is defaulted. The guarantor, on the other hand, must be notified by the creditor. Failure to give notice does not of itself discharge the guarantyship. If the guarantor is damaged by the failure to receive notice, he may offset the amount of the damage against the claim of the creditor.

> ▪ Hawkins was a surety on a debt for Crew for $150. When the debt came due, Crew was unable to pay. The creditor waited four months and then notified Hawkins of the default. Hawkins denied liability because of the delay in giving him notice of default. The court held he was not entitled to a notice of default since he was a surety and had a primary obligation to pay.

(3) Remedy. In the case of suretyship, the surety takes upon himself an original obligation. He binds himself to pay if the other party does not. The reason that the other party does not pay is immaterial. He is liable as fully and under the same conditions as if the debt were his from the beginning. The rule is different in many contracts of guaranty. If the guaranty is conditional, the guarantor is liable only if the other party cannot pay.

Arnold writes, "Let Brewer have a suit; if he is unable to pay you, I will." This guaranty depends upon Brewer's ability to pay. Therefore, the seller must make all reasonable efforts to collect from Brewer before he can look to Arnold. If Arnold had said, "Let Brewer have this suit, and I will pay you," he would have created an original obligation for which he would have been personally liable. Therefore, Arnold would be deemed a surety if the understanding was that Brewer was to pay for the suit, but the merchant could look to Arnold if Brewer merely did not pay, rather than if Brewer could not pay.

RIGHTS OF THE SURETY AND THE GUARANTOR

A guarantor and a surety have the following rights:

1. Indemnity
2. Subrogation
3. Contribution
4. Exoneration

(1) **Indemnity.** If the guarantor or the surety pays the debt or the obligation of the principal, he is entitled to be reimbursed by the principal. This right is known as the right of *indemnity*. The guarantor or the surety may be induced to pay the debt when it becomes due in order to avoid the accumulation of interest and other costs on the debt.

(2) **Subrogation.** When the guarantor or the surety pays the debt of his principal, the claim of the creditor is automatically assigned to the guarantor or surety by operation of law. He is also entitled to all property, liens, or securities that were held by the creditor to secure the payment of the debt. This right of subrogation does not arise until the creditor has been paid in full, but it does arise if the surety or the guarantor has paid a part of the debt and the principal has paid the remainder.

> ▪ Clayton wished to borrow $900 from the Bank of Elbert. The bank required Clayton to get a surety to go on the note with him, as well as give it a mortgage on his truck. Reed agreed to become a surety for Clayton. When Clayton defaulted, Reed paid the debt and then attempted to foreclose on the mortgage on the truck. The court ruled Reed could do this under the rule of subrogation. Reed was subrogated to the bank's rights since Reed paid the bank the amount of the debt.

(3) **Contribution.** When two or more persons are jointly held liable for the debt, default, or obligation of a certain person, they are

known as *coguarantors* or *cosureties*. When one of two or more guarantors or sureties has paid more than his proportionate share of the
debt, he is entitled to recover from the other guarantors or sureties
the amount in excess of his pro rata share of the loss. This right is
known as the right of *contribution*. It does not arise until the surety
or the guarantor has paid the debt in full or has otherwise settled
the debt.

(4) **Exoneration.** If one becomes a surety for the benefit of another, he may call upon the creditor to proceed to compel the payment of the debt; otherwise the surety will be released. This is known
as the right of *exoneration*. The creditor may delay in pressing the
debtor to pay because he has the security of the suretyship. In cases
where the debtor can pay, the surety is released from potential liability hanging over him for years.

DISCHARGE OF A SURETY OR A GUARANTOR

Both a surety and a guarantor may be discharged from their
obligation by the usual methods of discharging any obligation, including performance, voluntary agreement, and bankruptcy. There are,
however, some additional acts that will discharge the surety or the
guarantor. These are:

1. Extension of time
2. Alteration of the terms of the contract
3. Loss or return of collateral by the creditor

(1) **Extension of Time.** If the creditor extends the time of the
debt without the consent of the surety or the guarantor and for a
consideration, the surety or the guarantor is discharged from further
liability.

> ▪ Russel owed a note for $2,231 at the Bank of Omar. Lamar was
> surety on this note. When the note came due, the bank promised
> Russel it would renew the note if he would get Slack as an additional
> surety. This Russell did. Lamar did not consent to the renewal—in
> fact, he was not even aware of it. This extension of time released
> Lamar even though an added surety was to his advantage.

(2) **Alteration of the Terms of the Contract.** Any material
alteration of the contract by the creditor discharges the surety or the

guarantor. The change must be prejudicial to the surety or the guarantor. A reduction in the interest rate has been held not to discharge the surety, while a change in the place of payment has been held to be an act justifying a discharge of the surety. Even though the change is made for the convenience or the benefit of the surety, his obligation is discharged if the change is material. A material change in a contract is in fact substituting a new contract for the old. The surety guaranteed the payment of the old contract, not the new one.

(3) **Loss or Return of Collateral by the Creditor.** If the creditor through negligence loses collateral security given to secure the debt, a surety or a guarantor is discharged. The same is true if the creditor returns to the debtor any collateral security. This collateral must be held for the benefit of the surety until the debtor pays the debt in full.

▪ Black loaned Hendon $7,200. The loan was partially secured with $3,000 of bearer bonds deposited with Black by Hendon. Coe was a surety for the loan. Black used the bonds as collateral for a loan to buy stock for speculative purposes. He lost heavily on the stock market, and he lost the bonds as a result. Coe was released from his contract of suretyship by the amount of the bonds.

BONDING COMPANIES

In recent years *bonding companies* have taken over most of the business of guaranteeing the employer against losses due to the dishonesty of his employees. These bonding companies are paid sureties as distinguished from unpaid sureties or guarantors. The bonding company's obligation arises from its written contract with the employer. This contract of indemnity sets out in detail the conditions under which the surety will be liable.

QUESTIONS

1. What is the nature of a contract of guaranty or suretyship?
2. Name the parties to a contract of guaranty or suretyship.
3. When does the obligation of a surety arise?
4. When does the obligation of a guarantor arise?
5. What must be the form of a contract of guaranty? Of suretyship?
6. If the guarantor or the surety pays the debt of the principal, what is his right to payment called?

7. When does the right of subrogation of the guarantor or surety arise?

8. What is the right of *contribution*?

9. If the creditor extends the time of payment without the consent of the guarantor, what effect does this have on the contract of guaranty?

10. If a creditor loses any collateral held as security for a debt on which there is a surety, what effect does this loss have on the surety's liability?

11. What is a *bonding company*?

CASE PROBLEMS

1. Chapman was bookkeeper and credit manager of the Rowe Lumber Company, from which Mason purchased building materials amounting to $750. Reece, Mason's brother-in-law, entered into an oral contract of suretyship whereby he promised to be fully responsible for the debt. The original credit period was for 90 days. When the account came due, Mason paid $150 and asked to be allowed to give his 60-day note in payment of the balance. Chapman accepted the note and about two weeks later notified Reece of the new arrangement. Mason never paid the note, and the Rowe Lumber Company sued Reece. Reece denied liability for four reasons: first, oral contract; second, an extension of time; third, improper notice of default; and fourth, discharge of the debt which he had guaranteed. Were any of these defenses valid?

2. Coulter leased the Parkview Apartment Hotel for $1,500 a month. Denton deposited with the owner stock valued at $18,000 to be held as collateral to guarantee the payment of the rent by Coulter. When the lease was renewed at the end of the first year, the rent was increased to $1,850 a month, but Denton was not notified of this increase. Coulter defaulted in the payment of the rent, and demand was made upon Denton as guarantor to pay the rent. Was Denton liable for the rent?

3. Flannagan entered into a contract with WGAU Radio Broadcasting Company to carry on an advertising campaign over a period of 60 days. The total cost was $6,000. The radio station required Flannagan to provide some guaranty of payment of the $6,000 before the advertising campaign could start. Gill, a wealthy friend of Flannagan, orally agreed "to be personally responsible for this debt if for any reason Flannagan fails to pay it." There were three witnesses to this oral contract. Flannagan failed to pay any part of the $6,000, and the radio corporation demanded that Gill pay. Was Gill liable for this debt?

4. Huntley was a guarantor on a debt of $700 which Bartlet owed to Whitley. The debt was long past due; and though Whitley had never legally extended the time of payment, he was in no hurry to sue Bartlet. Huntley was confident that Bartlet would pay and release him from the potential liability if suit were instituted. What right does Huntley have?

5. Riley and Baker were cosureties on a debt of $1,000 which Ferguson owed Smallwood. They paid the debt off and then demanded that Ferguson pay them. When Ferguson refused, Riley wanted to bring suit, but Baker wished to charge it off as a bad debt and forget it. Riley offered Baker fifty cents for his half, and Baker accepted. Riley then sued Ferguson for $1,000. How much is he entitled to collect?

6. Ross promised to pay Fludd $5,000 to burn down Remley's residence because he claimed Remley had defrauded him. Fludd agreed to do this if Ross would get Lane to guarantee the payment of the $5,000. Although Lane was unaware of the illegal nature of the debt, he promised to pay the $5,000 if Ross did not. When Ross refused to pay, Fludd sued Lane. Must Lane pay?

SUMMARY CASES

PART 9

1. Simpson, a minor, purchased a $500 twenty-year endowment life insurance policy from the Prudential Life Insurance Company of America. After Simpson had paid $54, she attempted to disaffirm the contract and demanded a return of her $54. Is an endowment life insurance policy a necessary? (Simpson v. Prudential Insurance Co. of America, 184 Mass. 348, 68 N. E. 673)

2. Dr. Charles F. Clayton was a doctor employed by the Southern Mining Company to treat all the company's workers. The doctor's pay was deducted from the miners' wages. Some of the miners became very much dissatisfied with the arrangement. The dissatisfied miners made several threats against Dr. Clayton. Because of these threats, he renewed his insurance policy on his home and personal property. He also applied for and received two additional policies on the same property. In none of these applications did he make any reference to these threats. The property was destroyed, and the insurance companies denied liability on the ground of concealment. (a) Were these threats material? (b) Was there a concealment? (Great American Insurance Company of New York v. Clayton. 247 Ky. 612, 571 S. W. 2d 467)

3. Mrs. Veit purchased a $25,000 policy and made her husband the beneficiary. She understated her age by 16 years. More than 17 years after the policy was purchased she died, and Mr. Veit collected the $25,000. Soon thereafter the insurance company learned of the misstatement of age and sued Mr. Veit for a return of a portion of the $25,000. Had Mrs. Veit given her correct age, the amount of the premium she paid would have purchased a policy for only $15,077. The insurance company admitted liability for this amount but demanded a return of $9,923. Was this suit barred by the incontestability clause? (New York Life Insurance Company v. Veit, et al., 249 N. Y. 222, 62 N. E. 2d 45)

4. Rohde purchased an automobile public liability policy with a 20/50/5 coverage for each accident. The insured while driving negligently struck three motorcycles simultaneously. The drivers of the motorcycles were injured and their vehicles damaged. The total damages assessed were in excess of the limits of the policy if this was one accident. If there were three separate accidents, then the policy limits were adequate to cover all damages. Was this one accident or three accidents? (Truck Insurance Company v. Rohde, 49 Wash. 2d 465, 303 P. 2d 659)

5. Bruener purchased a comprehensive automobile policy that specifically excluded collision damage. While driving on a wet pavement, Bruener lost control of his car when it skidded on the highway, finally coming to a violent stop when it hit the road embankment. The car was badly damaged. The question arose as to whether the direct and proximate cause of the damage was the skidding or whether the proximate cause was the collision with the road embankment. If it were the latter, then it came within the exclusion clause and the insurance company was not liable. Was the skidding the proximate cause of the damage? (Bruener v. Twin City Fire Insurance Company, 37 Wash. 2d 181, 222 P. 2d 833)

6. Charles Roehm negligently injured Roy T. Caldwell in an automobile accident. Roehm carried a public liability automobile policy, purchased through Goldsmith, an insurance broker. The policy contained the usual clause that in the event of an accident, immediate notice must be given to the insurance company. On the day following the accident, Roehm notified Goldsmith by telephone and was assured that Goldsmith would take care of things. By mistake Goldsmith reported an entirely different accident, and the error was not discovered until 26 days after the accident. The insurance company denied liability on the grounds that Goldsmith was the agent of Roehm and therefore notice of the accident was not given to the company immediately. There was considerable evidence that the insurance company had on many previous occasions accepted Goldsmith as its agent to receive notices of accidents. Was notice to Goldsmith notice to the insurance company? (General Accident Insurance Company v. Caldwell, 59 F. 2d 473)

7. C. E. Youse purchased a fire insurance policy on her household goods and personal property. She removed a valuable ring from her finger and laid it on the table with some cleansing tissue. By mistake the maid threw the tissue and the ring into the wastepaper basket and then threw the contents of the basket into a backyard incinerator. She lighted the contents of the incinerator intentionally, and the ensuing fire stayed within the incinerator. About one week later the ring was discovered in the ashes in the incinerator. It had been damaged about $900 by the fire. The insurance company refused to pay on the ground this was a friendly fire. Was this a friendly fire or a hostile fire? (Youse v. Employers Fire Insurance Company, 238 P. 2d 472 Kan.)

8. Short and Sinai dissolved their partnership and left several creditors unpaid. Sinai owed Short some money, so he and DeVincenzi jointly agreed that Sinai would pay these creditors and thus relieve Short of the liability. DeVincenzi's promise was merely an accommodation to Sinai. The debts were never paid by Sinai, but Short gave no notice of the default to De-Vincenzi. When suit was instituted, DeVincenzi denied liability on the ground he had received no notice of default before suit was filed. Is a surety entitled to notice of default? (Short v. Sinai, et al., 50 Nev. 346, 259 P. 417)

9. Cuesta, Rey & Company drew a check for $1,887.60 on the Citizen's Bank and Trust Company. The check was payable to the Collector of Internal Revenue for federal taxes. Before the check was delivered, the drawer had it certified. Before it was collected, the bank failed. The drawer then paid it from another fund. Since the federal government had a first lien on the deposits of the insolvent bank for the face of the check, the drawer upon payment from another fund petitioned the court to be subro-gated to the rights of the federal government and thus given a preferred lien against the bank's assets for this check. Was Cuesta, Rey & Company entitled to subrogation? (Cuesta, Rey & Company v. Newsom, 102 Fla. 583, 136 S. 551)

Part 10.

PROPERTY

Preview Cases for Part 10: Property

■ The Hackney Mill Savings and Loan, by virtue of a financing assignment, claimed the wall-to-wall carpeting in a house built by Matthews. The case was defended on the ground that the carpeting was a fixture and belonged to the purchaser of the house. The carpeting could be removed without damage to the carpeting, but the removal of the padding might damage it and would leave the subflooring exposed. Was the defense successful?

■ Saul executed a general warranty deed conveying his home to his wife, Ilene. Since he did not want her to know of this act, he placed the deed in his safe deposit box. Only he had access to the box. Upon his death, the deed was discovered. John, Ilene's stepson, brought suit to have the deed nullified. Will the court declare the deed invalid?

■ Watson rented an apartment on the first floor of a three-story apartment building. The occupants on the second floor over Watson's apartment loved music and dancing. Every night they and some friends danced until after midnight. The noise from the dancing was loud and continuous. Watson demanded that the landlord evict the tenants, but the landlord refused. Watson moved seven months before his lease expired. The landlord sued for the balance of the rent. May he recover?

■ Graham provided in his will that his son, Henry, was to receive his lakeside home, Agua Vista, and the boat and boathouse. Before Graham died, he sold this property and purchased with the proceeds a beach home in Florida. He did not change his will. When he died, Henry demanded the beach home. Is he entitled to it?

■ Scott who was insolvent learned that three of his creditors were in the process of forcing him into involuntary bankruptcy. Scott immediately sold to his brother eight parcels of real estate for a total of Fifty Dollars. Scott was adjudicated bankrupt and the trustee sued to set aside the transfers as a fraud on the creditors. Will the trustee succeed?

These preview cases are designed to serve as a springboard for the study of this part. As you read through each chapter in this part, you will find the actual decisions for all these preview cases. Of course, there are many more such illustrative problems as well as case problems for decision at the end of each chapter. And there are also a number of even more challenging cases for review at the end of the part.

Chapter 44

NATURE OF PROPERTY

DEFINITION OF PROPERTY

Property is anything which may be owned, possessed, used, or disposed of. The right to use property is broader than ownership because one may enter into a contract with another to use property which does not belong to him. The law protects not only the right to own property but also the right to use it. Property includes not only physical things but such things as money, notes, and bonds which give the right to acquire either physical property or the use of such property.

Property may be classified according to its movability. In this sense all property falls into one of two classes, real property and personal property. If it is not movable it is real property; and if it is tangible, movable property, it is personal property.

REAL PROPERTY

Real property consists of land, which includes the actual soil, and all permanent attachments to the land, such as fences, walls, other man-made property, timber, and other growing things. It also includes minerals under the soil and the waters upon it. Through court interpretations we have accumulated a definite set of rules to guide us in distinguishing real property from personal property. The most important of these rules pertain to:

1. Trees and perennial crops
2. Rivers and streams
3. Fixtures
4. Emblements

(1) Trees and Perennial Crops. Trees that are growing on the land, orchards, vineyards, and perennial crops, such as clovers, grasses, and others that are not planted annually and cultivated, are classed as real property until they are severed from the land. When land is sold, if there is any doubt as to whether or not a particular item belongs to the land, or is personal property, the parties should agree before the sale is completed just how the item is to be classed.

> ▪ Howard owned a 40-acre farm on which was a substantial amount
> of timber. He was in the process of cutting down one 5-acre stand
> when he decided to move back to the city and sold the farm to
> Carson. At the time of the sale there were six cut walnut trees worth
> at least $300 on the property that Howard had not yet sold. Carson
> brought an action to prevent Howard from removing them, claiming
> they were sold with the farm. Carson lost since once the timber was
> cut it was no longer part of the realty.

(2) Rivers and Streams. If a nonnavigable river flows through a man's land, he owns the riverbed but not the water that flows over the bed. He cannot impound or divert the water to his own use in such a way as to deprive his neighbor of its use. If the river or the stream forms the boundary line, then the owner on each side of the river owns the land to the middle of the riverbed.

In most states where navigable rivers form the boundary, or flow through one's land, the owner of the adjoining land owns the land only to the low-water mark.

(3) Fixtures. Personal property attached to land or a building is known as a *fixture*. Generally, a fixture becomes part of the real estate. To determine whether or not personal property has become real estate, one or more of the following four rules may be applied:

1. How securely is it attached? If the personal property is so securely attached that it cannot be removed without damaging the real property to which it is attached, then it ceases to be personal property. A tenant cannot then remove fixtures when the lease expires.

2. What was the intention of the one installing the personal property? No matter what one's intention, the personal property becomes real property if it cannot be removed without damaging the property. But, if it is loosely attached and the person installing the fixture indicates his intention to make the fixture

real property, then this intention is the controlling factor. Kitchen refrigerators have been held to be real estate when the apartments were rented unfurnished but contained refrigerators.

3. For what purpose was the fixture attached? The purpose for which the fixture is to be used shows the intention of the one annexing it.

4. Who installed the fixture? If the owner of a building installs personal property to the building, this usually indicates his intention to make it a permanent addition to the real property. If the tenant makes the same improvements, the presumption is that he intended to keep the fixture as personal property unless a contrary intention can be shown.

■ The Hackney Mill Savings and Loan, by virtue of a financing assignment, claimed the wall-to-wall carpeting in a house built by Matthews. The case was defended on the ground that the carpeting was a fixture and belonged to the purchaser of the house. The carpeting could be removed without damage to the carpeting, but the removal of the padding might damage it and would leave the subflooring exposed. The court found that the carpeting was a fixture since it was annexed to the realty, and Matthews had intended it to become a fixture.

(4) **Emblements.** An *emblement* is an annual crop or a perennial which is produced primarily by the application of man's labor and industry. If the land is rented for a fixed period, the tenant must remove emblements before the expiration of the lease. If no definite time is fixed to terminate the lease, the tenant has a right to return and harvest emblements.

PERSONAL PROPERTY

Personal property is any property or property right which is not classified as real property. Personal property includes movable physical property and notes, bonds, and all written evidences of debt. Personal property is divided into two classes:

1. Tangible
2. Intangible

(1) **Tangible Personal Property.** *Tangible personal property* is personal property which can be seen, touched, and possessed. Animals, merchandise, furniture, annual growing crops, clothing, jewelry, and similar items are all classified as tangible personal property.

(2) Intangible Personal Property. Intangible personal property includes claims and debts, which are called *choses in action.* Some common forms of choses in action are checks, stocks, and savings account certificates.

REAL PROPERTY ESTATES

The interest which a person has in real estate may be:

1. A fee simple estate, or
2. A life estate

(1) Estate in Fee Simple. A *fee simple estate* is the largest and most complete right which one may possess in real property. It gives the owner the right to the surface of the land, the air above the land "all the way to heaven," and the subsoil beneath the surface all the way to the center of the earth. The courts have held, however, that the right to the air above the land is not absolute. One cannot prevent an airplane from flying over his land unless it flies too low.

One can own the surface of the land only, but not the minerals, oil, gas, and other valuable property under the topsoil. One may also own the soil but not the timber.

(2) Life Estate. One may have an estate in land by which he owns the land for his lifetime. This is known as a *life estate.* At the death of the owner, the title passes as directed by the original owner. The title may revert to the one who conveyed the life estate to the deceased, the interest of the grantor being called a *reversion,* or the property may go to someone other than the grantor, such interest being called a *remainder.*

■ John Dotson conveyed to his wife, Minnie, a life estate in all his real estate. At her death the property was to go to his three sons in equal parts. The interest of the sons was a remainder. Had the property at Minnie's death returned to her husband or to his estate, it would have been a reversion. In either case, the property right is real property, not personal property.

PERSONAL PROPERTY ESTATES

Any estate in land other than a fee simple or life estate is classified as personal property.

METHODS OF ACQUIRING OWNERSHIP

The title to property may be acquired by (1) purchase, (2) will, (3) gift, (4) descent, (5) accession, (6) confusion, (7) creation, and (8) original possession.

Acquiring ownership through purchase is a common occurrence. Acquiring property through a will or a gift is also well known.

One of the less common methods is *descent*. If a man dies *intestate*, that is, without leaving a will, his heirs acquire, as a matter of law, title to his personal property according to the law of descent existing in the decedent's state, and to his real property according to the law of descent in the state where the land is located.

One may get title to property by accretion or accession. *Accretion* takes place most commonly when the boundary line of property is a stream, river, lake, or ocean. If one's land extends to the low water mark of a navigable stream, he may get title to some land by the river's shifting its flow. This occurs slowly by the deposit of silt. Also the accretion may be the result of dredging or channeling of the river. If the silt and sand are thrown up on the riverbank thereby increasing the acreage of the upland contiguous to the river, the added acreage belongs to the owner of the upland.

If a nonnavigable stream is the dividing line between two property owners and the boundary follows the meandering of the stream, then one's line shifts with the river. One property owner, however, cannot take any action to encourage the river to change its course.

Accession is the acquiring of property by means of an addition to, or increase in, the property owned, such as the produce of land or the young of animals.

Confusion is the mixing of the goods of different owners so that the parts belonging to each owner cannot be identified and separated. Grain, lumber, oil, and coal are examples of the kinds of property that are susceptible to confusion. The property, belonging to different owners, may be mixed by common consent, by accident, or by the willful act of some wrongdoer.

When confusion of the property is brought about by common consent or by accident, each party will be deemed the owner of a proportionate part of the mass. If the confusion is willful, the title to the total mass passes to the innocent party, unless the one causing the confusion can clearly prove how much of his property was mingled with that of the other person; if he fails, the whole mass belongs to the other person.

Page 1   **FORM A**

CLASS	REGISTRATION NO.
A	DO NOT WRITE HERE

Application for Registration of a Claim to Copyright
in a published book manufactured in the United States of America

Instructions: Make sure that all applicable spaces have been completed before you submit the form. The application must be **SIGNED** at line 10 and the **AFFIDAVIT** (line 11) **must be COMPLETED AND NOTARIZED.** The application should not be submitted until after the date of publication given in line 4, and should state the facts which existed on that date. For further information, see page 4.

Pages 1 and 2 should be typewritten or printed with pen and ink. Pages 3 and 4 should contain exactly the same information as pages 1 and 2, but may be carbon copies. Mail all pages of the application to the Register of Copyrights, Library of Congress, Washington, D.C. 20540, together with 2 copies of the best edition of the work and the registration fee of $6. Make your remittance payable to the Register of Copyrights.

1. Copyright Claimant(s) and Address(es): Give the name(s) and address(es) of the copyright owner(s). Ordinarily the name(s) should be the same as in the notice of copyright on the copies deposited.

Name ...... South-Western Publishing Company

Address ...... 5101 Madison Road, Cincinnati, OH 45227

Name ......

Address ......

2. Title: ...... College Law, Seventh Edition
(Give the title of the book as it appears on the title page)

3. Authors: Citizenship and domicile information must be given. Where a work was made for hire, the employer is the author. The citizenship of organizations formed under U.S. Federal or State law should be stated as U.S.A. Authors may be editors, compilers, translators, illustrators, etc., as well as authors of original text. If the copyright claim is based on new matter (see line 5) give requested information about the author of the new matter.

Name ...... John D. Ashcroft ...... Citizenship ...U.S.A.
(Give legal name followed by pseudonym if latter appears on the copies)   (Name of country)

Domiciled in U.S.A. Yes ...X... No ...... Address Southwest Missouri State College, Springfield, Missouri

Name ...... A. Aldo Charles ...... Citizenship ...U.S.A.
(Give legal name followed by pseudonym if latter appears on the copies)   (Name of country)

Domiciled in U.S.A. Yes ...X... No ...... Address Late Professor of Business Law, University of Georgia, Athens, Georgia

Name ......
(Give legal name followed by pseudonym if latter appears on the copies) ...... Citizenship ......
(Name of country)

Domiciled in U.S.A. Yes ...... No ...... Address ......

4. Date of Publication of This Edition: Give the complete date when copies of this particular edition were first placed on sale, sold, or publicly distributed. The date when copies were made or printed should not be confused with the date of publication. **NOTE:** The full date (month, day, and year) must be given. For further information, see page 4.

...... May ...... 15, ... 1971 ......
(Month)   (Day)   (Year)

▶▶ (NOTE: Leave line 5 blank unless the following instructions apply to this work.) ◀◀

5. New Matter in This Version: If any substantial part of this work has been previously published anywhere, give a brief, general statement of the nature of the new matter published for the first time in this version. New matter may consist of compilation, translation, abridgment, editorial revision, and the like, as well as additional text or pictorial matter.

...... Additions and Revisions ......

▶▶ NOTE: Leave line 6 blank unless there has been a **PREVIOUS FOREIGN EDITION** in the English language. ◀◀

6. Book in English Previously Manufactured and Published Abroad: If all or a substantial part of the text of this edition was previously manufactured and published abroad in the English language, complete the following spaces:

Date of first publication of foreign edition ......
(Year)

Was registration for the foreign edition made in the U.S. Copyright Office? Yes ...... No ......

If your answer is "Yes," give registration number ......

EXAMINER

Complete all applicable spaces on next page

An Application for a Copyright

One may acquire personal property by *creation*. This is true of inventions, paintings, musical compositions, and other intellectual productions. Title to these is made secure through patents and copyrights.

The one who first applies for and obtains a patent gets title to the production. Creation alone does not give absolute title; it gives only the right to obtain absolute title by means of a patent. This is not true for songs, books, and other compositions that are copyrighted. This is a holdover from the common law which gave absolute title to one's mental creation but not to one who invented a new device. After one publishes a book, a song, or a painting, he must apply for and obtain a statutory copyright to replace his common-law right or he loses all right to his creation.

LOST AND ABANDONED PROPERTY

A person who discovers and takes possession of property that has been abandoned and has never been reclaimed by the owner acquires a right thereto. The prior owner, however, must have completely relinquished his ownership.

Property is considered to be *abandoned* when the owner actually discards it with no intention of reclaiming it. Property is considered to be *lost* when the owner, through negligence or accident, unintentionally leaves it somewhere. The difference between abandoned and lost property lies in the intention of the owner to part with title to it.

The finder of lost property has a right of possession against all but the true owner; he does not have the right of possession against the true owner except in instances when the owner cannot be found through reasonable diligence on the part of the finder and certain statutory requirements are fulfilled. The finder of abandoned goods, however, has an absolute right to possession since he has title to it.

In a few cases the courts have held that if an employee finds property in the course of his employment, the property belongs to the employer. Also if property is mislaid, not lost, then the owner of the premises has first claim against all but the true owner. This is especially true of property left on trains, airplanes, in restaurants, and in hotels.

QUESTIONS

1. What is *property*?
2. What is *real property*?
3. What is a *fixture*?
4. What is an *emblement*? Give an illustration.

5. If a tenant who has installed trade fixtures on the property moves away without removing the fixtures, to whom do the fixtures belong?

6. Name three types of personal property that are intangible.

7. What do we call the most complete right one can have in land?

8. If a man dies intestate, how may his heirs obtain title to his property?

9. If Young willfully mixes 1,000 pounds of his low-grade rice with 3,000 pounds of high-grade rice belonging to Harris, who owns the mixture?

CASE PROBLEMS

1. The Hermitage consisted of ten apartments. Each apartment contained an electric stove and an apartment-size refrigerator. The owner of the apartment building became insolvent, and his creditors levied on the stoves and refrigerators. The mortgagee who held the mortgage on the building claimed that his mortgage attached also to these appliances. Did it?

2. A nonnavigable stream was the dividing line between O'Keefe's farm and Coppage's farm. The river at one spot ran along the edge of a rich field, the field all being on Coppage's side of the river. O'Keefe felled some trees across the river at the upper end of the field, inducing the river to swing to the opposite side of the field. O'Keefe claims this field under the law of accretion. Is he entitled to it?

3. Ivey leased a farm for one year from Barton. The lease ran from January 1 to December 31. In October, Ivey sowed 100 acres of winter wheat which would not be ready to harvest until June of the following year. Barton refused on December 31 to renew the lease. Ivey contends he has a right to return and harvest the wheat. Is his contention correct?

4. Stewart went to Dr. Thor's office to have his aching tooth treated. He left a roll of canvas in the waiting room and forgot to pick it up. De-Pellet, an artist, found the canvas, took it home, and painted a portrait on the canvas. The painting proved to be excellent and was appraised at $5,000. Stewart learned that DePellet was the one who found his canvas and demanded the painting. Dr. Thor then claimed the painting because the canvas was found on his property. Who has title to the painting?

5. Holder was the only heir to his father's estate, consisting of tangible personal property and real estate. He signed a note that read: "90 days after I get title to my father's patents, etc." The question arose as to whether or not this note met the requirement that it must be payable at a due date absolutely certain to arrive. Does it?

6. Eberhart owned a textile mill which manufactured cordage material from cotton. Brewer left with Eberhart 20 bales of cotton for storage. Eberhart used the 20 bales of cotton together with several hundred of his own and processed it into cordage. Brewer demanded all the finished cordage. Is he entitled to it?

7. Coe owned a life interest in 80 acres of land. His brother John was to get the land upon Coe's death. Coe constructed a $40,000 home on the land. Three years later he died. Coe's son, Roger, demanded that his uncle pay him $40,000 for the home. Must the uncle pay for it?

Chapter 45

TRANSFER OF REAL PROPERTY

The three common ways of transferring title to real estate are by:

1. Sale
2. Will or descent
3. Adverse possession

(1) **Sale of Real Estate.** The most common way of transferring title to real estate is by sale. In the ordinary case there will be a contract of sale followed by delivery of a deed. One may transfer a leasehold title giving the rights to the use and possession of land for a limited period by means of a lease. The extent of the interest transferred is determined by the provisions of the deed or the lease.

Even when title to real property is conveyed as a gift, the transfer must be evidenced by a deed. As soon as the deed is executed and delivered, title vests fully in the donee. An executory promise to make a gift is unenforceable.

(2) **Transfer By Will or Descent.** The owner of real estate may convey title to another by will. Title is not transferred by will until the person making the will dies and his will is probated, meaning that it is officially accepted by the proper court or bureau.

(3) **Adverse Possession.** One may obtain title to real property by *adverse possession.* To do this one must occupy the land for the period fixed by statute. This statutory period varies from seven years

425

in some states to twenty-one in others. Occupancy must be continuous, open, hostile, visible, and exclusive. In colonial times this was known as "squatter's rights." To get title by adverse possession, one had to go one step further than the "squatter," that is, the adverse possession had to continue for the statutory period.

Possession for the statutory period then gave one clear title to all that land his color of title described. The color of title usually arises, but need not necessarily do so, from some defective document purporting to be a deed or a will, or even a gift.

> ▪ Mahan had used a path across certain land for quite a few years.
> Later Smithson purchased the land and even later he attempted to prevent Mahan's use of the land. Mahan brought an action to establish his right to use the land since he had already used the land for the statutory period. Smithson claimed Mahan's possession was not hostile since Mahan had not excluded Smithson from using the property also. The court found that the claimant of an easement does not have to exclude the owner from the land for all purposes in order for the claimant's use to be hostile; therefore Mahan had established an easement.

DEEDS

A *deed* is a sealed writing conveying title to real property. The law sets forth the form which the deed must have, and this form must be observed lest one's title prove defective. The parties to the deed are the *grantor* or seller and the *grantee* or buyer. There are two principal types of deeds:

1. Quitclaim deeds
2. Warranty deeds

(1) **Quitclaim Deeds.** A *quitclaim deed* is just what the name implies. The grantor quits any claim which he may have to the real property. He makes no warranty that he has any claim.

In the absence of a statute requiring a warranty deed, there is no reason why a quitclaim deed may not be used in making all conveyances of real property. The grantor's full and complete interest is as effectively transferred by a quitclaim deed as with a warranty deed. When one buys real property, however, he does not always want to buy merely the interest which the grantor has. He wants to buy a perfect and complete interest so that his title cannot be questioned by anyone. A quitclaim deed conveys only the interest of the grantor and no more. It contains no warranty that the grantor's title is good. In most real estate transactions, a quitclaim deed cannot be used because the contract will specify that a warranty deed must be delivered.

■ Cross owned land adjoining that of Barrow. The deeds called for a small stream to be the boundary line. A fence, over sixty years old, ran along the banks of the stream on Barrow's side. Former owners of both farms had for over forty years considered the fence the boundary line. Barrow wished to sell his land and the buyer refused to buy, claiming Barrow's title to the land between the fence and the stream defective. To remove this cloud, Cross executed and delivered to Barrow a quitclaim deed transferring to him whatever interest he might have in the boundary-line strip of land. This was effective in removing the cloud from the title.

(2) **Warranty Deeds.** A *warranty deed* not only conveys the grantor's interest in the real property but in addition warrants or guarantees that the buyer is receiving the interest he expected to get. The exact nature of the warranty or guarantee depends upon whether the deed is a general warranty or a special warranty deed.

A *general warranty deed* not only warrants that the grantor has good title to the real property but further warrants that the grantee "shall have quiet and peaceable possession, free from all encumbrances, and that the grantor will defend the grantee against all claims and demands from whomsoever made." This warranty, then, warrants that all prior grantors had good title and that there are no defects in any prior grantor's title. The grantee is not asked to assume any risks as the new owner of the property.

A *special warranty deed* warrants that the grantor has the right to sell the real property. He does not warrant the genuineness of any prior grantor's title. This type of deed is used by trustees and sheriffs who sell land at a foreclosure sale. It is also used by executors and administrators. There is no reason why these officials should warrant anything other than that they have the legal right to sell whatever interest the owner has.

CHARACTERISTICS OF A DEED

Unless statutes provide otherwise, a deed usually has the following characteristics:

WARRANTY DEED
Know All Men by These Presents:

That James L. Black and Louise A. Black, his wife

of   Butler   County,   Ohio,

in consideration of   twenty thousand (20,000) dollars

to   them   *in hand paid by*   Willis B. Crunk, the grantee, the receipt of
which is hereby acknowledged,

do   hereby **Grant, Bargain, Sell and Convey**
to the said   Willis B. Crunk

h is *heirs*

and assigns forever, the following described **Real Estate** *situate in the* City
of   Hamilton   *in the County of*   Butler   *and State of*   Ohio
Lot No. 10, Section 14, Range 62, Randall Subdivision, being a
portion of the estate of Horace E. Cresswell and Alice B. Cresswell

and all the **Estate, Right, Title and Interest** *of the said grantor*s *in and to said premises;* **To have and
to hold** *the same, with all the privileges and appurtenances thereunto belonging, to said grantee* , his
heirs and assigns forever. And the said James L. Black and Louise A. Black

do   hereby **Covenant and Warrant** *that the title so conveyed is* **Clear, Free and Unin-
cumbered,** *and that*   they   *will* **Defend** *the same against all lawful claims of all persons whomsoever.*

In Witness Whereof, *the said grantor*s ha ve *hereunto set*   their   *hand* s , *this*   first
day of   December   *in the year A. D. nineteen hundred and*   --

Signed and acknowledged in presence of us:

Michael R. Wiser | James L. Black
Antonio C. Petricelle | Louise A. Black

State of   Ohio,   Butler   **County, ss.**

On this   first   *day of*   December   *A. D. 19* 60 *, before me, a*   Notary Public
in and for said County, personally came   James L. Black and Louise A. Black
the grantor s *in the foregoing deed, and*
acknowledged the signing thereof to be   their   *voluntary act and deed.*

Witness *my official signature and seal on the day last above mentioned.*

Ronald R. Stelzer

Notary Public

A General Warranty Deed

1. Parties
2. Consideration
3. Covenants
4. Description
5. Signature
6. Acknowledgment

(1) **Parties.** The contract must have proper parties, the grantor and the grantee, and they must be named in the deed. If the grantor is married, his name and that of his wife should be written in the deed. If the grantor is unmarried, this fact should be indicated by using the word "single."

(2) **Consideration.** The amount paid to the grantor for the property is the consideration. The payment may be in money or in money's worth. A statement of the consideration must be made in the deed, although the amount specified need not be the actual price paid. In some localities the practice is to name a nominal amount, as one dollar, although a much larger sum was actually paid. The reason for stating a nominal amount as the consideration is to avoid tax liability on transfers.

(3) **Covenants.** There may be as many covenants as the grantor and the grantee wish to include. Some of these are *affirmative covenants* whereby the grantee is obligated to do something, such as maintaining a driveway used in common with adjoining property. Others are *negative covenants* whereby the grantee agrees to refrain from doing some event. Such covenants are very common in urban residential developments. The more common ones prohibit the grantee from using the property for business purposes and setting forth the types of homes that can or cannot be built on the property. Most covenants run with the land and are binding upon all future owners.

(4) **Description.** The property to be conveyed must be correctly described. Any description that will identify the property will suffice. Ordinarily, however, the description that was used in the deed by which the present owner acquired the title should be used if it is correct. The description may be by lots and blocks if the property is in a city; or it may be by metes and bounds, section, range, and township if the property is in a rural district.

(5) **Signature.** The deed should be signed by the grantor in the place provided for the signature. If the grantor is married, his wife also should sign for the purpose of giving up her statutory right. Her signature should be written below that of her husband. In some states the signatures must be attested by a witness or witnesses. If the grantor is incapable of signing his name, he may execute the deed by making his mark, thus:

James Smith
Witness of the mark of   Henry ⎰ His X Mark ⎱ Hoe
Henry Hoe

(6) **Acknowledgment.** The statutes in practically all the states require that the deed be formally acknowledged before a notary public or other officer authorized to take acknowledgments. The purpose of the acknowledgment is to make it possible for the deed to be recorded. After a deed has been recorded, it may be used as evidence in a court without further proof of its authenticity being given. Recording is not essential to the validity of the deed, but it is invaluable as security of the title of the grantee.

The *acknowledgment* is a declaration made by the properly authorized officer, in the form provided for that purpose, that the grantor has acknowledged the instrument as his act and deed. In some states it is further required that the grantor understand the nature and effect of the deed or that he be personally known to the acknowledging officer. These facts are attested by the officer, who affixes his official seal, and are further evidenced by his certificate.

DELIVERY

A deed is ineffective until it has been delivered. *Delivery* consists of giving up possession and control over the deed. So long as the grantor maintains control over the deed and reserves the right to demand its return before the deed is delivered to the grantee, then there has been no legal delivery. If the grantor executes a deed and leaves it with his own attorney to deliver to the grantee, there has been no delivery until his attorney delivers the deed to the grantee. Since the attorney is the agent of the grantor, he, the grantor, has the right to demand that his own agent return the deed to the grantor. If the grantor, however, delivers the deed to the grantee's attorney, then there has been an effective delivery.

■ Saul executed a general warranty deed conveying his home to his wife, Ilene. Since he did not want her to know of this act, he placed the deed in his safety deposit box. Only he had access to the box. Upon his death, the deed was discovered. John, Ilene's stepson, brought suit to have the deed nullified. He succeeded. There was never a valid delivery of the deed prior to Saul's death. No one has the authority to deliver it after his death.

MARRIAGE

Most state laws now provide that when an individual dies without leaving a will, his spouse is entitled to a set portion of all the property the deceased spouse owned at the time of his death. The spouse's portion varies depending on the number of children or other heirs who survive. If an individual leaves a will which does not provide for the surviving spouse to get the share provided by statute, the surviving spouse can usually reject the will and get the statutory share. The surviving spouse in some states may also claim an interest in property conveyed by the deceased spouse during the marriage without the consent of the surviving spouse.

RECORDING

A deed need not be recorded in order to complete one's title. Title is complete as soon as the deed is delivered. Recording the deed protects the grantee against a second sale by the grantor, and against any liens which may attach to the property while it is still recorded in the grantor's name.

When a deed is received for recording, the recording official will ordinarily be required to stamp the deed with the exact date and time that the deed is left with him for recording.

ABSTRACT OF TITLE

Before one buys real estate, it is advisable to have an abstract of title prepared. This may be done by a title abstract company or it may be done by an attorney. The *abstract of title* gives a complete history of the real estate. It also shows whether or not there are any unpaid taxes and assessments, mortgages, or deeds of trust outstanding, and any unpaid judgments or other unsatisfied liens of any type against the property. If an abstracting company makes the abstract, it is advisable to have an attorney read the abstract to see if it reveals any flaws in the title.

Some defects in the title to real estate cannot be detected by an abstract. Some of the most common of these defects are forgery of signatures in prior conveyances; claims by adverse possession; incompetency to contract by any prior party; fraud; duress; undue influence; defective wills; loss of real property by accretion; errors by title examiner, tax officials, surveyors, and many other public officials. A title insurance policy can be obtained that will cover these defects. The policy may expressly exclude any possible defects which the insurance company does not wish to be covered by the policy. With one premium, the insured is covered as long as he owns the property. The policy does not benefit a subsequent purchaser or a mortgagee.

QUESTIONS

1. If Hale wishes to transfer title to his land to his son by gift, what must he do?
2. If a person is left real estate by a will, when does he acquire title to it?
3. How may title to real estate be acquired by adverse possession?
4. What are the advantages and disadvantages of a quitclaim deed?
5. Define a warranty deed.
6. Who are the parties that must be named in a deed?
7. What is the difference between an affirmative covenant and a negative covenant?
8. When does a deed become effective?
9. (a) Is it necessary to record a deed in order to complete one's title to the land?
   (b) What does recording a deed do?
10. What is an abstract of title?

CASE PROBLEMS

1. Donaldson owned a home valued at $40,000 and personal property valued at $10,000. He desired that Mrs. Donaldson inherit all this property upon his death and wished to minimize the court costs and other expenses involved in transferring this property to her by will. Explain how he may do this and still retain full title until his death.

2. Donaldson purchased a house and lot. In a prior deed the grantor had inserted a covenant that the grantee would never use the property for commercial or business purposes. Such covenants were included by the original owner in the deeds for all the houses in that residential section. Donaldson wished to set up a dry-cleaning establishment in the basement of his house. A neighbor brought an equity suit to enjoin him from doing so. This action was based upon the original restrictive covenant. Was Donaldson bound by this covenant?

3. Morris, as a notary public, was authorized to acknowledge deeds. A man brought Morris a deed to be acknowledged. He represented himself as Sullivan, the grantor named in the deed, whereby Sullivan conveyed to William Peyton a valuable tract of real estate. Morris did not know Sullivan, the grantor, but he acknowledged the deed and certified that Sullivan personally appeared before him and signed the deed of conveyance. The man who claimed to be Sullivan was actually not Sullivan but William Peyton, the grantee. Peyton immediately sold the land to Ashby for cash. When Sullivan, the true owner, learned of Ashby's claim to the land, he denied him access to it and notified him that he had never signed the deed of conveyance to Peyton. Ashby produced an abstract of title that had been prepared by an attorney. Point out the mistakes the various people made in these transactions, and show how they might have been avoided.

4. Riley sold to the Ruark Lumber Company "all the timber now on my farm." The timber was cut, and about ten years later Riley contracted to sell his farm to Greeley. Greeley refused to complete the purchase, claiming that Riley did not own the timber. Thereupon Riley obtained a letter from the Ruark Lumber Company stating that it did not claim to own the timber. Was this adequate to clear the title?

5. Stewart sold Stern a house and lot, executing a special warranty deed. About a year later Sprouse sued Stern to recover the property, claiming that the signature of the grantor of the property ten years earlier was forged. The man who sold the property to Stewart was not a party to the forgery. Must Stewart make good the loss to Stern? Would your answer be different if he had made a general warranty deed?

6. Holcomb executed a deed to his home, conveying all the property to his son, John. The deed was delivered to John, but before he had it recorded, a brother, Roger, found the deed and burned it up. Before Holcomb could make another deed, he died; and John sought to have the court declare him the rightful owner of the house and lot. Was John entitled to the property?

7. Henry owned 600 acres of land which he had purchased by general warranty deed from Bell. He purchased title insurance on the property. He sold the land to Dawson and gave him a special warranty deed. He also agreed to assign the title insurance policy to Dawson. About two years after Dawson purchased the property, he learned an adjoining landowner claimed by adverse possession about 30 acres of the most valuable part of the land. In a court suit, the court awarded the 30 acres to the neighbor. What rights does Dawson have against Henry or the insurance company?

8. Walton in his young days was married to Margie for three years. He left Margie and married Eva though he never divorced Margie. He lived with Eva for thirty years and acquired a sizeable estate. Margie never remarried. When Walton died, Margie demanded her rights in Walton's real estate. Is she entitled to it?

9. Munson purchased lot "A" from Pepper. Through an error the deed actually conveyed title to lot "B." Munson built a house on lot "A" and lived on it for twenty-one years. Pepper's heirs attempted to dispossess Munson and take possession of lot "A" and the house on it. Were they entitled to the property?

Chapter 46

REAL ESTATE MORTGAGES

DEFINITION

A *mortgage* is a lien given upon real estate to secure a debt. The mortgage is not the debt itself but only the security for the debt. Land or any interest in land may be mortgaged. Land may be mortgaged separately from the improvements, or the improvements may be mortgaged apart from the land.

Under the common law a real estate mortgage was an absolute transfer of both title and possession of real property to the mortgagee. The mortgagor received in substance an option to repurchase the real estate, that is, the right to regain both title and the possession upon the payment of the debt. Under the modern plan the mortgagor does not give up possession of the property. In order for the mortgagee to obtain the benefit of the security, the mortgagee must take possession of the premises upon default; or he must sell the mortgaged property at a foreclosure sale. In some states, the mortgagee cannot take possession of the property upon default but may obtain the appointment of a receiver to collect the rents and income if the security will be inadequate to pay the debt. If the property brings more than the debt and the costs, the mortgagor is entitled to receive the balance.

THE MORTGAGE CONTRACT

A mortgage must be in writing. The contract, as a rule, must have the same form as a deed; that is, it must be acknowledged and must be under seal. The mortgage, like all other contracts, sets forth the rights and the duties of the contracting parties.

A mortgage is usually given to raise money for the purchase price of real estate but may be given for other reasons. One may borrow money for any reason and secure the loan by a mortgage. One may assume a contingent liability for another, such as going on his bond, and receive a mortgage as security.

The lien of the mortgage attaches to the property described in the mortgage. It is generally also provided that the lien attaches to additions thereafter made to the described property; for example, personal property which thereafter becomes a fixture is bound by the lien of the mortgage.

> ■ To finance the purchase of a new home, Roede needs to borrow $10,000. His bank refuses to lend $10,000 unless he conveys to the bank the right to sell the house to satisfy the debt in the event Roede fails to pay the debt. Roede, however, fully pays the debt and, as a result, the limited rights of the bank to sell the property expire.

RECORDING

Depending upon the law of the state where the land is situated, the mortgage gives the mortgagee either a lien on the land or title to the land. The title or lien is divested or destroyed when the debt is paid. Recording the mortgage protects the mortgagee against subsequent creditors since the public record is notice to the whole world as to the mortgagee's rights. There may be both a first mortgage and a second mortgage. Since the second mortgage recites the fact that a first mortgage exists, the second mortgage does not achieve priority over the first even though it is recorded first. The mortgage is also recorded to notify subsequent purchasers that the purchase price, or as much as is necessary, must be paid to the mortgagee.

> ■ Jarvis borrowed $10,000 from Sample and gave Sample a mortgage on his real estate to secure the debt. Sample forgot to record the mortgage. Anderson obtained a judgment of $5,000 against Jarvis and forced the sale of the real estate to pay off his judgment. The real estate was sold for $13,000. Sample sued to get $10,000 of the sale price, alleging that his mortgage was a first lien. The court found that since the mortgage was not recorded before Anderson obtained his judgment, Anderson was entitled to the full $5,000 and Sample was entitled to the remaining $8,000.

DUTIES OF THE MORTGAGOR

The mortgagor assumes three definite duties and liabilities when he places a mortgage upon his real estate. These pertain to:

1. Interest and principal
2. Taxes, assessments, and insurance premiums
3. Security of the mortgagee

(1) **Interest and Principal.** The mortgagor must make all payments of interest and principal as they become due. Most mortgages call for periodic payments, such as monthly, semiannual, or annual payments. These payments are used to pay all accrued interest to the date of payment, and the balance is applied on the principal. Other mortgages call for periodic payment of interest and for the payment of the entire principal at one time. In either case, a failure to pay either the periodic payments of interest and principal, or of interest only, is a default and gives the mortgagee the right to foreclose. Most mortgages contain a provision that if any interest or principal payments are not made when due or within a specified time after due the entire principal will become immediately due. This is known as an acceleration clause.

If the mortgagor wishes to pay off the mortgage debt before the due date so as to save interest, he must reserve that right at the time the mortgage is given. He can pay off the debt at any time, but the interest must be paid until the due date in the absence of an agreement to the contrary.

(2) **Taxes, Assessments, and Insurance Premiums.** As the mortgagor is the owner of the land regardless of the form of the mortgage, he must continue to make all such payments as would be expected of an owner of land. The mortgagor must pay taxes, assessments, and insurance premiums. If he does not do so, the mortgagee may pay them and compel a reimbursement from the mortgagor. If the mortgage contract requires the mortgagor to pay these charges, a failure to pay them becomes a default.

The law does not require the mortgagor to keep the property insured nor to insure it for the benefit of the mortgagee. This duty must be imposed on the mortgagor by contract. Both the mortgagor and the mortgagee have an insurable interest in the property to the extent of each one's interest or maximum loss.

(3) Security of the Mortgagee. The mortgagor must do no act that will materially impair the security of the mortgagee. Cutting timber, tearing down buildings, and all acts that waste the assets impair the security and give the mortgagee the right to seek legal protection. Some state statutes provide that any one of these acts is equivalent to a default. This gives the mortgagee the right to foreclose. Other statutes provide only that the mortgagee may obtain an injunction in a court of equity enjoining any further impairment. Many state laws also make it a criminal offense to impair willfully the security of mortgaged property.

RIGHTS OF THE MORTGAGOR

The mortgagor has four rights:

1. Possession of the property
2. Rents and profits
3. Cancellation of lien
4. Redemption

(1) Possession of the Property. The mortgagor usually has the right to retain possession of the mortgaged property. Upon default the mortgagee usually may take possession to collect rents and profits. In some states he cannot take possession, but may obtain the appointment of a receiver to collect rents and profits.

(2) Rents and Profits. The mortgagor is entitled to rents and profits. In the absence of an express agreement to the contrary, the mortgagor has the right to all rents and profits obtained from the mortgaged property. The mortgagor may retain the profits. This rule or any other rule may, of course, be superseded by a contract providing otherwise.

(3) Cancellation of Lien. The mortgagor has the right to have the lien canceled on final payment. As soon as the mortgage is delivered to the mortgagee, it becomes a lien upon the mortgaged real estate. A mortgage lien is canceled by having the clerk in the recorder's office enter a notation, usually on the margin, certifying that the debt has been paid and that the lien is canceled. The mortgagee, not the mortgagor, must have this done. If he fails or refuses to do so, the mortgagor may institute court action to have this cloud removed from his title so that he may have clear title.

(4) **Redemption.** The mortgagor has the right to free the mortgaged property from the lien of the mortgage after default. This is the right of *redemption*. Statutes in many states prescribe a specific time after the foreclosure and sale when this right may be exercised.

Usually the right of redemption may be exercised only by a person whose interests will be affected by foreclosure. This includes the executor or administrator and heirs of the mortgagor, and frequently a second mortgagee.

FORECLOSURE

If the mortgagor fails to pay the debt secured by the mortgage when it becomes due, or fails to perform any of the other terms set forth in the mortgage, the mortgagee has the right to foreclose for the purpose of collecting the debt. *Foreclosure* usually consists of a sale of the mortgaged property made under an order of a court and generally by an officer of the court.

Foreclose literally means a legal proceeding to shut out all other claims. A first mortgage may not necessarily constitute a first claim on the proceeds of the sale. The cost of foreclosure and taxes always takes precedence over the first mortgage. People who furnish materials for the construction of a house and workers who work on it have a claim under what is known as a *mechanics' lien* that takes precedence over a first mortgage. The foreclosure proceedings establish the existence of all prior claims and the order of their priority. Foreclosure proceedings are fixed by statutory law and therefore vary in different states.

If the proceeds of the sale of mortgaged property are greater than the amount of the debt and the expenses of foreclosure, the surplus must be given to the mortgagor. If a deficiency results, however, the mortgagee may secure a deficiency judgment for this amount. In that case the unpaid balance of the debt will stand as a claim against the mortgagor until the debt is paid.

> ▪ Heritage, who mortgaged his home in order to borrow money to start a new bookstore, is unable to pay off the note. The holder of the note forecloses but the proceeds are insufficient to cover the unpaid balance on the note. The holder of the note obtains a deficiency judgment. Heritage is personally liable for this amount even though his home was previously sold.

TRUST DEED

A trust deed is often used as a substitute for the ordinary form of mortgage for the purpose of securing a debt. A *trust deed* (sometimes called a *trust mortgage*) conveys the property to a disinterested third party, called a *trustee*, to be held in trust for the benefit of the creditor or creditors. If a default in payment occurs, the trustee must foreclose the property and apply the proceeds to the payment of the debt. The proceedings in the foreclosure of a trust deed are similar to those in the foreclosure of an ordinary mortgage. The right to redeem under a trust deed, when it exists, is similar to the right of redemption under a mortgage.

The trust deed may be employed when the mortgage debt is so large it is difficult or impossible to find one person or bank which is willing to lend so large a sum of money. By means of the trust deed the mortgage bond is broken up into a large number of smaller bonds, generally $1,000 each, which are then purchased by individual investors.

In the event that the mortgagor defaults in his payments, the mortgagee who holds an ordinary mortgage can foreclose, that is, have the mortgaged property sold to satisfy the debt. In most states, however, he must go into court and have a judicial court foreclosure. In some states the trustee in a trust deed may sell the mortgaged property on the mortgagor's default outside of court without going through a time-consuming court foreclosure. Hence, the property can be more quickly sold at a trustee's sale.

BUYING MORTGAGED PROPERTY

It is a common practice to buy property on which there is a mortgage or a trust deed. The purchaser may agree to "assume the mortgage," that is, to be primarily liable for its payment. He should understand the difference between "assuming" the mortgage and buying the property "subject to the mortgage." In the first case he binds himself to be liable for the mortgage obligation as fully as if he had been the original mortgagor. If he takes the property "subject to the mortgage," he may lose the property, but no more. Observe how a knowledge of this point of law may be worth several thousand dollars:

■ Ratcliffe sold Hurley a farm for $20,000, Hurley agreeing to pay $5,000 down and "assume a $15,000 mortgage." He held the farm a few years during which time the value of farmland declined considerably. The mortgagee foreclosed on the mortgage and sold the farm for $9,000. This left an unpaid balance of $3,000 which Hurley was compelled to pay. Had he purchased the property "subject to the mortgage," he would not have had to pay the balance of $3,000.

The original mortgagor is not automatically released when he sells mortgaged property whether the purchaser assumed the mortgage or bought it subject to the mortgage. He remains fully liable in both cases. He may be released from the mortgage by novation, i.e., the mortgagee agrees to release the mortgage by extending the time of payment without the mortgagor's consent. Courts have held that the acceptance of interest payment after the principal of the mortgage has become due constitutes an extension of the mortgage. If this is done without the mortgagor's consent, he is fully released from all liability under the mortgage.

ASSIGNMENT OF THE MORTGAGE

The mortgagee may assign his rights under the mortgage agreement. The assignee, that is, the purchaser, obtains no greater rights than the assignor had. To protect himself, the assignee should require the assignor to produce an estoppel certificate signed by the mortgagor. This certificate should acknowledge that the mortgagor has no claims of any kind in connection with the mortgage. This would bar him from subsequently claiming the right of offset.

The assignee of a mortgage should have his assignment recorded. In the event the mortgagee assigns the mortgage to more than one party, the one who records his assignment first has preference in case the proceeds are not adequate to pay both assignees.

QUESTIONS

1. (a) Define mortgage.
   (b) Does the mortgagor lose possession of the mortgaged property at the time the mortgage is executed?

2. If two mortgages are executed on the same land, which mortgagee has priority?

3. In executing a twenty-year mortgage on his home, what must the mortgagor do if he wishes to prepay the mortgage at some future date?

4. If there is a street assessment against mortgaged property for $1,000, who must pay this, the mortgagor or the mortgagee?

5. If the mortgagor tears down a garage worth $800, does this give the mortgagee the right to foreclose?

6. When the mortgage is paid in full, how is this fact indicated in the record books in the county clerk's office?

7. How may the mortgagor redeem his property after it has been sold under a foreclosure sale?

8. If the proceeds of a foreclosure sale of property are not enough to pay off the mortgage, how is the balance of the debt canceled?

9. Name two characteristics that distinguish a trust deed from a mortgage.

10. What is the difference in the liability of the purchaser when he buys mortgaged property "subject to the mortgage" and "assuming the mortgage"?

CASE PROBLEMS

1. Johnson owned a farm, which included 10 acres of growing cotton. He borrowed $5,000 from Dupree and executed a real estate mortgage on his farm to secure the debt. The mortgage contained the usual clause that the mortgagor must not commit any act that would decrease the mortgagee's risk. It also provided that if the mortgagor sold any timber, pulpwood, or any other part of the real property, the net proceeds must be applied on the $5,000 note. Johnson later sold the cotton for $1,500 but spent the money for living expenses. Dupree brought suit to foreclose on the mortgage, claiming that Johnson had violated his contract. Was Dupree entitled to foreclose?

2. Jensen, who had some extra money to invest, agreed to lend Bowen on a first mortgage $15,000 with which Bowen was to build a house on a lot he owned. Jensen agreed to let Bowen have $3,000 to start, and $3,000 a month as the construction progressed, the balance of the $15,000 to be loaned when the building was completed. About 30 days after the home was completed, Jensen and Bowen learned that the contractor had purchased on credit about $3,500 of materials for the house and had not paid for these materials out of the money Bowen paid him for building the house. In addition he owed $1,200 for labor that he had not paid. The materials supplier and the workers demanded that Bowen pay them. He had no money and could not pay. They threatened to sell the house unless Jensen paid them. Jensen contended his first mortgage took precedence over these items. Was this correct?

3. Dennison owned the timber on 1,000 acres of land but did not own the land or any other interest in the land. He borrowed $10,000 from Swanson and executed a first mortgage to Swanson on the timber as security for the loan. He sold about half of the timber to the Logan Lumber Company for $12,000 but did not pay any part of the proceeds on the $10,000 mortgage. Swanson indicted Dennison for willfully impairing the security

of his loan, and he brought an action to foreclose the mortgage. Was he legally justified in taking these actions?

4. Barbara and Donald Shea bought a home for $20,000 and financed it by paying $4,000 down and giving a 20-year first mortgage for $16,000 at 7 percent. Donald wished that in the event of his death his wife, Barbara, have the home free of debt. Consequently he purchased a mortgage life insurance policy whereby the insurance company agreed in event of Donald's death to pay off the balance of the principal of the mortgage plus accrued interest. Donald died one year later. At that time there was a balance of $15,860 principal and accrued interest on the loan. The life insurance company paid this. The mortgagee refused, however, to cancel the mortgage, claiming an additional $7,200 for interest for the next 19 years since the mortgage did not contain a prepayment clause. Must Barbara pay this $7,200?

5. Billy and Yvonne Rogers owned 80 acres of land with a modern dwelling. There was a first mortgage on the property for $12,000. The entire property was worth about $14,000. Yvonne's father was retired on a pension of $80 a month. Billy and Yvonne deeded him and his wife two acres of land so that he could take what cash he had and build himself a modest house for $6,000. Soon after the father-in-law completed his house, the country experienced a rather serious business recession. Real estate values declined about 25 percent. Billy lost his job and was unable to keep up his payments on the mortgage. The mortgagee foreclosed on the 78 acres and sold it at public auction. It brought only $9,000, leaving a balance on the mortgage of $3,000. The mortgagee threatened to sell the father-in-law's two acres and house if the father-in-law did not pay the $3,000. Was Billy's mortgage also a lien on the father-in-law's property?

6. Holleran borrowed $10,000 from Carswell and executed a first mortgage on his home as a security for the loan. Carswell later purchased a restaurant from Holcomb for $20,000 and, as part payment, assigned to Holcomb the first mortgage which he held on Holleran's home. At the time of the assignment Holleran had a claim against Carswell for $3,000 as a result of an automobile accident caused by Carswell's negligence. Holcomb did not know of this claim at the time he sold his restaurant to Carswell. When the mortgage came due and Holcomb demanded payment, Holleran contended he did not owe $10,000, but only $7,000 after taking credit for the $3,000 damage claim. May Holleran offset his claim of $3,000 against Holcomb's claim for $10,000?

7. Carlson placed a mortgage on his home for $12,000. He paid the mortgage in full. About one year later, he contracted to sell the property to Rowe. An abstract of title showed that the mortgage was still a lien on the house. The mortgagee refused to release the mortgage unless Carlson paid him $1,000. Rowe would not purchase the property until the title was cleared. What are Carlson's rights?

8. Mr. and Mrs. North purchased a home and agreed to pay $18,000 for it. They paid $3,000 down and assumed a $15,000 mortgage, which was to

be paid off at the rate of $100 a month. The company for which Mr. North worked moved away, and Mr. North therefore lost his job. As a result he was unable to keep up the payments on the mortgage. The property was foreclosed and sold. The purchaser paid $10,000. This left an unpaid balance of $2,000. Were Mr. and Mrs. North liable for the payment of this $2,000?

9. Rankell had a ten-year mortgage on his home, to be paid at the rate of $75 a month. He was discharged from his job and defaulted on two monthly payments before he obtained another job. The mortgagee foreclosed immediately upon the first default. What were Rankell's rights?

10. Cook wished to borrow his neighbor Fleeman's truck to haul cotton to the gin. Fleeman, fearing that Cook might have a wreck which would subject Fleeman to a suit for damages, had Cook execute and deliver to him a mortgage on Cook's farm for $5,000. Was this a valid mortgage?

11. Poe was the mortgagor and Corkrell the mortgagee to the extent of $2,500 upon certain real estate. Poe, before the mortgage was paid, sold the mortgaged property to a corporation, and the corporation in turn conveyed the property to Burke who assumed the mortgage. When Burke defaulted on the mortgage, Corkrell brought suit to foreclose and also secure a deficiency judgment against both Poe and Burke. Was Burke liable for the deficiency?

Chapter 47

LANDLORD AND TENANT

RELATION OF LANDLORD AND TENANT

The relation of landlord and tenant is created by a contract whereby one person agrees to lease land or a building to another. No special words or acts are necessary to create such an agreement unless the lease is for more than a year, in which case it must be in writing. The possession of the premises and the payment of rent for its use are the chief characteristics that determine the relation of landlord and tenant.

The owner or the holder of the property is known as the *landlord* or *lessor*. The person who is given possession of the property is the *tenant* or *lessee*. The contract between the two parties is called a *lease*. The amount the landlord is to receive for the use of the property is the *rent*.

A tenant is distinguished from a lodger or roomer in that the former has the exclusive legal possession of the property, while the latter has merely the right to use the premises subject to the control and supervision of the owner.

THE LEASE

A lease is a contract creating the relation of landlord and tenant. The lease may be oral or written, express or implied, formal or simple, subject, however, to the general statutory requirements that a lease of land for a term longer than one year must be in writing. If a dispute arises between the tenant and the landlord over their rights and duties, the court will look to the terms of the lease and the general body of landlord and tenant law to determine the decision.

445

House Lease

⌒

THIS INDENTURE, made the _____6th_____ day of _____April_____, 19 -- -

BETWEEN Daniel J. Slade , Lessor (whether one or more);
Cincinnati, Ohio

AND Jerry E. and Betty L. Sergent , Lessee (whether one or more);
Cincinnati, Ohio

WITNESSETH: *That for and in consideration of the payments of the rents, and the performance of the covenants contained herein, on the part of the said Lessee, and in the manner hereinafter specified, said Lessor does hereby lease, demise and let, unto the said Lessee, that certain* ___single-family_____ *dwelling house and its appurtenances situated at* 3780 Goodson Drive, Cincinnati, Ohio

for the term of _____one (1) year_____, *commencing on the*

_____1st_____*day of*_____May_____, 19 -- -, *and ending on the*

_____30th_____*day of*_____April_____, 19 -- -, *at the total rent or*

sum of ____Eighteen hundred (1800)_____ *Dollars,*

payable __monthly___ *in advance on the* _____1st_____ *day of each and every*

calendar month of said term in equal _____monthly_____ *payments of*

___One hundred fifty (150)_____ *Dollars,*

AND *the said Lessee does hereby promise and agree to pay to the said Lessor the said rent, herein reserved in the manner herein specified.*

AND *not to let or sublet the whole or any part of said premises, nor to assign this lease, and not to make or suffer any alteration to be made therein without the written consent of the said Lessor. And it is further agreed, that the said Lessor shall not be called upon to make any improvements or repairs whatsoever upon the said premises, or any part thereof, but the said Lessee agrees to keep the same in good order and condition at*__their_____ *own expense.*

AND *it is agreed, that if any rent shall be due and unpaid or if default shall be made in any of the covenants herein contained, then it shall be lawful for the said Lessor to re-enter the said premises and to move all persons therefrom.*

AND THAT *at the expiration of the said term or any sooner determination of this lease the said Lessee will quit and surrender the premises hereby demised, in as good order and condition as reasonable use and wear thereof will permit, damage by the elements excepted. And if the Lessee shall hold over the said term with the consent, expressed or implied, of the Lessor, such holding shall be construed to be a tenancy only from month to month, and said Lessee will pay the rent as above stated for such term as* _____they_____ *hold____ the same.* ____Lessee_____ *agrees to pay the water rate during the continuance of this lease.*

IN WITNESS WHEREOF: *the said parties have hereunto set their hands and seals the day and year first above written.*

_____*Daniel J. Slade*_____(Seal)_____

_____*Jerry E. Sargent*_____(Seal)_____

_____*Betty L. Sargent*_____(Seal)_____

A Lease

In order to avoid disputes, a lease should be in writing and should be complete and cover all the terms of the contract. Such items as the time and place of payment of rent, the notice required to vacate, the duration or the nature of the tenancy, and any specific provision desired by either party, such as the right of the landlord to show the property to prospective purchasers or agreement requiring the landlord to redecorate, should be included.

TYPES OF TENANCIES

There are four separate and distinct classes of tenancies, each having some rule of law governing it that does not apply to any other type of tenancy. The four classes of tenancies are:

1. Tenancy for years
2. Tenancy from year to year
3. Tenancy at will
4. Tenancy by sufferance

(1) Tenancy for Years. A *tenancy for years* is any tenancy for a definite period of time, whether it be one month, one year, or ninety-nine years. The termination date is fixed by the lease. The payment of the rent may be by the month even when the tenancy is for a specified number of years. Some states hold that no notice to terminate the tenancy is required when the termination date is fixed by the lease. Other states fix by statute the number of days' notice which must be given. The modern lease typically provides that it will continue to run on a year-to-year basis after the termination date, unless notice is given by the tenant to the landlord not less than a specified number of days before the termination date that the tenant intends to leave on that date.

(2) Tenancy from Year to Year. When the tenancy is for an indefinite period of time with rent due at stated intervals, it is known as a *tenancy from year to year*. Under such a tenancy, a tenant merely pays the rent periodically and the lease lasts until proper notice of termination has been given. A tenancy of this kind may be by the week, by the month, by the year, or any other period agreed upon.

Notice to terminate this type of tenancy must follow exactly the state law governing it. In a tenancy from month to month, notice is usually required thirty days before the rent due date.

▪   Larson rented an apartment which he paid for each month.
After three months of occupancy the landlord notified Larson
that commencing with the sixth month the rent would be doubled.
Larson objected. The increase in rent is in fact notice of a termination
of the existing lease and the onset of a new lease under different
terms.

(3) **Tenancy at Will.** A *tenancy at will* exists when the tenant
has possession of the property for an uncertain period. Either the
tenant or the landlord can terminate the tenancy at will. Of all the
types of tenancies, this is the only one that is automatically terminated
upon the death of the tenant or the landlord.

(4) **Tenancy by Sufferance.** When a tenant holds over his
tenancy after the expiration of the lease without permission of the
landlord, a *tenancy by sufferance* exists until the landlord elects to
treat the tenant as a trespasser or as a tenant. The landlord may treat
the tenant as a trespasser, sue him for damages, and have him removed by legal proceedings; or, if the landlord prefers, he may accept
payment of the rent due for another period and thus recognize the
tenant's possession as rightful.

RIGHTS OF THE TENANT

A lease gives the tenant certain rights, as follows:

1. Right to possession
2. Right to use the premises
3. Right to sublease

(1) **Right to Possession.** When the landlord signs the lease, he
warrants that he has the right to lease the premises and that the tenant
shall have quiet possession during the period of the lease. During the
term of the lease, the tenant has the same right to exclusive possession
of the premises as if he owned the property. If someone questions the
owner's right to lease the property, the landlord must defend the
tenant's right to exclusive possession. Failure of the landlord to give
possession on time or to protect the tenant's rights subjects the landlord to liability for damages.

A particular cause of dispute between landlord and tenant is the
existence of a nuisance that disturbs the tenant's quiet enjoyment of
the property. Failure to remove dead rats from the wall, failure to

stop disorderly conduct on the part of other tenants, and frequent and unnecessary entrances upon the property by the landlord or his agents are examples of acts which the courts have held destroy the tenant's right to quiet enjoyment and constitute a breach of warranty on the part of the landlord.

If the nuisance existed at the time the tenant leased the property and he was aware of its existence, he will be deemed to have waived his right to complain. Also if the nuisance is one over which the landlord has no control, the tenant cannot avoid his contract even though the nuisance arose subsequent to the signing of the lease. If the landlord fails or refuses to abate a nuisance over which he has control, the tenant not only may terminate the lease but may sue for damages also. In other cases he may seek an injunction compelling the landlord to abate a nuisance.

> Watson rented an apartment on the first floor of a three-story apartment building. The occupants on the second floor over Watson's apartment loved music and dancing. Every night they and some friends danced until after midnight. The noise from the dancing was loud and continuous. Watson demanded that the landlord evict the tenants, but the landlord refused. Watson moved seven months before his lease expired. The court held he was not liable for the rent since the dancing and music were a nuisance. The court found Watson was justified in terminating the lease.

(2) **Right to Use the Premises.** Unless this right is expressly restricted in the lease, the tenant has the right to use the premises in any way consistent with the nature of the property. He cannot convert a dwelling into a machine shop nor a clothing store into a restaurant. Damage to leased property other than that which results from ordinary wear and tear is not permissible. In the case of farming land the tenant may cut wood for his own use but not to sell.

(3) **Right to Assign or Sublease.** If the tenant assigns his entire lease to another party who agrees to comply with its terms, including the payment of the rent to the landlord, this is an *assignment*. In *subleasing,* the tenant usually collects the rent from the subtenant; in assignment, the rent is paid by the assignee directly to the landlord. Assignment must include the entire premises, although one may sublease to another person only a part of the property and retain the rest. Ordinarily the assigning or subleasing of the premises is prohibited unless the lessor's written consent thereto is first obtained.

Residential leases commonly restrict the use of the premises to the tenant and his family or to a certain number of persons. Unless the lease expressly prohibits both assignment and subleasing, either may be done. If only subleasing is prohibited, then the lease may be assigned.

Closely related to subleasing is joint occupancy. A provision in the lease prohibiting subleasing does not debar a contract for a joint occupancy. In joint occupancy the tenant does not give up exclusive control of any part of the premises. He merely permits another party to occupy all or a part of the premises jointly with him.

DUTIES OF THE TENANT

Duties of the tenant are:

1. To pay rent
2. To protect and preserve the premises

(1) To Pay Rent. The tenant's main duty is to pay the rent. This payment must be made in money unless the contract provides otherwise, such as a share of the crops. The rent is not due until the end of the term, but leases almost universally provide for rent in advance.

It is a common practice for the landlord to appoint an agent for the purpose of collecting the rent. The death of the principal automatically terminates the principal-agent relationship. If rent is paid to the agent after this termination and the agent does not remit to the proper party, the rent must be paid again.

If the rent is not paid on time, the landlord may terminate the lease and order the tenant to vacate, or he may permit the tenant to continue occupancy and sue for the rent. Under the common law the landlord could seize and hold any personal property found on the premises. This right has been either curtailed or abolished by statute. Most states permit the landlord to obtain a *distress warrant* and have the sheriff sell the property to pay the rent.

(2) To Protect and Preserve the Premises. The tenant must make all repairs necessary to prevent damage to or deterioration of the premises. He is not required to make repairs of a structural nature, however. If the roof blows off, the tenant need not put on a new roof unless he wishes to keep out the snow and rain. The landlord is under no obligation to put on a new roof, either, unless a state law requires the landlord to keep the property habitable.

RIGHTS OF THE LANDLORD

The landlord has three definite rights under the lease:

1. To regain possession
2. To enter upon the property to preserve it
3. To assign his rights

(1) **To Regain Possession.** Upon the termination of the lease, the landlord has the right to regain peaceable possession of the premises. If this possession is refused, the most common remedy is to bring an *action of ejectment* in a court of law. Upon the successful completion of this suit, the sheriff will forcibly remove the tenant and his property.

When the landlord repossesses the property, he may also retain all permanent improvements and fixtures. The test is whether or not the improvements have become a part of the real estate. If they have, they cannot be removed.

(2) **To Enter Upon the Property to Preserve It.** The landlord has a right to enter upon the property to preserve it. He cannot make extensive renovations that interfere with the tenant's peaceable occupancy. If the roof blows off or becomes leaky, the landlord may repair it or put on a new roof. He cannot use this occasion to add another story. If the landlord enters the property without permission, he may be treated as a stranger. He has no right to enter the premises to show the property to prospective purchasers or tenants. He may, and usually does, reserve this right in the lease itself.

(3) **To Assign His Rights.** The landlord has the right to assign his rights under the lease to a third party. The tenant cannot avoid any of his duties and obligations by reason of the assignment of the lease. Like all other assignments, the assignment does not release the assignor from the contract without the consent of the tenant. If, for example, the tenant was injured because of a concealed but defective water main cover, and the landlord knew of this condition, the landlord would be liable even though he assigned his rights before the injury.

DUTIES OF THE LANDLORD

The lease imposes certain duties upon the landlord:

1. To pay taxes
2. To protect the tenant from latent defects

(1) **To Pay Taxes.** Although the tenant occupies and uses the premises, the landlord must pay all taxes and special assessments. Sometimes the lease provides that the tenant shall pay the taxes. In such event, he is not liable for special assessments for sidewalks, street paving, and other improvements.

(2) **To Protect the Tenant from Concealed Defects.** The landlord is liable to the tenant if the tenant is injured by concealed defects which were known to the landlord or which should have been reasonably known to him at the time of giving the tenant possession of the premises. Such defects might be contamination from contagious germs, unfilled wells that are concealed, and rotten timbers in the dwelling. The tenant bears the risk of injury caused by defects which are apparent or reasonably discoverable by him upon inspection at the time that he enters into possession. Most cities and many states have tenement laws that require the landlord to keep all rental property habitable and provided with adequate fire escapes. Any damage due to a failure to observe these laws may subject the landlord to liability for damages.

TERMINATION OF THE LEASE

A lease that is to exist for a fixed time automatically terminates upon the expiration of that period. The death of either party does not ordinarily affect the lease. If the leased property consists of rooms or apartments in a building and they are destroyed by fire or any other accidental cause, the lease is terminated without liability on the part of the tenant. The landlord may agree to the voluntary surrender of the possession of the premises before the lease expires. An abandonment of the premises without the consent of the landlord is not a surrender, however, but a breach of contract.

If the lease is to run from year to year or from month to month, the party wishing to terminate it must generally give the other party a written notice of his intention. Statutes prescribe the time and the manner of giving notice; they may also specify other particulars, such as the grounds for a termination of the tenancy.

If either party fails to give proper notice, the other party may continue the tenancy for another period.

A tenant refusing to surrender possession of the property after the expiration of his lease may be liable in a summary action brought

NOTICE TO LEAVE THE PREMISES

To __Mr. C. Harold Whitmore_____

*You will please take notice that*__I_____*want you to leave the premises you now occupy, and which*

*you have rented of*__me____, *situated and described as follows:*

_____Suite 4_____

_____Lakeview Apartment_____

_____Lake Shore Drive at Overview Street_____

_____

_____

*in*___Cleveland_____, *County of*___Cuyahoga_____ *and State of*__,Ohio_____

Your compliance with this Notice ___by July 31_____

*will prevent legal measures being taken by*_me_*to obtain possession of the same, agreeably to law.*

                              Yours respectfully, *H. L. Simpson*

_____May 1_____*19*___.

A Landlord's Notice to Leave the Premises

by the landlord to regain possession. This is called a *forcible entry and detainer action.* In this matter the statutes of the different states have provided for the quick recovery of real property by the one legally entitled to it.

In the case of leases of entire buildings, serious problems arise if the property is destroyed by fire, tornado, or other causes. Under the common law the tenant had to continue to pay rent even though the property was destroyed. Many states retain this rule while other states have modified it. If the landlord has a ten-year lease on a

To _____Mr. George A. Hardwick_____

_____1719 Glenview Road, St. Louis, Missouri_____

*Take notice that I shall on the*_31st_____*day of*__March_____, *19*___,

*quit the possession and remove from the premises located at*_____

_____1292 Clarendon Road, St. Louis, Missouri_____

_____

.*which I now hold as your tenant. This*_2nd_____*day of*_January_____, *19*___.

                              John N. Richter

A Tenant's Notice That He Is Leaving the Premises

$100,000 building and it is destroyed by fire one year after the lease is signed, he would not be inclined to rebuild it if he has full fire insurance coverage. He would find it more profitable to invest his $100,000 and continue to collect the rent. To prevent this, statutes may provide that if the landlord refuses to restore the property, the lease is canceled. The lease itself may contain a cancellation clause. If it does not, the tenant can carry fire insurance for the amount of his possible loss. Even when the lease will thus terminate, the tenant will probably wish to carry fire insurance for his personal property which may be so destroyed and, if the premises are used for a business purpose, may also carry some form of insurance to protect him from business interruption or loss of business income.

IMPROVEMENTS

Tenants frequently make improvements during the life of the lease. Many disputes arise as to the tenant's right to take these improvements with him. The test is whether an improvement has become a fixture which must be left on the land or it remains personal property. If a farm tenant builds a fence in the normal way, the fence is a fixture, and he has no right to remove it when he leaves. A poultry house built in the usual way is a fixture and cannot be removed. In a similar case the tenant built the poultry house on sled-like runners. When he was ready to leave, he hitched his team to the poultry house and took it away. The court held he was within his rights because it had not become a fixture but remained personal property.

It is well to remember that one may freely contract away his rights or he may waive them. In one case a tenant built a permanent frame house on leased property with the landlord's agreement that he could remove the house at the end of the lease. The landlord was bound by this contract.

> ▪ Georg had leased an apartment for a year. After one month of occupancy he installed wall-to-wall carpeting. Upon termination of the lease Georg left the premises and desired to take the carpet with him. Since the carpeting is a fixture, it belongs to the landlord and Georg cannot remove it.

EASEMENTS AND LICENSES

An *easement* is an interest in land, such as a right-of-way across another's land or the use of another's driveway. An easement is not a tenancy because there is no exclusive right of possession, as distinguished from the right of intermittent use. It is classified as an interest in land. It is created by deed or by adverse use for a period of time similar to that required for the acquisition of title by adverse possession.

A *license* is a right to do certain acts on the land, but not a right to stay in possession of the land. A license does not create a leasehold interest.

QUESTIONS

1. Distinguish between a tenant and a lodger.
2. Explain the difference between subleasing and assigning.
3. Does a tenant have exclusive control of the leased premises?
4. May a tenant refuse to let the landlord enter upon the premises during the period of the lease?
5. What rights does the tenant have when he leases property?
6. (a) If a hurricane breaks all the windows in a dwelling, must the tenant replace these windows at his own expense?
   (b) If leased property is destroyed by fire, must the tenant continue to pay rent?
7. Who must pay the taxes on leased property, the landlord or the tenant?
8. Name three rights that a landlord has.
9. If a tenant builds a garage on the property, may he take the garage with him when he moves? Explain.
10. What is an easement?

CASE PROBLEMS

1. A storm blew off the roof of a farmhouse. At his own expense the tenant immediately put on a new roof. The contract was silent about repairs. The tenant refused to pay any more rent until the rent equaled the cost of the roof. The landlord brought suit to evict the tenant for nonpayment of rent. Who was entitled to win the suit?

2. Ellis leased a house from Hunt. About one month after moving in, Mrs. Ellis fell through the wooden floor of a back porch and was seriously injured. The floor was badly infested with termites, but this fact could not be detected by a casual inspection. Ellis sued Hunt for damages. Is he entitled to them?

3. Arnold rented a building in a new shopping center for a dress shop. The lease was for five years with an option for renewal. One year later

Arnold sold the business in bulk to Redwine who agreed to take over the lease and make all rent payments to the landlord. The lease contained a clause prohibiting subleasing. The landlord demanded that Redwine vacate the premises. Must Redwine do so?

4. West leased a building for ten years to be used for a men's clothing store. The rent was $1,000 a month. There was no cancellation clause in the lease, and the state law followed the common law. Due to the rapid growth of the city, five years later similar property would rent for $1,500 a month. The building was damaged by fire so badly it could not be used until restored. (a) Must the landlord restore the property? (b) Must the tenant restore the property? (c) Could West protect himself for the monthly rent by carrying a fire insurance policy? (d) If there had been a clause providing for cancellation of the lease upon destruction of the premises, what would your answer be to (c)? (e) Under (d) would the landlord be inclined to cancel the lease? (f) If the landlord does cancel the lease, does West have an insurable interest to protect him against having to pay $1,500 a month for the restored building?

5. Harrel rented an apartment for one year starting September 1. The rent was $150 a month. The state law stipulated that if either party did not wish to renew the lease, he must give notice to that effect ninety days before the lease expires. The following June 1 Harrel thought he wanted to keep the apartment for another year and did not give notice of intent to terminate it. On July 1, he was told by his employer he was being transferred to another state on August 1. What might Harrel do to minimize his loss in this case?

6. On May 15 Pauly rented a house by oral agreement for one year; the occupancy was to begin on June 1. In the state where this property was located, when property is rented from month to month, a thirty-day notice of intention to vacate is required. If the rental contract is for one year or more, a ninety-day notice must be given in order to terminate the lease. On April 28 of the following year, Pauly gave written notice that he intended to vacate the house on June 1. The landlord contended that the lease ran for one more year. Was this correct?

7. Rex purchased the timber on Howington's farm. He could save considerable time and expense by crossing Brown's land. Brown agreed orally to let Rex cross his land upon the payment of $10. The next morning Brown attempted to prevent Rex from crossing his land. Did he have the right to stop him?

Chapter 48

WILLS AND INHERITANCES

WILLS

Title to all property, both real and personal, may be transferred by a will. A *will* is an instrument, prepared in the form prescribed by law, which provides for the disposition of a person's property to take effect after death.

The testator does not have to meet as high a standard of capacity to make a will as he would in order to make a contract. He must have the mental capacity at the time of making the will to know the natural objects of his bounty, understand the nature and extent of his property, understand that he is making a will, and have the ability to dispose of his property by means of a plan he has formulated. Even if he does not have the mental capacity to carry on a business or if he makes unusual provisions in his will, this does not necessarily mean that he does not have capacity to make a will. A person who is insane lacks sufficient capacity; however, an insane person who has intervals of sanity has capacity during those intervals to make a will. Any person, other than a minor, of sound mind ordinarily is competent to make a will. In a few states minors can, under limited circumstances, make a will.

LIMITATIONS ON FREEDOM TO DISPOSE OF PROPERTY BY WILL

The right to dispose of property by will is a highly prized right and but few restrictions are placed upon it. These restrictions are:

(1) A spouse may elect to take the share he would receive had his spouse died without leaving a will, or the share provided by statute, if his spouse's will does not leave him as large a share. However, this right to take against the will can be barred by actions of

the surviving spouse. If the surviving spouse is guilty of conduct which would have justified the deceased spouse in securing a divorce, the surviving spouse generally cannot elect to take against the will.

Except for the cases of a surviving spouse electing to take against the will and in some cases of a subsequent marriage, birth, or adoption, the testator may exclude or disinherit any person he choses from receiving any portion of his estate. If the testator gives his entire estate to someone else, all persons who would inherit in the absence of a will are excluded. The testator does not even have to mention in his will those who are disinherited with the exception of children, nor does he have to leave a nominal sum to those disinherited.

(2) One cannot control by will the distribution of his property in perpetuity. The rule against perpetuities requires that an interest in property must vest within 21 years after the death of persons living on the date the owner of the property creates the interest. When the interest is created by will, the date of creation is the date of death of the owner. For example, if he has no nephews or nieces at his death, he cannot create an interest for the children (not yet born) of the nephews and nieces (not yet born).

TERMS COMMON TO WILLS

The person making the will is called a *testator*, if a man, and a *testatrix*, if a woman. If the gift is real estate, the one receiving the gift (the beneficiary) is called the *devisee;* if it is personal property, he is called the *legatee*. A *bequest* is a gift of personal property in general. A *legacy* is a gift of a sum of money. The person named in a will as the one to administer the estate is an *executor* (man) or an *executrix* (woman). One who dies without having made a will is said to die *intestate*. A person appointed by a court to settle the affairs of an intestate is an *administrator* (man) or an *administratrix* (woman).

DISTINGUISHING CHARACTERISTICS OF A WILL

A will has the following outstanding characteristics that distinguish it from many other legal instruments:

(1) A will is construed by the courts with less technical strictness than a deed or any other kind of written document.

(2) A will devising real property must be executed in conformity with the law of the state in which the property is situated. A will

bequeathing personal property is governed by the law of the state in which the testator was domiciled at the time of his death.

(3) A will may be revoked at any time during the life of the testator.

FORMALITIES

All states prescribe formalities for wills. The formalities for executing must be satisfied.

When property is left by will, title does not vest in the devisee until the will is probated. If a will is written in the testator's own handwriting and is dated, it need not be witnessed in more than a third of the states. In many states the will must be witnessed by at least two, and in some states three, witnesses regardless of how it is written. The usual requirement is for the witnesses and the testator to sign in the presence of each other. Many states also require the testator to inform the witnesses that the instrument he is signing is his will. This is called *publication.*

When subscribing witnesses are required, they will be required at the time that the will is offered for probate to identify their signatures and the signature of the testator and to state that they were present when the signature was made. In states which do not require subscribing witnesses for a will, it is generally required that two persons identify the signature of the testator on the will, basing their opinion that it is his signature upon their experience through prior correspondence or business records involving the testator's signature. If a person's will is not drawn according to the legal requirements, the court may disregard it and the property may be disposed of in a manner entirely foreign to the testator's wishes.

SPECIAL TYPES OF WILLS

There are at least three special types of wills to meet special circumstances. First, there are *holographic wills,* which are written entirely in longhand by the testator. Many states make no distinction between holographic and other wills. In other states variations of the general law of wills are established for holographic wills. Second, there are *nuncupative wills,* which are oral wills declared by the testator in the presence of witnesses to be his will. Usually such a will can only be made during the testator's last illness and only

LAST WILL AND TESTAMENT OF F. J. ROSE

I, F. J. Rose, of the City of Chicago and State of Illinois, do make, publish, and declare this to be my Last Will and Testament in manner following:

FIRST: I direct that all my just debts, funeral expenses, and the cost of administering my estate be paid by my executrix hereinafter named.

SECOND: I give, devise, and bequeath to my beloved daughter, Anna Rose Scott, now residing in Englewood, New Jersey, that certain piece of real estate, with all improvements thereon, situated in the same city and at the corner of Hudson Avenue and Tenafly Road.

THIRD: All the remainder and residue of my property, real, personal, and mixed, I give to my beloved wife, Mary Ellen Rose, for her use and forever.

FOURTH: I hereby nominate and appoint my wife, Mary Ellen Rose, executrix of this, my Last Will and Testament, and I direct that she not be required to give bond or security for the performance of her duties as such.

LASTLY: I hereby revoke any and all former wills by me made.

IN WITNESS WHEREOF, I have hereunto set my hand this tenth day of October, in the year nineteen hundred

F. J. Rose
F. J. Rose

We, the undersigned, certify that the foregoing instrument was, on the date thereof, signed and declared by F. J. Rose as his Last Will and Testament, in the presence of us who, in his presence and in the presence of each other, have, at his request, hereunto signed our names as witnesses of the execution thereof, this tenth day of October, 19--; and we hereby certify that we believe the said F. J. Rose to be of sound mind and memory.

C. O. Moore residing at 4316 Cottage Grove Avenue Chicago, Illinois

Sarah J. King residing at 1313 East 63 Street Chicago, Illinois

S. S. Samuels residing at 2611 Elm Street Joliet, Illinois

A Will

applies to personal property, and sometimes only a limited value of personal property may be so disposed. The witnesses frequently must reduce the will to writing within a specified number of days. Third, most states make special provision for soldiers and seamen. They are allowed to make oral or written wills of personal property without complying with the formalities required of other wills. These wills are in force even after the testator returns to civilian life. They must be revoked in the same manner as other wills.

THE WORDING OF A WILL

Any words that convey the intention of the testator are sufficient. No matter how rough and ungrammatical the language may be, if the intention of the testator can be ascertained, the court will order that the provisions of the will be carried out. Since the court will order the terms of a will to be carried out exactly, the wording of the will should express the exact wishes of the testator.

■ A well-to-do man, who had provided for his children previously, inserted into his will this provision: "To my brother, Kirby, I leave $8,000." By the time the testator died, his estate had shrunk from $80,000 to $10,000. He had intended to leave his brother one tenth of his estate; but, because of the wording used in the will, his brother received almost the entire estate after the expenses were paid. The testator should have written, "To my brother, Kirby, I leave one tenth of my estate, which sum in no event is to exceed $8,000."

■ Two sisters drew wills, each leaving the other all her property. It was their intention that the survivor was to use the estate until her death, at which time she would devise it so that a worthless brother would not get any part of it. They both died at the same time in an automobile accident, and the brother inherited the entire estate. Their prime purpose in making a will had been to keep their property from going to "laughing heirs," those who are delighted when the testator dies because they receive property for nothing and without being caused any personal grief by the event which resulted in their increased wealth. They could have prevented this by including a "common disaster" clause, stipulating how their estate should be distributed if both died simultaneously. Had they done this, the brother would not have gained the entire estates of his sisters.

REVOCATION

A will may be revoked at any time prior to the death of the testator. The revocation may take any one of several forms.

(1) **Destruction or Alteration.** If the testator deliberately destroys a will, this constitutes a revocation. If the testator merely alters the will, this may or may not revoke it depending upon the nature and the extent of the alteration. If he merely obliterates a part of the will, this in most states does not revoke the will.

(2) **Marriage and Divorce.** If a single person makes a will and later marries, the marriage may revoke the will in whole or part; or the will may be presumed to be revoked unless it was made in contemplation of the marriage, or made provision for a future spouse. In some states a marriage will not revoke the will completely, but only so that the spouse will get the estate she would have been entitled to in the absence of a will. A divorce automatically revokes a will to the extent of the property left to the divorced spouse if there is a property settlement; otherwise, a divorce usually in no way affects the will.

(3) **Execution of a Later Will.** The execution of a later will automatically revokes a prior will if the terms of the second will are inconsistent with the first will. If the second will merely changes a few provisions in the first will and leaves the bulk of it intact, then a second only revokes the first will to the extent of such inconsistency.

(4) **After-Born Child.** A child may be born or adopted after the will is made. If no codicil is added to provide for the child, then this will revoke or partially revoke the will.

ABATEMENT AND ADEMPTION

If a testator leaves $20,000 to his son John, $10,000 to his sister Mary, and a painting to his brother Adam, it is possible there will be both an abatement and an ademption in the will. When the will is probated, there may not be enough money after all debts are paid to comply with the terms of the will. If there is only $15,000 in cash left, then the cash gifts to John and Mary will *abate*. This means each will receive a proportionate share, in this case fifty percent, or $10,000 and $5,000 respectively. If the painting was sold, stolen, or destroyed before the death of the testator, then Adam would get nothing. The gift to him is *adeemed* since the property is not in existence at the time of the testator's death. He is not entitled to its cash value or any other substitute item of property.

- Graham provided in his will that his son, Henry, was to receive his lakeside home, Agua Vista, and the boat and boathouse. Before Graham died, he sold this property and purchased with the proceeds a beach home in Florida. He did not change his will. When he died, Henry demanded the beach home. He was not entitled to it since his devise was adeemed.

PROBATE OF A WILL

When the testator dies leaving a will, the will must be probated. Probate is a very simple process if there is no contest of the will. If the will does not name an executor, then upon petition of one of the beneficiaries the court will appoint an administrator.

If the will is contested, the court must hear the contest to determine if it is valid. A contest of the will is to be distinguished from litigation over the meaning or interpretation to be given the will. If the contest alleges and proves fraud, undue influence, improper witnessing, mental incapacity of the testator, revocation of the will, or any other infirmity in the will affecting its legality, the will is nullified and the property of the testator distributed according to the law of descent described later in this chapter.

WHEN ADMINISTRATION IS UNNECESSARY

Of course, if an individual does not own any property at the time of his death, there is no need for administration. Also, if all of his property is jointly owned with someone else who acquired his interest by right of survivorship, there is no need for administration.

Some states have special statutes allowing the administration procedures to be shortened when only a small estate is involved, usually under $1,000. It is also possible in many states to have a *settlement agreement* by which the estate is divided without formal court proceedings. This occurs if all the persons interested in the estate, relatives and creditors, can agree on the shares each one is to receive.

CODICIL

A *codicil* is a separate writing that modifies a will. Except for the part modified, the original will remains the same. A codicil must be executed with all the formalities of the original will.

TITLE BY DESCENT

When a person dies intestate, his property is distributed in accordance with the state law of descent. Every state has such a law. Although these laws vary slightly, on the whole they provide as follows: The property of the intestate goes to his children subject to the rights of the surviving spouse. If there are no surviving children or grandchildren, the father and the mother, as the next of kin, receive the property. If they are not living, the brothers and sisters become the next of kin; and they are followed by grandparents, aunts and uncles, and so on. Some statutes permit any person related by blood to inherit when no nearer related relative exists. Some statutes do not permit those beyond first cousins to inherit. In any case, if there is not a proper person to inherit, the property passes to the state.

If the owner of property makes no will but leaves his property to be distributed according to the law of descent in force in his state, he has no assurance that his property will be distributed as he desires.

> ▪ A man gave his wife a $50,000 home which he had bought with money he had inherited from his parents. Shortly afterward, his wife died without leaving a will survived only by the husband and her brother. Under the state law, the brother was entitled to receive half of the house as his share of the wife's estate.

PER CAPITA AND PER STIRPES DISTRIBUTION

The lineal descendants of a testator are his children and his grandchildren. If all his children are living at the time of the father's death, and his wife has predeceased him, his property will be distributed *per capita,* meaning per head, or equally. If one child predeceased the father and left three surviving children, then the property would be divided into three equal parts and the dead child's part would then be divided into three equal parts with one of these parts going to each of the grandchildren. When this is done, the property is said to be divided *per stirpes.* If the deceased child left no children or other lineal descendants, then the surviving children would take its share.

EXECUTORS AND ADMINISTRATORS

For the most part the duties and responsibilities of executors and administrators are similar, but there are two significant differences.

(1) With but few exceptions anyone may be appointed an executor; but in the appointment of an administrator, there is a clear order of priority in most states. The surviving spouse has first priority, followed by children, grandchildren, parents, and brothers or sisters. (2) The executor may be excused by the testator from furnishing a bond, but an administrator must in all cases execute a bond guaranteeing his faithful performance of his duties. In some cases the court may require a bond of an executor even when the will expressly exempts him.

The prime duty of an executor or an administrator is to preserve the estate and distribute it to the rightful parties. Any loss due to negligence, bad faith, or breach of trust subjects him to liability. He is required to act in good faith, with prudence, and within the powers conferred on him by will or by law. If any part of the estate is a going business, with but few exceptions the business must be liquidated. A will may expressly provide that the executor continue the business; and frequently the executor or administrator will obtain leave of court to continue the business for either a limited time or an indefinite time, depending largely upon the wishes of those who are entitled to receive the estate. Third parties dealing with executors and administrators are charged with knowledge of limitations upon their authority.

QUESTIONS

1. What is a *will*?
2. What restrictions are there upon one's right to leave his property by will to anyone he chooses?
3. How does one get title to property left to him by will?
4. (a) Do all states require all wills to be witnessed?
   (b) How many witnesses are required to validate a will when witnesses are required?
5. What is the difference between ademption and abatement?
6. What is the difference between distributing property per capita and per stirpes?
7. Does a second will automatically revoke a first will?
8. Do the devisees under a will inherit the real property or the right to get the real property? Explain.
9. If a testator has real estate in California and personal property in Georgia, the laws of which state apply to the will if he was living in Georgia at the time of his death?

10. Must the testator obtain the consent of the beneficiaries of the will before he can revoke it?

11. Must a codicil be witnessed in the same way as a will?

CASE PROBLEMS

1. Kirkland, sales manager for the Langford Furniture Company, received an order for furniture amounting to $10,285 from the John Quarles Furniture Mart. The order was signed by John Knowles, executor for John Quarles. Kirkland shipped the merchandise promptly. When the account was long past due, it was found upon investigation that Quarles' will had never authorized Knowles to continue the business. The heirs of Quarles demanded that the bill not be paid. Kirkland sued both the estate and John Knowles, executor. There were no bondsmen. Knowles was insolvent. Could Kirkland look to the estate for this debt?

2. Tom Middlebrooks, age twenty-nine and unmarried, made a will and left all of his property, both personal and real, to his church since he had not planned to get married. Later he married Cynthia, but he failed to revoke his will. Over a period of twenty years he accumulated a considerable estate. After his death, the church pastor found the will and presented it to the court for probate since Tom had left his wife and children ample property by gift for their needs. Will the court order the property to be transferred to the church?

3. Joseph made a will and left his son, Johnathon, 1,000 shares of stock in the United States Steel Corporation. Before Joseph died, he sold the stock and purchased with the proceeds from the sale stock in the Atlantic Steel Corporation. When the will was offered for probate after Joseph's death, Johnathon petitioned the court to have the stock in the Atlantic Steel Corporation transferred to him. Is he entitled to his stock?

4. Bunting died intestate, leaving an estate of $300,000. He had two children, John and Harold, who survived him. One child, Bentley, had predeceased him, leaving three minor children. In addition, Bunting had raised his brother's son James but had never formally adopted him. How will this property be distributed?

5. Henry's father died leaving an estate of $200,000. Henry was named as the executor in the will. When the fire insurance policies on two of the houses belonging to the estate expired, Henry failed to have them renewed. Several months later one of the houses was totally destroyed by fire. The beneficiaries of the estate demanded that this loss be borne by Henry. Are they correct in their demand?

6. Welch, a single man, sold a patent for $50,000. He then married Evaline and gave her $25,000 in government E bonds as a wedding present. Shortly after their marriage Evaline died. They had no children, and Evaline left no will. Welch's mother-in-law demanded one half of the E bonds. Was she entitled to them?

7. Over the years Harvey and his wife, Lydia, accumulated an estate of $200,000. Harvey made a will leaving all his property, both personal and real, to Lydia. Two or three years later they were divorced, but no property settlement was made. Harvey remarried. Soon after his remarriage, he died without having changed or revoked his will. Sally, his second wife, demanded all his estate since there were no children. Lydia claimed that all the estate belonged to her. Who was entitled to the estate, Sally or Lydia?

8. McKay, who was seriously injured in an automobile accident, was convinced that he would die. He told two of his friends how he wanted his property distributed. The next day these two men wrote down what McKay told them and both signed it. McKay recovered in about three weeks but then died of a heart attack about two weeks later. There was no connection between his heart attack and his injury in the automobile accident. McKay did nothing before he died to change his oral will. One son, Todd, was dissatisfied with his share of the estate and took legal action to bar a probate of the oral will. Was the will valid?

9. At the time of his death Cohen lived in Georgia. He owned personal property worth over $1,000,000, most of which was kept in Virginia. The Georgia law requires three witnesses to a will, while the Virginia law requires only two witnesses. Cohen made a will just one month before his death and obtained two witnesses to his signature. He left $500,000 to a charitable organization. His two sons brought an action to invalidate the will because it did not meet the requirements of the Georgia law. Was this a valid will?

Chapter 49

BANKRUPTCY

Insolvency is a fact or condition and is to be distinguished from bankruptcy which is a judicial declaration as to the debtor's financial condition. The Bankruptcy Act defines *insolvency* as insufficient assets to pay all debts outstanding, or an inability to pay one's debts when they come due.

The bankruptcy law has two very definite purposes:

1. To give the debtor a new start
2. To give creditors an equal chance in the collection of their claims

(1) To Give Debtor a New Start. If an honest debtor is hopelessly insolvent, he may be tempted to cease trying even to earn a living. Hope is the great stimulant to enterprise and honest endeavor. If hope vanishes, effort diminishes or may even vanish. By permitting an insolvent debtor to give up all his assets with a few minor exceptions and thereby get forgiveness of his debts, he can at least start anew with the hope of success. The court prescribes an equitable settlement under the circumstances; and when these conditions are fully met, the debtor may resume full control of his business.

(2) To Give Creditors an Equal Chance. If one is bankrupt, it is unfair to permit some unsecured creditors to get paid in full while others receive nothing. By appointing a trustee to take over the bankrupt's property and to pay each creditor in proportion to his claim, a more equitable settlement is achieved. Not only is this arrangement more equitable, but it is also less wasteful and less expensive than for each creditor to sue the debtor in separate suits.

WHO MAY FILE A PETITION FOR BANKRUPTCY

Today any business or person may become a bankrupt, either voluntarily or involuntarily, except banks, insurance companies, savings and loan associations, railroads, and municipalities. All of these exempted institutions except municipalities may be thrown into what is known as *receivership* but cannot be declared bankrupt. In receivership a receiver is appointed to take charge of the assets and if possible to restore the firm to financial solvency.

KINDS OF BANKRUPTCY

There are two kinds of bankruptcy:

1. Voluntary
2. Involuntary

(1) **Voluntary Bankruptcy.** Anyone, except a city, a railroad, an insurance company, or a bank, may file a voluntary petition to be adjudicated a bankrupt.

(2) **Involuntary Bankruptcy.** Under certain conditions one may be forced into involuntary bankruptcy. Three or more creditors, whose aggregate claims amount to $500 in excess of any collateral held as security, are necessary to file a petition to have an insolvent debtor declared a bankrupt if there are twelve or more creditors.

If the debtor is declared a bankrupt, the procedure in liquidating his estate is the same whether it is a voluntary bankruptcy proceeding or an involuntary one.

ACTS OF BANKRUPTCY

Before one may be declared an involuntary bankrupt, he must have committed an act of bankruptcy. Any one of the following six acts, if committed within the four months immediately preceding the filing of a petition in bankruptcy, is sufficient to warrant the court in declaring the debtor an involuntary bankrupt:

1. A fraudulent transfer
2. Giving preference to creditors
3. Permitting a lien to be obtained
4. Assignment of claims for the benefit of creditors

5. Appointing a receiver for assets
6. Admitting insolvency in writing

(1) Fraudulent Transfers. When a debtor realizes he is in financial difficulty, he may attempt to transfer some of his property beyond the reach of his creditors. If these transfers are made without an adequate consideration with the intent that he will later get the property back, the transfer is fraudulent. If the transfer is made within four months immediately preceding the filing of a petition in bankruptcy, the court may presume intent to defraud existing creditors. If the transfer is made within twelve months preceding the filing of the petition, the trustee in bankruptcy may have the transfers declared null and void if they can prove intent to defraud.

■ Scott who was insolvent learned that three of his creditors were in the process of forcing him into involuntary bankruptcy. Scott immediately sold to his brother eight parcels of real estate for a total of $50. Scott was adjudicated bankrupt and the trustee set aside the transfers as being in defraud of the creditors.

(2) Giving Preference to Creditors. If within four months immediately preceding the filing of the petition in bankruptcy the debtor transfers property to a creditor with the intent to prefer one creditor over another creditor, this is an act of bankruptcy. Not only is it an act of bankruptcy, but the trustees in bankruptcy may petition the court to have the transfer avoided and the property restored to the debtor's estate. Before the transfer can be avoided, the trustee must prove not only that the debtor had the intent to prefer one creditor over another but also that the creditor at the time of the transfer had reasonable cause to believe that the debtor was insolvent.

(3) Permitting a Lien to Be Obtained. If an insolvent debtor permits a lien to be obtained against him through a legal proceeding, he has committed an act of bankruptcy. The debtor may redeem himself, however, by paying the lien within thirty days, or at least five days before the enforcement of the lien.

■ Spivak owed ten various creditors $75,000. He had assets of $30,000 in real property and $10,000 in personal property. One of the creditors obtained judgment for $5,000 and had the judgment recorded. He also attached two trucks worth $3,000. Both these liens are acts of bankruptcy. To avoid being declared an involuntary bankrupt, Spivak must pay them within thirty days or sooner if the property is to be sold at a sheriff's sale.

(4) Assignment of Claims for the Benefit of Creditors. If an insolvent debtor makes an assignment of claims due him for the benefit of some of his creditors, he commits an act of bankruptcy.

(5) Appointing a Receiver for Assets. An insolvent debtor may have the court appoint a receiver for his estate. Also, under some state laws the creditors may have a receiver appointed. For either this voluntary or involuntary appointment of a receiver to be an act of bankruptcy, the debtor must be insolvent.

(6) Admitting Insolvency in Writing. The debtor may admit his insolvency in writing and express his willingness to be declared a bankrupt. The chief difference between this type and a voluntary petition is that the creditors must employ the counsel and advance the necessary costs for bringing the action.

PROCEDURE IN A BANKRUPTCY CASE

After the court declares a debtor bankrupt, the first step is to call a meeting of all creditors. These creditors then elect a trustee to take over all the assets of the bankrupt. The trustee steps into the shoes of the bankrupt. He collects all debts due the bankrupt, preserves all physical assets, sues all delinquent creditors of the estate, and finally distributes all money realized according to a definite priority which will be discussed later in this chapter.

EXEMPT PROPERTY

Each state has laws exempting certain property from seizure for the payment of debts. The most common types of property that are excluded are household effects, tools of the trade, such as a carpenter's tools, a dentist's equipment, and similar items within reasonable limits. If the bankrupt is the insured and if he reserved the right to change the beneficiary of an insurance policy, the general rule is that he owns the cash surrender value; and this asset must be included in his assets which he turns over to the trustee. If he did not reserve the right to change the beneficiary, the cash surrender value does not belong to him. If the policy were bought, however, in contemplation of bankruptcy and for the purpose of defrauding creditors, the trustee may order the cash surrender value included.

Most states specifically exempt all necessary wearing apparel for the bankrupt and members of his family, and such items as the family

Bible, and all pictures of the members of the family even though some of these may be portraits of some value.

CORPORATE REORGANIZATION

Bankruptcy proceedings result in the liquidation and distribution of the assets of an enterprise. The national bankruptcy law provides a special reorganization system for corporations so that they may be reorganized rather than liquidated.

A corporation, indenture trustee, or three or more creditors of the corporation with specific claims which total $5,000 or more may file a petition for a reorganization. The petition must state that the corporation is insolvent or unable to pay its debts as they mature and that reorganization is necessary. The proposed plan of reorganization may be included. The court will confirm a plan if it is fair, equitable, feasible, has been proposed and accepted in good faith, and all the payments made or proposed are found to be reasonable. If the plan is approved, the management of the corporation is returned to the corporation. If no acceptable plan of reorganization can be worked out, the corporation is adjudged bankrupt; and the business is liquidated like all other bankrupt firms.

ARRANGEMENTS

If the insolvent debtor is not a corporation but a person, partnership, sole proprietorship, real property owner, or wage earner, he may work out an arrangement or composition of creditors that attempts to achieve for him the same advantages the corporate reorganization act gives to corporations. Under the common law, one unwilling creditor could prevent a composition among creditors of an insolvent debtor. Under the present law a majority of creditors can impose a settlement upon the dissenting minority. The debtor is as fully released from his debts as if he had been formally declared a bankrupt. The purpose of these arrangements or compositions is to prevent the hardship of an immediate liquidation of all of the debtor's assets and to give the debtor time in which to pay the obligations as agreed to in the composition. This plan benefits the creditors because they are likely, in the long run, to receive a greater percentage of the money owed them.

DUTIES OF THE BANKRUPT

The bankrupt must cooperate fully with the trustee. He must attend all creditors' meetings when requested and furnish all relevant evidence about debts due him. He must file with the trustee a schedule of all his assets and all his liabilities. This schedule must be in sufficient detail so that the trustee can list the secured creditors, the partially secured creditors, and the unsecured creditors. Failure of the bankrupt to cooperate with the trustee and to obey all orders of the referee not only may prevent his being discharged from bankruptcy, but may also subject him to criminal prosecution for contempt of court.

PROOF OF CLAIMS

All creditors of the bankrupt must present proof of their claims to the trustee. A maximum of six months is allowed for presenting proof of claims, after which time all right to the claim is lost. This is true even though the creditor had no knowledge of the bankruptcy proceedings.

RECLAMATIONS

Frequently the bankrupt has in his possession at the time he is adjudicated a bankrupt property that does not belong to him. This property takes the form of bailed goods, or property held in trust for another, or as security for a loan. The true owner of the property is not technically a creditor of the bankrupt. He should file a reclamation claim for the specific property.

If one is in possession of a check drawn by the bankrupt, he may or may not lose depending on the circumstances. If the check is an uncertified check, the holder is a mere creditor of the bankrupt and is not entitled to have it cashed. This is so because a check is not an assignment of the money on deposit, and the creditor merely holds the unpaid claim which the check was intended to discharge. If the check has been certified, the creditor has the obligation of the drawee bank on the check, which he may assert in reference to proceeding upon the claim against the drawer of the check.

PRIORITY OF CLAIMS

Claims of a bankrupt may be classified as fully secured claims, partially secured claims, and unsecured claims.

Fully secured creditors may have their claims satisfied in full from the proceeds of the assets used for security. If these assets sell for more than enough to satisfy the secured debts, the remainder must be surrendered to the trustee in bankruptcy of the debtor.

Partially secured creditors are those with a lien on some assets but not enough to satisfy the debts in full. The proceeds of the security held by a partially secured creditor are used to pay his claim; and, to the extent that any portion of a debt remains unpaid, the creditor is entitled to claim as a general creditor for the balance.

The priority of claims is as follows:

(1) The expenses of preserving and administering the estate (filing fees paid by creditors in involuntary proceedings, expenses of creditors in recovering property transferred or concealed by the bankrupt, and reasonable expenses of creditors in resisting a refused or set-aside composition).

(2) Wage claims not exceeding $600 for any one wage earner provided the wages were earned not more than three months prior to bankruptcy proceedings

(3) Creditors' expenses incurred in opposing a plan for the discharge of a bankrupt, or in convicting a person of violating the bankruptcy law

(4) Tax claims

(5) Debts owed persons who by law are entitled to priority

DEBTS NOT DISCHARGED

Certain obligations cannot be avoided by bankruptcy. The most important of these claims are:

(1) Claims for alimony and child support

(2) All taxes—federal, state, and local

(3) Debts owed by reasons of embezzlement

(4) Debts due on a judgment for malicious injury to others, such as a judgment obtained for assault and battery

(5) Wages earned within three months of the bankruptcy proceedings

(6) Deposits left with the bankrupt as an employer who accepted a cash deposit from an employee as a fidelity bond

There are some other circumstances under which certain debts are not discharged by bankruptcy, but the list above includes the most common ones.

DISCHARGE FROM BANKRUPTCY

When the court adjudicates one a bankrupt, this operates as an application for a discharge in bankruptcy. If the bankrupt cooperates fully with the court and the trustee in bankruptcy and meets all other requirements for discharge, the application will be granted. The bankrupt is then free to engage in all types of business transactions, and his contracts are fully binding upon him. If the bankrupt is a corporation, it must wait at least six months after it is declared bankrupt before it can file an application for discharge.

> ▪ Baker, who filed a voluntary petition of bankruptcy, concealed the fact that he owned a substantial number of rare coins of high value. After a discharge in bankruptcy was granted, one of Baker's prior creditors sought to enforce his claim on the ground that Baker was not discharged because of his fraudulent concealment. The creditor prevailed.

QUESTIONS

1. Is bankruptcy a legal or a financial status?
2. State two purposes of the law permitting one to be adjudicated a bankrupt.
3. Who may be adjudicated a bankrupt?
4. What is the difference between a voluntary and an involuntary bankrupt?
5. Give an illustration of a fraudulent transfer that will be considered null and void.
6. If a business firm is insolvent, is every payment on its liabilities a preference to creditors that renders the payment an act of bankruptcy?
7. John, a bankrupt, had a portrait of his wife done by an artist of some note. At the time of the application for bankruptcy, the portrait had a sale value of $500. May he keep this portrait?
8. What is a reclamation in bankruptcy?

CASE PROBLEMS

1. Henderson held a check drawn by Sellers for $700. He held this check two weeks before presenting it to the bank for payment. When he did present it, he was told that Sellers had been declared a bankrupt two days before, and for that reason the check could not be paid although Sellers had ample funds in the bank to pay it. Henderson contended that by the check Sellers had assigned $700 to him before he became bankrupt and therefore this $700 did not belong to Sellers. Was this contention correct?

2. Rachels conducted a jewelry business. He put on a big sale and took in $25,000 in cash. About thirty days later he asked the court to declare him a voluntary bankrupt. He refused to tell the trustee what he did with the $25,000. Did he have to reveal this information?

3. The three Hill brothers were laborers for Mayberry, a bankrupt. Mayberry owed each of them $300 earned in the last two months. Mayberry's assets amounted to only $1,100 after all costs of the bankruptcy proceedings were paid. His debts amounted to $11,000. How much were the Hill brothers able to collect?

4. O'Hara was in extreme financial difficulties and realized he could not avoid eventual bankruptcy. He accumulated $50,000 in cash by selling much of his property at a large discount. He then purchased a ten-year endowment insurance policy on himself and made his wife the beneficiary. He reserved the right to change the beneficiary. He paid for the policy with a single premium payment of $50,000. The creditors contended the cash value belonged to them since the policy was purchased while insolvent and for the purpose of defrauding the creditors. Could the trustee demand that the cash surrender value of this policy be included in the bankrupt's assets?

5. Henderson was the payee of a certified check for $2,000 given to him by Donaldson. Before the check was cashed, Donaldson was adjudicated a bankrupt. Henderson claimed that he was entitled to be paid the full $2,000 by Donaldson's bank before the creditors should receive anything. Is that contention correct? Why?

6. Davis borrowed $5,000 from Harrell and deposited with him 125 shares of U. S. Steel common stock as collateral security. Before Davis paid the debt, Harrell was declared bankrupt. Should Davis file a reclamation or a proof of claim? Why?

7. Middlebrooks was the accountant for the Three Minute Wash Corporation. The company owed Middlebrooks $3,000 for his salary for the past six months. After all assets were converted into cash and the cost of administration paid, there remained only $4,000 in cash. How much of this, if any, is Middlebrooks entitled to, assuming there are $30,000 in total debts, unsecured?

8. Presley had assets valued at $18,000 and liabilities of $12,000. Most of his assets were "frozen" so that he could not meet his current liabilities. To persuade one creditor not to sue him, Presley gave the creditor a deed of trust on his stock of merchandise. The other creditors sought to have Presley declared a bankrupt. Was this an act of bankruptcy?

9. Short's wife divorced him, and the court ordered Short to pay his wife $200 a month indefinitely as alimony. Short sought to avoid this claim by being adjudicated a bankrupt. Could he do this?

10. Dr. McAlpin was declared an involuntary bankrupt. His offices were equipped with the most modern X-ray machines and other equipment, valued at $30,000. The state law stipulated that the tools of one's trade could not be attached by creditors, but the law was not specific as to what constituted tools of trade. Dr. McAlpin contended that none of his equipment need be turned over to the trustee in bankruptcy. The creditors contended that all but the bare minimum needed for general practice of medicine should be turned over. How much of this equipment could Dr. McAlpin keep?

SUMMARY CASES

PART 10

1. Jacobson by oral contract sold some standing timber to Sorenson. Sorenson started immediately to cut and haul the timber. Since there was no time limit set on when the timber was to be removed, two years later much timber remained to be cut. Jacobson then served written notice on Sorenson that he had only ten days more to complete the contract. When the ten days expired, there were about 70,000 board feet of logs on the ground that had not been removed. Jacobson refused to let him haul these away even though Sorenson was willing to pay for them. The question was raised to what extent an oral contract for the sale of interest in land can be enforced. Was this oral contract enforceable? (Sorensen et al. v. Jacobson, 125 Mont. 148, 232 P. 2d 332)

2. A Plymouth sedan was stolen from the owner, Skellinger. The thief installed in it a motor from an older Plymouth to which he had legal title. The insurance company paid Skellinger for the theft of his Plymouth sedan and was subrogated to his rights. Merlin Motors later purchased the Plymouth sedan containing the older car's motor from the thief and later sold it to Gambino, an innocent purchaser. Gambino admits he does not have good title to the entire newer car but contends he has title to the older motor. The insurance company contended that the accession in value made by the thief to the car owned by Skellinger became the property of Skellinger and thus to the insurance company by subrogation. Is the insurance company entitled to the entire Plymouth sedan? (National Retailers Mutual Insurance Company v. Gambino, 1 N.J. Sup. 627, 64 A.2d 927)

3. Over a period of several years, Jessie Gordon sent money to Joseph Bryan for safekeeping. In her last letter just before her death, she wrote Bryan: ". . . and at my death the money I have down there you take it and divide it among your sisters, your brother, and yourself." Jessie had made a will devising her estate to several parties, including Bryan, his sisters, and his brother. Bryan contended the $5,000 was not a part of her estate but that he, his brother, and sisters had acquired title to it by gift before Jessie's death. Was this a gift? (In re Gordon's Will, 27 N.W. 2d 900)

4. Moretti, a pedestrian, received a very painful injury from an electric fan blade projecting from the outside of the wall of the building. The building was occupied by a tenant who installed the fan. The lease was on a month-to-month basis so that the landlord could have re-entered the premises for the purpose of removing the fan by giving the tenant 30 days' notice to vacate. He did not do this, nor did he order the tenant to remove the fan. Moretti sued the landlord for damages for his injury. Is the landlord liable in this case for the injury to Moretti? (Moretti v. C. S. Realty Co., 78 R. I. 341, 82 A. 2d 608)

5. Arthur H. Kelley executed a deed to his home to his son. The deed was complete in every detail. When Kelly handed it to his son, he said, "Here is the deed to the home property. . . . The only request I want

to make is that you do not record the deed until after my death." The father made many statements after this to the effect he had not given his son the property except on the condition that he die from a serious operation he was to undergo. The son's acts corroborated these statements by his failure to assume possession of the property, pay tax on it, or in any way assert ownership during his father's lifetime. Since a deed cannot serve as a will, this deed was not effective unless there was a delivery for the purpose of passing title. Was there a valid delivery? (Kelley v. Bank of America, National Trust and Savings Association, 112 Col. App. 2d 388, 246 P. 2d 92)

6. Halliday constructed an apartment building of several stories on his lot. On one side were windows to admit light and air. Hibbard, who owned the adjoining lot, constructed a building up against Halliday's lot with a solid brick wall facing the windows of Halliday's apartment building, thereby greatly reducing the value of his property. The evidence showed that Hibbard did this out of malice toward Halliday. Hibbard contended he could use his property any way he wished. Is Halliday entitled to damages for the reduced value of his property? (Hibbard v. Halliday, 58 Okla. 244, 158 P. 1158)

7. The People's Savings and Trust Company held a first mortgage on a building. Munsert sold and installed, subsequent to the mortgage, an expensive sprinkler system. The owner of the building defaulted in his payments, and the mortgagee brought suit to foreclose on the mortgage. The question arose as to whether or not the real estate mortgage attached to the sprinkler system. Did the sprinkler system become a part of the real estate? (People's Savings and Trust Company v. Munsert, 212 Wis. 449, 249 N. W. 527)

8. The Whellkin Coat Co. sent an expensive fur coat to Silberstein to be treated. While in Silberstein's possession, it was badly damaged due to a leaky roof which permitted water to enter the room where the coat was stored. Silberstein had rented only a portion of the building, so he had no control over the roof, hallways, and other parts of the building. The Whellkin Coat Co. sued the landlord for the damage to the coat. The landlord denied liability, claiming the tenant if anyone should be held liable. Who is liable in this case? (Whellkin Coat Co. v. Long Branch Trust Co., 1-21 N. J. L. 106, 1 A. 2d 394)

9. Stevens and Co. leased warehouses, wharves, and docks to Pratt. The lease provided that the lessor would keep the premises in a good state of repair. He failed to do this even though several demands were made upon him to do so. The lessee then abandoned the property and refused to pay any more rent. Must the tenant pay rent? (John B. Stevens & Co. v. Pratt, 119 Wash. 232, 205 Pac. 10)

Glossary of Legal Terms

(Other legal terms are defined elsewhere in the text. Refer to the Index for them.)

A

Abandon: give up or leave employment; relinquish possession of personal property with intent to disclaim title.

Abrogate: recall or repeal; abolish entirely.

Absolute liability: liability for an act that causes harm even though the doer was not at fault.

Abstract of title: history of the transfers of title to a given piece of land, briefly stating the parties to and the effect of all deeds, wills, and judicial proceedings relating to the land.

Acceleration clause: provision in a contract or any legal instrument that upon a certain event the time for the performance of specified obligations shall be advanced.

Acceptance: an accepted draft; the assent by the person on whom a draft is drawn to pay it when due.

Acceptor: one who assents to an order or a draft.

Accession: acquisition of title to property by virtue of the fact that it has been attached to property already owned.

Accessory after the fact: one who after the commission of a felony knowingly assists the felon.

Accessory before the fact: one who is absent at the commission of the crime but who aided and abetted its commission.

Accident: an event that occurs even though a reasonable man would not have foreseen its occurrence, because of which the law holds no one legally responsible for the harm caused.

Accommodation party: a person who signs a negotiable instrument as a favor to another.

Accord and satisfaction: an agreement made and executed in satisfaction of the rights one has acquired under a former contract.

Accretion: acquisition of title to additional land when the owner's land is built up by gradual deposits made by the natural action of water.

Acknowledgment: the admission of the execution of a writing made before a competent officer; the formal certificate made by an officer.

Acquittal: the action of a jury in a finding of not guilty.

Action: proceeding at law.

Act of bankruptcy: any of the acts specified by the national bankruptcy law which, when committed by the debtor within the four months preceding the filing of the petition in bankruptcy, is proper ground for declaring the debtor a bankrupt.

Act of God: an act of nature that is not reasonably foreseeable.

Adjudication: a judicial determination.

Administrative agency: a governmental commission or board given authority to regulate particular matters.

Administrator—administratrix: the person (man—woman) appointed by a court to take charge of the estate of a deceased person.

Adult: one who has reached full legal age.

Adverse possession: the hostile possession of real estate, which when actual, visible, notorious, exclusive, and continued for the required number of years, will place title to the land in the person in possession.

Affidavit: a voluntary sworn statement in writing.

Affirm: to declare to tell the truth under a penalty of perjury; to confirm.

Affirmative covenant: an express under-taking or promise in a contract or deed to do an act.

Agency: the relationship that exists be-tween a person identified as a prin-cipal and another by virtue of which the latter may make contracts with third persons on behalf of the prin-cipal.

Agency coupled with an interest in the authority: an agency in which the agent has given a consideration or has paid for the right to exercise the authority granted to him.

Agency coupled with an interest in the subject matter: an agency in which for a consideration the agent is given an interest in the property with which he is dealing.

Agency shop: a union contract provision requiring that nonunion employees pay to the union the equivalent of union dues in order to retain their employment.

Agent: one who is authorized by the principal to make contracts with third persons on behalf of the prin-cipal.

Alien: a citizen of one country resid-ing in another.

Alienate: to transfer voluntarily the title to real property.

Alimony: an allowance made to a woman living apart from her hus-band.

Allegation: a statement of a fact in a legal proceeding.

Alteration: any material change of the terms of a writing fraudulently made by a party thereto.

Ambiguity: doubtfulness; the state of having two or more possible mean-ings.

Annexation: attachment of personal property to realty in such a way as to make it become real property and part of the realty.

Annuity: a contract by which the in-sured pays a lump sum to the insurer and later receives fixed annual pay-ments.

Annulment: the act of making void.

Answer: a written statement of the de-fendant's claim, as to the facts in a suit in equity; response; reply.

Antedate: a date prior to the true one; an earlier date.

Anti-injunction acts: statutes prohibit-ing the use of injunctions in labor disputes except under exceptional circumstances; notably the Federal Norris-LaGuardia Act of 1932.

Appeal: taking the case to a reviewing court to determine whether the judgment of the lower court was correct.

Appellate jurisdiction: the power of a court to hear and decide a given class of cases on appeal from an-other court or administrative agency.

Arbitration: the settlement of disputed questions, whether of law or fact, by one or more arbitrators by whose decision the parties agree to be bound. Increasingly used as a pro-cedure for labor dispute settlement.

Arraign: to accuse; to impeach; to read the charge of an indictment.

Assault: to attempt to do harm to an-other by physical violence.

Assent: to consent; to concur.

Assets: property available for the pay-ment of debts.

Assign: to transfer property or a right to another.

Assignee: one to whom property has been assigned.

Assignment: transfer of a right. Used in connection with personal property rights, as rights under a contract, a negotiable instrument, an insurance policy, or a mortgage.

Assumption of risk: the common-law rule that an employee could not sue the employer for injuries caused by the ordinary risks of employment on the theory that he had assumed such risks by undertaking the work. Abolished in those areas governed by workmen's compensation laws and most employers' liability stat-utes.

Attachment: the legal process by which property is seized in process of a debt settlement.

Attest: to bear witness.

Attorney: one legally appointed to act for another.

Attractive nuisance doctrine: a rule imposing liability on a landowner for injuries sustained by small children playing on his land when the landowner permits a condition to exist or maintains equipment that he should realize would attract small children who could not realize the danger. The rule does not apply if an unreasonable burden would be imposed on the landowner in taking steps to protect the children.

Avoid: to make void; to annul.

Award: the decision of arbitrators.

B

Bad check laws: laws making it a crime to issue a bad check with intent to defraud.

Baggage: articles of necessity or personal convenience usually carried for personal use by passengers of common carriers.

Bail: security given for the appearance of a person in court.

Bailee's lien: a specific, possessory lien of the bailee on the goods for work done to them. Commonly extended by statute to any bailee's claim for compensation and eliminating the necessity of retention of possession.

Bailment: the relation that exists when personal property is delivered into the possession of another under an agreement, express or implied, that the identical property will be returned or will be disposed of in accordance with the agreement.

Bankrupt: one who has been judicially discharged from the obligations of certain past claims.

Bankruptcy: a procedure by which one unable to pay his debts may be declared a bankrupt, after which all his assets in excess of his exemption claim are surrendered to the court for administration and distribution to his creditors, and the debtor is given a discharge that releases him from the unpaid balance due on most debts.

Battery: the unlawful touching of another.

Bearer: the person in physical possession of a negotiable instrument payable to bearer.

Beneficiary: the person to whom the proceeds of a life insurance policy are payable, a person for whose benefit property is held in trust, or a person given property by a will.

Bequest: a gift of personal property by will.

Bilateral: a contract executory on both sides.

Bill of exchange (draft): an unconditional order in writing by one person upon another, signed by the person giving it, and ordering the person to whom it is directed to pay or deliver on demand or at a definite time a sum certain in money to order or to bearer.

Bill of lading: a document issued by a carrier showing the receipt of goods and the terms of the contract of transportation.

Bill of sale: a writing signed by the seller showing that he has sold to the buyer the personal property described.

Binder: a memorandum delivered to the insured stating the essential terms of a policy to be executed in the future, when it is agreed that the contract of insurance is to be effective before the written policy is executed.

Blank indorsement: an indorsement that does not state to whom the instrument is to be paid.

Blue-sky laws: statutes designed to protect the public from the sale of worthless stocks and bonds.

Boardinghouse keeper: one regularly engaged in the business of offering living accommodations to permanent lodgers or boarders as distinguished from transient guests.

Bona fide: in good faith; without deceit or fraud; genuine.

Bond: an obligation or promise in writing and sealed, generally of corporations, personal representatives, trustees; fidelity bonds.

Boycott: a combination of two or more persons to cause harm to another by refraining from patronizing or dealing with such other person in any way or inducing others to so refrain; commonly an incident of labor disputes.

Breach: in contracts, the violation of an agreement or obligation.

Brief: written or printed arguments or authorities furnished by a lawyer to a court.

Bulk sales acts: statutes to protect creditors of a bulk seller by preventing him from obtaining cash for his goods and then leaving the state. Notice must be given creditors, and the bulk sale buyer is liable to the seller's creditors if the statute is not satisfied. Expanded to "bulk transfers" under the Code.

Burglary: the breaking open and entering of a dwelling with the intent to commit a felony.

Business trust: a form of business organization in which the owners of the property to be devoted to the business transfer the title of the property to trustees with full power to operate the business.

C

Cancellation: a crossing out of a part of an instrument or a destruction of all legal effect of the instrument, whether by act of party, upon breach by the other party, or pursuant to agreement or decree of court.

Capital: net assets of a corporation.

Capital stock: the declared money value of the outstanding stock of the corporation.

Case: an occurrence upon which an action in court is based.

Cash surrender value: the sum that will be paid the insured if he surrenders his policy to the insurer.

Cause of action: the right to damages or other judicial relief when a legally protected right of the plaintiff is violated by an unlawful act of the defendant.

Caveat emptor: let the buyer beware.

Certificate of protest: a written statement by a notary public setting forth the fact that the holder had presented the commercial paper to the primary party and that the latter had failed to make payment.

Charter: the grant of authority from a government to exist as a corporation.

Chattel: any article of personal property.

Chattel mortgage: a security device by which the owner of personal property transfers the title to a creditor as security for the debt owed by the owner to the creditor.

Check: an order by a depositor on his bank to pay a sum of money to a payee; also defined as a bill of exchange drawn on a bank and payable on demand.

Circumstantial evidence: relates to circumstances surrounding the facts in dispute from which the trier of fact may deduce what had happened.

Civil action: in many states a simplified form of action combining all or many of the former common-law actions.

Civil court: a court with jurisdiction to hear and determine controversies relating to private rights and duties.

Client: one who employs a lawyer to represent him in legal matters.

Closed shop: a place of employment in which only union members may be employed. Now generally prohibited by statutes.

Code: a compilation of laws by public authority.

Collateral note: a note accompanied by collateral security.

Collective bargaining: the process by which the terms of employment are agreed upon through negotiations between the employer or employers within a given industry or industrial area and the union or the bargaining representative of the employees.

Collective bargaining unit: the employment area within which employees are by statute authorized to select a bargaining representative, who is then to represent all the employees in bargaining collectively with the employer.

Collusion: a secret agreement between two or more persons, designed to obtain an object forbidden by law or to defraud another.

Commission merchant: a bailee to whom goods are consigned for sale.

Common carrier: a carrier that holds out its facilities to serve the general public for compensation without discrimination.

Common law: the body of unwritten principles originally based on the usages and customs of the community which were recognized and enforced by the courts.

Common stock: stock that has no right or priority over any other stock of the corporation as to dividends or distribution of assets upon dissolution.

Community property: the cotenancy held by husband and wife in property acquired during their marriage under the law of some of the states, principally in the southwestern United States.

Competency: legal power, adequacy, or ability.

Complaint: the initial pleading filed by the plaintiff in many actions which in many states may be served as original process to acquire jurisdiction over the defendant.

Composition of creditors: an agreement among creditors that each shall accept a part payment as full payment in consideration of the other creditors doing the same.

Compromise: a settlement reached by mutual concessions.

Concealment: the failure to volunteer information not requested.

Conditional sale: a credit transaction by which the buyer purchases on credit and promises to pay the purchase price in installments, while the seller retains the title to the goods, together with the right of repossession upon default, until the condition of payment in full has been satisfied.

Conflict of laws: the body of law that determines the law of which state is to apply when two or more states are involved in the facts of a given case.

Confusion of goods: the mixing of goods of different owners that under certain circumstances results in one of the owners becoming the owner of all the goods.

Consanguinity: relationship by blood.

Consideration: the promise or performance by the other party that the promisor demands as the price of his promise.

Consignee: one to whom goods are shipped.

Consignment: a bailment made for the purpose of sale by the bailee. (Parties—consignor, consignee)

Contingent beneficiary: the person to whom the proceeds of a life insurance policy are payable in the event that the primary beneficiary dies before the insured.

Contract: a binding agreement based upon the genuine assent of the parties, made for a lawful object, between competent parties, in the form required by law, and generally supported by consideration.

Contract carrier: a carrier who transports on the basis of individual contracts that it makes with each shipper.

Contract of record: name sometimes given to a judgment of a court.

Contract to sell: a contract to make a transfer of title in the future as contrasted with a present sale.

Contributory negligence: negligence of the plaintiff that contributes to his injury and at common law bars him from recovery from the defendant although the defendant may have been more negligent than the plaintiff.

Conveyance: a transfer of an interest in land, ordinarily by the execution and delivery of a deed.

Cooperative: a group of two or more persons or enterprises that act through a common agent with respect to a common objective, as buying or selling.

Corporation: an artificial legal person or being created by law, which for many purposes is treated as a natural person.

Corporeal: material; tangible; substantial.

Counterclaim: a claim that the defendant in an action may make against the plaintiff.

Covenant: a promise contained in a sealed instrument; a solemn compact.

Coverture: the status or condition of a woman during marriage.

Crime: a violation of the law that is punished as an offense against the state or government.

Cumulative voting: a system of voting for directors in which each stockholder has as many votes as the number of voting shares he owns multiplied by the number of directors to be elected, which votes he can distribute for the various candidates as he desires.

Custody: care, possession, or keeping of property.

D

Damages: a sum of money recovered to redress or make amends for the legal wrong or injury done.

Deceit: a device of false representation by which one person misleads another to the latter's injury.

Decree: the decision of a court of equity or admiralty.

Dedication: acquisition by the public or a government of title to land when it is given over by its owner to use by the public and such gift is accepted.

Deed: an instrument by which the grantor (owner of land) conveys or transfers the title to a grantee.

Default: the nonperformance of a duty or an obligation.

Defendant: a person against whom a suit is brought.

Defense: that which is relied upon by a defendant to defeat an action; the resistance to an attack.

Delegation: the transfer of the power to do an act to another.

Demurrage: a charge made by the carrier for the unreasonable detention of cars by the consignor or consignee.

Deposition: the testimony of a witness taken out of court before a person authorized to administer oaths.

Descent: the hereditary succession to an estate.

Devise: a gift of real estate made by will.

Directors: the persons vested with control of the corporation, subject to the elective power of the shareholders.

Disability: incapacity for the performance of a legal act.

Disaffirm: to repudiate; to refuse to confirm.

Discharge in bankrupty: an order of the bankruptcy court discharging the bankrupt debtor from the unpaid balance of most of the claims against him.

Discharge of contract: termination of a contract by performance, agreement, impossibility, acceptance of breach, or operation of law.

Dishonor by nonacceptance: the refusal of the drawee to accept a draft (bill of exchange).

Dishonor by nonpayment: the refusal to pay a commercial paper when properly presented for payment.

Divorce: the dissolution of the marriage ties.

Domestic bill of exchange: a draft drawn in one state and payable in the same or another state.

Domestic corporation: a corporation that has been incorporated by the state as opposed to incorporation by another state.

Domicile: the home of a person or the state of incorporation of a corporation, to be distinguished from a place where a person lives but which he does not regard as his home, or a state in which a corporation does business but in which it was not incorporated.

Double indemnity: a provision for payment of double the amount specified by the insurance contract if death is caused by an accident and occurs under specified circumstances.

Double jeopardy: the principle that a person who has once been placed in jeopardy by being brought to trial at which the proceedings progressed at least as far as having the jury sworn cannot thereafter be tried a second time for the same offense.

Draft: see bill of exchange.

Due care: the degree of care that a reasonable man would exercise to prevent the realization of harm, which under all the circumstances was reasonably foreseeable in the event that such care were not taken.

Duress: constraint or compulsion.

E

Easement: the right that one person has to use the land of another for a special purpose.

Eleemosynary corporation: a corporation organized for a charitable or benevolent purpose.

Embezzlement: the fraudulent appropriation of property by a person to whom it has been entrusted.

Emblements: growing crops that have been sown or planted.

Eminent domain: the power of a government and certain kinds of corporations to take private property against the objection of the owner, provided the taking is for a public purpose and just compensation is made therefor.

Enact: to make into a law.

Encumbrance: a right held by a third person in or a lien or charge against property, as a mortgage or judgment lien on land.

Equitable: just; fair; right; reasonable.

Equity: the body of principles that originally developed because of the inadequacy of the rules then applied by the common-law courts of England.

Erosion: the loss of land through a gradual washing away by tides or currents, with the owner losing title to the lost land.

Escrow: a conditional delivery of property or of a deed to a custodian or escrow holder, who in turn makes final delivery to the grantee or transferee when a specified condition has been satisfied.

Estate: an interest in property.

Estate in fee simple: the largest estate possible in which the owner has the absolute and entire property in the land.

Estoppel: the principle by which a person is barred from pursuing a certain course of action or of disputing the truth of certain matters when his conduct has been such that it would be unjust to permit him to do so.

Eviction: the expulsion of an occupant of real property.

Evidence: that which is presented to the trier of fact as the basis on which the trier is to determine what had happened.

Execution: the carrying out of a judgment of a court, generally directing that property owned by the defendant be sold and the proceeds first used to pay the execution or judgment creditor.

Executor: the person named by the maker of a will to carry out its provisions.

Ex parte: upon or from one side only.

Extradition: the surrender by one government to another of a person charged with a crime.

Extraordinary bailment: a bailment in which the bailee is subject to unusual duties and liabilities, as a hotelkeeper or common carrier.

F

Factor: a bailee to whom goods are consigned for sale.

Fair employment practice acts: statutes designed to eliminate discrimination in employment in terms of race, religion, natural origin, or sex.

Fair labor standards acts: statutes, particularly the federal statute, designed to prevent excessive hours of employment and low pay, the employment of young children, and other unsound practices.

Fair trade acts: statutes that authorize the making of resale price maintenance agreements as to trademark and brand name articles, and generally provide that all persons in the industry are bound by such an agreement whether they have signed it or not.

Featherbedding: the exaction of money for services not performed or not to be performed, which is made an unfair labor practice generally and a criminal offense in connection with radio broadcasting.

Fellow-servant rule: a common-law defense of the employer that barred an employee from suing an employer for injuries caused by a fellow employee.

Felony: a criminal offense that is punishable by confinement in prison or by death, or that is expressly stated by statute to be a felony.

Fiduciary: involving a relation of trust or confidence.

Financial responsibility laws: statutes that require a driver involved in an automobile accident to prove his financial responsibility in order to retain his license, which responsibility may be shown by procuring public liability insurance in a specified minimum amount.

Firm offer: an offer stated to be held open for a specified time, which must be so held in some states even in the absence of an option contract, or under the Code, with respect to merchants.

Fixture: personal property that has become so attached to or adapted to real estate that it has lost its character as personal property and is part of the real estate.

Forbearance: refraining from doing an act.

Foreclosure: procedure for enforcing a mortgage resulting in the public sale of the mortgaged property and less commonly in merely barring the right of the mortgagor to redeem the property from the mortgage.

Foreign (international) bill of exchange: a bill of exchange made in one nation and payable in another.

Foreign corporation: a corporation incorporated under the laws of another state.

Forfeiture: the loss of some right or privilege.

Forgery: the fraudulent making or altering of an instrument that apparently creates or alters a legal liability of another.

Franchise: a right or privilege conferred by law.

Fraud: the making of a false statement of a past or existing fact with knowledge of its falsity or with reckless indifference as to its truth with the intent to cause another to rely thereon, and he does rely thereon to his injury.

Fungible goods: goods of a homogenous nature of which any unit is the equivalent of any other unit or is treated as such by mercantile usage.

G

Garnishment: a process whereby property is attached.

General partnership: a partnership in which the partners conduct as co-owners a business for profit, and each partner has a right to take part in the management of the business and has unlimited liability.

Grant: convey real property; an instrument by which such property has been conveyed, particularly in the case of a government.

Gratuitous bailment: a bailment in which the bailee does not receive any compensation or advantage.

Guarantor: one who undertakes the obligation of guaranty.

Guaranty: an undertaking to pay the debt of another if the creditor first sues the debtor and is unable to recover the debt from the debtor or principal.

Guardian: one who has the care of a person or property.

H

Hedging: the making of simultaneous contracts to purchase and to sell a particular commodity at a future date with the intention that the loss on one transaction will be offset by the gain on the other.

Heirs: those persons specified by statute to receive the estate of a decedent not disposed of by will.

Holder: the person in possession of a commercial paper payable to him as payee or indorsee, or the person in possession of a commercial paper payable to bearer.

Holder in due course: the holder of a commercial paper under such circumstances that he is treated as favored and is given an immunity from certain defenses.

Holder through a holder in due course: a person who is not himself a holder in due course but is a holder of the paper after it was held by some prior party who was a holder in due course, and who is given the same rights as a holder in due course.

Holographic will: a will written by the testator in his own hand.

Hotelkeeper: one regularly engaged in the business of offering living accommodations to all transient persons.

I

Implied contract: a contract expressed by conduct or implied or deduced from the facts. Also used to refer to a quasi-contract.

Incidental authority: authority of an agent that is reasonably necessary to execute his express authority.

Incontestable clause: a provision that after the lapse of a specified time the insurer cannot dispute the policy on the ground of misrepresentation or fraud of the insured or similar wrongful conduct.

Indemnity: compensation for loss sustained.

Independent contractor: a contractor who undertakes to perform a specified task according to the terms of a contract but over whom the other contracting party has no control except as provided for by the contract.

Indictment: a formal accusation of crime made by a grand jury which accusation is then tried by a petty or trial jury.

Infant: any person not of full legal age.

Inheritance: the estate which passes from the decedent to his heirs.

Injunction: a judicial order or decree forbidding the doing of a certain act.

Insolvency: the state of being unable to pay one's debts as they become due.

Instrument: a written document.

Insurable interest: an interest in the nonoccurrence of the risk insured against, generally because such occurrence would cause financial loss, although sometimes merely because of the close relationship between the insured and the beneficiary.

Insurance: a plan of security against risks by charging the loss against a fund created by the payments made by policyholders.

Intangible personal property: an interest in an enterprise, such as an interest in a partnership or stock of a corporation, and claims against other persons, whether based on contract or tort.

International bill of exchange: an instrument made in one nation and payable in another.

Intestate: one who dies without having made a valid will.

Invalid: void, of no legal effect.

J

Joint and several contract: a contract in which two or more persons are jointly and severally obligated or are jointly and severally entitled to recover.

Joint contract: a contract in which two or more persons are jointly liable or jointly entitled to performance under the contract.

Joint stock company: an association in which the shares of the members are transferable and control is delegated to a group or board.

Joint tenancy: the estate held by two or more jointly with the right of survivorship as between them.

Joint venture: a relationship in which two or more persons combine their labor or property for a single undertaking and share profits and losses equally unless otherwise agreed.

Judgment: a decision of a court.

Judgment note: a promissory note containing a clause authorizing the holder of the note to enter judgment against the maker of the note if it is not paid when due. Also called cognovit note.

Jurisdiction: the power of a court to hear and determine a given class of cases; the power to act over a particular defendant.

L

Land: earth, including all things imbedded in or attached thereto, whether naturally or by act of man.

Lease: an agreement between the owner of property and a tenant by which the former agrees to give possession of the property to the latter in consideration of the payment of rent. (Parties—landlord or lessor, tenant or lessee)

Leasehold: the estate or interest which the tenant has in land rented to him.

Legacy: a gift of personal property by will.

Legal: authorized or prescribed by law.

Legal tender: such form of money as the law recognizes as lawful and declares that a tender thereof in the proper amount is a proper tender which the creditor cannot refuse.

Legatee: one to whom a legacy is given.

Levy: to take possession of property to satisfy a judgment.

Libel: defamation of another without legal justification.

License: a personal privilege to do some act or series of acts upon the land of another not amounting to an easement or a right of possession, as the placing of a sign thereon.

Lien: a right to control, hold, and retain, or enforce a charge against another's property as security for a debt or claim.

Life estate: an estate for the duration of a life.

Limited liability: loss of contributed capital as maximum liability.

Limited partnership: a partnership in which at least one partner has a liability limited to the loss of the capital contribution that he has made to the partnership, and such a partner neither takes part in the management of the partnership nor appears to the public to be a partner.

Liquidated damages: the amount agreed upon in advance by the parties to a contract, to be paid in case of a breach.

Liquidation: the process of converting property into money whether of particular items of property or all the assets of a business.

Litigation: a suit at law, a judicial contest.

Lobbying contract (illegal): a contract by which one party agrees to attempt to influence the action of a legislature or Congress, or any members thereof, by improper means.

Lottery: any plan by which a consideration is given for a chance to win a prize.

M

Majority: of age, as contrasted with being a minor; more than half of any group, as a majority of stockholders.

Malfeasance: the doing of some wrongful act.

Malice: ill will towards some person.

Mechanics' lien: protection afforded by statute to various types of laborers and persons supplying materials, by giving them a lien on the building and land that has been improved or added to by them.

Merger: an absorption, union, or extinguishment of one contract or interest in another.

Merger of corporations: a combining of corporations by which one absorbs the other and continues to exist, preserving its original charter and identity while the other corporation ceases to exist.

Minor: any person not of full legal age.

Misdemeanor: a criminal offense which is neither treason nor a felony.

Misrepresentation: a false statement of fact although made innocently without any intent to deceive.

Mortgage: an interest in land given by the owner to his creditor as security for the payment to the creditor of a debt, the nature of the interest depending upon the law of the state where the land is located. (Parties—mortgagor, mortgagee)

N

Negative covenant: an undertaking in a deed to refrain from doing an act.

Negligence: the omission to do what a reasonable, prudent person would do, or doing what such a person would not have done.

Negotiable instruments: drafts, promissory notes, checks, and certificates of deposit in such form that greater rights may be acquired thereunder than by taking an assignment of a contract right.

Negotiation: the transfer of a negotiable instrument by indorsement and delivery by the person to whom then payable in the case of order paper, and by physical transfer in the case of bearer paper.

Nominal damages: a small sum given for the violation of a right where no actual loss has resulted.

Nominal partner: a person who in fact is not a partner but who holds himself out as a partner or permits others to do so.

Notice of dishonor: notice given to parties secondarily liable that the primary party to the instrument has refused to accept the instrument or to make payment when it was properly presented for that purpose.

Novation: the discharge of a contract between two parties by their agreeing with a third person that such third person shall be substituted for one of the original parties to the contract, who shall thereupon be released.

Nuisance: something which wrongfully disturbs, annoys, or injures another.

Nuncupative will: an oral will made and declared by the testator in the presence of witnesses to be his will and generally made during the testator's last illness.

O

Obligation: a duty.

Occupation: taking and holding possession of property; a method of acquiring title to personal property which has been abandoned.

Open-end mortgage: a mortgage given to secure additional loans to be made in the future as well as the original loan.

Option contract: a contract to hold an offer to make a contract open for a fixed period of time.

Ordinance: a rule of law passed by the legislative body of a city.

P

Parole: the promise of a prisoner that in return for conditional freedom he will follow certain requirements.

Parol evidence rule: the rule that prohibits the introduction in evidence of oral or written statements made prior to or contemporaneously with the execution of a complete written contract, deed, or instrument, in the absence of clear proof of fraud, accident, or mistake.

Past consideration: something that has been performed in the past and which therefore cannot be consideration for a promise made in the present.

Patent: the grant to an inventor of an exclusive right to make and sell his invention for a nonrenewable period of 17 years; a deed to land given by government to a private person.

Pawn: a pledge of tangible personal property.

Perjury: willful false testimony under oath in a judicial proceeding.

Perpetual succession: a phrase describing the continuing life of the corporation unaffected by the death of any stockholder or the transfer by stockholders of their stock.

Per se: in, through, or by itself.

Person: a term that includes both natural persons, or living people, and artificial persons, as corporations which are created by act of government.

Per stirpes: according to the root or by way of representation. Distribution among heirs related to the decedent in different degrees, the property being divided into lines of descent from the decedent and the share of each line then divided within the line by way of representation.

Picketing: the placing of persons outside of places of employment or distribution so that by words or banners they may inform the public of the existence of a labor dispute.

Plaintiff: one who brings an action in a court.

Pledge: a bailment given as security for the payment of a debt or the performance of an obligation owed to the pledgee. (Parties—pledgor, pledgee)

Police power: the power to govern; the power to adopt laws for the protection of the public health, welfare, safety, and morals.

Policy: the paper evidencing the contract of insurance.

Possession: exclusive domain and control of property.

Possessory lien: a right to retain possession of property of another as security for some debt or obligation owed the lienor which right continues only as long as possession is retained.

Postdate: to insert or place a later date on an instrument than the actual date on which it was executed.

Power of attorney: a written authorization to an agent by the principal.

Preferred stock: stock that has a priority or preference as to payment of dividends or upon liquidation, or both.

Prescription: the acquisition of a right to use the land of another, as an easement, through the making of hostile, visible, and notorious use of the land, continuing for the period specified by the local law.

Price: the consideration for a sale of goods.

Prima facie: at first view, apparently true; on the first appearance.

Primary beneficiary: the person designated as the first one to receive the proceeds of a life insurance policy, as distinguished from a contingent beneficiary who will receive the proceeds only if the primary beneficiary dies before the insured.

Principal: one who employs an agent to act on his behalf; the person who as between himself and the surety is primarily liable to the third person or creditor.

Private carrier: a carrier owned by the shipper, such as a company's own fleet of trucks.

Privileged communication: information which the witness may refuse to testify to because of the relationship with the person furnishing the information, as husband-wife, attorney-client.

Privity: a succession or chain of relationship to the same thing or right, as a privity of contract, privity of estate, privity of possession.

Probate: a court having jurisdiction over estates.

Process: a writ or order of court generally used as a means of acquiring jurisdiction over the person of the defendant by serving him with process.

Promissory estoppel: the doctrine that a promise will be enforced although not supported by consideration when the promisor should have reasonably expected that his promise would induce action or forbearance of a definite and substantial character on the part of the promisee, and injustice can only be avoided by enforcement of the promise.

Promissory note: an unconditional promise in writing made by one person to another, signed by the maker, engaging to pay on demand, or at a definite time, a sum certain in money to order or to bearer. (Parties—maker, payee)

Promoters: the persons who plan the formation of the corporation and sell or promote the idea to others.

Property: the rights and interests one has in anything subject to ownership.

Prosecute: to proceed against by legal means.

Protest: formal certification that proper presentment of a commercial paper was made to the primary party and that he defaulted.

Proximate cause: the act which is the natural and reasonably foreseeable cause of the harm or event which occurs and injures the plaintiff.

Proximate damages: damages which in the ordinary course of events are the natural and reasonably foreseeable result of the defendant's violation of the plaintiff's rights.

Proxy: a written authorization by a shareholder to another person to vote the stock owned by the shareholder; the person who is the holder of such a written authorization.

Public domain: public or government-owned lands.

Punitive damages: damages in excess of those required to compensate the plaintiff for the wrong done, which are imposed in order to punish the defendant because of the particularly wanton or willful character of his wrongdoing.

Purchase-money mortgage: a mortgage given by the purchaser of land to the seller to secure the seller for the payment of the unpaid balance of the purchase price, which the seller purports to lend the purchaser.

Purchaser in good faith: a person who purchases without any notice or knowledge of any defect of title, misconduct, or defense.

Q

Qualified acceptance: an acceptance of a draft that varies the order of the bill in some way.

Qualified indorsement: an indorsement that includes words such as "without recourse" evidencing the intent of the indorser that he shall not be held liable for the failure of the primary party to pay the instrument.

Quantum meruit: an action brought for the value of the services rendered the defendant when there was no express contract as to the payment to be made.

Quasi: as if, as though it were, having the characteristics of; a modifier employed to indicate that the subject is to be treated as though it were in fact the noun which follows the word "quasi:" as in quasi-contract, quasi-corporation, quasi-public corporation.

Quitclaim deed: a deed by which the grantor purports only to give up whatever right or title he may have in the property without specifying or warranting that he is transferring any particular interest.

Quorum: the minimum number of persons, shares represented, or directors who must be present at a meeting in order that business may be lawfully transacted.

R

Ratification: confirming an act which was executed without authority or an act which was voidable.

Ratification by minor: the approval of a contract given by a minor after attaining majority.

Ratification of agency: the approval of the unauthorized act of an agent or of a person who is not an agent for any purpose after the act has been done, which has the same effect as though the act had been authorized before it was done.

Real property: land and all rights in land.

Realty: real property.

Reasonable care: that degree of care that a reasonable man would take under all the circumstances then known.

Receiver: a person appointed by a court to take charge of property pending litigation.

Redemption: the buying back of one's property which has been sold because of a default.

Referee: an impartial person selected by the parties or appointed by a court to determine facts or decide matters in dispute.

Referee in bankruptcy: a referee appointed by a bankruptcy court to hear and determine various matters relating to bankruptcy proceedings.

Reimbursement: the right of one paying money on behalf of another, which such other person should have himself paid, to recover the amount of the payment from him.

Release: the surrender or relinquishment to another of a right, claim, interest, or estate.

Remedy: the action or procedure that is followed in order to enforce a right or to obtain damages for injury to a right.

Reorganization of corporation: procedure devised to restore insolvent corporations to financial stability through readjustment of debt and capital structure either under the supervision of a court of equity or of bankruptcy.

Replevin: an action to recover possession of property unlawfully detained.

Repossession: any taking again of possession although generally used in connection with the act of a secured seller in taking back the property upon the default of the credit buyer.

Representations: statements, whether oral or written, made to give the insurer the information which it needs in writing the insurance, and which if false and relating to a material fact will entitle the insurer to avoid the contract.

Representative capacity: action taken by one not on his own behalf but on behalf of another, as an executor acting on behalf of the decedent's estate, or action taken both on one's behalf and on behalf of others, as a stockholder bringing a representative action.

Resale price maintenance agreement: an agreement that the buyer will not resell a trademark or brand name article below a stated minimum price which agreement, by virtue of fair trade laws, is valid not only as between the contracting parties but may also bind other persons in the trade who know of the agreement although they did not sign it.

Rescission: cancelling, annulling, avoiding.

Reservation: the creation by the grantor of a right that did not exist before, which he reserves or keeps for himself upon making a conveyance of property.

Res ipsa loquitur: the rebuttable presumption that the thing speaks for itself when the circumstances are such that ordinarily the plaintiff could not have been injured had the defendant not been at fault.

Respondeat superior: the doctrine that the principal or employer is vicariously liable for the unauthorized torts committed by his agent or employee while acting within the scope of his agency or the course of his employment, respectively.

Restrictive covenants: covenants in a deed by which the grantee agrees to refrain from doing specified acts.

Restrictive indorsement: an indorsement that prohibits the further transfer, constitutes the indorsee the agent of the indorser, vests the title in the indorsee in trust for or to the use of some other person, is conditional, or is for collection or deposit.

Revocation: the annulment or cancellation of an instrument, act, or promise by one doing or making it.

Rider: a slip of paper executed by the insurer and intended to be attached to the insurance policy for the purpose of changing it in some respect.

Riparian rights: the right of a person through whose land runs a natural watercourse to use the water free from unreasonable pollution or diversion by the upper riparian owners and from blocking by lower riparian owners.

Risk: the peril or contingency against which the insured is protected by the contract of insurance.

S

Sale or return: a sale in which the title to the property passes to the buyer at the time of the transaction but he is given the option of returning the property and restoring the title to the seller.

Scope of employment: the area within which the employee is authorized to act with the consequence that a tort committed while so acting imposes liability upon the employer.

Seal: at common law an impression on wax or other material attached to the instrument. Under modern law, any mark not ordinarily part of the signature is a seal when so intended, including the letters "L. S." and the word "seal," or a pictorial representation of a seal.

Secret partner: a partner who takes an active part in the management of the partnership but is not known to the public as a partner.

Secured transaction: a credit sale of goods or a secured loan that provides special protection for the creditor.

Sentence: the penalty pronounced upon a person convicted of a crime.

Severable contract: a contract the terms of which are such that one part may be separated or severed from the other, so that a default as to one part is not necessarily a default as to the entire contract.

Several contracts: separate or independent contracts made by different persons undertaking to perform the same obligation.

Severalty: sole ownership of property by one person.

Shareholder's action: an action brought by one or more shareholders on behalf of the shareholders generally and of the corporation to enforce a cause of action of the corporation against third persons.

Sight draft: a draft or bill of exchange payable on sight or when presented for payment.

Silent partner: a partner who takes no active part in the business, without regard to whether he is known to the public as a partner.

Sitdown strike: a strike in which the employees remain in the plant and refuse to allow the employer to operate it.

Slander: defamation of character by spoken words or gestures.

Slowdown: a slowing down of production by employees without actual stopping of work.

Special agent: an agent authorized to transact a specific transaction or to do a specific act.

Special damages: damages that do not necessarily result from the injury to the plaintiff but at the same time are not so remote that the defendant should not be held liable therefor, provided that the claim for special damages is properly made in the action.

Special indorsement: an indorsement that specifies the person to whom the instrument is indorsed.

Specific (identified) goods: goods which are so identified to the contract that no other goods may be delivered in performance of the contract.

Specific lien: the right of a creditor to hold particular property or assert a lien on any particular property of the debtor because of the creditor's having done work on or having some other association with the property, as distinguished from having a lien generally against the assets of the debtor merely because the debtor is indebted to him.

Specific performance: an action brought to compel the adverse party to perform his contract on the theory that merely suing him for damages for its breach will not be an adequate remedy.

SS. or ss.: abbreviation for the Latin word scilicet, meaning, to wit; namely; that is to say.

Stare decisis: the principle that the decision of a court should serve as a guide or precedent and control the decision of a similar case in the future.

Statute of Frauds: a statute which, in order to prevent fraud through the use of perjured testimony, requires that certain types of transactions be evidenced in writing in order to be binding or enforceable.

Statute of Limitations: a statute that restricts the period of time within which an action may be brought.

Stop payment: an order by a depositor to his bank to refuse to make payment of his check when presented for payment.

Sublease: a transfer of the premises by the lessee to a third person, the sublessee or subtenant, for a period less than the term of the original lease.

Subpoena: a writ commanding a person to appear as a witness.

Subrogation: the right of a party secondarily liable to stand in the place of the creditor after he has made payment to the creditor and to enforce the creditor's right against the party primarily liable in order to obtain indemnity from him.

Subsidiary corporation: a corporation that is controlled by another corporation through the ownership by the latter of a controlling amount of the voting stock of the former.

Substantial performance: the equitable doctrine that a contractor substantially performing a contract in good faith is entitled to recover the contract price less damages for noncompletion or defective work.

Substantive law: the law that defines rights and liabilities.

Substitution: discharge of contracts by substituting another in its place.

Subtenant: one who rents the leased premises from the original tenant for a period of time less than the balance of the lease to the original tenant.

Suit: the prosecution of some claim in a court of justice.

Summons: a notice to a person to appear in court.

Suretyship: an undertaking to pay the debt or be liable for the default of another.

Surrender: the yielding up of the tenant's leasehold estate to the lessor in consequence of which the lease terminates.

Survivorship: the right by which a surviving joint tenant or tenant by the entireties acquires the interest of the predeceasing tenant automatically upon his death.

Syndicate: an association of individuals formed to conduct a particular business transaction, generally of a financial nature.

T

Tenancy at sufferance: the holding over by a tenant after his lease has expired of the rented land without the permission of the landlord and prior to the time that the landlord has elected to treat him as a trespasser or a tenant.

Tenancy at will: the holding of land for an indefinite period that may be terminated at any time by the landlord or by the landlord and tenant acting together.

Tenancy for years: a tenancy for a fixed period of time, even though the time is less than a year.

Tenancy from year to year: a tenancy which continues indefinitely from year to year until terminated.

Tenancy in common: the relation that exists when two or more persons own undivided interests in property.

Tender of payment: an unconditional offer to pay the exact amount of money due at the time and place specified by the contract.

Tender of performance: an unconditional offer to perform at the time and in the manner specified by the contract.

Testamentary: designed to take effect at death, as by disposing of property or appointing an executor.

Testate: the condition of leaving a will upon death.

Testator—testatrix: a man—woman who makes a will.

Testimony: the answers of witnesses under oath to questions given at the time of the trial.

Third-party beneficiary: a third person whom the parties to a contract intend to benefit by the making of the contract.

Time draft: a bill of exchange payable at a stated time after sight or a stated time after a certain date.

Title insurance: a form of insurance by which the insurer insures the buyer of real property against the risk of loss should the title acquired from the seller be defective in any way.

Tort: a private injury or wrong arising from a breach of a duty created by law.

Trade acceptance: a draft or bill of exchange drawn by the seller of goods on the purchaser at the time of sale and accepted by the purchaser.

Trade fixtures: articles of personal property which have been attached to the freehold by a tenant and which are used for or are necessary to the carrying on of the tenant's trade.

Trademark: a name, device, or symbol used by a manufacturer or seller to distinguish his goods from those of other persons.

Trade name: a name under which a business is carried on and, if fictitious, it must be registered.

Treasury stock: stock of the corporation which the corporation has reacquired.

Trespass: an unwarranted invasion of another's right.

Trust: a transfer of property by one person to another with the understanding or declaration that such property be held for the benefit of another, or the holding of property by the owner in trust for another, upon his declaration of trust, without a transfer to another person.

Trust deed: a form of deed which transfers the trust property to the trustee for the purposes therein stated, particularly used as a form of mortgage when the trustee is to hold the title to the mortgagor's land in trust for the benefit of the mortgage bondholders.

Trustee: one who holds property for the benefit of another.

Trustee in bankruptcy: an impartial person elected to administer the bankrupt's estate.

U

Ultra vires: an act or contract which the corporation does not have authority to do or make.

Underwriter: an insurer.

Undisclosed principal: a principal on whose behalf an agent acts without disclosing to the third person the fact that he is an agent nor the identity of the principal.

Undue influence: the influence that is asserted upon another person by one who dominates that person.

Unfair competition: the wrong of employing competitive methods that have been declared unfair by statute or an administrative agency.

Unfair labor practice acts: statutes that prohibit certain labor practices and declare them to be unfair labor practices.

Unilateral: one-sided, applied to contracts where only one promise is still unperformed.

Unincorporated association: a combination of two or more persons for the furtherance of a common nonprofit purpose.

Union contract: a contract between a labor union and an employer or group of employers prescribing the general terms of employment of workers by the latter.

Union shop: under present unfair labor practice statutes, a place of employment where nonunion men may be employed for a trial period of not more than 30 days after which the nonunion worker must join the union or be discharged.

Universal agent: an agent authorized by the principal to do all acts that can lawfully be delegated to a representative.

Usury: the lending of money at greater than the maximum rate allowed by law.

V

Valid: legal.

Venue: the place where the trial is held.

Verdict: a decision rendered by a jury.

Void: no legal effect and not binding on anyone.

Voidable: a transaction that may be set aside by one party because of fraud or similar reason but which is binding on the other party until the injured party elects to set the contract aside.

Voting trust: the transfer by two or more persons of their shares of stock of a corporation to a trustee who is to vote the shares and act for such shareholders.

W

Waiver: the voluntary surrender or relinquishment of a right or privilege.

Warehouseman: a person regularly engaged in the business of storing the goods of others for compensation. If he holds himself out to serve the public without discrimination, he is a public warehouseman.

Warehouse receipt: a receipt issued by the warehouseman for goods stored with him. Regulated by the Uniform Commercial Code, which clothes the receipt with some degree of negotiability.

Warranty deed: a deed by which the grantor conveys a specific estate or interest to the grantee and covenants that he has transferred the estate or interest by making one or more of the covenants of title.

Waste: damage or destruction to property done or permitted by a tenant.

Watered stock: stock issued by a corporation as fully paid when in fact it is not.

Will: an instrument executed with the formality required by law, by which a person makes a disposition of his property to take effect upon his death.

Witness: a person who gives testimony in court; one who sees a document executed and signs his name thereto.

Workmen's compensation: a system providing for payments to workmen because they have been injured from a risk arising out of the course of their employment while they were employed at their employment or have contracted an occupational disease in that manner, payment being made without consideration of the negligence of any party.

Works of charity: in connection with Sunday laws, acts involved in religious worship or aiding persons in distress.

Works of necessity: in connection with Sunday laws, acts that must be done at the particular time in order to save life, health, or property.

Writ: a formal written command issued by a court of law.

Z

Zoning restrictions: restrictions imposed by government on the use of property for the advancement of the general welfare.

Index

497